BARRON'S

LAST/ATS-W

HOW TO PREPARE FOR THE LIBERAL ARTS AND SCIENCES TEST ASSESSMENT OF TEACHING SKILLS-WRITTEN

WITH AN INTRODUCTION TO THE CST AND THE ATS-P

NEW YORK STATE TEACHER CERTIFICATION EXAMINATIONS (NYSTCE)

BARRON'S

LAST/ATS-W

HOW TO PREPARE FOR THE LIBERAL ARTS AND SCIENCES TEST ASSESSMENT OF TEACHING SKILLS-WRITTEN

WITH AN INTRODUCTION TO THE CST AND THE ATS-P

NEW YORK STATE TEACHER CERTIFICATION EXAMINATIONS (NYSTCE)

Dr. Robert D. Postman
Professor, Mercy College, Westchester County, New York

BARRON'S

To my wife
Liz
and my children
Chad, Blaire, and Ryan
This book is dedicated to you.

All inquiries should be addressed to:
Barron's Educational Series, Inc.
250 Wireless Boulevard
Hauppauge, New York 11788
http://www.barronseduc.com

Library of Congress Catalog Card No. 98-38301

International Standard Book No. 0-7641-0446-2

Library of Congress Cataloging-in-Publication Data

Postman, Robert D.
    How to prepare for LAST ATS-W, Liberal Arts and Sciences Test
  Assessment of Teaching Skills-Written, New York State teacher
  certifications examinations with an introduction to the CST and the
  ATS-P / Robert D. Postman
          p.   cm.
    ISBN 0-7641-0446-2
    1. Teaching—New York (State)—Examinations.   2. Teachers—
  Certification—New York (State)   I. Title
  LB1763.N7P67   1998   98-38301
  371.12'09747—dc21   CIP

PRINTED IN THE UNITED STATES OF AMERICA

19 18 17 16 15 14 13 12 11 10

CONTENTS

PREFACE

This book shows you how to get a passing score on the LAST and ATS-W, introduces you to the other New York Teacher Certification Examination, and helps you get started in a teaching career. The book has been field-tested by college students and prospective teachers and reviewed by experienced teachers and subject matter specialists.

The practice tests in this book have the same question types and the same question-and-answer formats as the real tests. Review sections provide a clear overview of subject matter, strategies for passing the LAST and ATS-W, and extra LAST and ATS-W practice questions.

My wife, Liz, a teacher and a constant source of support, made significant contributions to this book. I hope she accepts my regrets for the lost months. My children Chad, Blaire, and Ryan have also been supportive as I worked on this and other books over the years.

I can attest that Barron's is simply the best publisher of test preparation books. The editorial department, under the leadership of Grace Freedson, spared no effort to assure that this book is most helpful to you, the test-taker.

Max Reed, the senior editor for Barron's, did another masterful job with this manuscript. This is the fourth book that Max and I have worked on together. As usual, many special touches in the book are due to her caring attention.

Special thanks to the undergraduate and graduate students and those changing careers who field-tested sections of this book, and to those at the Metropolitan Museum of Art for their assistance. Thanks also to Hardy Ropes for his wisdom, intelligence, and insight. I am also grateful to those at the New York Education Department for taking the time to talk with me about the LAST and ATS-W, and to those at other New York colleges who talked to me about their experiences with the testing.

You are entering teaching during a time of tremendous opportunity, and I wish you well in your pursuit of a rewarding and fulfilling career. The next generation awaits. You will help them prepare for a vastly different, technological world.

Robert D. Postman
August 1998

PART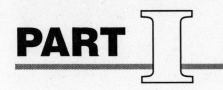

Introduction

LAST and ATS-W TEST DATES

Test Date	Regular Registration	Late Registration	Emergency Registration	Score Report Deadline
03/02/02	01/18/02	02/08/02	02/13–02/22/02	04/05/02
05/11/02	03/29/02	04/19/02	05/21–05/31/02	06/14/02
07/20/02	06/07/02	06/28/02	07/03–07/12/02	08/23/02

THE LAST, ATS-W, AND OTHER NEW YORK TEACHER CERTIFICATION TESTS

| TEST INFO BOX |

Every chapter begins with a Test Info Box. Read it for information about the LAST and the ATS-W.

The New York State Teacher Certification Tests are offered by National Evaluation Systems (NES). Contact NES for information about registration, admission tickets, testing accommodations, and test scores.

National Evaluation Systems
300 Gatehouse Road
Amherst, MA 01004-9008
413-256-2882
TTY for the deaf: 413-256-8032

THE TESTS

Passing scores on the Liberal Arts and Sciences Test (LAST) and the Assessment of Teaching Skills-Written (ATS-W) are required for most New York teaching certificates.

The LAST consists of 80 multiple-choice items and a written assignment. The multiple-choice items are drawn from these broad subareas: Mathematics/Science, History/Social Science, Art/Literature/Humanities, and Communication. The written assignment is about a topic given on the test.

The ATS-W consists of 80 multiple-choice items and a written assignment. There is an elementary and a secondary version of the ATS-W. The multiple-choice items are drawn from these broad subareas: Knowledge of the Learner, Planning and Assessment, Instructional Delivery, and The Professional Environment. The written assignment is about teaching or a school-related situation

PASSING SCORES

An overall scale score of 220 is passing for each test. The multiple-choice items contribute 80 percent to the final score, while the written assignment contributes 20 percent. About 50–54 correct answers on the multiple-choice section and 3 or 4 out of 6 points on the written assignment should earn a passing score.

OTHER NEW YORK STATE TESTS

The Content Specialty Test (CST) and the Assessment of Teaching Skills-Performance (ATS-P) are also discussed in this chapter.

READ ME FIRST

NEW YORK STATE TEACHER CERTIFICATION TESTS

This section gives a brief overview of the tests required for New York teacher certification.

The LAST and the ATS-W

This book is about the LAST and the ATS-W. Passing scores on the LAST and the ATS-W are required for most initial New York State teaching certificates. These tests are summarized on the previous pages, and this book provides a comprehensive review for the LAST and the ATS-W. You will find two LAST practice tests and two ATS-W practice tests in Chapters 11–14.

The CST and the ATS-P

A Content Specialty Test (CST) is required for most permanent New York teaching certificates. There is a separate CST for each certificate. A CST focuses on the subject matter of the certificate. Most CST's consist only of multiple-choice items, although tests in languages other than English include listening and speaking sections. The material in this book will prepare you to take the CST for elementary school certification. Undergraduate major courses are the best preparation for subject matter CST's.

The Assessment of Teaching Skills-Performance (ATS-P) consists of a 30-minute videotape made in your classroom. You must be employed as a teacher in a public or nonpublic school to complete the ATS-P. The testing authorities recommend that you complete the ATS-P after two years of classroom experience. The ATS-W chapter in this book will help you understand the teaching skills assessed on the ATS-P. The best preparation for the ATS-P is to make a series of practice tapes and to have these tapes reviewed by peers, college faculty, or others who can help you improve your teaching performance.

TESTS REQUIRED FOR NEW YORK TEACHER CERTIFICATION

The chart on the next page shows the tests required for New York teacher certification. These requirements change from time to time. Confirm these requirements with the New York State Department of Education.

NEW YORK STATE TEACHER CERTIFICATION TESTING REQUIREMENTS

Teaching Certificates	Current Requirements		Projected Requirements	
PreK–6 Common Branch Subjects	LAST ATS-W CST (Elementary Education) ATS-P	Provisional Provisional Permanent Permanent	Same as current requirements except	
7–9 Extension	Same as base certificate, PLUS: CST in academic subject	Permanent	CST	Provisional
Early Childhood Annotation (PreK–3)	CST in annotation	Permanent		
7–12 Academic Subjects English, Languages other than English, Mathematics, Science (Biology, Chemistry, Earth Science, Physics), Social Studies	LAST ATS-W CST (in academic subject) ATS-P	Provisional Provisional Permanent Permanent	Same as current requirements except	
5–6 Extension	Same as base certificate		CST	Provisional
Bilingual Education (Extension)	Same as base certificate, PLUS: LPA in English (oral) LPA in Target Language (oral & written)	Prov./Perm. Prov./Perm.	Same as current requirements	
English to speakers of other languages (ESOL)	LAST ATS-W LPA in English (oral) CST (ESOL) ATS-P	Provisional Provisional Provisional Permanent Permanent	Same as current requirements except CST	 Provisional
Occupational Subjects, e.g., Agricultural Subjects, Business/Distributive Education, Health Occupations, Trade Subjects, Technical Subjects, Home Economics Subjects	Baccalaureate-based certificates: LAST + ATS-W Associate & non-degree-based certificate titles: LAST + ATS-W	Provisional Permanent	Baccalaureate-based certificates: LAST ATS-W CST ATS-P Associate & non-degree-based certificate titles: ATS-W ATS-P LAST CST	 Provisional Provisional Provisional Permanent Permanent Permanent Permanent Permanent
Special Education, e.g., Special Education, Blind/Partially Sighted, Deaf/Hearing Impaired Speech/Hearing Handicapped	LAST + ATS-W	Provisional	LAST ATS-W CST ATS-P	Provisional Provisional Provisional Permanent
Reading	LAST + ATS-W	Provisional	Same as for PreK–6 or 7–12 certificate PLUS: CST in Reading	Provisional
School Media Specialist(s)	LAST + ATS-W	Provisional	LAST ATS-W CST ATS-P	Provisional Provisional Provisional Permanent
Special Subjects, e.g., Art, Business/Distributive Education, Dance, Health, Home Economics, Music, Physical Education, Recreation, Speech, Technology Education	LAST + ATS-W	Provisional	LAST ATS-W CST ATS-P	Provisional Provisional Provisional Permanent

* NTEs will no longer be accepted as of September 2, 1999.

LAST = Liberal Arts and Sciences Test
ATS-W = Assesment of Teaching Skills-Written

CST = Content Specialty Test
ATS-P = Assesment of Teaching Skills-Performance (video)
LPA = Language Proficiency Assessment

This section explains the steps you should take in the beginning of your preparation.

What Is the LAST All About?

The LAST is a test about the introductory level liberal arts courses you took in college. The tests consist of 80 multiple-choice items and a written assignment. You have four hours to complete the LAST. You decide how much time to spend on the multiple-choice items, and how much time to spend on the written assignment.

The LAST items are based on four broad liberal arts subareas. The test yields a score for each liberal arts area, a score for the written assignment, and a score for the entire test. The multiple-choice items contribute 80 percent to the final score, while the written assignment score contributes 20 percent to the final score. Even so, you may encounter the most difficulty with the written assignment.

Multiple-Choice Items

The number and percent of items drawn from each liberal arts subarea is shown below. Some areas include several subjects. The number of items in each area is approximate and the distribution of items varies from test to test. You get one raw score point for each correct answer. There is no penalty for incorrect answers.

APPROXIMATE LAST ITEM DISTRIBUTION

Subarea		Number	Percentage
I	Mathematics	12	15%
	Science	12	15%
II	History/Social Science	20	25%
III	Art	8	10%
	Literature	8	10%
	Humanities	4	5%
IV	English/Communication	16	20%

Each review chapter discusses in more detail the topics covered and the types of items you will find for each topic.

Written Assignment

Each LAST contains a written assignment. Usually, you are asked to summarize the topic or situation and then give your opinion or point of view. Written assignments are rated 0–3 by two readers based on how well you write edited English. The final written assignment score of 0–6 is the sum of these two scores.

What Is the ATS-W All About?

The ATS-W is a test about the education courses you took in college and about your experience in schools. The test consists of 80 multiple-choice items and a written assignment. You have four hours to complete the ATS-W. You decide how much time to spend on the multiple-choice items and how much time to spend on the written assignment.

The ATS-W items are based on four broad education-related subareas. The test yields a score for each subarea, a score for the written assignment, and a score for the entire test. The multiple-choice items contribute 80 percent to the final score, while the written assignment score contributes 20 percent to the final score. Even so, you may encounter the most difficulty with the written assignment.

Multiple-Choice Items

The number and percent of items drawn from each subarea is shown below. The number of items in each area is approximate and the distribution of items varies from test to test. You get one raw score point for each correct answer. There is no penalty for incorrect answers.

APPROXIMATE ATS-W ITEM DISTRIBUTION

Subarea		Number	Percentage
I	Knowledge of the Learner	20	25%
II	Instructional Planning/Assessment	15	19%
III	Instructional Delivery	25	31%
IV	The Professional Environment	20	25%

Each review chapter discusses in more detail the areas covered and the types of items you will find for each topic.

Written Assignment

The ATS-W includes a written assignment. This written assignment may not be an essay. For example, past written assignments have asked for the outline of a curriculum and a lesson plan.

You may be asked to respond to a classroom situation, or some other education related situation. The written assignment must be written clearly enough to be understood, but the readers do not evaluate your writing ability. However, a well-written assignment always makes the best impression.

The written assignment is rated 0–3 by two readers based on the appropriateness of your response. Your final written assignment score is the sum of these two scores. The final written assignment score of 0–6 is the sum of these two scores.

The Good News

The good news is that the LAST and ATS-W focus on a central core of information. The information covered by the tests is at an introductory level. You frequently do not have to go beyond the information in an item to answer it correctly. You can successfully prepare for these tests. This book will show you how.

At the end of the book we show you how to begin your career in teaching, how to get certified, how to write your first resume, and how to look for your first job.

GETTING A PASSING SCORE
Raw Scores and Scale Scores

Your raw score is the number of items you answer correctly, or the number of points you actually earn. Your scale score shows your raw score on a single scale compared to everyone else who has taken the LAST or the ATS-W.

It works this way. LAST and ATS-W test items and different forms of the test have different difficulty levels. For example, a mathematics item on one form of the LAST might be harder than a mathematics item on another form. To make up for this difference in difficulty, the harder mathematics item might earn 0.9 scale points, while the easier item might earn 0.8 scale points.

This is the fair way to do it. To maintain this fairness, LAST and ATS-W passing scores are given as scale scores. The scale scores for the LAST and the ATS-W, as well as for each area on the test and for the written assignment, range from 100 to 300.

Passing Scores

Passing these tests is about your ability to use, apply, and integrate information. Just memorizing the information isn't good enough.

Scale Scores
You pass if your overall scale score is 220 or better.

PASSING SCALE SCORES

LAST   220

ATS-W   220

Raw Scores
The table below shows the raw scores likely to earn minimum scale scores. These are estimates and somewhat higher or somewhat lower raw scores may be passing for the test you take.

ESTIMATED RAW SCORES NEEDED FOR PASSING SCALE SCORES

	Minimum
LAST	50–54 multiple-choice items correct and
	3 or 4 out of 6 written assignment points
ATS-W	50–54 multiple-choice items correct and
	3 or 4 out of 6 written assignment points

You can make up for a lower score on the multiple-choice items or the written assignment with a higher score on the other part of the test.

Follow These Steps

Follow the chapters in this book—one after another. They are arranged to take you right through the review process and right up to test day. First you'll find out how to register for the tests, how to set up a study plan, and how to use test-taking strategies that work.

Then you'll go through chapters that review the LAST and ATS-W subject matter. Review chapters provide a clear overview of subject matter and specific strategies for passing the LAST and ATS-W. These chapters also give you extra multiple-choice practice items and practice written assignments.

Finally there are two complete practice LAST and ATS-Ws to get you ready for the real thing. These practice tests give you a chance to find out how well you will do on the actual LAST and ATS-W. An extra section at the end of the book helps you get started in a teaching career.

So just relax. Make connections among the information you review. Put this book on autopilot and in a short time the LAST and ATS-W will be behind you.

REGISTERING FOR THE LAST AND THE ATS-W

The New York State Teacher Certification Registration Bulletin contains registration forms for the LAST, ATS-W, and other New York Certification Tests. The bulletin is usually available in the summer for the following school year. If you are attending a college in New York State, you can usually find copies of the bulletin in the school or department of education.

When you get the bulletin, complete the registration form and send it in with the correct fee. Pay close attention to the registration deadlines in the bulletin.

ON THE WEB

The New York State Office of Teaching has a web site with up-to-date information about teacher certification requirements and teacher tests (**http://www.nysed.gov/tcert/homepage.htm**). You can request a test application through this site. You can also request information by e-mail from the New York State Education Department. Test scores are not available through this site.

TEST SITE

Recent tests have been given at the sites listed below. Some sites offer tests on only a few test dates.

Albany	New York City – Brooklyn
Binghamton	New York City – Manhattan
Buffalo	New York City – Queens
Cortland	Plattsburgh
Geneseo	Potsdam
Long Island – Nassau	Rochester
Long Island – Suffolk	Syracuse
New Paltz	Westchester
Niagara	Puerto Rico

Check the bulletin for sites near you and list as your first choice the site at which you will feel the most comfortable. List acceptable second and third choice alternatives, but never list an alternative you really don't want to go to. If you do, you may end up there.

Send in the registration form as soon as possible. Early registrants are more likely to get their first choice site.

REGISTRATION DEADLINES

There are regular, late, and emergency registration periods. Your registration form must be *postmarked* by the registration deadline shown in the bulletin. Emergency registration is by phone. The regular registration deadline is about six weeks before the test date. You will pay about 40 percent more to register during the late registration period, which ends about three weeks before the test date. You will double your registration costs during the emergency registration period, which ends about a week before the test date.

Regular registrants should receive an admissions ticket about three weeks before the test. Late registrants should receive the ticket about a week before the test. Emergency registrants complete their registration at the test site. If you don't get your registration ticket in a timely manner, or the ticket has errors, contact National Evaluation Systems at the phone number in the registration booklet.

TEST SCHEDULE

The LAST and the ATS-W each take four and a half hours with four hours of testing time and 30 minutes for instructions. The LAST is given from 8:00 A.M. to 12:30 P.M. and the ATS-W from 1:00 P.M. to 5:30 P.M. It takes nine hours if you take two tests. Most students take just one test at a time, unless it is an emergency.

ALTERNATIVE TEST ARRANGEMENTS

You may qualify for special test arrangements if your religious beliefs do not permit you to take tests on Saturday, or if you have a physical, cognitive, or emotional disability. All requests for alternative testing arrangements must be made during the regular registration period.

Alternative tests for religious reasons are given on the Sunday following the regular test dates at selected test sites. You should submit a regular registration form, an Alternative Testing Arrangements Request Form, and a letter from a clergy member on official letterhead.

If you have a disability, you can request more time on a regular test date or request alternative test arrangements. Some disabilities can be accommodated at all test sites, while others require a separate test site. You should submit a regular registration form, an Alternative Testing Arrangements Request Form, and complete documentation of your disability.

As a practical matter, you or your counselor should contact National Evaluation Systems well in advance of the registration deadline to explain your needs and to find out the sort of documentation they require.

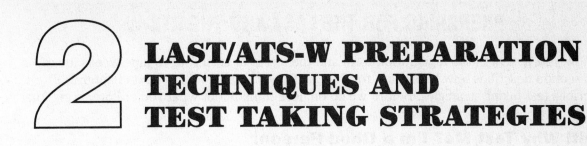

2 LAST/ATS-W PREPARATION TECHNIQUES AND TEST TAKING STRATEGIES

TEST INFO BOX

This chapter shows you how to set up a test preparation schedule and shows you some test taking strategies that will help you improve your score. It includes steps for written assignments and scored written assignment examples. The important strategies are discussed below.

MULTIPLE-CHOICE
Eliminate and then guess. There is no penalty for wrong answers. Never leave any answer blank.

Suppose you eliminate just one incorrect answer choice on all the items and you guess every answer. On average you would get about 26 correct. Suppose you eliminate two incorrect answer choices on all the items and you guess every answer. On average, you would get 40 correct.

WRITTEN ASSIGNMENT
Write an outline first, then complete the written assignment. Write 4, 5, or 6 paragraphs with 60 to 75 words in each paragraph.

The LAST written assignment is used to evaluate your writing ability. The ATS-W written assignment is used to evaluate your ability to respond to education related situations. ATS-W written assignments may not be essays.

Topic Paragraph: Begin the written assignment with an introduction to orient the reader to the topic. The first paragraph should clearly state the main idea of your entire written assignment.
Topic Sentence: Begin each paragraph with a topic sentence that supports the main idea.
Details: Provide details, examples, and arguments to support the topic sentence.
Grammar, Punctuation, Spelling: Edit sentences to conform to standard usage. Avoid passive construction; write actively and avoid the passive voice.
Conclusion: End the written assignment with a paragraph that summarizes your main points.

PREPARING FOR THE LAST AND THE ATS-W

By now you've sent in the registration form and the test is at least four to nine weeks away. This section describes how to prepare for the LAST and the ATS-W. The next chapter describes test taking strategies. Before we go on, let's think about what you are preparing for.

Wait! Why Test Me? I'm a Good Person!

Why indeed? Life would be so much easier without tests. If anyone tells you that they like to take tests, don't believe them. Nobody does. Tests are imperfect. Some people pass when they should have failed, while others fail when they should have passed. It may not be fair, but it is very real. So sit back and relax. You're just going to have to do it, and this book will show you how.

Who Makes Up These Tests and How Do They Get Written?

Consider the following scenario. It is late in the afternoon. Around a table sit teachers, deans of education, parents, and representatives of the state education department. In front of each person is a preliminary list of skills and knowledge that teachers should possess. The list comes from comments by an even larger group of teachers and other educational professionals.

Those around the table are regular people just like the ones you might run into in a store or on the street. They all care about education. They also bring to the table their own strengths and weaknesses—their own perspectives and biases. What's that? An argument just broke out. People are choosing up sides and, depending on the outcome, one item on the list will stay or go.

The final list goes to professional test writers to prepare test items. These items are tried out, refined, and put through a review process. Eventually the test question bank is established, and a test is born. These test writers are not geniuses. They just know how to write questions. You might get a better score on this test than some of them would.

The test writers want to write a test that measures important things. They try not to ask dumb or obscure questions that have strange answers. For the most part, they are successful. You can count on the test questions to ask about things you should know.

You can also be sure that the test writers will ask questions that will make you think. Their questions will ask you to use what you know. They will not ask for rote responses.

Keep those people around the table and the test writers in mind as you use this book. You are preparing for their test. Soon, you will be like one of those people around the table. You may even contribute to a test like this one.

Get Yourself Ready for the Test

Most people feel at least a little bit uncomfortable about tests. You are probably one of them. No book is going to make you feel comfortable. But here are some suggestions.

Most people are less tense when they exercise. Set up a reasonable exercise program for yourself. The program should involve exercising in a way that is appropriate for you 30 to 45 minutes each day. This exercise may be just as important as other preparation.

Prepare with another person. You will feel less isolated if you have a friend or colleague to study with.

Accept these important truths. You are not going to get all the answers correct. You don't have to. You can take this test over again if you have to. Remember the score you have to get. There is no penalty for taking the test again. This is not a do or die, life or death situation.

WHAT COLLEGE STUDENTS SAY ABOUT THE TESTS

About 100 students were surveyed just after they took the LAST and the ATS-W. Their reactions to the tests and their advice to future test-takers are summarized below.

What College Students Say About the LAST

Students say you should take the LAST after the sophomore year. Most students say answer the multiple-choice items first and then write the essay. Check with your education advisor for advice about when to take the LAST.

Multiple Choice

Students say the LAST is primarily a reading comprehension test. Much of the test consists of passages followed by items about the passage. Some passages are difficult and some items are tricky. Passages and items may integrate liberal arts concepts.

Students say you need to know the essential ideas in mathematics, reading graphs, charts and maps, and English usage. The visual arts items often show a picture and ask for some common sense interpretation. Items related to these topics are not reading comprehension items.

Students say you should have a broad general background in history, science, and social science.

Students say that between 50 percent and 75 percent of the items can be answered just from the information in the passage.

Written Assignment

Students say the most important thing is to write an outline before you start to write. They say to be sure to write about the topic. The written assignment can be about anything. It is how you write, not your point of view that matters.

Students' Advice to You About Preparing for the LAST

1. Learn how to answer reading comprehension items and how to write an essay. Practice reading and writing.
2. Learn about mathematics, reading graphs, charts and maps, and English usage.
3. Get a broad overview of science, history, social studies, literature, and the arts.
4. Take practice tests in a realistic situation.

What College Students Say About the ATS-W

Students say you should take the ATS-W after you finish most of your education courses and after you have several semesters of field experience. Most students say answer the multiple-choice items first and then complete the written assignment. Check with your education advisor about when to take the ATS-W.

Multiple Choice

Students say the ATS-W is just as much about your teaching experience as about your college education courses. Most of the test consists of passages describing teaching or other education-related situations followed by items about the passage.

Students say the test is a reading comprehension test with most of the information needed to answer the items found in the passage.

Students say you need to use common sense based on your education experience as you answer the questions. They say that between 35 percent and 55 percent of the items can be answered using informed common sense.

Students say you should have a broad general background in education related areas.

Written Assignment

Students say the most important thing is to write at least a brief outline before you start to write the assignment. They say to be sure to write about the topic. The written assignment will be about a teaching or school-related situation. Be prepared to write an essay, a lesson plan, or a curriculum. It is how well you respond to the education-related situation, not your writing ability, that matters on this written assignment.

Students' Advice to You About Preparing for the ATS-W

1. Get lots of teaching experience.
2. Learn how to answer reading comprehension items and how to write essays, lesson plans, and curricula. Practice reading and writing.
3. Get a broad overview of education related areas.
4. Take practice tests in a realistic situation.

Follow This Study Plan

Begin to work six to thirteen weeks before the test. Use the study plan that follows.

Most review chapters start with a review quiz. Take each review quiz. Use the answer key to mark the review quiz. Each incorrect answer will point to a specific portion of the chapter review. Go over the subject matter review indicated by the review quiz. Don't spend your time reviewing things you already know.

Each review chapter ends with practice items. Complete these items to help you get ready for the Practice LASTs and Practice ATS-Ws.

LAST AND ATS-W STUDY PLAN

This plan starts thirteen weeks before the test. It assumes you are taking both the LAST and the ATS-W. Adjust the time line if you are taking only one test, if you have less time to study or if you have particular subject matter strengths or needs. Write your target completion date for each step of the review in the space provided. Try to read and write every day as you prepare for the test(s).

Thirteen weeks to go   Target Completion Date_____
Review the test preparation on pages 27–323. (Both tests)
Review the test taking strategies on pages 16–21. (Both tests)

Twelve weeks to go   Target Completion Date_____
Review Chapter 3—Reading (Both tests)

Eleven weeks to go   Target Completion Date_____
Review Chapter 4—Writing (Both tests)

Ten weeks to go   *Target Completion Date_____*
Review Chapter 5—Mathematics

Nine weeks to go   *Target Completion Date_____*
Review Chapter 6—Science

Eight weeks to go   *Target Completion Date_____*
Review Chapter 7—History and Social Science

Seven weeks to go   *Target Completion Date_____*
Review Chapter 8—Visual and Performing Arts
Review Chapter 9—Literature and Humanities

Six weeks to go   *Target Completion Date_____*
Review Chapter 10—ATS-W

Five weeks to go   *Target Completion Date_____*
Review Chapter 10—ATS-W
Review the test taking strategies on pages 16–21.
Review the special test taking strategies in each chapter.

Four weeks before the actual test   *Target Completion Date_____*
Take Practice LAST I and ATS-W I (pages 327 and 397).
Try to take the test on Saturday under exact test conditions.

Four weeks to go and
Three weeks to go   *Target Completion Date_____*
Score the test and review the answer explanations.
Go over the review chapters and do more writing to help correct the errors on the practice test.
Review the test taking strategies on pages 16–21.

Two weeks before the actual test   *Target Completion Date_____*
Take Practice LAST II and Practice ATS-W II.
Try to take the test on Saturday under exact test conditions.
Score the test and review the answer explanations.

Two weeks to go   *Target Completion Date_____*
During this week look over those areas you got wrong on the second practice LAST. Go over tests, the answer explanations and go back to the review sections. Read the newspaper every day until the day before the test.

One week to go   *Target Completion Date_____*
The hard work is over. You're coasting in for a landing. You know the material on the test. You don't even have to get an A. You just have to pass.

Get up each day at the time you will have to get up the following Saturday. Sit down at the time the test will start and spend about one hour answering questions on practice tests. It's okay that you have answered these questions before.

MONDAY

Make sure you have your admission ticket.
Make sure you know where the test is given.
Make sure you know how you're getting there.

TUESDAY

Visit the test site, if you haven't done it already. You don't want any surprises this Saturday.

WEDNESDAY

Get some sharpened No. 2 pencils, a digital watch or pocket clock, and a good big eraser and put them aside.

THURSDAY

Take a break from preparing for the test, and relax.

FRIDAY

Complete any forms you have to bring to the test.
Prepare any snacks or food you want to bring with you.
Talk to someone who makes you feel good or do something enjoyable and relaxing.
Have a good night's sleep.

SATURDAY—TEST DAY

Dress comfortably. There are no points for appearance.
Eat the same kind of breakfast you've been eating each morning.
Don't stuff yourself. You want your blood racing through your brain, not your stomach.
Get together things to bring to the test including: registration ticket, identification forms, pencils, calculator, eraser, and snacks or food.

Get to the test room, not the parking lot, about 10 to 15 minutes before the start time.
Remember to leave time for parking and walking to the test site.
Hand in your forms—you're in the door. You're ready. This is the easy part.
Follow the test taking strategies in the next section.

PROVEN TEST TAKING STRATEGIES

Testing companies like to pretend that test taking strategies don't help that much. They act like that because they want everyone to think that their tests only measure your knowledge of the subject. Of course, they are just pretending; knowing test taking strategies can make a big difference.

However, there is nothing better than being prepared for the subject matter on this test. These strategies will do you little good if you lack this fundamental knowledge. If you are prepared, then these strategies can make a difference. Use them. Other people will be. Not using them may very well lower your score.

Be Comfortable

Get a good seat. Don't sit near anyone or anything that will distract you. Stay away from your friends. If you don't like where you are sitting, move or ask for another seat. You paid money for this test, and you have a right to favorable test conditions.

You Will Make Mistakes

You are going to make mistakes on this test. The people who wrote the test expect you to make them.

You Are Not Competing with Anyone

Don't worry about how anyone else is doing. Your score does not depend on theirs. When the score report comes out it doesn't say, "Nancy got a 661, but Blaire got a 670." You just want to get the score required for your certificate. If you can do better, that's great. Stay focused. Remember your goal.

MULTIPLE-CHOICE STRATEGIES

It's Not What You Know That Matters, It's Just Which Circle You Fill In

No one you know or care about will see your test. An impersonal machine scores all multiple-choice questions. The machine just senses whether the correct circle on the answer sheet is filled in. That is the way the test makers want it. If that's good enough for them, it should be good enough for you. Concentrate on filling in the correct circle.

You Can Be Right but Be Marked Wrong

If you get the right answer but fill in the wrong circle, the machine will mark it wrong. We told you that filling in the right circle was what mattered. We strongly recommend that you follow this strategy.

Write the letter for your answer big in the test booklet next to the number for the problem. If you change your mind about an answer, cross off the "old" letter and write the "new" one. At the end of each section, transfer all the answers together from the test booklet to the answer sheet.

Do Your Work in the Test Booklet

You can write anything you want in your test booklet. The test booklet is not used for scoring and no one will look at it. You can't bring scratch paper to the test so use your booklet instead.

Some of the strategies we recommend involve writing in and marking up the booklet. These strategies work and we strongly recommend that you use them.

Do your work for a question near that question in the test booklet. You can also do work on the cover or wherever else suits you. You may want to do calculations, underline important words, mark up a picture, or draw a diagram.

Watch That Answer Sheet

Remember that a machine is doing the marking. Fill in the correct answer circle completely. Don't put extra pencil marks on the answer section of the answer sheet. Stray marks could be mistaken for answers.

Some Questions Are Traps

Some questions include the words *not*, *least*, or *except*. You are being asked for the answer that doesn't fit with the rest. Be alert for these types of questions.

Save the Hard Questions for Last

You're not supposed to get all the questions correct, and some of them will be too difficult for you. Work through the questions and answer the easy ones. Pass the other ones by. Do these more difficult questions the second time through. If a question seems really hard, draw a circle around the question number in the test booklet. Save these questions until the very end.

They Show You the Answer

Every multiple-choice test shows you the correct answer for each question. The answer is staring right at you. You just have to figure out which one it is. There is a 20 or 25 percent chance you'll get it right by just closing your eyes and pointing.

Some Answers Are Traps

When someone writes a test question, they often include distracters. Distracters are traps—incorrect answers that look like correct answers. It might be an answer to an addition problem when you should be multiplying. It might be a correct answer to a different question. It might just be an answer that catches your eye. Watch out for this type of incorrect answer.

Eliminate the Incorrect Answers

If you can't figure out which answer is correct, then decide which answers can't be correct. Choose the answers you're sure are incorrect. Cross them off in the test booklet. Only one left? That's the correct answer.

Guess, Guess, Guess

If there are still two or more answers left, then guess. Guess the answer from those remaining. Never leave any item blank. There is no penalty for guessing.

WRITTEN ASSIGNMENT STRATEGIES

Here's How They Score You

Written assignments are rated 0–3. The raters use these general guidelines.

3 A well developed, complete written assignment. Shows a thorough response to all parts of the topic. Clear explanations that are well supported. An assignment that is free of significant grammatical, punctuation, or spelling errors.

2 A fairly well developed, complete written assignment. It may not thoroughly respond to all parts of the topic. Fairly clear explanations that may not be well supported. It may contain some significant grammatical, punctuation, or spelling errors.

1 A poorly developed, incomplete written assignment. It does not thoroughly respond to most parts of the topic. Contains many poor explanations that are not well supported. It may contain some significant grammatical, punctuation, or spelling errors.

0 A very poorly developed, incomplete written assignment. It does not thoroughly respond to the topic. Contains only poor, unsupported explanations. Contains numerous significant grammatical, punctuation, or spelling errors

Unscorable Written Assignments

A written assignment is rated unscorable (U) if it is blank; unrelated to the topic, no matter how well written; not long enough to score; written in a language other than English; or illegible. A rating of U means the test is a failure regardless of the score on the multiple-choice section.

Your Responses Are Graded Holistically

Holistic rating means the raters assign a score based on their informed sense about your writing. Raters have a lot of answers to look at and they do not do a detailed analysis.

After each test date, National Evaluation Systems gets together a group of readers in Albany, New York. These readers typically consist of teachers and college professors. They put these readers up in an Albany area motel. At first, representatives of NES show the readers the topics for the recent test and review the types of responses that should be rated 0, 1, 2, or 3. The readers are trained to evaluate the responses according to the NES guidelines.

Each written assignment is evaluated twice, without the second reader knowing the evaluation given by the first reader. If the two evaluations differ significantly, other readers review the assignment.

Using this Section

This section shows you how to write passing essays. It goes without saying that readers have a tedious, tiring assignment. Think about those readers as you write. Write a response that makes it easy for them to give you a high score.

Steps for Writing Passing Written Assignments

Follow these steps to write a passing essay. You should allow about two hours to complete all the steps.

1. **Understand the assignment. (5 minutes)**
   Each topic provides a subject and then describes the subject in more detail.
   Read the topic carefully to ensure that you understand each of these parts.

2. **Choose thesis statement. Write it down. (5 minutes)**
   Readers expect you to have one clear main point of view about the topic.
   Choose yours; make sure it addresses the entire topic, and stick to it.

3. **Write an outline. (20 minutes)**
   Write a brief outline summarizing the following essay elements.
   - Thesis statement
   - Introduction
   - Topic sentence and details for each paragraph
   - Conclusion
   Use this time to plan your essay.

4. **Write the assignment. (40–60 minutes)**
   Essays scoring 2 or 3 higher typically have five, six, or seven paragraphs totaling 300–600 words. Writing an essay this long does not guarantee a passing score, but most passing essays are about this long.
   Use this time to write well.

5. **Proofread and edit your writing. (15 minutes)**
   Read your essay over and correct any errors in usage, spelling, or punctuation. The readers understand that your essay is a first draft and they expect to see corrections.

Apply the Steps

Here's how to apply these steps for a particular written assignment. Follow along and write in your own ideas when called for. Remember, for any written assignment, there are many different thesis statements and essays that would receive a passing score.

WRITTEN ASSIGNMENT

Some people say that machines cause difficulty for people. Others say that machines help people.

Choose one of these positions. Give a specific example of a machine that causes difficulty or one that helps people. Write an essay that explains how the machine you chose is a difficulty for people or helps people.

1. **Understand the written assignment. (5 minutes)**
   The assignment is about machines. I have to decide whether to write about machines that causes difficulty for people OR about machines that help people. I have to give a specific example of a machine that is a difficulty or a machine that helps.

   I've got to stick to this topic.

   I'm going to choose machines that help people.

   A complete response to the topic is an essay about a machine that helps people. There are many machines to choose from. An incomplete response will significantly lower the score.

2. **Choose thesis statement. Write it down. (5 minutes)**
   This important step sets the stage for your entire essay. Work through this section actively. Write down the names of several machines that help people. There is no one correct answer, so it does not have to be an exhaustive list.

   > Computers
   > Escalator
   > Car
   > Heart-lung machine
   > Fax machine

   Suppose you choose the heart-lung machine.

   Now write how, what, and why heart-lung machines help people.
   How: Circulate blood in place of the heart?
   What: Replaces the heart during heart surgery.
   Why: The heart is unable to pump blood when it is being operated on.

   Now write the choice from your list of machines. _____

   Thesis statement.

   My thesis statement is: Heart-lung machines are machines that help people by taking the place of the heart during heart surgery.

   The thesis statement identifies the heart-lung machine as a machine that helps people and explains the basis for my choice of the heart-lung machine. Both parts are needed for an effective thesis statement.

   Write your thesis statement.

3. Write an outline. (20 minutes)
  - Introduction, including the thesis statement
  - A heart-lung machine saves lives.
    People would die if the machines were not available.

  - The machine circulates and filters blood during operations.
    Special membranes filter the blood, removing impurities.
  - The heart can literally stop while the heart-lung machine is in use
    Doctors have to restart the heart.
  - Conclusion

  My outline consists of an introduction, topic sentences and supporting
  details for three paragraphs, and a conclusion. That's five paragraphs in all.

Write an outline for your written assignment.

_____

_____

_____

_____

_____

_____

_____

_____

_____

_____

4. Write the assignment. (40–60 minutes)

I spent the time writing an outline to plan my essay. I am going to rely on that plan as I
write my essay.
Use a separate piece of paper.
Write your own essay about the heart-lung machine—a machine that helps people.

5. Proofread and edit your essay. (15 minutes)
Edit your essay. Remember that readers expect to see changes.

Check

You will find five rated sample essays on this topic on this and the following pages. Compare your essays to these sample essays. Rate your essay 0–3 using these samples and the scoring guide on page 19.

Practice

Write, proofread, and edit an essay on your topic. Rate your essay 0–3. Try to show your essays to an English professor or an experienced essay evaluator. Ask that person to evaluate your essays and make recommendations for improving your writing.

You'll have more opportunities to practice written assignments in Chapter 4—English and Writing and Chapter 10—ATS-W.

SAMPLE WRITTEN ASSIGNMENTS

ESSAY 1

Heart-lung machines are a medical miracle. Heart-lung machines are used in hospitals all over the country. Doctors rely on this machine during surgery. Heart-lung machines keep people alive during surgery and they use them to do open heart surgery. Lots of people can thank the heart-lung machine for keeping them alive. Some people say that there are too many bypass surgeries done every year and this may cause more problems than it fixes. However lots of people would die without the machine. It is a good thing that the heart-lung machine was invented.

Total score from both readers—1 or 2 out of 6.

ESSAY 2

Heart-lung machines are use in hospital all over the world. They get use every day. People are hook up to them when they are having surgry like if they are in open heart surgery.

I will now present one of way heart lung-machines are use. Once we did't have heart-lung machines to help a doctor. When the machine was invent we see lots of changes in surgry that a doctor can do. The doctor can oprate during the person heart not work. My gran-mothr went to the hospital for have surgry and they use the machine. Where she would have been without the machine.

And the machine keep blood move through the body. The doctor can take their time to fix a person heart while they are laying their on the operating room. I know someone who work in a hospital and they said don't know how it was possible befour the machine.

Last, that machine clean a bodies blood as it foes through. The blood won't poison the person who blood it is. But it wood be better if the body could clean it's own blood. A body is better than a machine.

I did tell about how the machine work and what it did. The machine can save a lifes.

Total score from both readers—2 or 3 out of 6.

ESSAY 3

Heart lung machines are a medical miracle. They are used in hospitals all over the world. Heart lung machines are used during open heart surgery to circulate a patients blood and clean the blood. These machines can save lots of lives.

Heart-lung machines have made open heart surgery possible. Before they were invented, many people died because of disaese or during surgery. Surgery would not have been possible before then. And many people are alive today because of them. Besides surgery can now go on for hours. Sometimes the surgry can last as long as 12 hours. The heart lung machine makes things possible and saves lives.

Heart-lung machines circulate blood through the body. It pumps like a heart. The heart can stop and the heart lung machine will pump instead. Then the blood moves through the body just like the heart was pumping. So the blood gets to all the viens. It is unbelievable how the heart-lung machine can work and to keep people from dying.

The heart-lung machine can clean a persons blood. All the bad stuff gets taken out of the blood before it goes back into the body. That way the body won't get poison. I know of someone who had their blood cleaned by the machine while they were operated on. The person was unconscience. The doctor fixed his heart. Since the machine was going the persons heart was stopped. The doctor had to start it up again. It was pretty scary to think about that happening to a person. But the machine took all the bad stuff out of the blood and the person lived.

To conclude, I believe that the heart lung machine is great for people who need open heart surgery. It pumps and cleans their blood too. They are a medical miracle.

Total score from both readers—4 or 5 out of 6.

ESSAY 4

Every day the heart-lung machine saves someone's life. Each day we walk by someone who is alive because of a heart-lung machine. Each day in hospitals throughout the world, skilled surgeons perform difficult surgery with the aid of a heart-lung machine. Some day, we may be kept alive by a heart-lung machine. The heart-lung machine is a wonderful machine that makes open-heart surgery possible by pumping and cleaning a person's blood. Surgeons use the machine during open heart surgery.

The heart-lung machine makes open-heart surgery possible. Open-heart surgery means the doctor is operating on the inside of the heart. In order to operate on the inside of a heart, the flow of blood through the heart must be stopped. But without blood flow, the patient will die. Researchers worked for decades to find a way to keep a person alive while the heart was stopped. Many of their early attempts failed; however, during this century the researchers and inventors were successful. They named their invention the heart-lung machine. The first heart-lung machines were probably very primitive, but today's machines are very sophisticated.

The heart-lung machine circulates blood while the heart is not pumping. The machine is hooked up to a person's circulatory system and acts just like a heart. The blood is taken from the body into one side of the machine and pumped back into the body through the other side of the machine. Blood returning to the heart is taken into the machine. The blood pumped out travels to every part of the body. The heart-lung machine helps the patient by replacing blood while the heart is stopped during open-heart surgery.

However, just pumping blood is not enough. As blood passes through a person's body, the body takes oxygen stored in the blood. Blood starts through the body full of oxygen and returns from the body without much oxygen. Normally, the lungs would take in oxygen and place that oxygen in the blood. But since the person's heart is stopped, the lungs are not working. The heart-lung machine does the lung's work and places oxygen in the blood as the blood passes through the machine.

The heart-lung machine makes open-heart surgery possible. The machine circulates and oxygenates a person's blood while their heart is stopped. Without the machine, many people would die from heart disease or would die during surgery. The heart-lung machine is a machine that helps people by keeping them alive and holds the promise for even more amazing machines to come.

Total score from both readers—6 out of 6.

Handwritten Essay

This is what Essay 3 looked like in handwritten form. This is the essay that the raters would actually see. Note the editorial changes that the student has made during writing and editing. The raters expect to see these changes and marks.

Heart lung machines are a ~~medicine~~ medical miracle. They are used in hospitals all over the world. Heart lung machines are used during open heart surgery to circulate a patients blood and clean the blood. These machines can save lots of ~~lives~~ lives.

Heart-lung machines have made open heart surgery possible. Before they were invented, many people died because of disease or during surgery. Surgery would not have been ~~impossible~~ possible before then. And many people are alive ~~here~~ today because of them. Besides surgery can now go on for hours. Sometimes the surgry can last as long as 12 hours. The heart lung machine makes things ~~very~~ possible and saves lives.

Heart-lung machines circulate blood ~~thru~~ through a body. It pumps like a heart. The heart can stop and the heart lung machine will pump instead. Then the blood moves through the body just like the heart ~~is~~ was pumping. So the blood gets to all the viens. It is ~~too~~ unbelievable ~~why~~ how the heart-lung machine can work and to keep people from dying.

The heart-lung machine can clean a persons blood. All the bad stuff gets taken out of the blood before it goes back into the body. That way the body won't get poison. I know of someone who had their blood cleaned by the machine while they were operated on. The person was ~~unconscience~~ unconscious. The doctor fixed his heart. ~~Since~~ Because the machine was going the persons heart was stopped. The doctor had to start it up again. It was pretty scary to think about that happening to a person. But the machine took all the bad stuff out of the blood and the person lived.

To conclude, I believe that the heart lung machine is great for people who need open heart surgery. It pumps and cleans their blood too. They are a medical miracle.

PART II

Subject Matter Preparation, Strategies, and Practice for the LAST and the ATS-W

3 READING

TEST INFO BOX

This review chapter comes first because it contains the most important review for both of the multiple-choice tests. Most of the LAST and ATS-W multiple-choice items are reading comprehension items.

This is not to say that skilled reading comprehension alone will earn a passing score. However, all the test-takers this writer talked to agree that reading comprehension is the single most important skill for passing the multiple-choice tests.

The chapter ends with reading practice items.

MULTIPLE-CHOICE TEST
There are about 8 items on the LAST that specifically measure reading comprehension.

USING THIS CHAPTER

❑ Review the entire Reading section.
❑ Complete the Reading Practice Items on page 49.

VOCABULARY REVIEW

You can't read if you don't know the vocabulary. But you don't have to know every word in the dictionary. Follow this reasonable approach to developing a good vocabulary for these tests.

CONTEXT CLUES

Many times you can figure out a word from its context. Look at these examples. Synonyms, antonyms, examples, or descriptions may help you figure out the word.

1. The woman's mind wandered as her two friends *prated* on. It really did not bother her though. In all the years she had known them, they had always *babbled* about their lives. It was almost comforting.
2. The wind *abated* in the late afternoon. Things were different yesterday when the wind had *picked up* toward the end of the day.
3. The argument with her boss had been her *Waterloo*. She wondered if the *defeat* suffered by Napoleon *at this famous place* had felt the same.
4. The events swept the politician into a *vortex* of controversy. The politician knew what it meant to be spun around like a toy boat in the *swirl of water* that swept down the bathtub drain.

Passage 1 gives a synonym for the unknown word. We can tell that *prated* means babbled. *Babbled* is used as a synonym of *prated* in the passage.

Passage 2 gives an antonym for the unknown word. We can tell that *abated* means slowed down or diminished because *picked up* is used as an antonym of *abated*.

Passage 3 gives a description of the unknown word. The description of *Waterloo* tells us that the word means *defeat*.

Passage 4 gives an example of the unknown word. This example of a *swirl of water* going down the bathtub drain gives us a good idea of what a *vortex* is.

ROOTS

A root is the basic element of a word. The root is usually related to the word's origin. Roots can often help you figure out the word's meaning. Here are some roots that may help you.

Root	Meaning	Examples
bio	life	biography, biology
circu	around	circumference, circulate
frac	break	fraction, refract
geo	earth	geology, geography
mal	bad	malicious, malcontent
matr, mater	mother	maternal, matron
neo	new	neonate, neoclassic
patr, pater	father	paternal, patron
spec	look	spectacles, specimen
tele	distant	telephone, television

PREFIXES

Prefixes are syllables that come at the beginning of a word. Prefixes usually have a standard meaning. They can often help you figure out the word's meaning. Here is a list of prefixes that may help you figure out a word.

Prefix	Meaning	Examples
a-	not	amoral, apolitical
il-, im-, ir-	not	illegitimate, immoral, incorrect
un-	not	unbearable, unknown
non-	not	nonbeliever, nonsense
ant-, anti-	against	antiwar, antidote
de-	opposite	defoliate, declaw
mis-	wrong	misstep, misdeed
ante-	before	antedate, antecedent
fore-	before	foretell, forecast
post-	after	postfight, postoperative
re-	again	refurbish, redo
super-	above	superior, superstar
sub-	below	subsonic, subpar

THE VOCABULARY LIST

Here is a list of a few hundred vocabulary words. This list includes everyday words and a few specialized education terms. Read through the list and visualize the words and their definitions. After a while you will become very familiar with them.

Of course, this is not anywhere near all the words you need to know for the exams. But they will give you a start. These words also will give you some idea of the kinds of words you may encounter on the examinations.

Another great way to develop a vocabulary is to read a paper every day and a news magazine every week, in addition to the other reading you are doing. There are also several inexpensive books, including *1100 Words You Need to Know*, *Pocket Guide to Vocabulary*, and *Vocabulary Success* from Barron's, which may help you develop your vocabulary further.

abhor To regard with horror
I abhor violence.

abstain To refrain by choice
Ray decided to abstain from fattening foods.

abstract Not related to any object, theoretical
Mathematics can be very abstract.

acquisition An addition to an established group or collection
The museum's most recent acquisition was an early Roman vase.

admonish To correct firmly but kindly
The teacher admonished the student not to chew gum in class.

adroit Skillful or nimble in difficult circumstances
The nine year old was already an adroit gymnast.

adversary A foe or enemy
The wildebeast was ever-alert for its ancient adversary, the lion.

advocate To speak for an idea; a person who speaks for an idea
Lou was an advocate of gun control.

aesthetic Pertaining to beauty
Ron found the painting a moving aesthetic experience.

affective To do with the emotional or feeling aspect of learning
Len read the Taxonomy of Educational Objectives: Affective Domain.

alias An assumed name
The check forger had used an alias.

alleviate To reduce or make more bearable
The hot shower helped alleviate the pain in her back.

allude To make an indirect reference to, hint at
Elaine only alluded to her previous trips through the state.

ambiguous Open to many interpretations
That is an ambiguous statement.

apathy Absence of passion or emotion
The teacher tried to overcome their apathy toward the subject.

apprehensive Fear or unease about possible outcomes
Bob was apprehensive about visiting the dentist.

aptitude The ability to gain from a particular type of instruction
The professor pointed out that aptitude alone was not enough for success in school.

articulate To speak clearly and distinctly, present a point of view
Chris was chosen to articulate the group's point of view.

assess To measure or determine an outcome or value
There are many informal ways to assess learning.

attest To affirm or certify
I can attest to Cathy's ability as a softball pitcher.

augment To increase or add to
The new coins augmented the already large collection.

belated Past time or tardy
George sent a belated birthday card.

benevolent Expresses good will or kindly feelings
The club was devoted to performing benevolent acts.

biased A prejudiced view or action
The judge ruled that the decision was biased.

bolster To shore up, support
The explorer sang to bolster her courage.

candid Direct and outspoken
Lee was well known for her candid comments.

caricature Exaggerated, ludicrous picture, in words or a cartoon
The satirist presented world leaders as caricatures.

carnivorous Flesh eating or predatory
The lion is a carnivorous animal.

censor A person who judges the morality of others; act on that judgment
Please don't censor my views!

censure Expression of disapproval, reprimand
The senate acted to censure the congressman.

cessation The act of ceasing or halting
The eleventh hour marked the cessation of hostilities.

chronic Continuing and constant
Asthma can be a chronic condition.

clandestine Concealed or secret
The spy engaged in clandestine activities.

cogent Intellectually convincing
He presented a cogent argument.

cognitive Relates to the intellectual area of learning
Lou read the Taxonomy of Educational Objectives: Cognitive Domain.

competency Demonstrated ability
Bert demonstrated the specified mathematics competency.

complacent Unaware self-satisfaction
The tennis player realized she had become complacent.

concept A generalization
The professor lectured on concept development.

congenital Existing at birth but non-hereditary
The baby had a small congenital defect.

contemporaries Belonging in the same time period, about the same age
Piaget and Bruner were contemporaries.

contempt Feeling or showing disdain or scorn
She felt nothing but contempt for their actions.

contentious Argumentative
Tim was in a contentious mood.

corroborate To make certain with other information, to confirm
The reporter would always corroborate a story before publication.

credence Claim to acceptance or trustworthiness
They did not want to lend credence to his views.

cursory Surface, not in depth
Ron gave his car a cursory inspection.

daunt To intimidate with fear
Harry did not let the difficulty of the task daunt him.

debacle Disastrous collapse or rout
The whole trip had been a debacle.

debilitate To make feeble
He was concerned that the flu would debilitate him.

decadent Condition of decline/decay
Joan said in frustration, "We live in a decadent society."

deductive Learning that proceeds from general to specific
He proved his premise using deductive logic.

demographic Population data
The census gathers demographic information.

denounce To condemn a person or idea
The diplomat rose in the United Nations to denounce the plan.

deter To prevent or stop an action, usually by some threat
The president felt that the peace conference would help deter aggression.

diligent A persistent effort; a person who makes such an effort
The investigator was diligent in her pursuit of the truth.

discern To perceive or recognize, often by insight
The principal attempted to discern which student was telling the truth.

discord Disagreement or disharmony
Gail's early promotion led to discord in the office.

discriminate To distinguish among people or groups based on their characteristics
It is not appropriate to discriminate based on race or ethnicity.

disdain To show or act with contempt
The professional showed disdain for her amateurish efforts.

disseminate To send around, scatter
The health organization will disseminate any new information on the flu.

divergent Thinking that extends in many directions, is not focused
Les was an intelligent but divergent thinker.

diverse Not uniform, varied
Alan came from a diverse neighborhood.

duress coercion
He claimed that he confessed under duress.

eccentric Behaves unusually, different from the norm
His long hair and midnight walks made Albert appear eccentric.

eclectic Drawing from several ideas or practices
Joe preferred an eclectic approach to the practice of psychology.

eloquent Vivid, articulate expression
The congregation was spellbound by the eloquent sermon.

emanate To flow out, come forth
How could such wisdom emanate from one so young?

embellish To make things seem more than they are
Art loved to embellish the truth.

empirical From observation or experiment
The scientist's conclusions were based on empirical evidence.

employment A job or professional position (paid)
You seek employment so you can make the big bucks.

enduring Lasting over the long term
Their friendship grew into an enduring relationship.

enhance To improve or build up
The mechanic used a fuel additive to enhance the car's performance.

enigma A mystery or puzzle
The communist bloc is an "enigma wrapped inside a mystery." (Churchill)

equity Equal attention or treatment
The workers were seeking pay equity with others in their industry.

equivocal Uncertain, capable of multiple interpretations
In an attempt to avoid conflict, the negotiator took an equivocal stand.

expedite To speed up, facilitate
Hal's job at the shipping company was to expedite deliveries.

exploit Take maximum advantage of, perhaps unethically
Her adversary tried to exploit her grief to gain an advantage.

extrinsic Coming from outside
The teacher turned to extrinsic motivation.

farce A mockery
The attorney objected, saying that the testimony made the trial a farce.

feign To pretend, make a false appearance of
Some people feign illness to get out of work.

fervent Marked by intense feeling
The spokesman presented a fervent defense of the company's actions.

fiasco Total failure
They had not prepared for the presentation, and it turned into a fiasco.

formidable Difficult to surmount
State certification requirements can present a formidable obstacle.

fracas A noisy quarrel or a scrap
The debate turned into a full-fledged fracas.

gamut Complete range or extent
Waiting to take the test, her mind ran the gamut of emotions.

glib Quickness suggesting insincerity
The glib response made Rita wonder about the speaker's sincerity.

grave Very serious or weighty
The supervisor had grave concerns about the worker's ability.

guile Cunning, crafty, duplicitous
When the truth failed, he tried to win his point with guile.

handicapped Having one or more disabilities
The child study team classified Loren as handicapped.

harass Bother persistently
Some fans came to harass the players on the opposing team.

heterogeneous A group with normal variation in ability or performance
Students from many backgrounds formed a heterogeneous population.

homogeneous A group with little variation in ability or performance
The school used test scores to place students in homogeneous groups.

hypocrite One who feigns a virtuous character or belief
Speaking against drinking and then driving drunk make him a hypocrite!

immune Protected or exempt from disease or harm
The vaccination made Ray immune to measles.

impartial Fair and objective
The contestants agreed on an objective, impartial referee.

impasse Situation with no workable solution
The talks had not stopped, but they had reached an impasse.

impede To retard or obstruct
Mason did not let adversity impede his progress.

implicit Understood but not directly stated
They never spoke about the matter, but they had an implicit understanding.

indifferent Uncaring or apathetic
The teacher was indifferent to the student's pleas for an extension.

indigenous Native to an area
The botanist recognized it as an indigenous plant.

inductive Learning that proceeds from specific to general
Science uses an inductive process, from examples to a generalization.

inevitable Certain and unavoidable
After the rains, the collapse of the dam was inevitable.

infer To reach a conclusion not explicitly stated
The advertisement sought to infer that the product was superior.

inhibit To hold back or restrain
The hormone was used to inhibit growth.

innovate To introduce something new or change established procedure
Mere change was not enough, they had to innovate the procedure.

inquiry Question-based Socratic learning
Much of science teaching uses inquiry-based learning.

intrinsic inherent, the essential nature
The teacher drew on the meaning of the topic for an intrinsic motivation.

inundate To overwhelm, flood
It was December, and mail began to inundate the post office.

jocular Characterized by joking or good nature
The smiling man seemed to be a jocular fellow.

judicial Relating to the administration of justice
His goal was to have no dealings with the judicial system.

knack A talent for doing something
Ron had a real knack for mechanical work.

languid Weak, lacking energy
The sunbather enjoyed a languid afternoon at the shore.

liaison An illicit relationship or a means of communication
The governor appointed his chief aid liaison to the senate.

lucid Clear and easily understood
The teacher answered the question in a direct and lucid way.

magnanimous Generous in forgiving
Loretta is a magnanimous to a fault.

malignant Very injurious, evil
Crime is a malignant sore on our society.

malleable Open to being shaped or influenced
He had a malleable position on gun control.

meticulous Very careful and precise
Gina took meticulous care of the fine china.

miser A money hoarder
The old miser had more money than he could ever use.

monotonous Repetitive and boring
Circling the airport, waiting to land, became monotonous.

mores Understood rules of society
Linda made following social mores her goal in life.

motivation Something that creates interest or action
Most good lessons begin with good motivation.

myriad Large indefinite number
Look skyward and be amazed by the myriad of stars.

naive Lacking sophistication
Laura is unaware, and a little naive, about the impact she has on others.

nemesis A formidable rival
Lex Luthor is Superman's nemesis.

novice A beginner
Her unsteady legs revealed that Sue was a novice skater.

nullified Removed the importance of
The penalty nullified the 20-yard gain made by the running back.

objective A goal
The teacher wrote an objective for each lesson.

oblivious Unaware and unmindful
Les was half asleep and oblivious to the racket around him.

obscure Vague, unclear, uncertain
The lawyer quoted an obscure reference.

ominous Threatening or menacing
There were ominous black storm clouds on the horizon.

palatable Agreeable, acceptable
Sandy's friends tried to make her punishment more palatable.

panorama A comprehensive view or picture
The visitors' center offered a panorama of the canyon below.

pedagogy The science of teaching
Part of certification tests focus on pedagogy.

perpetuate To continue or cause to be remembered
A plaque was put up to perpetuate the memory of the retiring teacher.

pompous Exaggerated self-importance
Rona acted pompous, but Lynne suspected she was very empty inside.

precarious Uncertain, beyond one's control
A diver sat on a precarious perch on a cliff above the water.

precedent An act or instance that sets the standard
The judge's ruling set a precedent for later cases.

preclude To act to make impossible or impracticable
Beau did not want to preclude any options.

precocious Very early development
Chad was very precocious and ran at six months.

prolific Abundant producer
Isaac Asimov was a prolific science fiction writer.

prognosis A forecast or prediction
The stock broker gave a guarded prognosis for continued growth.

provoke To stir up or anger
Children banging on the cage would provoke the circus lion to growl.

psychomotor Relates to the motor skill area of learning
I read the Taxonomy of Behavioral Objectives: Psychomotor Domain.

quagmire Predicament or difficult situation
The regulations were a quagmire of conflicting rules and vague terms.

qualm Feeling of doubt or misgiving
The teacher had not a single qualm about giving the student a low grade.

quandary A dilemma
The absence of the teacher aide left the teacher in a quandary.

quench To put out, satisfy
The glass of water was not enough to quench his thirst.

rancor Bitter continuing resentment
A deep rancor had existed between the two friends since the accident.

rationale The basis or reason for something
The speeder tried to present a rationale to the officer who stopped her.

reciprocal Mutual interchange
Each person got something out of their reciprocal arrangement.

refute To prove false
The lawyer used new evidence to refute claims made by the prosecution.

remedial Designed to compensate for learning deficits
Jim spent one period a day in remedial instruction.

reprove Criticize gently
The teacher would reprove students for chewing gum in class.

repudiate To reject or disown
The senator repudiated membership in an all male club.

resolve To reach a definite conclusion
A mediator was called in to resolve the situation.

retrospect Contemplation of the past
Ryan noted, in retrospect, that leaving home was his best decision.

revere To hold in the highest regard
Citizens of the town revere their long time mayor.

sanction To issue authoritative approval or a penalty
The boxing commissioner had to sanction the match.

scrutinize To inspect with great care
You should scrutinize any document before signing it.

siblings Brothers or sisters
The holidays give me the chance to spend time with my siblings.

skeptical Doubting, questioning the validity
The principal was skeptical about the students' reason for being late.

solace Comfort in misfortune
Her friends provided solace in her time of grief.

solitude Being alone
Pat enjoyed her Sunday afternoon moments of solitude.

stagnant Inert, contaminated
In dry weather the lake shrank to a stagnant pool.

stereotype An oversimplified generalized view or belief
We are all guilty of fitting people into a stereotype.

subsidy Financial assistance
Chris received a subsidy from her company so she could attend school.

subtle Faint, not easy to find or understand
Subtle changes in the teller's actions alerted the police to the robbery.

subterfuge A deceptive strategy
The spy used subterfuge to gain access to the secret materials.

superficial Surface, not profound
The inspector gave the car a superficial inspection.

tacit Not spoken, inferred
They had a tacit agreement.

taxonomy Classification of levels of thinking or organisms
I read each Taxonomy of Educational Objectives.

tenacious Persistent and determined
The police officer was tenacious in pursuit of a criminal.

tentative Unsure, uncertain
The athletic director set up a tentative basketball schedule.

terminate To end, conclude
He wanted to terminate the relationship.

transition Passage from one activity to another
The transition from college student to teacher was not easy.

trepidation Apprehension, state of dread
Erin felt some trepidation about beginning her new job

trivial Unimportant, ordinary
The seemingly trivial occurrence had taken on added importance.

ubiquitous Everywhere, omnipresent
A walk through the forest invited attacks from the ubiquitous mosquitoes.

ultimatum A final demand
After a trying day, the teacher issued an ultimatum to the class.

usurp To wrongfully and forcefully seize and hold, particularly power
The association vice president tried to usurp the president's power.

vacillate To swing indecisively
He had a tendency to vacillate in his stance on discipline.

valid Logically correct
The math teacher was explaining a valid mathematical proof.

vehement Forceful, passionate
The child had a vehement reaction to the teacher's criticism.

vestige A sign of something no longer there or existing
Old John was the last vestige of the first teachers to work at the school.

vicarious Experience through the activities or feelings of others
He had to experience sports in a vicarious way through his students.

virulent Very poisonous or noxious
The coral snake has a particularly virulent venom.

vital Important and essential
The school secretary was a vital part of the school.

waffle To write or speak in a misleading way
The spokesperson waffled as she tried to explain away the mistake.

wary Watchful, on guard
The soldiers were very wary of any movements in the field.

Xanadu An idyllic, perfect place
All wished for some time in Xanadu.

yearned Longed or hoped for
Liz yearned for a small class.

zeal Diligent devotion to a cause
Ron approached his job with considerable zeal.

STEPS FOR ANSWERING MULTIPLE-CHOICE READING ITEMS

Most of the LAST and the ATS-W consists of passages followed by multiple-choice questions. You do not have to know what an entire reading passage is about. You just have to know enough to get the answer correct. Less than half, often less than 25 percent, of the information in any passage is needed to answer all the questions.

You do not have to read the passage in detail. In fact, careful slow reading will almost certainly get you into trouble. Strange as it seems, follow this advice—avoid careful, detailed reading at all costs.

Buried among all the false gold in the passage are a few valuable nuggets. Follow these steps to hit pay dirt and avoid the fool's gold.

READING ABOUT READING

Reading seems to be a natural process. Reading about reading and about steps to taking reading tests can seem contrived and confusing. However, we know that these steps and techniques work. Once you apply the steps to the practice exercises, your reading ability and scores will improve. Refer also to the section on Reading and Interpreting Literature on page 254.

FIVE STEPS TO TAKING A READING TEST

During a reading test follow these steps.

1. Skim to find the topic of each paragraph.
2. Read the questions and answers.
3. Eliminate incorrect answers.
4. Scan the details to find the answer.
5. Choose the answer that is absolutely correct.

Skim to Find the Topic of Each Paragraph

Your first job is to find the topic of each paragraph. The topic is what a paragraph or passage is about.

The topic of a paragraph is usually found in the first and last sentences. Read the first and last sentences just enough to find the topic. You can write the topic in the margin next to the passage. Remember, the test booklet is yours. You can mark it up as much as you like.

Reading Sentences

Every sentence has a subject that tells what the sentence is about. The sentence also has a verb that tells what the subject is doing or links the subject to the complement. The sentence may also contain a complement that receives the action or describes what is being said about the subject. The words underlined in the following examples are the ones you would focus on as you preview.

1. The famous educator <u>John Dewey founded</u> an educational movement called <u>progressive education.</u>

2. Sad to say, we have learned <u>American school children</u> of all ages <u>are poorly nourished.</u>

You may occasionally encounter a paragraph or passage in which the topic can't be summarized from the first and last sentences. This type of paragraph usually contains factual information. If this happens, you will have to read the entire paragraph.

Fact, Opinion, or Fiction

If it is a factual passage, the author will present the fact and support it with details and examples. If the passage presents an opinion, the author will give the opinion and support it with arguments, examples, and other details. Many passages combine fact and opinion. If it is a fictional passage, the author will tell a story with details, descriptions, and examples about people, places, or things.

Once you find the topic, you will probably need more information to answer the questions. But don't worry about this other information and details now. You can go back and find it after you have read the questions.

Read the Questions and the Answers

Now read the questions—one at a time. Read the answers for the question you are working on. Be sure that you understand what each question and its answer mean.

Before you answer a question, be sure you know whether it is asking for a fact or an inference. If the question asks for a fact, the correct answer will identify a main idea or supporting detail. We'll discuss more about main ideas and details later. The correct answer may also identify a cause-and-effect relationship among ideas or be a paraphrase or summary of parts of the passage. Look for these.

If the question asks for an inference, the correct answer will identify the author's purpose, assumptions, or attitude and the difference between fact and the author's opinion. Look for these elements.

Eliminate Incorrect Answers

Read the answers and eliminate the ones that you absolutely know are incorrect. Read the answers literally. Look for words such as *always, never, must, all*. If you can find a single exception to this type of sweeping statement, then the answer can't be correct. Eliminate it.

Scan the Details to Find the Answer

Once you have eliminated answers, compare the other answers to the passage. When you find the answer that is confirmed by the passage—stop. That is your answer choice. Follow these other suggestions for finding the correct answer.

You will often need to read details to find the main idea of a paragraph. The main idea of a paragraph is what the writer has to say about the topic. Most questions are about the main idea of a paragraph. Scan the details about the main idea until you find the answer. Scanning means skipping over information that does not answer the question.

Look at this paragraph.

> There are many types of boats. Some are very fast while others could sleep a whole platoon of soldiers. I prefer the old putt-putt fishing boat with a ten-horsepower motor. That was a boat with a purpose. You didn't scare many people, but the fish were sure worried.

The topic of this paragraph is boats. The main idea is that the writer prefers small fishing boats to other boats.

Unstated Topic and Main Idea

Sometimes the topic and main idea are not stated. Consider this passage.

> The Chinese were the first to use sails thousands of years ago, hundreds of years before sails were used in Europe. The Chinese also used the wheel and the kite long before they were used on the European continent. Experts believe that many other Chinese inventions were used from three hundred to one thousand three hundred years before they were used in Europe.

The topic of this paragraph is inventions. The main idea of the paragraph is that the Chinese invented and used many things hundreds and thousands of years before they appeared in Europe.

Some Answers Are Not Related to the Main Idea

Some answers are not related to the main idea of a paragraph. These questions may be the most difficult to answer. You just have to keep scanning the details until you find the correct answer.

Who Wrote This Answer?

People who write tests go to great lengths to choose a correct answer that cannot be questioned. That is what they get paid for. They are not paid to write answers that have a higher meaning or include great truths.

Test writers want to be asked to write questions and answers again. They want to avoid valid complaints from test takers like you who raise legitimate concerns about their answers.

They usually accomplish this difficult task in one of two ways. They may write answers that are very specific and based directly on the reading. They may also write correct answers that seem very vague.

A Vague Answer Can Be Correct

How can a person write a vague answer that is correct? Think of it this way. If I wrote that a person is 6 feet 5 inches tall, you could get out a tape measure to check my facts. Since I was very specific, you are more likely to be able to prove me wrong.

On the other hand, if I write that the same person is over 6 feet tall you would be hard pressed to find fault with my statement. So my vague statement was hard to argue with. If the person in question is near 6 feet 5 inches tall, then my vague answer is most likely to be the correct one.

Don't choose an answer just because it seems more detailed or specific. A vague answer may be just as likely to be correct.

Choose the Answer That Is Absolutely Correct

Be sure that your choice answers the question. Be sure that your choice is based on the information contained in the paragraph. Don't choose an answer to another question. Don't choose an answer just because it sounds right. Don't choose an answer just because you agree with it.

There is no room on tests like these for answers that are partially wrong. It is not enough for an answer to be 99.9 percent correct. It must be absolutely, incontrovertibly, unquestionably, indisputably, and unarguably correct.

APPLYING THE STEPS

Let's apply the five steps to this passage and questions.

> Many vocational high schools in the United States give off-site work experience to their students. Students usually work in local businesses part of the school day and attend high school the other part. These programs have made American vocational schools world leaders in making job experience available to teenage students.

According to this paragraph, American vocational high schools are world leaders in making job experience available to teenage students because they
(A) have students attend school only part of the day.
(B) were quick to move their students to schools off-site.
(C) require students to work before they can attend the school.
(D) involve their students in cooperative education programs.

Step 1: Skim to find the topic of each paragraph. Both the first and last sentences tell us that the topic is vocational schools and work experience.

Step 2: Read the questions and answers. Why are American vocational education high schools the world leaders in offering job experience?

Step 3: Eliminate incorrect answers. Answer (C) is obviously wrong. It has to do with work before high school. Answer (B) is also incorrect. This has to do with attending school off-site. This leaves answers (A) and (D).

Step 4: Scan the details to find the answer. Scan the details and find that parts of answer (A) are found in the passage. In answer (D) you have to know that cooperative education is another name for off-site work during school.

Step 5: Choose the answer that is absolutely correct. It is down to answer (A) or answer (D). But answer (A) contains only part of the reason that vocational education high schools have gained such acclaim. Answer (D) is the absolutely correct answer.

Here's how to apply the steps to the following passage.

Problem Solving

Problem solving has become the main focus of mathematics learning. Students learn problem-solving strategies and then apply them to problems. Many tests now focus on problem solving and limit the number of computational problems. The problem-solving movement is traced to George Polya who wrote several problem-solving books for high school teachers.

Problem Solving Strategies

Problem-solving strategies include guess and check, draw a diagram, and make a list. Many of the strategies are taught as skills, which inhibits flexible and creative thinking. Problems in textbooks can also limit the power of the strategies. However, the problem-solving movement will be with us for some time, and a number of the strategies are useful.

Step 1: Skim to find the topic of each paragraph. The topic of the first paragraph is problem solving. You find the topic in both the first and last sentences. Write the topic next to the paragraph. The topic for the second paragraph is problem-solving strategies. Write the topic next to the paragraph.

Now we are ready to look at the questions. If the question is about problem solving "in general" we start looking in the first paragraph for the answer. If the question is about strategies, we start looking in the second paragraph for the answer.

Step 2: Read the questions and answers.

> According to this passage, a difficulty with teaching problem-solving strategies is:
> (A) The strategies are too difficult for children.
> (B) The strategies are taught as skills.
> (C) The strategies are in textbooks.
> (D) The strategies are part of a movement.

Step 3: Eliminate incorrect answers. Answer (A) can't be right because difficulty is not mentioned in the passage. That leaves (B), (C), and (D) for us to consider.

Step 4: Scan the details to find the answer. The question asks about strategies so we look immediately to the second paragraph for the answer. The correct answer is (B). Choice (C) is not correct because the passage does not mention strategies in textbooks. There is no indication that (D) is correct.

Step 5: Choose the answer that is absolutely correct. The correct choice is (B).

PRACTICE PASSAGE

Apply the five steps to this practice passage. Darken the letter of the correct answer. Follow the directions given below. The answers to these questions are found on pages 45–48. Do not look at the answers until you complete your work.

Read the following passage. After reading the passage, choose the best answer to each question from among the four choices. Answer all the questions following the passage on the basis of what is stated or implied in the passage.

> Today's students have hand-held calculators that can graph one or even many equations. Students can even type in several equations and the calculator will "solve" them. This is the best way just to see a plotted graph quickly.
>
> This is the worst way to learn about graphing and equations. The calculator can't tell the student anything about the process of graphing and does not teach them how to plot a graph.
>
> Left to this electronic graphing process, students will not have the hands-on experience patterns needed to see the patterns and symmetry that characterize graphing and equations. They may become too dependent on the calculator and be unable to reason effectively about equations and the process of graphing.
>
> It may be true that graphing and solving equations is taught mechanically in some classrooms. There is also something to be said for these electronic devices, which give students the opportunity to try out several graphs and solutions quickly before deciding on a final solution.
>
> For all their electronic accuracy and patience, these graphing calculators cannot replace the process of graphing and solving equations on your own. For mastery of equations and graphing comes not just from seeing the graph automatically displayed on a screen; it also comes from a hands-on involvement with graphing.

1. The main idea of the passage is that:
   (A) a child can be good at graphing equations only through hands-on experience.
   (B) teaching approaches for graphing equations should be improved.
   (C) accuracy and patience are the keys to effective graphing instruction.
   (D) the new graphing calculators have limited ability to teach students about graphing.

2. According to this passage, what negative impact will graphing calculators have on students who use them?
   (A) They will not have experience with four-function calculators.
   (B) They will become too dependent on the calculator.
   (C) They can quickly try out several graphs before coming up with a final answer.
   (D) They will get too much hands-on experience with calculators.

3. According to the passage, which of the following is a major drawback of the graphing calculator?
   (A) It graphs too many equations with their solutions.
   (B) It does not give students hands-on experience with graphing.
   (C) It does not give students hands-on experience with calculators.
   (D) This electronic method interferes with the mechanical method.

4. The passage includes information that would answer which of the following questions?
   (A) What are the shortcomings of graphing and solving equations as it sometimes takes place?
   (B) How many equations can you type into a graphing calculator?
   (C) What hands-on experience should students have as they learn about graphing equations?
   (D) What is the degree of accuracy and speed that can be attained by a graphing calculator?

5. The description of a graphing calculator found in this passage tells about which of the following?
   I.   The equations that can be graphed
   II. The approximate size of the calculator
   III. The advantages of the graphing calculator
   (A) I only
   (B) II only
   (C) I and II only
   (D) II and III only

Practice Passage Answers

Don't read this section until you have completed the practice passage.
   Here's how to apply the steps.

   Step 1: Skim to find the topic of each paragraph. You should have written a topic next to each paragraph. Suggested topics are shown next to the following selection. Your topics don't have to be identical, but they should accurately reflect the paragraph's content.

Graphing Calculators

Today's students have hand-held calculators that can graph one or even many equations. Students can even type in several equations and the calculator will "solve" them. This is the best way to see a plotted graph quickly.

This is the worst way to learn about graphing and equations. The calculator can't tell the student anything about the process of graphing and does not teach them how to plot a graph.

Problem with Graphing Calculators

Left to this electronic graphing process, students will not have the hands-on experience needed to see the patterns and symmetry that characterize graphing and equations. They may become too dependent on the calculator and be unable to reason effectively about equations and the process of graphing.

Why its a Problem

It may be true that graphing and solving equations is taught mechanically in some classrooms. There is also something to be said for these electronic devices, which give students the opportunity to try out several graphs and solutions quickly before deciding on a final solution.

Good Points

For all their electronic accuracy and patience, these graphing calculators cannot replace the process of graphing and solving equations on your own. For mastery of equations and graphing comes not just from seeing the graph automatically displayed on a screen; it also comes from a hands-on involvement with graphing.

Apply Steps 2 through 5 to each of the questions.

1. The main idea of the passage is that:
   (A) a child can be good at graphing equations only through hands-on experience.
   (B) teaching approaches for graphing equations should be improved.
   (C) accuracy and patience are the keys to effective graphing instruction.
   (D) the new graphing calculators have limited ability to teach students about graphing.

Step 2: Read the question and answers. You have to identify the main idea of the passage. This is a very common question on reading tests. Remember that the main idea is what the writer is trying to say or communicate in the passage.

Step 3: Eliminate incorrect answers. Answers (B) and (C) are not correct. Answer (C) is not at all correct based on the passage. Even though (B) may be true, it does not reflect what the writer is trying to say in this passage.

Step 4: Scan the details to find the answer. As we review the details we see that both answer (A) and answer (D) are both stated or implied in the passage. A scan of the details, alone, does not reveal which is the main idea. We must determine that on our own.

Step 5: Choose the answer that is absolutely correct. Which answer is absolutely correct? The whole passage is about graphing calculators, and they must be an important part of the main idea. The correct answer is (D). The author certainly believes that (A) is true, but uses this point to support the main idea.

2. According to this passage, what negative impact will graphing calculators have on students who use them?
   (A) They will not have experience with four-function calculators.
   (B) They will become too dependent on the calculator.
   (C) They can quickly try out several graphs before coming up with a final answer.
   (D) They will get too much hands-on experience with calculators.

Step 2: Read the questions and answers. This is a straightforward comprehension question. What negative impact will calculators have on students who use them? The second and third paragraphs have topics related to problems with calculators. We'll probably find the answer there.

Step 3: Eliminate incorrect answers. Answer (C) is not a negative impact of graphing calculators. Scan the details to find the correct answer from (A), (B), and (D).

Step 4: Scan the details to find the answer. The only detail that matches the question is in paragraph 3. The authors says that students may become too dependent on the calculators. That's our answer.

Step 5: Choose the answer that is absolutely correct. Answer (B) is the only correct choice.

3. According to the passage, which of the following is a major drawback of the graphing calculator?
   (A) It graphs too many equations with their solutions.
   (B) It does not give students hands-on experience with graphing.
   (C) It does not give students hands-on experience with calculators.
   (D) This electronic method interferes with the mechanical method.

Step 2: Read the question and answers. This is another straightforward comprehension question. This question is somewhat different from Question 2. Notice that the question asks for a drawback of the calculator. It does not ask for something that is wrong with the calculator itself. The topics indicate that we will probably find the answer in paragraph 1 or paragraph 2.

Step 3: Eliminate incorrect answers. Answer (C) is obviously wrong. Graphing calculators do give students hands-on experience with calculators. Be careful! It is easy to mix up (C) and (B). Answer (A) is a strength of the calculator and is also incorrect. Let's move on to the details.

Step 4: Scan the details to find the answer. Choices (B) and (D) remain. The details in paragraph 2 reveal that the correct answer is (B).

Step 5: Choose the answer that is absolutely correct. Answer (B) is the only absolutely correct answer. Notice that answers (B) and (C) are similar. The absolutely correct answer for this question was a possible correct answer for the previous question. Just because an answer seems correct doesn't mean that it is the absolutely correct answer.

4. The passage includes information that would answer which of the following questions?
   (A) What are the shortcomings of teaching about graphing equations as it some-times takes place?
   (B) How many equations can you type into a graphing calculator?
   (C) What hands-on experience should students have as they learn about graphing equations?
   (D) What is the degree of accuracy and speed that can be attained by a graphing cal-culator?

Step 2: Read the question and answers. This is yet another type of reading comprehension question. You are asked to identify the questions that could be answered from the passage.

Step 3: Eliminate incorrect answers. Choices (B) and (D) are not correct. None of this information is included in the passage. This is not to say that these questions are not important. Rather it means that the answers to these questions are not found in this passage.

Step 4: Scan the details to find the answer. Both (A) and (C) are discussed in the passage. However, a scan of the details reveals that the answer to (C) is not found in the passage. The passage mentions hands-on experience, but it does not mention what types of hands-on experience students should have. There is an answer for (A). Graphing is taught mechanically in some classrooms.

Step 5: Choose the answer that is absolutely correct. Answer (A) is the absolutely correct answer. This is the only question that can be answered from the passage. The answer is not related to the writer's main idea and this may make it more difficult to answer.

5. The description of a graphing calculator found in this passage tells about which of the following?
   I.   The equations that can be graphed
   II.   The approximate size of the calculator
   III. The advantages of the graphing calculator
   (A) I only
   (B) II only
   (C) I and II only
   (D) II and III only

Step 2: Read the question and answers. This is another classic type of reading comprehension question. You are given several choices. You must decide which combination of these choices is the absolutely correct answer.

Step 3: Eliminate incorrect answers. If you can determine that Statement I, for example, is not addressed in the passage, you can eliminate ALL answer choices that include Statement I.

Step 4: Scan the details to find which of the original three statements are true.

    I. No, there is no description of which equations can be graphed.

   II. Yes, paragraph 1 mentions that the calculators are hand-held.

  III. Yes, paragraph 4 mentions the advantages.

Both II and III are correct.

Step 5: Choose the answer that is absolutely correct. Choice (D) is absolutely correct. It lists both II and III.

READING PRACTICE ITEMS

The practice items are designed to help you practice the concepts and skills presented in this chapter. For that reason, questions may have a different emphasis than the actual test, and the actual test will certainly be more complete.

Mark your choice, then check your answers. Use the test-taking strategies on pages 39–43.

1 Ⓐ Ⓑ Ⓒ Ⓓ	5 Ⓐ Ⓑ Ⓒ Ⓓ	9 Ⓐ Ⓑ Ⓒ Ⓓ	13 Ⓐ Ⓑ Ⓒ Ⓓ	17 Ⓐ Ⓑ Ⓒ Ⓓ
2 Ⓐ Ⓑ Ⓒ Ⓓ	6 Ⓐ Ⓑ Ⓒ Ⓓ	10 Ⓐ Ⓑ Ⓒ Ⓓ	14 Ⓐ Ⓑ Ⓒ Ⓓ	18 Ⓐ Ⓑ Ⓒ Ⓓ
3 Ⓐ Ⓑ Ⓒ Ⓓ	7 Ⓐ Ⓑ Ⓒ Ⓓ	11 Ⓐ Ⓑ Ⓒ Ⓓ	15 Ⓐ Ⓑ Ⓒ Ⓓ	19 Ⓐ Ⓑ Ⓒ Ⓓ
4 Ⓐ Ⓑ Ⓒ Ⓓ	8 Ⓐ Ⓑ Ⓒ Ⓓ	12 Ⓐ Ⓑ Ⓒ Ⓓ	16 Ⓐ Ⓑ Ⓒ Ⓓ	20 Ⓐ Ⓑ Ⓒ Ⓓ

While becoming a teacher, I spent most of my time with books. I read books about the subjects I would teach in school and books that explained how to teach the subjects. As a new teacher, I relied on books to help my students learn. But I learned, and now the basis for my teaching is to help students apply what they have learned to the real world.

1. Which of the following would most likely be the next line of this passage?
   (A) The world is a dangerous and intimidating place; be wary of it.
   (B) Children should be taught to seek whatever the world has to offer.
   (C) A teacher has to be in the world, not just study about the world.
   (D) But you can't forget about books.

2. Which of the following is the underlying moral of this passage?
   (A) Teaching art is very rewarding.
   (B) Children learn a lot from field trips.
   (C) There is much to be said for teachers who think of their students' experiences first.
   (D) Firsthand experiences are important for children's learning and develoment.

The American alligator is found in Florida and Georgia, and has also been reported in other states, including North and South Carolina. Weighing in at more than 400 pounds, the length of an adult alligator is twice that of its tail. Adult alligators eat fish and small mammals while young alligators prefer insects, shrimp, and frogs.

An untrained person may mistake a crocodile for an alligator. Crocodiles are found in the same areas as alligators and both have prominent snouts with many teeth. The crocodile has a long thin snout with teeth in both jaws. The alligator's snout is wider with teeth only in the upper jaw.

3. Which of the following would be a good title for this passage?
   (A) Large Reptiles
   (B) Eating Habits of Alligators
   (C) The American Alligator
   (D) How Alligators and Crocodiles Differ

4. Which of the following would be a way to distinguish an alligator from a crocodile?
   (A) number of teeth
   (B) shape of snout
   (C) habitat
   (D) diet

5. Which of the following best describes the purpose of the passage?
   (A) All animals are noteworthy.
   (B) Reptiles are interesting animals.
   (C) To educate readers about differences in similar animals.
   (D) To describe the life cycle of wetland creatures.

Remove the jack from the trunk. Set the jack under the car. Use the jack to raise the car. Remove the lug nuts. Remove the tire and replace it with the doughnut. Reset the lug nuts loosely and use the jack to lower the chassis to the ground. Tighten the lug nuts once the tire is touching the ground.

6. Which of the following is the main idea of this passage?
   (A) using a jack
   (B) changing a tire on a car
   (C) maintaining a car
   (D) following directions

Farmers and animals are fighting over rain forests. The farmers are clearing the forests and driving out the animals to make room for crops. If this battle continues, the rain forest will disappear. Both the farmers and the animals will lose, and the soil in the cleared forest will form a hard crust.

Of course, there are global implications as well. Clearing the forests increases the amount of carbon dioxide in the atmosphere. The most promising solution to the problems caused by clearing the rain forests is the education of the local farmers.

7. Which information below is not provided in the passage?
   (A) reasons the animals are being run out
   (B) reasons the farmers need more land
   (C) effects of lost rain forests
   (D) ways that people can help globally

8. What most likely would the opinion of the author be about wildlife conservation?
   (A) All animals must fend for themselves.
   (B) Damage to the earth affects both people and animals.
   (C) Our greatest resource on earth is the human intellect.
   (D) Testing products on animals is a practice that should be outlawed.

I love gingerbread cookies, which are flavored with ginger and molasses. I can remember cold winter days when my brother and I huddled around the fire eating gingerbread cookies and sipping warm apple cider. In those days, gingerbread cookies came in many shapes and sizes. When you eat a gingerbread cookie today, you have to bite a "person's" head off.

9. Why did the author of the passage above put quotes around the word *person*?
   (A) to emphasize the difference between gingerbread cookies that appear as people rather than windmills
   (B) because gingerbread cookies often don't look like people
   (C) to emphasize the most popular current shape of gingerbread cookies
   (D) to emphasize the choice of this word rather than the word *man*

Use this fable attributed to Aesop to answer questions 10 and 11.

The Frogs Who Wanted a King

The frogs lived a happy life in the pond. They jumped from lily pad to lily pad and sunned themselves without a care. But a few of the frogs were not satisfied with this relaxed and enjoyable life. These frogs thought that they needed a king to rule them. So they sent a note to the god Jupiter requesting that he appoint a king.

Jupiter was amused by this request. In a good-natured response, Jupiter threw a log into the pond, which landed with a big splash. All the frogs jumped to safety. Some time passed and one frog started to approach the log, which lay still in the pond. When nothing happened, the other frogs jumped on the floating giant, treating it with disdain.

The frogs were not satisfied with such a docile king. They sent another note to Jupiter asking for a strong king to rule over them. Jupiter was not amused by this second request and he was tired of the frogs' complaints.

So Jupiter sent a stork. The stork immediately devoured every frog in sight. The few surviving frogs gave Mercury a message to carry to Jupiter pleading for Jupiter to show them mercy.

Jupiter was very cold. He told Mercury to tell the frogs that they were responsible for their own problems. They had asked for a king to rule them and they would have to make the best of it.

10. Which of the following morals fits the passage?
    (A) Let well enough alone.
    (B) Familiarity breeds contempt.
    (C) Slow and steady wins the race.
    (D) Liberty is too high a price to pay for revenge.

11. Why did the frogs treat the log with contempt?
    (A) The log was sent by Jupiter.
    (B) The log floated in the pond.
    (C) The log was not alive.
    (D) The log was not assertive.

You may want to go to a park on a virgin prairie in Minnesota. The park borders Canada and is just west of the Mississippi River. The thousands of acres of parkland are home to hundreds of species of birds and mammals. In the evening, a sotto wind sweeps across the prairie, creating wave-like ripples in the tall grasses. This prairie park is just one of the wonders you can see when you visit marvelous Minnesota.

12. Where might you find this excerpt?
    (A) cook book
    (B) travel brochure
    (C) hunting magazine
    (D) national parks guide

13. In which part of the United States is this park located?
    (A) Midwest
    (B) Northeast
    (C) Southeast
    (D) Northwest

14. What does the author mean by "virgin prairie"?
    (A) desolate taiga
    (B) untouched grasslands
    (C) wooded plains
    (D) Indian reservation

There was a time in the United States when a married woman was expected to take her husband's last name. Most women still follow this practice, but things are changing. In fact, Hawaii is the only state with a law requiring a woman to take her husband's last name when she marries.

Many women look forward to taking their husband's surname. They may enjoy the bond it establishes with their husband, or want to be identified with their husband's professional status. Other women want to keep their own last name. They may prefer their original last name, or want to maintain their professional identity.

Some women resolve this problem by choosing a last name that hyphenates their surname and their husband's surname. This practice of adopting elements of both surnames is common in other cultures.

15. What would be the best title for this passage?
    (A) Women Have Rights
    (B) Determining a Woman's Name after Marriage
    (C) Determining a Woman's Name after Divorce
    (D) Legal Aspects of Surname Changing

16. What position is the author taking on women's rights?
    (A) for women but against men
    (B) for women and against equality
    (C) for women and for men
    (D) against women but for men

17. The passage would LEAST likely be found in a
    (A) fashion magazine.
    (B) woman's corporate magazine.
    (C) teen magazine aimed at girls.
    (D) fitness magazine.

18. What is the main idea of this passage?
    (A) Women are at the mercy of the law.
    (B) Women in Hawaii have no options.
    (C) Women today have many options related to surnames.
    (D) Children should have the same name as their mother.

In recent years, cooperative learning, which involves students in small group activities, has gained popularity as an instructional approach. Cooperative learning provides students with an opportunity to work on projects presented by the teacher. This type of learning emphasizes group goals, cooperative learning, and shared responsibility. All students must contribute in order for the group to be successful.

19. What is the main idea of this passage?
    (A) to show different learning styles
    (B) to examine the best way to teach
    (C) to explain why cooperative learning is the best method for eliminating classrooms
    (D) to illustrate the method of cooperative learning

20. According to this passage what would be a good definition of cooperative learning?
    (A) An instructional arrangement in which children work in small groups in a manner that promotes student responsibility.
    (B) An instructional arrangement in which the teacher pairs two students in a tutor- tutee relationship to promote learning of academic skills or subject content.
    (C) An instructional arrangement consisting of three to seven students that represents a major format for teaching academic skills.
    (D) An instructional arrangement that is appropriate for numerous classroom activities, such as show and tell, discussing interesting events, taking a field trip, or watching a movie.

Answers

1. C	5. C	9. D	13. A	17. D
2. D	6. B	10. A	14. B	18. C
3. D	7. B	11. D	15. D	19. D
4. B	8. C	12. B	16. B	20. A

ENGLISH AND WRITING

The LAST and the ATS-W each include a written assignment. The written assignment contributes 20 percent to your overall score for each test. This chapter contains a thorough English review and sample LAST written assignments. Chapter 10 contains sample ATS-W written assignments. Refer to Chapter 2 to review the Steps for Writing Passing Written Assignments.

WRITTEN ASSIGNMENTS

LAST
LAST written assignments usually ask you to summarize a topic or situation and then give your opinion or point of view. Written assignments are rated 0–3 by two readers based on how well you write edited English. The final written assignment score of 0–6 is the sum of these two scores.

ATS-W
ATS-W written assignments might not be an essay. For example, past written assignments have asked for the outline of a curriculum and a lesson plan. You may be asked to respond to a classroom situation, or some other education-related situation. The written assignment must be written clearly enough to be understood, but the readers do not evaluate your writing ability. However, a well-written assignment always makes the best impression.

The written assignment is rated 0–3 by two readers based on the appropriateness of your response. The final written assignment score of 0–6 is the sum of these two scores.

USING THIS CHAPTER

Choose one of these approaches.

I want all the English/Writing review I can get.

❑ Skip the English Review Quiz on page 57 and read the entire review section.
❑ Take the English Review Quiz on page 57.
❑ Correct the Review Quiz and reread the indicated parts of the review.
❑ Complete the English Practice Items on pages 83–86.
❑ Complete the Practice LAST Written Assignment on page 87.

I want a thorough English/Writing review.

❑ Take the English Review Quiz on page 57.
❑ Correct the Review Quiz and read the indicated parts of the review.
❑ Complete the English Practice Items on pages 83–86.
❑ Complete the Practice LAST Written Assignment on page 87.

I want a quick English/Writing review.

❑ Take the English Review Quiz on page 57.
❑ Complete the English Practice Items on pages 83–86.
❑ Complete the Practice LAST Written Assignment on page 87.

I want to practice English/Writing activities.

❑ Complete the English Practice Items on pages 83–86.
❑ Complete the Practice LAST Written Assignment on page 87.

ENGLISH REVIEW QUIZ

The English Review Quiz assesses your knowledge of the English topics included in the tests. The quiz also provides an excellent way to refresh your memory about these topics. The first part of the quiz consists of sentences to mark or correct. Make your marks or corrections right on the sentences. In the second part of the quiz, you are asked to write a brief essay.

This quiz will be more difficult than the questions on the actual certification test. The idea here is to find out what you do know and what you don't know. It's not important to answer all these questions correctly and don't be concerned if you miss many of them.

The answers are found immediately after the quiz. It's to your advantage not to look at them until you have completed the quiz. Once you have completed and marked this review quiz, use the checklist to decide which sections to study.

PART I—SENTENCE CORRECTION

> Correct the sentence. Some sentences may not contain errors.

1. Ron and James fathers each sent them to players camp to learn the mysterys of sport.

2. They go the camp, ridden horses while they were there, and had write letters home.

3. Ron and James called his coach. The operator never answered, and they wondered what happened to her.

4. Bob and Liz went to the store and got some groceries.

5. Dad want me to do my homework. My sisters try their best to help me.

> Underline the subject in each sentence.

6. Chad's project that he showed the teacher improved his final grade.

7. The legs pumped hard, and the racer finished in first place.

8. Through the halls and down the stairs ran the harried student.

9. Where is the dog's leash?

> Correct the sentence. Some sentences may not contain errors.

10. Chad was sure correct; the food tastes bad and the singer sang bad but Ryan played really well. Ryan was more happy than Chad, who sat closer to the stage than Ryan.

11. The waiter brought food to the table on a large tray. The waiter wanted a job in the suburbs that paid well.

12. Waiting for the food to come, the complaining began.

13. After three weeks in the suburbs, the job was lost.

14. Juan and Rita spent two days at the beach before going to the mountains.

15. Neither Ryan or Bob wanted to shovel the drive. However, some things must be done not only when you want to but when you have to do them.

| Underline the prepositional phrases. |

16. The two friends walked among the flowers before the sunset. They stepped without fear beside the waterfall as they thought about the future.

| Correct the sentence. Some sentences may not contain errors. |

17. Ryan knew that the coach wouldn't do anything that would not be helpful. The coach thought it was better to do nothing than to make a mistake. Ryan thought there was no truth to the belief that nothing could be done.

18. Ryan hoped his coach, professor Lois Minke, would help him get a tryout with the United States national team. Dr. Minke, a professor of physical education recommended that Ryan read *Sports: a Guide to Survival*.

19. The coach realized that new selection rules to go into effect in May. She also knew what it would take for Ryan to be selected. Ryan winning every game. But the coach and Ryan had a common goal. To see Ryan on the team.

20. Ryan's parents wanted a success rather than see him fail. They knew he stayed in shape by eating right and exercising daily. Ryan was a person who works hard and has talent.

21. Chad was dog tired after soccer practice. He became a coach for the purpose of helping the college to the soccer finals. During the rein of the former coach, the team had miserable seasons. Chad would stay at the job until such time as he could except the first place trophy.

22. Chad was satisfied but the players were grumbling. The players wanted to practice less have more free time. The players didn't like their light blue uniforms. The finals began in May 1996. The first game was scheduled for Tuesday May 9 at 1:00 P.M. The time for the game was here the players were on the field. Chad had the essential materials with him player list score book soccer balls and a cup of hope.

PART II—ESSAY

Time yourself for 30 minutes. Use the following lined page to write a brief essay that answers this question.

Should high school students have to pass a standardized test before they graduate?

Write a brief outline below.

ANSWER CHECKLIST

PART I—Sentence Correction

The answers are organized by review sections. Check your answers. If you miss any item in a section, check the box and review that section.

❏ *Nouns, page 64*
 1. Ron's and James's fathers each sent them to players' camp to learn the mysteries of sport.

❏ *Verbs, page 64*
 2. They went to the camp, rode horses while they were there, and wrote letters home.

❏ *Pronouns, page 66*
 3. Ron and James called (Ron's, James's, their) coach. The operator never answered, and they wondered what happened to him or her.

❏ *Subject-Verb Agreement, page 68*
 4. No error
 5. Dad wants me to do my homework. My sisters try their best to help me.
 6. Chad's project that he showed the teacher improved his final grade.
 7. The legs pumped hard, and the racer finished in first place.
 8. Through the halls and down the stairs ran the harried student.
 9. Where is the dog's leash?

❏ *Adjectives and Adverbs, page 69*
 10. Chad was surely correct; the food tastes bad and the singer sang badly but Ryan played really well. Ryan was happier than Chad, who sat closer to the stage than Ryan did.

 11. The waiter brought food on a large tray to the table. The waiter wanted a well-paying job in the suburbs.
 12. Waiting for the food to come, the (patrons, diners) complained. The (patrons, diners) complained about waiting for the food to come.
 13. After (he, the waiter) was in the suburbs for three weeks (his) job was lost. He lost his job after he was in the suburbs for three weeks.

❏ *Conjunctions, page 71*
 14. No error
 15. Neither Ryan nor Bob wanted to shovel the drive. However, some things must be done not only when you want to but also when you have to do them.

❏ *Prepositions, page 72*
 16. The two friends walked among the flowers before the sunset. They stepped without fear beside the waterfall as they thought about the future.

❏ *Negation, page 72*
 17. Ryan knew that the coach would be helpful. The coach thought it was better to do nothing than to make a mistake. Ryan thought something could be done.

❏ *Capitalization, page 73*
 18. Ryan hoped his coach, Professor Lois Minke, would help him get a tryout with the United States National Team. Dr. Minke, a professor of physical education, recommended that Ryan read *Sports: A Guide to Survival.*

❏ *Sentence Fragments, page 74*

19. The coach realized that new selection rules <u>would</u> go into effect in May. She also knew what it would take for Ryan to be selected. Ryan <u>would have to win</u> every game. But the coach and Ryan had a common goal. <u>They wanted</u> to see Ryan on the team.

❏ *Parallelism, page 75*

20. Ryan's parents wanted a success rather than <u>a failure</u>. (wanted success rather than failure) They knew he stayed in shape <u>by</u> eating right and by exercising daily. Ryan was a person who works hard and <u>who</u> has talent. (Ryan is hardworking and talented.)

❏ *Diction, page 75*

21. Chad was [delete "dog"] tired after soccer practice. He became a coach <u>to help</u> the college <u>ascend</u> to the soccer finals. During the <u>reign</u> of the former coach, the team had miserable seasons. Chad would stay at the job until [delete "such time as"] he could <u>accept</u> the first place trophy.

❏ *Punctuation, page 77*

22. Chad was satisfied, but the players were grumbling. The players wanted to practice less <u>and</u> have more free time. The players didn't like their light blue uniforms. The finals began in May 1996. The first game was scheduled for Tuesday, May 9, at 1:00 P.M. The time for the game was here; the players were on the field. Chad had the essential materials with him: player list, score book, soccer balls, (optional) and a cup of hope.

PART II—ESSAY

Evaluation Guidelines

Find an English professor or a high school English teacher. Ask that person to *rigorously* rate your essay using the criteria below.

A rating of 3 indicates your writing is acceptable.

A rating of 2 indicates that you need help writing essays. You should practice writing essays and get help at a writing center or from a writing tutor.

A rating of 1, 0, or U indicates you need a significant amount of help writing essays. You should practice writing essays until you can consistently achieve a rating of 2. You should get regular help at a writing center or from a writing tutor. Ask the person who rated your essay for other recommendations. Follow these recommendations.

Raters use these general guidelines

3 A well developed, complete written assignment.
   Shows a thorough response to all parts of the topic.
   Clear explanations that are well supported.
   The assignment is free of significant grammatical, punctuation, or spelling errors.

2 A fairly well developed, complete written assignment.
   It may not thoroughly respond to all parts of the topic.
   Fairly clear explanations that may not be well supported.
   It may contain some significant grammatical, punctuation, or spelling errors.

1 A poorly developed, incomplete written assignment.
   It does not thoroughly respond to most parts of the topic.
   Contains many poor explanations that are not well supported.
   It may contain some significant grammatical, punctuation, or spelling errors.

0 A very poorly developed, incomplete written assignment.
   It does not thoroughly respond to the topic.
   Contains only poor, unsupported explanations.
   Contains numerous significant grammatical, punctuation, or spelling errors.

U Any of these factors leads to a "U" rating
   A blank paper
   An essay unrelated to the topic no matter how well written
   An essay not long enough to score
   An essay written in a language other than English
   An illegible essay

ENGLISH REVIEW

NOUNS AND VERBS

Every sentence has a subject and a predicate. Most sentences are statements. The sentence usually names something (subject). Then the sentence describes the subject or tells what that subject is doing (predicate). Sentences that ask questions also have a subject and a predicate. Here are some examples.

Subject	Predicate
The car	moved.
The tree	grew.
The street	was dark.
The forest	teemed with plants of every type and size.

Many subjects are nouns. Every predicate has a verb. A list of the nouns and verbs from the preceding sentences follows.

Noun	Verb
car	moved
tree	grew
street	was
forest, plants	teemed

Nouns

Nouns name a person, place, thing, characteristic, or concept. Nouns give a name to everything that is, has been, or will be. Here are some simple examples.

Person	Place	Thing	Characteristic	Concept (Idea)
Abe Lincoln	Lincoln Memorial	beard	mystery	freedom
judge	courthouse	gavel	fairness	justice
professor	college	chalkboard	intelligence	number

Singular and Plural Nouns

Singular nouns refer to only one thing. Plural forms refer to more than one thing. Plurals are usually formed by adding an *s* or dropping a *y* and adding *ies*. Here are some examples.

Singular	Plural
college	colleges
professor	professors
Lincoln Memorial	Lincoln Memorials
mystery	mysteries

Possessive Nouns

Possessive nouns show that the noun possesses a thing or a characteristic. Make a singular noun possessive by adding *'s*. Here are some examples.

> The *child's* sled was in the garage ready for use.
> The *school's* mascot was loose again.
> The rain interfered with *Jane's* vacation.
> *Ron's* and *Doug's* fathers were born in the same year.
> Ron and *Doug's* teacher kept them after school.

Make a singular noun ending in *s* possessive by adding *'s* unless the pronunciation is too difficult.

> The teacher read *James's* paper several times.
> The angler grabbed the *bass'* fin.

Make a plural noun possessive by adding an apostrophe (') only.

> The *principals'* meeting was delayed.
> The report indicated that *students'* scores had declined.

Verbs

Some verbs are action verbs. Other verbs are linking verbs that link the subject to words that describe it. Here are some examples.

Action Verbs	Linking Verbs
Blaire *runs* down the street.	Blaire *is* tired.
Blaire *told* her story.	The class *was* bored.
The crowd *roared*.	The players *were* inspired.
The old ship *rusted*.	It *had been* a proud ship.

Tense

A verb has three principal tenses: present tense, past tense, and future tense. The present tense shows that the action is happening now. The past tense shows that the action happened in the past. The future tense shows that something will happen. Here are some examples.

Present:	I *enjoy* my time off.
Past:	I *enjoyed* my time off.
Future:	I *will enjoy* my time off.

Present: I *hate* working late.
Past: I *hated* working late.
Future: I *will hate* working late.

Regular and Irregular Verbs

Regular verbs follow the consistent pattern noted previously. However, a number of verbs are irregular. Irregular verbs have their own unique forms for each tense. A partial list of irregular verbs follows. The past participle is usually preceded by *had, has* or *have*.

SOME IRREGULAR VERBS

Present Tense	Past Tense	Past Participle
am, is, are	was, were	been
begin	began	begun
break	broke	broken
bring	brought	brought
catch	caught	caught
choose	chose	chosen
come	came	come
do	did	done
eat	ate	eaten
give	gave	given
go	went	gone
grow	grew	grown
know	knew	known
lie	lay	lain
lay	laid	laid
raise	raised	raised
ride	rode	ridden
see	saw	seen
set	set	set
sit	sat	sat
speak	spoke	spoken
take	took	taken
tear	tore	torn
throw	threw	thrown
write	wrote	written

PRONOUNS

Pronouns take the place of nouns or noun phrases and help avoid constant repetition of the noun or phrase. Here is an example.

Blaire is in law school. *She* studies in *her* room every day.
[The pronouns *she* and *her* refer to the noun *Blaire*.]

Clear Reference

The pronouns must clearly refer to a particular noun or noun phrase. Here are some examples.

Unclear

Ashley and Blaire took turns feeding *her* cat.
[We can't tell which person *her* refers to.]

Ashley gave it to Blaire. [The pronoun *it* refers to a noun that is not stated.]

Clear

Ashley and Blaire took turns feeding Blaire's cat. [A pronoun doesn't work here.]

Ashley got the book and gave it to Blaire. [The pronoun works once the noun is stated.]

Agreement

Each pronoun must agree in number (singular or plural) and gender (male or female) with the noun it refers to. Here are some examples.

Nonagreement in Number

The children played all day, and *she* came in exhausted.
[*Children* is plural, but *she* is singular.]

The child picked up the hat and brought *them* into the house.
[*Child* is singular, but *them* is plural.]

Agreement

The children played all day, and *they* came in exhausted.

The child picked up the hat and brought *it* into the house.

Nonagreement in Gender

The lioness picked up *his* cub. [*Lioness* is female, and *his* is male.]

A child must bring in a doctor's note before she comes to school.
[The child may be a male or female but *she* is female.]

Agreement

The lioness picked up *her* cub.

A child must bring in a doctor's note before *he* or *she* comes to school.

SUBJECT-VERB AGREEMENT

Singular and Plural

Singular nouns take singular verbs. Plural nouns take plural verbs. Singular verbs usually end in *s*, and plural verbs usually do not. Here are some examples.

Singular:	My father want*s* me home early.
Plural:	My parents want me home early.
Singular:	Ryan runs a mile each day.
Plural:	Ryan and Chad run a mile each day.
Singular:	She tries her best to do a good job.
Plural:	Liz and Ann try their best to do a good job.

Correctly Identify Subject and Verb

The subject may not be in front of the verb. In fact, the subject may not be anywhere near the verb. Say the subject and the verb to yourself. If it makes sense, you probably have it right.

- Words may come between the subject and the verb.

    Chad's final exam score, which he showed to his mother, improved his final grade.

The verb is *improved*. The word *mother* appears just before improved.

Is this the subject? Say it to yourself. [Mother improved the grade.]

That can't be right. Score must be the subject. Say it to yourself. [Score improved the grade.] That's right. *Score* is the subject, and *improved* is the verb.

    The racer running with a sore arm finished first.

Say it to yourself. [Racer finished first.] *Racer* is the noun, and *finished* is the verb.

It wouldn't make any sense to say the arm finished first.

- The verb may come before the subject.

    Over the river and through the woods romps the merry leprechaun.

Leprechaun is the subject, and *romps* is the verb. [Think: Leprechaun romps.]

    Where are the car keys?

Keys is the subject, and *are* is the verb. [Think: The car keys are where?]

Examples of Subject-Verb Agreement

Words such as *each, neither, everyone, nobody, someone,* and *anyone* are singular pronouns. They always take a singular verb.

> Everyone *needs* a good laugh now and then.
> Nobody *knows* more about computers than Bob.

Words that refer to number such as *one-half, any, most,* and *some* can be singular or plural.

> One-fifth of the students *were* absent. [*Students* is plural.]
> One-fifth of the cake *was* eaten. [There is only one cake.]

ADJECTIVES AND ADVERBS

Adjectives

Adjectives modify nouns and pronouns. Adjectives add detail and clarify nouns and pronouns. Frequently, adjectives come immediately before the nouns or pronouns they are modifying. At other times, the nouns or pronouns come first and are connected directly to the adjectives by linking verbs. Here are some examples.

Direct	With a Linking Verb
That is a *large* dog.	That dog is *large*.
He's an *angry* man.	The man seems *angry*.

Adverbs

Adverbs are often formed by adding *ly* to an adjective. However, many adverbs don't end in *ly* (for example, *always*). Adverbs modify verbs, adjectives, and adverbs. Adverbs can also modify phrases, clauses, and sentences. Here are some examples.

Modify verb:	Ryan *quickly* sought a solution.
Modify adjective:	That is an *exceedingly* large dog.
Modify adverb:	Lisa told her story *quite* truthfully.
Modify sentence:	*Unfortunately*, all good things must end.
Modify phrase:	The instructor arrived *just* in time to start the class.

Avoiding Adjective and Adverb Errors

• Don't use adjectives in place of adverbs.

Correct	Incorrect
Lynne read the book quickly.	Lynne read the book quick.
Stan finished his work easily.	Stan finished the book easy.

• Don't confuse the adjectives *good* and *bad* with the adverbs *well* and *badly*.

Correct	Incorrect
Adverbs	
She wanted to play the piano well.	She wanted to play the piano good.
Bob sang badly.	Bob sang bad.
Adjectives	
The food tastes good.	The food tastes well.
The food tastes bad.	The food tastes badly.

• Don't confuse the adjectives *real* and *sure* with the adverbs *really* and *surely*.

Correct	Incorrect
Chuck played really well.	Chuck played real well.
He was surely correct.	He was sure correct.

Comparison

Adjectives and adverbs can show comparisons. Avoid clumsy modifiers.

Correct	Incorrect
Jim is more clingy than Ray.	Jim is clingier than Ray.
Ray is much taller than Jim.	Ray is more taller than Jim.
Jim is more interesting than Ray.	Jim is interesting than Ray.
Ray is happier than Jim.	Ray is more happy than Jim.

Word comparisons carefully to be sure that the comparison is clear.

Unclear:	Chad lives closer to Ryan than Blaire.
Clear:	Chad lives closer to Ryan than Blaire does.
Clear:	Chad lives closer to Ryan than he does to Blaire.

Unclear:	The bus engine is bigger than a cars.
Clear:	The bus engine is bigger than a car's engine.

Misplaced and Dangling Modifiers

Modifiers may be words or groups of words. Modifiers change or qualify the meaning of another word or group of words. Modifiers belong near the words they modify.

Misplaced modifiers appear to modify words in a way that doesn't make sense.

The modifier in the following sentence is *in a large box*. It doesn't make sense for *in a large box* to modify *house*. Move the modifier near *pizza* where it belongs.

> Misplaced: Les delivered pizza to the house in a large box.
> Revised: Les delivered pizza in a large box to the house.

The modifier in the next sentence is *paid well. Paid well* can't modify *city*. Move it next to *the job* where it belongs.

> Misplaced: Gail wanted the job in the city that paid well.
> Revised: Gail wanted the well-paying job in the city.

Dangling modifiers modify words not present in the sentence. The modifier in the following sentence is *waiting for the concert to begin.*

This modifier describes the audience, but *audience* is not mentioned in the sentence. The modifier is left dangling with nothing to attach itself to.

> Dangling: Waiting for the concert to begin, the chanting started.
> Revised: Waiting for the concert to begin, the audience began chanting.
> Revised: The audience began chanting while waiting for the concert to begin.

The modifier in the next sentence is *after three weeks in the country*. The modifier describes the person, not the license. But the person is not mentioned in the sentence. The modifier is dangling.

> Dangling: After three weeks in the country, the license was revoked.
> Revised: After he was in the country for three weeks, his license was revoked.
> Revised: His license was revoked after he was in the country three weeks.

CONJUNCTIONS

Conjunctions are words that connect and logically relate parts of a sentence.

- These conjunctions connect words: *and, but, for, or, nor.*

  Dan *and* Dorie live in Pittsburgh.

  Tim *or* Sarah will get up to feed the baby.

- These conjunctive pairs establish a relationship among words: *either–or, neither–nor, not only–but also*. Words in these pairs should not be mixed.

  Neither David *nor* Noel wants to get up to feed the baby.

  The baby cries *not only* when she is hungry, *but also* when she is thirsty.

- These conjunctions connect and modify clauses in a sentence: *nevertheless, however, because, furthermore.*

> Matt's mother was coming to visit; *however*, a snow storm prevented the trip.

> *Because* the baby was sleeping, Julie and Bill decided to get some sleep too.

PREPOSITIONS

Prepositions connect a word to a pronoun, noun, or noun phrase called the object of the preposition. A partial list of prepositions follows.

PREPOSITIONS

above	across	after	among
as	at	before	below
beside	by	except	for
from	in	into	near
of	on	over	to
toward	up	upon	without

A prepositional phrase consists of a preposition, its object and any modifiers. Here are some examples.

Preposition	Object
in	the book
with	apparent glee
without	a care

Some sentences with prepositional phrases follow.

> Chad found his book *in the room*.
> Liz rode *on her horse*.
> Trix is the dog *with the brown paws*.
> *Over the river* and *through the woods to grandmother's house* we go.

NEGATION

Words such as *no, never, nobody, nothing,* and *not* (with contractions such as *would not—wouldn't*) are used to express a negative. However, only one of these words is needed to express a negative thought. Two negative words create a double negative, which is not standard English.

Incorrect:	The politician *didn't say nothing* that made sense.
Revised:	The politician *didn't say anything* that made sense.
Revised:	The politician *said nothing* that made any sense.
Incorrect:	The politician *wouldn't do nothing* that did no good. [A triple negative.]
Revised:	The politician *would do nothing* good.
Revised:	The politician *wouldn't do* good things.

CAPITALIZATION

- Capitalize the first word in each sentence.
- Capitalize *I*.
- Capitalize proper nouns. In a title, capitalize proper and common nouns, but not articles or short prepositions. Proper nouns are specific names for people, places, or things.
- Capitalize proper adjectives. Proper adjectives can be formed from some proper nouns.

PROPER NOUNS

Bill Clinton	Taj Majal
Bob Postman	Thanksgiving
Alabama	July
North America	Wednesday

COMMON NOUNS

president	building
author	fall
state	month
continent	day

PROPER NOUNS AND PROPER ADJECTIVES

Pennsylvania	Pennsylvanian
California	Californian
New York	New Yorker
Italy	Italian

PROPER NOUNS WITH COMMON NOUNS AND ARTICLES

United States of America
the Mississippi River
Lake Michigan

- Capitalize titles before, but not after, proper nouns.

Professor Jeremy Smails	Jeremy Smails, professor of history
President Otto Smart	Otto Smart, president of Limelight Ltd.

- Titles, alone, may be capitalized if they indicate a very high rank.

President of the United States

Secretary of State

- Capitalize titles of books except for short articles, prepositions, and conjunctions unless they are the first or last words or follow a colon (:).

How to Prepare for the Praxis Examinations

The How to Survive in College Book

Derek: A Study in Perseverance

SENTENCE FRAGMENTS

English sentences require a subject and a verb. Fragments are parts of sentences written as though they were sentences. Fragments are writing mistakes that lack a subject, a predicate, or both subject and predicate. Here are some examples.

Since when.
To enjoy the summer months.
Because he isn't working hard.
If you can fix old cars.
What the principal wanted to hear.

Include a subject and/or a verb to rewrite a fragment as a sentence.

Fragment	Sentence
Should be coming up the driveway now.	The *car* should be coming up the driveway now.
Both the lawyer and her client.	Both the lawyer and her client *waited* in court.
Which is my favorite subject.	I *took math*, which is my favorite subject.
If you can play.	If you can play, *you'll improve with practice.*

Verbs such as *to be, to go, winning, starring,* etc., need a main verb.

Fragment	Sentence
The new rules to go into effect in April.	The new rules *will* go into effect in April.
The team winning every game.	The team *was* winning every game.

Often, a fragment is related to a complete sentence. Combine the two to make a single sentence.

Fragment:	Reni loved vegetables. *Particularly corn, celery, lettuce, squash, and eggplant.*
Revised:	Reni loved vegetables, particularly corn, celery, lettuce, squash, and eggplant.
Fragment:	*To see people standing on Mars.* This could happen in the 21st century.
Revised:	To see people standing on Mars is one of the things that could happen in the 21st century.

Sometimes short fragments can be used for emphasis. However, you should not use fragments in your essay. Here are some examples.

Stop! Don't take one more step toward that apple pie.

I need some time to myself. *That's why.*

PARALLELISM

When two or more ideas are connected, use a parallel structure. Parallelism helps the reader follow the passage more clearly. Here are some examples.

Not Parallel:	Toni stayed in shape by eating right and exercising daily.
Parallel:	Toni stayed in shape by eating right and *by* exercising daily.
Not Parallel:	Lisa is a student who works hard and has genuine insight.
Parallel:	Lisa is a student who works hard and *who* has genuine insight.
Not Parallel:	Art had a choice either to clean his room or take out the garbage.
Parallel:	Art had a choice either to clean his room or *to* take out the garbage.
Not Parallel:	Derek wanted a success rather than failing.
Parallel:	Derek wanted a success rather than a failure.
Parallel:	Derek wanted success rather than failure.

DICTION

Diction is choosing and using appropriate words. Good diction conveys a thought clearly without unnecessary words. Good diction develops fully over a number of years; however, there are some rules and tips you can follow, especially when writing for the LAST.

• Do not use slang, colloquialisms, or other nonstandard English. One person's slang is another person's confusion. Slang is often regional, and slang meanings change rapidly. We do not give examples of slang here for that very reason. Do not use slang words in your formal writing.

   Colloquialisms are words used frequently in spoken language. This informal use of terms such as *dog tired*, *kids*, and *hanging around*, is not generally accepted in formal writing. Save these informal terms for daily speech and omit or remove them from your writing except as quotations.

Omit any other non-standard English. Always choose standard English terms that accurately reflect the thought to be conveyed.

- Avoid wordy, redundant, or pretentious writing. Good writing is clear and economical.

Wordy: I chose my career as a teacher because of its high ideals, the truly self-sacrificing idealism of a career in teaching, and for the purpose of receiving the myriad and cascading recognition that one can receive from the community as a whole and from its constituents.

Revised: I chose a career in teaching for its high ideals and for community recognition.

Given below is a partial list of wordy phrases and the replacement word.

WORDY PHRASES AND REPLACEMENTS

at the present time	now	because of the fact that	because
for the purpose of	for	in the final analysis	finally
in the event that	if	until such time as	until

Choosing the Correct Word

Homonyms

Homonyms are words that sound alike but do not have the same meaning. These words can be confusing and you may use the incorrect spelling of a word. If words are homonyms, be sure you choose the correct spelling for the meaning you intend.

HOMONYMS

accept (receive)	ascent (rise)
except (other than)	assent (agreement)
board (wood)	fair (average)
bored (uninterested)	fare (a charge)
led (guided)	lessen (make less)
lead (metal)	lesson (learning experience)
past (gone before)	peace (no war)
passed (moved by)	piece (portion)
rain (precipitation)	to (toward)
reign (rule)	too (also)
rein (animal strap)	two (a number)
their (possessive pronoun)	its (shows possession)
there (location)	it's (it is)
they're (they are)	

Idioms

Idioms are expressions with special meanings, and they often break the rules of grammar. Idioms are acceptable in formal writing, but they must be used carefully. Here are some examples.

IDIOMS	
in accordance with	inferior to
angry with	occupied by (someone)
differ from (someone)	occupied with (something)
differ about (an issue)	prior to
independent of	rewarded with (something)

PUNCTUATION

The Period (.)

Use a period to end every sentence, unless the sentence is a direct question, a strong command, or an interjection.

> You will do well on the LAST.

The Question Mark (?)

Use a question mark to end every sentence that is a direct question.

> What is the passing score for the ATS-W?

The Exclamation Point (!)

Use an exclamation point to end every sentence that is a strong command or interjection. Do not overuse exclamation points.

> Interjection: Oh, please!
> Command: Avalanche, head for cover!

The Comma (,)

The comma may be the most used punctuation mark. This section details a few of these uses.
  A clause is part of a sentence that could be a sentence itself. If a clause begins with a conjunction, use a comma before the conjunction.

> Incorrect: I was satisfied with the food but John was grumbling.
> Correct: I was satisfied with the food, but John was grumbling.

> Incorrect: Larry was going fishing or he was going to paint his house.
> Correct: Larry was going fishing, or he was going to paint his house.

A clause or a phrase often introduces a sentence. Introductory phrases or clauses should be set off by a comma. If the introductory element is very short, the comma is optional. Here are some examples.

However, there are other options you may want to consider.

When the de-icer hit the plane's wing, the ice began to melt.

To get a driver's license, go to the motor vehicle bureau.

It doesn't matter what you want, you have to take what you get.

Parenthetical expressions interrupt the flow of a sentence. Set off the parenthetical expression with commas. Do not set off expressions that are essential to understanding the sentence. Here are some examples.

Tom, an old friend, showed up at my house the other day.

I was traveling on a train, in car 8200, on my way to Florida.

John and Ron, who are seniors, went on break to Florida.
[Use a comma. The phrase "who are seniors" is extra information.]

All the students who are seniors take an additional course.
[Don't use a comma. The phrase "who are seniors" is essential information.]

Commas are used to set off items in a list or series. Here are some examples.

Jed is interested in computers, surfing, and fishing.
[Notice the comma before the conjunction *and*. You may omit this comma.]

Mario drives a fast, red car.
[The sentence would make sense with *and* in place of the commas.]

Andy hoped for a bright, sunny, balmy day.
[The sentence would make sense with *and* in place of the commas.]

Lucy had a pale green dress.
[The sentence would not make sense with *and*. The word *pale* modifies *green*. Don't use a comma.]

Randy will go to the movies, pick up some groceries, and then go home.
[Remember, the comma before *and* is optional.]

Commas are used in other writing. Here are some examples.

Dates
Tuesday, February 8, 1994

July 4, 1776, was the first Independence Day.

School begins on Wednesday, September 6, at 8:00 A.M.

His parents immigrated in October 1936.
[No comma is needed.]

Addresses

Closter, New Jersey 07624

321 Forest Street, Phoenix, Arizona

The distance to Hauppauge, Long Island is 37 miles.

16 Martins Avenue, Room 220

The Semicolon (;)

Use the semicolon to connect main clauses not connected by a conjunction. Include a semicolon with very long clauses connected by a conjunction. Here are some examples.

The puck was dropped; the hockey game began.

The puck was dropped, and the hockey game began.

The general manager of the hockey team was not sure what should be done about the player who was injured during the game; but he did know that the player's contract stipulated that his pay would continue whether he was able to play or not.

The Colon (:)

Use the colon after a main clause to introduce a list. Here are some examples.

Liz kept these items in her car: spare tire, jack, flares, and a blanket.

Liz kept a spare tire, jack, flares, and a blanket in her car.

ENGLISH PRACTICE ITEMS

These questions are designed to help you practice the concepts and skills presented in this chapter. For that reason, questions 1–20 are not at all like the items on the real LAST. The other questions may have a different emphasis than the real test.

Mark your choice, then check your answers on page 90.

PART A

1 Ⓐ Ⓑ Ⓒ Ⓓ Ⓔ   5 Ⓐ Ⓑ Ⓒ Ⓓ Ⓔ   9 Ⓐ Ⓑ Ⓒ Ⓓ Ⓔ   13 Ⓐ Ⓑ Ⓒ Ⓓ Ⓔ   17 Ⓐ Ⓑ Ⓒ Ⓓ Ⓔ
2 Ⓐ Ⓑ Ⓒ Ⓓ Ⓔ   6 Ⓐ Ⓑ Ⓒ Ⓓ Ⓔ   10 Ⓐ Ⓑ Ⓒ Ⓓ Ⓔ   14 Ⓐ Ⓑ Ⓒ Ⓓ Ⓔ   18 Ⓐ Ⓑ Ⓒ Ⓓ Ⓔ
3 Ⓐ Ⓑ Ⓒ Ⓓ Ⓔ   7 Ⓐ Ⓑ Ⓒ Ⓓ Ⓔ   11 Ⓐ Ⓑ Ⓒ Ⓓ Ⓔ   15 Ⓐ Ⓑ Ⓒ Ⓓ Ⓔ   19 Ⓐ Ⓑ Ⓒ Ⓓ Ⓔ
4 Ⓐ Ⓑ Ⓒ Ⓓ Ⓔ   8 Ⓐ Ⓑ Ⓒ Ⓓ Ⓔ   12 Ⓐ Ⓑ Ⓒ Ⓓ Ⓔ   16 Ⓐ Ⓑ Ⓒ Ⓓ Ⓔ   20 Ⓐ Ⓑ Ⓒ Ⓓ Ⓔ

PART B

21 Ⓐ Ⓑ Ⓒ Ⓓ Ⓔ
22 Ⓐ Ⓑ Ⓒ Ⓓ Ⓔ
23 Ⓐ Ⓑ Ⓒ Ⓓ Ⓔ
24 Ⓐ Ⓑ Ⓒ Ⓓ Ⓔ
25 Ⓐ Ⓑ Ⓒ Ⓓ Ⓔ

PART C

26 Ⓐ Ⓑ Ⓒ Ⓓ Ⓔ
27 Ⓐ Ⓑ Ⓒ Ⓓ Ⓔ
28 Ⓐ Ⓑ Ⓒ Ⓓ Ⓔ
29 Ⓐ Ⓑ Ⓒ Ⓓ Ⓔ
30 Ⓐ Ⓑ Ⓒ Ⓓ Ⓔ

PART A

> Choose the letter that indicates an error, or choose (E) for no error.

1. <u>Kitty and Harry's</u> <u>anniversary will fall on</u>
         (A)   (B)
   <u>Father's Day</u> <u>this year</u>. <u>No error</u>.
      (C)   (D)   (E)

2. <u>The trees leaves</u> <u>provide</u> a fall festival
         (A)   (B)
   called <u>"Fall Foliage"</u>
              (C)
   <u>in most New England states</u>. <u>No error</u>.
                (D)   (E)

3. <u>Most colleges</u> <u>require</u>
        (A)   (B)
   a <u>specific number</u>
          (C)
   <u>of academic credits for admission</u>.
                   (D)
   <u>No error</u>.
     (E)

4. <u>My brother Robert</u>
          (A)
   <u>loves to read novels</u> <u>but would enjoy</u>
            (B)   (C)
   <u>good mystery's more</u>. <u>No error</u>.
            (D)   (E)

5. <u>Louise had lay</u> <u>her mitt</u> <u>on</u> the bench
         (A)   (B)   (C)
   <u>when she got a glass of water</u>.
                 (D)
   <u>No error</u>.
     (E)

6. <u>It seems to me</u> that <u>I had spoke</u> to my
         (A)   (B)
   landlord <u>about the crack</u> in the ceiling
                   (C)
   <u>about two months ago</u>. <u>No error</u>.
              (D)   (E)

7. <u>The committee</u> <u>on fund-raising</u>
          (A)   (B)
   <u>gathers in the hall</u>,
            (C)
   <u>but Joe went to the</u> room. <u>No error</u>.
            (D)   (E)

8. <u>The administrator</u> <u>wanted</u>
          (A)   (B)
   <u>all lesson plan books</u>
            (C)
   <u>handed in by Friday</u>. <u>No error</u>.
            (D)   (E)

9. Behind the tree, she was reading a book,
   <u>(A)</u>   <u>(B)</u>
   eating a banana, and she waited for the
   <u>(C)</u>   <u>(D)</u>
   sunset. No error.
          <u>(E)</u>

10. Is Washington, D.C. closer to Arlington
    <u>(A)</u>   <u>(B)</u>   <u>(C)</u>
    Cemetery than Charleston? No error.
            <u>(D)</u>   <u>(E)</u>

11. The student would not do nothing
        <u>(A)</u>   <u>(B)</u>
    to redeem himself
    <u>(C)</u>
    in the eyes of the principal. No error.
            <u>(D)</u>   <u>(E)</u>

12. Good teachers are distinguished by
    <u>(A)</u>   <u>(B)</u>
    their enthusiasm and organization.
          <u>(C)</u>   <u>(D)</u>
    No error.
      <u>(E)</u>

13. The principle of the middle school
    <u>(A)</u>   <u>(B)</u>
    wanted to reorganize
    <u>(C)</u>
    the lunch schedule. No error.
          <u>(D)</u>   <u>(E)</u>

14. Grandmother's shopping list consisted of
    <u>(A)</u>   <u>(B)</u>
    mustard, green beans, buttermilk, and
                          <u>(C)</u>
    included some eggs. No error.
          <u>(D)</u>   <u>(E)</u>

15. Unless you arm yourself with
           <u>(A)</u>
    insect repellent, you will get a bight.
                       <u>(B)</u>   <u>(C)</u>   <u>(D)</u>
    No error.
      <u>(E)</u>

16. Graduation exercises will be held on _
               <u>(A)</u>   <u>(B)</u>
    Friday _ June 19th at 7:00 P.M. No error.
    <u>(C)</u>   <u>(D)</u>   <u>(E)</u>

17. With a quick glance the noisy room
    <u>(A)</u>   <u>(B)</u>   <u>(C)</u>
    was silenced. No error.
    <u>(D)</u>   <u>(E)</u>

18. Without even trying, the sprinter
    <u>(A)</u>   <u>(B)</u>
    passed the world record
          <u>(C)</u>
    by five tenths of a second. No error.
    <u>(D)</u>   <u>(E)</u>

19. Prior to the passage of PL 94–142,
    <u>(A)</u>   <u>(B)</u>
    special-education students
            <u>(C)</u>
    were not unrepresented legally.
            <u>(D)</u>
    No error.
      <u>(E)</u>

20. Combine the sugar, waters, cornstarch,
    <u>(A)</u>   <u>(B)</u>   <u>(C)</u>
    and eggs. No error.
        <u>(D)</u>   <u>(E)</u>

PART B

Choose the letter of the best choice for the underlined section, without changing the meaning of the sentence. If the original is best, choose (A). Otherwise, select one of the suggested changes.

21. Postman's talents were missed <u>not any more</u> as a student but also in his extracurricular activities on campus.
    (A) not any more
    (B) not
    (C) not only
    (D) never any
    (E) any

22. <u>Piled on the table, the students started sorting through their projects</u>.
    (A) Piled on the table, the students started sorting through their projects.
    (B) The students started sorting through their projects, which were piled on the table.
    (C) Piled on the table, the students sorted through their projects.
    (D) The students sorted through their projects as they piled on the table.
    (E) Students started sorting through the table piled with projects.

23. All the soccer players, <u>who are injured,</u> must not play the game.
    (A) , who are injured,
    (B) , who are injured
    (C) who are injured,
    (D) who are injured
    (E) (who are injured)

24. The plumber kept these tools in his <u>truck; plunger, snake, washers and faucets</u>.
    (A) truck; plunger, snake, washers and faucets
    (B) truck (plunger, snake, washes and faucets)
    (C) truck: plunger; snake; washers and faucets
    (D) truck; plunger, snake, washers and faucets
    (E) truck: plunger, snake, washers, and faucets.

25. The two <u>attorneys meet</u> and agreed on an out-of-court settlement.
    (A) attorneys meet
    (B) attorney's meet
    (C) attorney's met
    (D) attorneys met
    (E) attorney meets

PART C

Read the passage and answer the questions.

(1) Shop-at-home networks are the latest television craze. (2) You can order just about anything you want from the comfort of your home. (3) I heard a story recently about someone who claims to have picked up the phone and ordered while this person was _____. (4) It seems to me that television shopping is the final step in our descent to an isolated society. (5) Malls will be like ghost towns, libraries will be empty, town centers will be deserted, and we will, each of us, be alone in our own cubicles, glued to our television sets.

26. How does the writer of the passage intend the word glued in the last sentence to be interpreted?
(A) literally
(B) ironically
(C) figuratively
(D) emphatically
(E) metaphorically

27. Which of the following best fits in the blank in Sentence 3?
(A) flying
(B) asleep
(C) undecided
(D) shopping
(E) driving

28. Which of the following sentences contain opinions?
(A) 1 only
(B) 4 and 5 only
(C) 3 only
(D) 1 and 3 only
(E) 1, 2, 3, 4, and 5

29. Which of the following best describes the technique the author uses in this paragraph?
(A) argumentation
(B) exposition
(C) description
(D) characterization
(E) intonation

30. Which sentence contains a simile?
(A) 1
(B) 2
(C) 3
(D) 4
(E) 5

PRACTICE WRITTEN ASSIGNMENT

Use the following lined pages to write a brief essay based on this topic.

**Which of your elementary teachers do you think of most often?
What was there about that teacher's style or classroom that you would either
use the most or avoid the most in your own classroom?**

Write a brief outline below.

ANSWERS

Part A

1. **E**	5. **A**	9. **D**	13. **A**	17. **E**
2. **A**	6. **B**	10. **D**	14. **D**	18. **C**
3. **E**	7. **C**	11. **B**	15. **D**	19. **D**
4. **D**	8. **E**	12. **E**	16. **C**	20. **C**

Part B

21. **C**   22. **B**   23. **D**   24. **E**   25. **D**

Part C

26. **C**   27. **B**   28. **B**   29 **A**   30. **E**

Practice Essay

Show your essay to two people for evaluation. Ask an English teacher or English professor to look at it. Use the rating scale shown on page 63. Add their rating together to find your total score.

Example of an Essay That Might Receive a Total Score of 3 or 4 out of 6.

It's been a long time since I was in elementary school. The school that I attended isn't even there anymore. But I remember most of my elementary school teachers.

Who would I choose as my favorite teacher. When I was in fifth grade, my teacher was Miss Stendel. Even though it was a long time ago, I can almost see her now.

Miss Stendel is probably the teacher I think about the most. She liked Indians, and she used to spend a lot of time in the western states.

Miss Stendel was very nice to me while I was in her classroom. She seemed to understand boys, which many teachers did not. I would say that she is the teacher I think about the most, but of course there are lots of other teachers whom I liked and still like.

Even though I liked her the most, she had an approach to teaching that I will probably avoid when I am a teacher. She used to have piles of mathematics worksheets all around the window sill in the classroom. You had to work your way around the window sill to do the math program. The sheets were boring and I hated them.

I don't know where Miss Stendel is today, but I would like to be able to thank her for being so nice.

Example of an Essay That Might Receive a Total Score of 2 or 3 out of 6.

Miss Willis was my second grade teacher who I respected very much.

I remember her the most of all of my teachers. Good teachers are very important if we expect to have good students.

Miss Willis would have come to school every day with a very sunny attitude even when there was some other problem at home or in the school. She never got mad at us or yeled when we did stuff that was not good.

That was the style which Miss Willis had that I would use if I was a teacher. She never made me feel bad and she was always trying to be helpful and nice. I would try my very best to be as nice as she was and to follow her examples to. If I could be as good a teacher as she was that when I was a teacher my superviser would have to say that she thought that I was doing all the things that she had done to make her a good teacher.

So Miss Willis is the most favorite teacher I can remember.

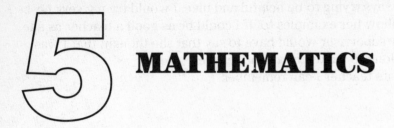

5 MATHEMATICS

USING THIS CHAPTER

This chapter prepares you to do the Mathematics items on the LAST. Choose one of the approaches.

I want all the Mathematics review I can get.

❑ Skip the Review Quiz and read the entire review section.
❑ Take the Mathematics Review Quiz on page 94.
❑ Correct the Review Quiz and reread the indicated parts of the review.
❑ Go over the Special Strategies for Answering the Mathematics Items on pages 130–133.
❑ Complete the Mathematics LAST Practice Items on page 135.

I want a thorough Mathematics review.

❑ Take the Mathematics Review Quiz on page 94.
❑ Correct the Review Quiz and reread the indicated parts of the review.
❑ Go over the Special Strategies for Answering the Mathematics Items on pages 130–133.
❑ Complete the Mathematics LAST Practice Items on page 135.

I want a quick Mathematics review. (Best for most students.)

❑ Take and correct the Mathematics Review Quiz on page 94.
❑ Go over the Special Strategies for Answering the Mathematics Items on pages 130–133.
❑ Complete the Mathematics LAST Practice Items on page 135.

I want to practice Mathematics questions.

❑ Go over the Special Strategies for Answering the Mathematics Items on pages 130–133.
❑ Complete the Mathematics LAST Practice Items on page 135.

MATHEMATICS REVIEW QUIZ

This quiz uses a short answer format to help you find out what you know about the Mathematics topics reviewed in this chapter. The quiz results direct you to the portions of the chapter you should reread.

This quiz will also help focus your thinking about Mathematics, and these questions and answers are a good review in themselves. It's not important to answer all these questions correctly, and don't be concerned if you miss many of them.

The answers are found immediately after the quiz. It's to your advantage not to look at them until you have completed the quiz. Once you have completed and corrected this review quiz, use the answer checklist to decide which sections of the review to study.

> Write the answers in the space provided or on a separate sheet of paper.

1. Which number is missing from this sequence?

    3 6 _____ 12

Questions 2–4: *Use symbols for less than, greater than, and equal to, and compare these numbers:*

2. 23 _____ 32

3. 18 _____ 4 + 14

4. 9 _____ 10 _____ 11

5. Write the place value of the digit 7 in the numeral 476,891,202,593.

    _____

6. Write this number in words: 6,000,000,000,000.

    _____

7. $4^3 =$ _____

8. $2^2 \times 2^3 =$ _____

9. $6^9 \div 6^7 =$ _____

10. $3^2 \times 2^3 =$ _____

11. Write the place value of the digit 4 in the numeral 529.354.

    _____

Questions 12–13: *Use symbols for less than, greater than, and equal to, and compare these numbers:*

12. 9,879 _____ 12,021

13. 98.1589 _____ 98.162

Questions 14–17:

    Round 234,489.0754 to the:

14. thousands place _____

15. hundredths place _____

16. tenths place _____

17. hundreds place _____

18. Write these fractions from least to greatest.

    $^7/_8$, $^{11}/_{12}$, $^{17}/_{20}$

    _____, _____, _____

19. $5 + 7 \times 3^2$ _____

20. $5 \times 8 - (15 - 7 \times 2)$ _____

21. Write a seven-digit number divisible by 4.

    _____

22. Write the GCF and LCM of 6 and 14.

    _____

23. Ron had 20 more baseball cards than he started out with. Then he gave half the cards away and was left with 19. How many baseball cards did Ron start out with?

    _____

24. 203.61 + 9.402 + 0.78 _____

25. 30.916 − 8.72 _____

26. 3.4 × 0.0021 _____

27. 0.576 ÷ 0.32 _____

28. $1\frac{2}{3} \times 3\frac{3}{4}$ _____

29. $1\frac{2}{3} \div \frac{3}{8}$ _____

30. $1\frac{4}{9} + \frac{5}{6}$ _____

31. $4\frac{5}{6} - 2\frac{3}{5}$ _____

32. Simplify this square root $\sqrt{98}$ = _____

33. Complete the following ratio so that it is equivalent to 4 : 5:

    28 : _____

34. Use a proportion and solve this problem. Bob uses jelly and peanut butter in a ratio of 5 : 2. He uses 10 teaspoons of jelly. How much peanut butter will he use?

    _____

Questions 35–40: *Change among decimals, percents, and fractions to complete the table.*

Decimal	Percent	Fraction
0.56	35. _____	36. _____
37. _____	15.2%	38. _____
39. _____	40. _____	$\frac{3}{8}$

41. What is 35 percent of 50? _____ 5

42. What percent of 120 is 40? _____

43. 15 percent of what number is 6? _____

44. What is the probability of rolling one die and getting a 7? _____

45. You flip a fair coin five times in a row and it comes up heads each time. What is the probability that it will come up tails on the next flip?

    _____

46. You pick one card from a deck. Then you pick another one without replacing the first. Are these dependent or independent events? Explain.

    _____

Questions 47–49: *Find the mean, median, and mode of this set of data*

    10, 5, 2, 1, 8, 5, 3, 0

47. Mean _____

48. Median _____

49. Mode _____

50. Draw a stem and leaf plot that shows these data: 12, 12, 23, 25, 36, 38.

51. $^-8 + {}^+4$ = _____

52. $^+85 + {}^-103$ = _____

53. $^-12 - {}^+7$ = _____

54. $^-72 - {}^-28$ = _____

55. $^-9 \times {}^+8$ = _____

56. $^-12 \times {}^-6$ = _____

57. $^-28 \div {}^+7$ = _____

58. $^-72 \div {}^-9$ = _____

59. Find the area of a triangle with a base of 3 and a height of 2.

    _____

60. Find the area of a square with a side of 5.

    _____

61. Find the area of a circle with a radius of 6.

    _____

62. Find the volume of a cube with a side of 5.

    _____

Write the value of the variable.

63. $x - 35 = 26$ _____

64. $x + 81 = 7$ _____

65. $y \div 8 = 3$ _____

66. $3z = 54$ _____

67. $4y - 9 = 19$ _____

68. $k \div 6 + 5 = 17$ _____

Questions 69–75: *Draw a model of:*

69. a point

70. a line

71. a ray

72. an acute angle

73. complementary angles

74. an isosceles triangle

75. a rectangle

76. Use this coordinate grid and plot these points: A (3,2) B (−4, −2).

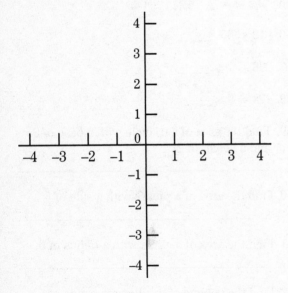

77. Draw a diagram to show that all vowels (*a, e, i, o, u*) are letters and that all consonants are letters, but that no vowels are consonants.

78. What is the difference between the mass of an object on earth and the mass of the same object on the moon?

    _____

79. How many inches would it take to make 5 yards? _____

80. How many cups would it take to make 3 quarts? _____

81. A kilogram is how many grams? _____

82. A centimeter is how many meters? _____

83. It's 1:00 P.M. in Los Angeles. What time is it in New York? _____

84. It's 32° Celsius. How would you describe a day with that temperature?

    _____

ANSWER CHECKLIST

The answers are organized by review sections. Check your answers. If you miss any questions in a section, check the box and review that section.

Number Sense and Numeration

❏ *Understanding and Ordering Whole Numbers, page 100*
1. 9
2. <
3. =
4. <, <

❏ *Place Value, page 100*
5. 10 billion
6. six trillion

❏ *Positive Exponents, page 101*
7. 64
8. 32
9. 36
10. 72

❏ *Understanding and Ordering Decimals, page 101*
11. thousandths

❏ *Comparing Whole Numbers and Decimals, page 101*
12. <
13. <

❏ *Rounding Whole Numbers and Decimals, page 102*
14. 234,000
15. 234,489.08
16. 234,489.1
17. 234,500

❏ *Understanding and Ordering Fractions, page 102*
18. $^{17}/_{20}$, $^{7}/_{8}$, $^{11}/_{12}$

❏ *How and When to Add, Subtract, Multiply, and Divide, page 104*
19. 68
20. 39

❏ *Number Theory, page 105*
21. The last 2 digits have to be divisible by 4.
22. GCF is 2. LCM is 42.

Real Number Systems and Subsystems

❏ *Add, Subtract, Multiply, and Divide Decimals, page 108*
23. 18
24. 213.792
25. 22.196
26. 0.00714
27. 1.8

❏ *Multiplying, Dividing, Adding, and Subtracting Fractions and Mixed Numbers, page 109*
28. $6^{1}/_{4}$
29. $4^{4}/_{9}$
30. $2^{5}/_{18}$
31. $2^{7}/_{30}$

❏ *Square Roots, page 110*
32. $7\sqrt{2}$

❏ *Ratio and Proportion, page 110*
33. 35
34. 4

❏ *Percent, page 111*

Decimal	Percent	Fraction
0.56	**35.** 56%	**36.** 14/25
37. 0.152	15.2%	**38.** 19/125
39. 0.375	**40.** 37.5%	3/8

❏ *Three Types of Percent Problems, page 112*
41. 17.5
42. $33^{1}/_{3}$%
43. 40

Probability and Simple Statistics

❑ *Probability, page 113*
   44. Zero
   45. $\frac{1}{2}$

❑ *Dependent and Independent Events, page 114*
   46. Dependent. The outcome of one event affects the probability of the other event.

❑ *Statistics, page 114*
   47. 4.25
   48. 4
   49. 5

❑ *Stem-and-Leaf and Box-and-Whisker Plots, page 115*
   50.

1	2,2
2	3,5
3	6,8

Algebra

❑ *Adding and Subtracting Integers, page 116*
   51. –4
   52. –18
   53. –19
   54. –44

❑ *Multiplying and Dividing Integers, page 116*
   55. –72
   56. +72
   57. –4
   58. +8

❑ *Formulas, page 117*
   59. 3
   60. 25
   61. about 113 (113.097...)
   62. 125

❑ *Equations, page 118*
   63. 61
   64. –74
   65. 24
   66. 18
   67. 7
   68. 72

Geometry

❑ *Two-Dimensional Geometry, page 120*
   69. .
   70.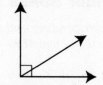
   71.

72. Acute angle   **73.** Complementary angles

74. Isosceles triangle   **75.** Rectangle

❑ *Coordinate Grid, page 123*
76.

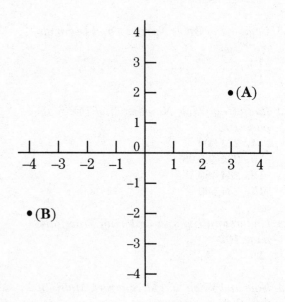

❑ *Using Diagrams, page 123*
   77.

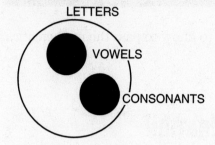

Measurement

❑ *Measuring with a Ruler and a Protractor,*
   page 124

❑ *Weight and Mass, page 125*
   78. None. Mass remains constant.

❑ *Customary (English) Units, page 125*
   79. 180 inches
   80. 12

❑ *Metric System, page 126*
   81. 1,000
   82. 0.01

❑ *Time and Temperature, page 126*
   83. 4:00 P.M.
   84. Hot — about 90°F.

❑ *Problem Solving, page 128*

MATHEMATICS REVIEW

This review section targets the skills and concepts you need to know to pass the mathematics part of the LAST.

NUMBER SENSE AND NUMERATION

UNDERSTANDING AND ORDERING WHOLE NUMBERS

Whole numbers are the numbers you use to tell how many. They include 0, 1, 2, 3, 4, 5, 6 . . . . The dots tell us that these numbers keep going on forever. There are an infinite number of whole numbers, which means you will never reach the last one.

Cardinal numbers such as 1, 9, and 18 tell how many. There are 9 players on the field in a baseball game. Ordinal numbers such as 1st, 2nd, 9th, and 18th tell about order. For example, Lynne batted 1st this inning.

You can visualize whole numbers evenly spaced on a number line.

You can use the number line to compare numbers. Numbers get smaller as we go to the left and larger as we go to the right. We use the terms *equal to* (=), *less than* (<), *greater than* (>), and *between* to compare numbers.

12 equals 10 +2	2 is less than 5	9 is greater than 4	6 is between 5 and 7
12 = 10 + 2	2 < 5	9 > 4	5 < 6 < 7

PLACE VALUE

We use ten digits, 0–9 to write out numerals. We also use a place value system of numeration. The value of a digit depends on the place it occupies. Look at the following place value chart.

millions	hundred thousands	ten thousands	thousands	hundreds	tens	ones
3	5	7	9	4	1	0

The value of the 9 is 9,000. The 9 is in the thousands place. The value of the 5 is 500,000. The 5 is in the hundred thousands place. Read the number three million, five hundred seventy-nine thousand, four hundred ten.

Some whole numbers are very large. The distance from earth to the planet Pluto is about six trillion (6,000,000,000,000) yards. The distance from earth to the nearest star is about 40 quadrillion (40,000,000,000,000,000) yards.

POSITIVE EXPONENTS

You can show repeated multiplication as an exponent. The exponent shows how many times the factor appears.

$$\text{Base}-3^{5} = 3 \times 3 \times 3 \times 3 \times 3 = 243$$

[Exponent]

[Factors]

Rules for Exponents

Use these rules to multiply and divide exponents with the *same base*.

$$7^{8} \times 7^{5} = 7^{13} \qquad a^{n} \times a^{m} = a^{m+n}$$
$$7^{8} \div 7^{5} = 7^{3} \qquad a^{n} \div a^{m} = a^{n-m}$$

Scientific Notation

Sometimes we use scientific notation to represent very large numbers. For example, 6,000,000,000,000 has 12 zeros. We can write 6,000,000,000,000 as 6×10^{12}.

UNDERSTANDING AND ORDERING DECIMALS

Decimals are used to represent numbers between 0 and 1. Decimals can also be written on a number line.

We also use ten digits 0–9 and a place value system of numeration to write decimals. The value of a digit depends on the place it occupies. Look at the following place value chart.

ones	tenths	hundredths	thousandths	ten-thousandths	hundred-thousandths	millionths	ten-millionths	hundred-millionths	billionths
0.	3	6	8	7					

The value of 3 is three tenths. The 3 is in the tenths place. The value of 8 is eight thousandths. The 8 is in the thousandths place.

COMPARING WHOLE NUMBERS AND DECIMALS

To compare two numbers line up the place values. Start at the left and keep going until the digits in the same place are different.

Compare	9,879 and 16,459	23,801 and 23,798	58.1289 and 58.132
Line up the place values	9,879 16,459 9,879 < 16,459 Less than	23,**8**01 23,798 23,801 > 23,798 Greater than	58.1289 58.132 58.1289 < 58.132 Less than

ROUNDING WHOLE NUMBERS AND DECIMALS

Follow these steps to round a number to a place.

- Look at the digit to the right of that place.
- If the digit to the right is 5 or more, round up. If the digit is less than 5, leave the numeral to be rounded as written.

> *Round 859,465 to the thousands place.*
>
> Underline the thousands place.
>
> Look to the right. The digit 4 is less than 5 so leave as written.
>
> 859,465 rounded to the thousands place is 859,000.
>
> 859,465 rounded to the ten-thousands place 860,000.
>
> *Round 8.647 to the hundredths place.*
>
> Underline the hundredths place.
>
> Look to the right. The digit 7 is 5 or more so you round up.
>
> 8.647 rounded to the *hundredths* place is 8.65.
>
> 8.647 rounded to the *tenths* place is 8.6.

UNDERSTANDING AND ORDERING FRACTIONS

A fraction names a part of a whole or of a group. A fraction has two parts, a numerator and a denominator. The denominator tells how many parts in all. The numerator tell how many parts you identified.

$$\frac{3}{4} \begin{array}{l} \text{Numerator} \\ \text{Denominator} \end{array}$$

Equivalent Fractions

Two fractions that stand for the same number are called equivalent fractions. Multiply or divide the numerator and denominator by the same number to find an equivalent fraction.

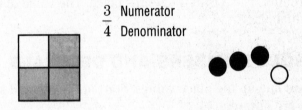

$$\frac{2 \times 3}{5 \times 3} = \frac{6}{15} \qquad \frac{6 \div 3}{9 \div 3} = \frac{2}{3} \qquad \frac{6 \times 4}{8 \times 4} = \frac{24}{32} \qquad \frac{8 \div 2}{10 \div 2} = \frac{4}{5}$$

Fractions can also be written and ordered on a number line. You can use the number line to compare fractions. Fractions get smaller as we go to the left and larger as we go to the right. We use the terms equivalent to (=), less than (<), greater than (>), and between to compare fractions.

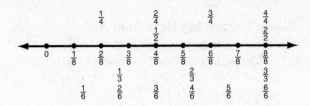

$\frac{1}{2}$ is equivalent to $\frac{2}{4}$ $\frac{2}{3}$ is less than $\frac{3}{4}$ $\frac{5}{8}$ is greater than $\frac{1}{2}$ $\frac{1}{3}$ is between $\frac{1}{4}$ and $\frac{3}{8}$

$$\frac{1}{2} = \frac{2}{4} \qquad\qquad \frac{2}{3} < \frac{3}{4} \qquad\qquad \frac{5}{8} > \frac{1}{2} \qquad\qquad \frac{1}{4} < \frac{1}{3} < \frac{3}{8}$$

Compare Two Fractions

Use this method to compare two fractions. For example, compare $\frac{13}{18}$ and $\frac{5}{7}$. First write the two fractions and cross multiply as shown. The larger cross product appears next to the larger fraction. If cross products are equal then the fractions are equivalent.

$$91 = \qquad\qquad = 90$$
$$\frac{13}{18} \times \frac{5}{7}$$

$$91 > 90 \text{ so } \frac{13}{18} > \frac{5}{7}$$

Mixed Numbers and Improper Fractions

Change an improper fraction to a mixed number:

$$\frac{23}{8} = 8\overline{)23}^{\,2\frac{7}{8}}$$

Change a mixed number to an improper fraction:

$$3\frac{2}{5} = \frac{17}{5}$$

Multiply denominator and whole number. Then add the numerator.

$$\frac{(3 \times 5) + 2}{5} = \frac{15 + 2}{5} = \frac{17}{5}$$

HOW AND WHEN TO ADD, SUBTRACT, MULTIPLY, AND DIVIDE

Order of Operations

Use this phrase to remember the order in which we do operations:

Please Excuse My Dear Aunt Sally

(1) **P**arentheses (2) **E**xponents (3) **M**ultiplication or **D**ivision (4) **A**ddition or **S**ubtraction

For example,

$$4 + 3 \times 7^2 = 4 + 3 \times 49 = 4 + 147 = 151$$
$$(4 + 3) \times 7^2 = 7 \times 7^2 = 7 \times 49 = 343$$
$$(6 - 10 \div 5) + 6 \times 3 = (6 - 2) + 6 \times 3 = 4 + 6 \times 3 = 4 + 18 = 22$$

Decide Whether to Add, Subtract, Multiply, or Divide

Before you can solve a problem, you should know which operation to use. You can use key words to decide which operation to use, or you can use a problem-solving strategy called choosing the operation. We'll discuss both of them here.

Key Words

Addition	sum, and, more, increased by
Subtraction	less, difference, decreased by
Multiplication	of, product, times
Division	per, quotient, shared, ratio
Equals	is, equals

You can't just use these key words without thinking. You must check to be sure that the operation makes sense when it replaces the key word. For example,

19 and 23 is 42	16 is 4 more than 12	What percent of 19 is 5.7
$19 + 23 = 42$	$16 = 4 + 12$	$\_\_\_\_\% \times 19 = 5.7$

Choosing the Operation

To use the choosing-the-operation strategy, you think of each situation in this way. What do I know? What am I trying to find? The answers to these questions lead you directly to the correct operation.

You Know	You Want to Find
Add	
1. How many in two or more groups	How many in all
2. How many in one group How many join it	The total amount
3. How many in one group How many more in the second group	How many in the second group
Subtract	
4. How many in one group Number taken away	How many are left
5. How many in each of two groups	How much larger one group is than the other
6. How many in one group How many in part of that group	How many in the rest of the group
Multiply	
7. How many in each group There is the same number in each group How many groups	How many in all
Divide	
8. Same number in each group How many in all How many in each group	How many groups
9. Same number in each group How many in all How many groups	How many in each group

NUMBER THEORY

Number theory explores the natural numbers {1, 2, 3, 4, . . .}. We'll review just a few important number theory concepts.

Factors

The factors of a number evenly divide the number with no remainder. For example, 2 is a factor of 6, but 2 is not a factor of 5.

The number 1 is a factor of every number. Each number is a factor of itself.

1 The only factor is 1
2 Factors 1, 2
3 1, 3

4   1, 2, 4
5   1, 5
6   1, 2, 3, 6
7   1, 7
8   1, 2, 4, 8
9   1, 3, 9
10 1, 2, 5, 10

Prime Numbers and Composite Numbers

A prime number has exactly two factors, itself and 1.

2 is prime. The only factors are 1 and 2.
3 Prime. Factors 1, 3.
5 Prime. Factors 1, 5.
7 Prime. Factors 1, 7.

A composite number has more than two factors.

4 is composite. The factors are 1, 2, 4.
6 is composite. Factors: 1, 2, 3, 6.
8 is composite. Factors: 1, 2, 4, 8.
9 is composite. Factors: 1, 3, 9.
10 is composite. Factors: 1, 2, 5, 10.

The number 1 has only one factor, itself. The number 1 is neither prime nor composite.

Least Common Multiple (LCM), Greatest Common Factor (GCF)

Multiples. The multiples of a number are all the numbers you get when you count by that number. Here are some examples.

Multiples of 1: 1, 2, 3, 4, 5, . . .
Multiples of 2: 2, 4, 6, 8, 10, . . .
Multiples of 3: 3, 6, 9, 12, 15, . . .
Multiples of 4: 4, 8, 12, 16, 20, . . .
Multiples of 5: 5, 10, 15, 20, 25, . . .

Least Common Multiple is the smallest multiple shared by two numbers.

The least common multiple of 6 and 8 is 24.

List the multiples of 6 and 8. Notice that 24 is the smallest multiple common to both numbers.

Multiples of 6: 6, 12, 18, **24**, 30, 36
Multiples of 8: 8, 16, **24**, 32, 40

Greatest Common Factor is the largest factor shared by two numbers.

> The greatest common factor of 28 and 36 is 4.
> List the factors of 28 and 36.
>
> Factors of 28: 1, 2, **4**, 7, 28
> Factors of 36: 1, 2, 3, **4**, 9, 12, 18, 36

Divisibility Rules

Use these rules to find out if a number is divisible by the given number. *Divisible* means the given number divides evenly with no remainder.

2 Every even number is divisible by 2.

3 If the sum of the digits is divisible by 3, the number is divisible by 3.

> 347   3 + 4 + 7 = 14   14 is not divisible by 3 so 347 is not divisible by 3
>
> 738   7 + 3 + 8 = 18   18 is divisible by 3 so 738 is divisible by 3

4 If the last two digits are divisible by 4, the number is divisible by 4.

> 484,8<u>42</u>   42 is not divisible by 4 so 484,842 is not divisible by 4.
>
> 371,9<u>56</u>   56 is divisible by 4 so 372,956 is divisible by 4.

5 If the last digit is 0 or 5, then the number is divisible by 5.

6 If the number meets the divisibility rules for both 2 *and* 3 then it is divisible by 6.

8 If the last three digits are divisible by 8, then the number is divisible by 8.

> 208,513,<u>114</u>   114 is not divisible by 8 so 208,513,114 is not divisible by 8.
>
> 703,628,<u>920</u>   920 is divisible by 8 so 703,628,920 is divisible by 8.

9 If the sum of the digits is divisible by 9 then the number is divisible by 9.

> 93,163   9 + 3 + 1 + 6 + 3 = 22   22 is not divisible by 9 so 93,163
>   is not divisible by 9.
>
> 86,715   8 + 6 + 7 + 1 + 5 = 27   27 is divisible by 9 so 86,715 is
>   divisible by 9.

10 If a number ends in 0, the number is divisible by 10.

REAL NUMBER SYSTEMS AND SUBSYSTEMS

ADD, SUBTRACT, MULTIPLY, AND DIVIDE DECIMALS

Add and Subtract Decimals

Line up the decimal points and add or subtract.

Add: $14.9 + 3.108 + 0.16$ Subtract $14.234 - 7.14$

$$
\begin{array}{r}
14.9 \\
3.108 \\
+\ 0.16 \\
\hline
18.168
\end{array}
\qquad
\begin{array}{r}
14.234 \\
-7.14 \\
\hline
7.094
\end{array}
$$

Multiply Decimals

Multiply as with whole numbers. Count the total number of decimal places in the factors. Put that many decimal places in the product. You may have to write leading zeros.

Multiply: 17.4×1.3 Multiply: 0.016×1.7

$$
\begin{array}{r}
17.4 \\
\times\ 1.3 \\
\hline
522 \\
174 \\
\hline
22.6\,2
\end{array}
\qquad
\begin{array}{r}
0.016 \\
\times\ 1.7 \\
\hline
112 \\
16 \\
\hline
0\,2\,7\,2
\end{array}
$$

Divide Decimals

Make the divisor a whole number. Match the movement in the dividend and then divide.

$$
0.16\overline{)1.328} \qquad 0.16\overline{)1.328} \qquad
\begin{array}{r}
8.3 \\
16\overline{)132.8} \\
128 \\
\hline
48 \\
48 \\
\hline
0
\end{array}
$$

MULTIPLYING, DIVIDING, ADDING, AND SUBTRACTING FRACTIONS AND MIXED NUMBERS

Multiplying Fractions and Mixed Numbers

Write any mixed number as an improper fraction. Multiply numerator and denominator. Write the product in simplest form. For example, Multiply $^3/_4$ and $^1/_6$.

$$\frac{3}{4} \times \frac{1}{6} = \frac{3}{24} = \frac{1}{8}$$

Now, multiply $3^1/_3$ times $^3/_5$.

$$3\frac{1}{3} \times \frac{3}{5} = \frac{10}{3} \times \frac{3}{5} = \frac{30}{15} = 2$$

Dividing Fractions and Mixed Numbers

To divide $1^4/_5$ by $^3/_8$:

$$1\frac{4}{5} \div \frac{3}{8} = \frac{9}{5} \div \frac{3}{8} = \frac{9}{5} \times \frac{8}{3} = \frac{72}{15} = 4\frac{12}{15} = 4\frac{4}{5}$$

Write any mixed numbers as improper fractions   Invert the divisor and multiply   Write the product   Write in simplest form

Adding Fractions and Mixed Numbers

Write fractions with common denominators. Add and then write in simplest form.

Add: $\dfrac{3}{8}+\dfrac{1}{4}$

$$\frac{3}{8}=\frac{3}{8}$$
$$+\frac{1}{4}=\frac{2}{8}$$
$$\frac{5}{8}$$

Add: $\dfrac{7}{8}+\dfrac{5}{12}$

$$\frac{7}{8}=\frac{21}{24}$$
$$+\frac{5}{12}=\frac{10}{24}$$
$$\frac{31}{24}=1\frac{7}{24}$$

Add: $2\dfrac{1}{3}+\dfrac{5}{7}$

$$2\frac{1}{3}=2\frac{7}{21}$$
$$+\frac{5}{7}=\frac{15}{21}$$
$$2\frac{22}{21}=3\frac{1}{21}$$

Subtracting Fractions and Mixed Numbers

Write fractions with common denominators. Subtract and then write in simplest form.

Subtract: $\dfrac{5}{6}-\dfrac{1}{3}$

$$\frac{5}{6}=\frac{5}{6}$$
$$-\frac{1}{3}=\frac{2}{6}$$
$$\frac{3}{6}=\frac{1}{2}$$

Subtract: $\dfrac{3}{8}-\dfrac{1}{5}$

$$\frac{3}{8}=\frac{15}{40}$$
$$-\frac{1}{5}=\frac{8}{40}$$
$$\frac{7}{40}$$

Subtract: $3\dfrac{1}{6}-1\dfrac{1}{3}$

$$3\frac{1}{6}=3\frac{1}{6}=2\frac{7}{6}$$
$$-1\frac{1}{3}=1\frac{2}{6}=1\frac{2}{6}$$
$$1\frac{5}{6}$$

SQUARE ROOTS

The square root of a given number, when multiplied by itself, equals the given number. This symbol means the square root of 25 $\sqrt{25}$. The square root of 25 is 5. $5 \times 5 = 25$.

Some Square Roots Are Whole Numbers

The numbers with whole-number square roots are called perfect squares.

$$\sqrt{1} = 1 \quad \sqrt{4} = 2 \quad \sqrt{9} = 3 \quad \sqrt{16} = 4 \quad \sqrt{25} = 5 \quad \sqrt{36} = 6$$

$$\sqrt{49} = 7 \quad \sqrt{64} = 8 \quad \sqrt{81} = 9 \quad \sqrt{100} = 10 \quad \sqrt{121} = 11 \quad \sqrt{144} = 12$$

Use This Rule to Write a Square Root in Its Simplest Form

$$\sqrt{a \times b} = \sqrt{a} \times \sqrt{b} \qquad\qquad \sqrt{5 \times 3} = \sqrt{5} \times \sqrt{3}$$

$$\sqrt{72} = \sqrt{36 \times 2} = \sqrt{36} \times \sqrt{2} = 6 \times \sqrt{2}$$

RATIO AND PROPORTION

Ratio

A ratio is a way of comparing two numbers with division. It conveys the same meaning as a fraction. There are three ways to write a ratio.

Using words   3 to 4   As a fraction   3/4   Using a colon   3 : 4

Proportion

A proportion shows two ratios that have the same value; that is, the fractions representing the ratios are equivalent. Use cross multiplication. If the cross products are equal, then the two ratios form a proportion.

$^{3}/_{8}$ and $^{27}/_{72}$ form a proportion. The cross products are equal. ($3 \times 72 = 8 \times 27$)

$^{3}/_{8}$ and $^{24}/_{56}$ do not form a proportion. The cross products are not equal.

Solving a Proportion

You may have to write a proportion to solve a problem. For example, the mason mixes cement and sand using a ratio of 2 : 5. Twelve bags of cement will be used. How much sand is needed?

To solve, use the numerator to stand for cement. The denominator will stand for sand.

$$\frac{2}{5} = \frac{12}{S} \qquad\qquad \frac{2}{5} = \frac{12}{S}$$

$$2 \times S = 5 \times 12$$
$$2S = 60$$
$$S = 30$$

Write the proportion   Cross multiply to solve

Thirty bags of sand are needed.

PERCENT

Percent comes from per centum, which means per hundred. Whenever you see a number followed by a percent sign it means that number out of 100.

Decimals and Percents

To write a decimal as a percent, move the decimal point two places to the right and write the percent sign.

$$0.34 = 34\% \qquad 0.297 = 29.7\% \qquad 0.6 = 60\% \qquad 0.001 = 0.1\%$$

To write a percent as a decimal, move the decimal point two places to the left and delete the percent sign.

$$51\% = 0.51 \qquad 34.18\% = 0.3418 \qquad 0.9\% = 0.009$$

Fractions and Percents

Writing Fractions as Percents

• Divide the numerator by the denominator. Write the answer as a percent.

Write $^3/_5$ as a percent.   Write $^5/_8$ as a percent.

$$5\overline{)3.0} = 0.6 \qquad 0.6 = 60\% \qquad\qquad 8\overline{)5.000} = 0.625 \qquad 0.625 = 62.5\%$$

- Write an equivalent fraction with 100 in the denominator. Write the numerator followed by a percent sign.

$$\text{Write } {}^{13}\!/_{25} \text{ as a percent.}$$

$$\frac{13}{25} = \frac{52}{100} = 52\%$$

- Use these equivalencies.

$$\frac{1}{4} = 25\% \qquad \frac{1}{2} = 50\% \qquad \frac{3}{4} = 75\% \qquad \frac{4}{4} = 100\%$$

$$\frac{1}{5} = 20\% \qquad \frac{2}{5} = 40\% \qquad \frac{3}{5} = 60\% \qquad \frac{4}{5} = 80\%$$

$$\frac{1}{6} = 16\frac{2}{3}\% \qquad \frac{1}{3} = 33\frac{1}{3}\% \qquad \frac{2}{3} = 66\frac{2}{3}\% \qquad \frac{5}{6} = 83\frac{1}{3}\%$$

$$\frac{1}{8} = 12\frac{1}{2}\% \qquad \frac{3}{8} = 37\frac{1}{2}\% \qquad \frac{5}{8} = 62\frac{1}{2}\% \qquad \frac{7}{8} = 87\frac{1}{2}\%$$

Writing Percents as Fractions

Write a fraction with 100 in the denominator and the percent in the numerator. Simplify.

$$18\% = \frac{18}{100} = \frac{9}{50} \qquad 7.5\% = \frac{7.5}{100} = \frac{75}{1000} = \frac{3}{40}$$

THREE TYPES OF PERCENT PROBLEMS

Finding a Percent of a Number

To find a percent of a number, write a number sentence with a decimal for the percent and solve.

$$\text{Find } 40\% \text{ of } 90.$$

$$0.4 \times 90 = 36$$

It may be easier to write a fraction for the percent.

$$\text{Find } 62\frac{1}{2}\% \text{ of } 64.$$

$$\frac{5}{8} \times 64 = 5 \times 8 = 40$$

Finding What Percent One Number Is of Another

To find what percent one number is of another, write a number sentence and solve to find the percent.

What percent of 5 is 3?

$$n \times 5 = 3$$

$$n = \frac{3}{5} = 0.6 = 60\%$$

Finding a Number When a Percent of It Is Known

To find a number when a percent of it is known, write a number sentence with a decimal or a fraction for the percent and solve to find the number.

5% of what number is 2?

$$0.05 \times n = 2$$

$$n = 2 \div 0.05$$

$$n = 40$$

PROBABILITY AND SIMPLE STATISTICS

PROBABILITY

The probability of an occurrence is the likelihood that it will happen. Most often, we write probability as a fraction.

Flip a fair coin and the probability that it will come up heads is 1/2. The same is true for tails. Write the probability this way.

$$P(H) = 1/2 \qquad P(T) = 1/2$$

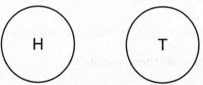

If something will never occur the probability is 0. If something will always occur, the probability is 1. Therefore, if you flip a fair coin,

$$P(7) = 0 \qquad P(H \text{ or } T) = 1$$

DEPENDENT AND INDEPENDENT EVENTS

Events are *independent* when the outcome of one event does not affect the probability of the other event. Each coin flip is an independent event. No matter the outcome of one flip, the probability of the next flip remains the same.

Flip heads 10 times in a row with a fair coin. On the next flip, the P (H) is still 1/2. Coin flips are independent events.

Events are *dependent* where the outcome of one event does affect the probability of the other event. For example, you have a full deck of cards. The probability of picking the Queen of Hearts is 1/52.

You pick one card and it's not the Queen of Hearts. You don't put the card back. The probability of picking the Queen of Hearts is now 1/51. Cards picked without replacement are dependent events.

STATISTICS

Descriptive statistics are used to explain or describe a set of numbers. Most often we use the mean, median, or mode to describe these numbers.

Mean (Average)

The mean is a position midway between two extremes. To find the mean:

1. Add the items or scores.

2. Divide by the number of items.

    For example, find the mean of 24, 17, 42, 51, 36.

$$24 + 17 + 42 + 51 + 36 = 170 \qquad 170 \div 5 = 34$$

The mean or average is 34.

Median

The median is the middle number. To find the median:

1. Arrange the numbers from least to greatest.

2. If there are an odd number of scores, then find the middle score.

3. If there is an even number of scores, average the two middle scores.

    For example, find the median of these numbers.

$$6, 9, 11, \underline{17}, \underline{21}, 33, 45, 71$$

There are an even number of scores.

$$17 + 21 = 38 \qquad 38 \div 2 = 19$$

The median is 19.

Don't forget to arrange the scores in order before finding the middle score!

Mode

The mode is the number that occurs most often.
   For example, find the mode of these numbers.

$$6, 3, 7, 6, 9, 3, 6, 1, 2, 6, 7, 3$$

The number 6 occurs most often so 6 is the mode.

Not all sets of numbers have a mode. Some sets of numbers may have more than one mode.

STEM-AND-LEAF AND BOX-AND-WHISKER PLOTS

Stem-and-Leaf Plots

Stem-and-leaf plots represent data in place value-oriented plots. Each piece of data is shown in the plot. The following stem-and-leaf plot shows test scores. The stem represents 10, and the leaves represent 1. You can read each score. In the 50s the scores are 55, 55, and 58. There are no scores in the 60s. You can find the lowest score, 40, and highest score, 128.

Stem	Leaves
4	0, 7
5	5, 5, 8
6	
7	1, 4, 4, 6
8	2, 3, 4, 5
9	9, 9
10	
11	
12	3, 4, 8

Example: 7 | 4   means 74 people

Box-and-Whisker Plots

Box-and-whisker plots show the range and quartiles of scores. The plot is a box divided into two parts with a whisker at each end. The ends of the left and right whiskers show the lowest and highest scores. Quartiles partition scores into quarters. The left and right parts of the box show the upper and lower quartiles; the dividing line shows the median.

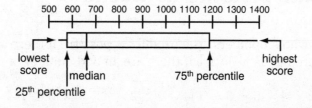

ALGEBRA

The number line can also show negative numbers. There is a negative whole number for every positive whole number. Zero is neither positive nor negative. The negative whole numbers and the positive whole numbers together are called integers.

ADDING AND SUBTRACTING INTEGERS

Addition

When the signs are the same keep the sign and add.

$$
\begin{array}{r} ^+7 \\ +\,^+8 \\ \hline ^+15 \end{array}
\qquad
\begin{array}{r} ^-3 \\ +\,^-11 \\ \hline ^-14 \end{array}
$$

When the signs are different, disregard the signs, subtract the numbers, and keep the sign of the larger number.

$$
\begin{array}{r} ^+28 \\ +\,^-49 \\ \hline ^-21 \end{array}
\qquad
\begin{array}{r} ^-86 \\ +\,^+135 \\ \hline ^+49 \end{array}
$$

Subtraction

Change the sign of the number being subtracted. Then add using the preceding rules.

$$
\begin{array}{r} ^+13 \\ -\,^-18 \\ \downarrow \\ ^+13 \\ +\,^+18 \\ \hline ^+31 \end{array}
\qquad
\begin{array}{r} ^-43 \\ -\,^-17 \\ \downarrow \\ ^-43 \\ +\,^+17 \\ \hline ^-26 \end{array}
\qquad
\begin{array}{r} ^+29 \\ -\,^-49 \\ \downarrow \\ ^+29 \\ +\,^+49 \\ \hline ^+78 \end{array}
\qquad
\begin{array}{r} ^-92 \\ -\,^+135 \\ \downarrow \\ ^-92 \\ +\,^-135 \\ \hline ^-227 \end{array}
$$

MULTIPLYING AND DIVIDING INTEGERS

Multiply

Multiply as you would whole numbers. The product is *positive* if there are an even number of negative factors. The product is *negative* if there are an odd number of negative factors.

$$^-2 \times {}^+4 \times {}^-6 \times {}^+3 = {}^+144 \qquad {}^-2 \times {}^-4 \times {}^+6 \times {}^-3 = {}^-144$$

Divide

Forget the signs and divide. The quotient is *positive* if both integers have the same sign. The quotient is *negative* if the integers have different signs.

$$^+24 \div {}^+4 = {}^+6 \qquad {}^-24 \div {}^-4 = {}^+6 \qquad {}^+24 \div {}^-4 = {}^-6 \qquad {}^-24 \div {}^+4 = {}^-6$$

FORMULAS

Evaluating an Expression

Evaluate an expression by replacing the variables with values. Remember to use the correct order of operations. For example, evaluate

$$3x - \frac{y}{z} \text{ for } x = 3, y = 8, \text{ and } z = 4$$

$$3\left(3\right) - \frac{8}{4} = 9 - 2 = 7$$

Using Formulas

Using a formula is like evaluating an expression. Just replace the variables with values. Here are some important formulas to know. The area of a figure is the amount of space it occupies in two dimensions. The perimeter of a figure is the distance around the figure. Use 3.14 for π.

Figure	Formula	Description
Triangle	Area = $\frac{1}{2} bh$ Perimeter = $s_1 + s_2 + s_3$	
Square	Area = s^2 Perimeter = $4s$	
Rectangle	Area = lw Perimeter = $2l + 2w$	
Parallelogram	Area = bh Perimeter = $2s + 2h$	
Trapezoid	Area = $\frac{1}{2} h(b_1 + b_2)$ Perimeter = $b_1 + b_2 + s_1 + s_2$	

Figure	Formula	Description
Circle	Area = πr^2 Circumference = $2\pi r$ or = πd	
Cube	Volume = s^3	
Rectangular Prism	Volume = lwh	
Sphere	Volume = $\frac{4}{3}\pi r^3$	

Pythagorean Formula

The Pythagorean formula for right triangles states that the sum of the square of the legs equals the square of the hypotenuse:

$$a^2 + b^2 = c^2$$

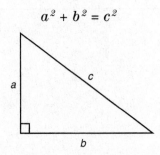

EQUATIONS

The whole idea of solving equations is to isolate the variable on one side of the equal sign. The value of the variable is what's on the other side of the equal sign. Substitute your answer into the original equation to check your solution.

Solving Equations by Adding or Subtracting

Solve: $y + 19 = 23$

Subtract 19 $y + 19 - 19 = 23 - 19$

$$y = 4$$

Check: Does **4** + 19 = 23? Yes. It checks.

Solve: $x - 23 = 51$

Add 23　$x - 23 + 23 = 51 + 23$

$$x = 74$$

Check: Does **74** $- 23 = 51$. Yes. It checks.

Solving Equations by Multiplying or Dividing

Solve: $\dfrac{z}{7} = 6$

Multiply by 7　$\dfrac{z}{7} \times 7 = 6 \times 7$

$$z = 42$$

Check: Does $\dfrac{42}{7} = 6$? Yes. It checks.

Solve: $21 = -3x$

Divide by ⁻3　$\dfrac{21}{-3} = \dfrac{-3x}{-3}$

$$-7 = x$$

Check: Does $21 = (-3)(-7)$? Yes. It checks.

Solving Two-Step Equations

Add or subtract before you multiply or divide.

Solve: $3x - 6 = 24$

Add 6　$3x - 6 + 6 = 24 + 6$

$$3x = 30$$

Divide by 3　$\dfrac{3x}{3} = \dfrac{30}{3}$

$$x = 10$$

Check: Does $3 \times \mathbf{10} - 6 = 24$? Yes. It checks.

$$\text{Solve: } \frac{y}{7} + 4 = 32$$

Subtract 4 $\quad \dfrac{y}{7} + 4 - 4 = 32 - 4$

$$\frac{y}{7} = 28$$

Multiply by 7 $\quad \dfrac{y}{7} \times 7 = (28)(7)$

$$y = 196$$

Check: Does $\dfrac{196}{7} + 4 = 32$? Yes. It checks.

GEOMETRY

TWO-DIMENSIONAL GEOMETRY

We can think of geometry in two or three dimensions. A two-dimensional model is this page. A three-dimensional model is the room you'll take the test in.

Definition	Model	Symbol
Point—a location	. A	A
Plane—a flat surface that extends infinitely in all directions		plane ABC
Space—occupies three dimensions and extends infinitely in all directions		space xyz
Line—a set of points in a straight path that extends infinitely in two directions		$\overleftrightarrow{AB}$
Line segment—part of a line with two endpoints		$\overline{AB}$
Ray—part of a line with one endpoint		$\overrightarrow{AB}$
Parallel lines—lines that stay the same distance apart and never touch		

Definition	Model	Symbol

Perpendicular lines—lines that meet at right angles

Angle—two rays with a common endpoint, which is called the vertex

$\angle ABC$

Acute angle—angle that measures between 0° and 90°

Right angle—angle that measures 90°

Obtuse angle—angle that measures between 90° and 180°

Complementary angles—angles that have a total measure of 90°

Supplementary angles—angles that have a total measure of 180°

Polygon—a closed figure made up of line segments; if all sides are the same length, the figure is a regular polygon

    Pentagon

Five Sides

    Hexagon

Six Sides

Octagon

Eight Sides

Triangle—polygon with three sides and three angles; the sum of the angles is always 180°.

Equilateral triangle—all the sides are the same length; all the angles are the same size, 60°.

Isosceles triangle—two sides the same length; two angles the same size.

Scalene triangle—all sides different lengths; all angles different sizes.

Quadrilateral—polygon with four sides

Square

Rhombus

Rectangle

Parallelogram

Trapezoid

COORDINATE GRID

You can plot ordered pairs of numbers on a coordinate grid.

The x axis goes horizontally from left to right. The first number in the pair tells how far to move left or right from the origin. A minus sign means move left. A plus sign means move right.

The y axis goes vertically up and down. The second number in the pair tells how far to move up or down from the origin. A minus sign means move down. A plus sign means move up.

Pairs of numbers show the x coordinate first and the y coordinate second (x, y). The origin is point $(0, 0)$ where the x axis and the y axis meet.

Plot these pairs of numbers on the grid.

A $(^+3, ^-7)$ **B** $(^+5, ^+3)$ **C** $(^-6, ^+2)$ **D** $(^-3, ^-6)$

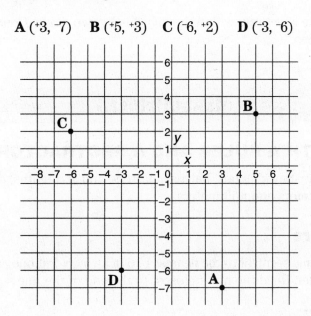

USING DIAGRAMS

All, Some, and None

Diagrams can show the logical connectives all, some, and none. View the following diagrams for an explanation.

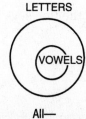

All—
All vowels are letters.

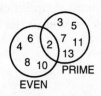

Some—
Some prime numbers are even.

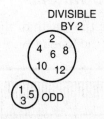

None—
No odd numbers are divisible by two.

Deductive Reasoning

Deductive reasoning draws conclusions from statements or assumptions. Diagrams may help you draw a conclusion. Consider this simple example.

Assume that all even numbers are divisible by two and that all multiples of ten are even. Draw a diagram:

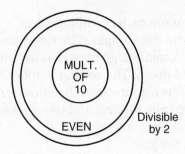

The multiple of ten circle is entirely within the divisible by two circle. Conclusion: All multiples of ten are divisible by two.

MEASUREMENT

MEASURING WITH A RULER AND A PROTRACTOR

You may use a ruler that shows inches, halves, quarters, and sixteenths, or you may use a ruler that shows centimeters and millimeters.

Customary Rulers

Measure the length of a line segment to the nearest 1/16 of an inch. Put one end of the line segment at the 0 point on the ruler. Read the mark closest to the end of the line

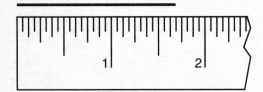

The line segment is $1^{11}/_{16}$ inches long.

Metric Rulers

Measure the length of the line segment to the nearest millimeter. Put one end of the line segment at the 0 point on the ruler. Read the mark closest to the end of the line.

The line segment is 45 mm long.

Protractors

Most protractors are half circles and show degrees from 0° to 180°.

Put the center of the protractor on the vertex of the angle. Align one ray of the angle on the inner or outer 0° point on the scale. Read the measure of the angle on that scale.

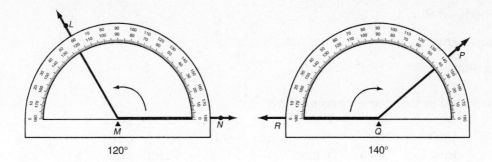

120°   140°

WEIGHT AND MASS

Mass is the amount of matter in a body. Weight is a measure of the force of gravity on a body. Mass is the same everywhere, but weight depends on its location in a gravitational field. That is, an object has the same mass whether on the moon or on earth. However, the object weighs less on the moon than on earth.

CUSTOMARY (ENGLISH) UNITS

Length

12 inches (in.) = 1 foot (ft)
3 feet = 1 yard (yd)
36 inches = 1 yard
1,760 yards = 1 mile (mi)
5,280 feet = 1 mile

Weight

16 ounces (oz) = 1 pound (lb)
2,000 pounds = 1 ton (T)

Capacity

2 cups = 1 pint (pt)
2 pints = 1 quart (qt)
4 quarts = 1 gallon (gal)

METRIC SYSTEM

The metric system uses common units of measure. The system uses prefixes that are powers of 10 or 0.1.

The common units used in the metric system follow:

Length—meter

Mass—gram

Capacity—liter

The prefixes used in the metric system follow:

1000	100	10	Unit	0.1	0.01	0.001
Kilo	Hecto	Deka		Deci	Centi	Milli

Notice that prefixes less than 1 end in i.

References for commonly used metric measurements

Unit	Description
Length	
Meter	A little more than a yard
Centimeter (0.01 meter)	The width of a paper clip (About 2.5 per inch)
Millimeter (0.001 meter)	The thickness of the wire on a paper clip
Kilometer (1000 meters)	About 0.6 of a mile
Mass	
Gram	The weight of a paper clip
Kilogram (1000 grams)	About 2.2 pounds
Capacity	
Liter	A little more than a quart
Milliliter	The amount of water in a cubic centimeter

TIME AND TEMPERATURE

Time

Each of the 24 hours in a day is partitioned into 60 minutes. Each minute is partitioned into 60 seconds. In the United States we use a 12-hour clock. The time between midnight and noon is called A.M., while the time between noon and midnight is called P.M. In other countries and in the scientific and military communities, a 24-hour clock is used. Both analog and digital clocks are used to keep track of time.

Digital 12-hour clock
5:15 P.M.

Analog 24-hour clock
1715 hours (5:15 P.M.)

There are 24 time zones in the world and four time zones in the continental United States. The United States time zones are shown in the following map. As you travel west, the sun rises later and the time gets earlier—11 A.M. in New York is 8 A.M. in Los Angeles.

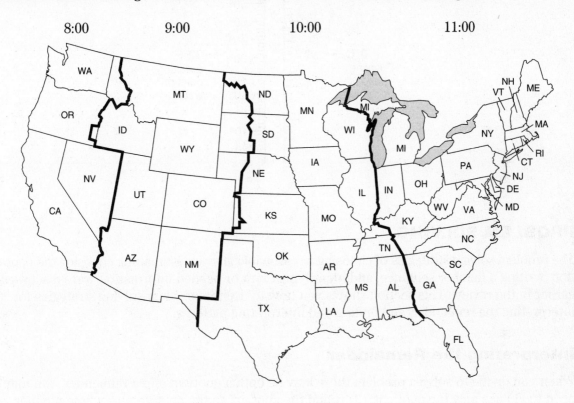

Temperature

Temperature is the degree of warmth or cold. We use Fahrenheit and Celsius thermometers to measure warmth. On a Fahrenheit thermometer water freezes at 32° and boils at 212°. A temperature of 98.6° Fahrenheit is normal body temperature and 90° Fahrenheit is a hot day. On the Celsius thermometer water freezes at 0° and boils at 100°. A temperature of 37° is normal body temperature and about 32° is a hot day.

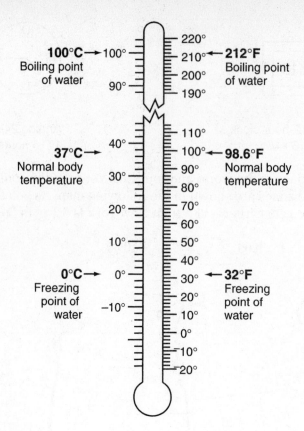

PROBLEM SOLVING

The problem-solving strategies of choosing a reasonable answer, estimating, choosing the operation, writing a number sentence, and identifying extra or needed information were discussed earlier in the review. This section shows you how to use the problem-solving strategies for interpreting the remainder, and finding and interpreting patterns.

Interpreting the Remainder

When you divide to solve a problem there may be both a quotient and a remainder. You may need to (1) use only the quotient, (2) round the quotient to the next greater whole number, or (3) use only the remainder.

Example:

Stereo speakers are packed 4 to a box. There are 315 stereo speakers to be packed.

Questions:

1. How many boxes can be filled?

2. How many boxes would be needed to hold all the stereo speakers?

3. How many stereo speakers will be in the box that is not completely full?

Divide 315 by 4.

$$4 \overline{\smash{\big)}315} \quad \begin{array}{r} 78 \text{ R3} \\ \end{array}$$

$$\begin{array}{r} 78 \text{ R3} \\ 4 \overline{\smash{\big)}315} \\ \underline{28} \\ 32 \\ \underline{32} \\ 3 \end{array}$$

Answers:

1. Use only the quotient—78 of the boxes can be filled.

2. Round the quotient to the next higher number. It would take 79 boxes to hold all the stereo speakers.

3. Use only the remainder. Three stereo speakers would be in the partially filled box.

Finding and Interpreting Patterns

Sometimes you may be able to use a pattern to find a rule or make a generalization and solve a problem. This approach is also called inductive reasoning. You proceed from information, data, to the rule.

For example, a meteorologist placed remote thermometers at sea level and up the side of the mountain at 1,000, 2,000, 5,000, and 6,000 feet. Readings were taken simultaneously and entered in the following table. What temperatures would you predict for the missing readings?

TEMPERATURE

0	1,000	2,000	3,000	4,000	5,000	6,000	7,000	8,000	9,000	10,000
52°	49°	46°			37°	34°				

The temperatures drops 3° from 52° to 49°. If it drops at the same rate, the temperature drop at 3,000 would be 43° and 4,000 feet would be 40° (followed by 37° and 34°). Continue to fill in the table accordingly, as follows.

TEMPERATURE

0	1,000	2,000	3,000	4,000	5,000	6,000	7,000	8,000	9,000	10,000
52°	49°	46°	*43°*	*40°*	37°	34°	*31°*	*28°*	*25°*	*22°*

Consider another example. A space capsule is moving in a straight line and is being tracked on a grid. The first four positions on the grid are recorded in the following table. Where will the capsule be on the grid when the x position is 13?

x Value	*1*	*2*	*3*	*4*
y Value	1	4	7	10

To solve, multiply three times the x value, subtract 2, and that gives the y value. The rule is y equals three times $x - 2$ so that the equation is $y = 3x - 2$. Substitute 13 for x:

$$y = 3(13) - 2 = 39 - 2 = 37$$

The capsule will be at position (13, 37).

STRATEGIES FOR ANSWERING MATHEMATICS ITEMS

The mathematics tested is the kind you probably had in high school and in college. It is the kind of mathematics you will use as you teach and go about your everyday life. Computational ability alone is expected but is held to a minimum. Remember to use the general test strategies discussed in the Introduction.

WRITE IN THE TEST BOOKLET

It is particularly important to write in the test booklet while taking the mathematics portion of the test. Use these hints for writing in the test booklet.

Do Your Calculations in the Test Booklet

Do all your calculations in the test booklet to the right of the question. This makes it easy to refer to the calcuations as you choose the correct answer.

This example should make you feel comfortable about writing in the test booklet.

What number times 0.00708 is equal to 70.8?

(A) ~~100,000 × 0.00708 = 708~~

(B) $10,000 \times 0.00708 = 70.8$

(C) 1,000

(D) 0.01

(E) 0.0001

The correct answer is (B) 10,000

Draw Diagrams and Figures in the Test Booklet

When you come across a geometry problem or related problem, draw a diagram in the test booklet to help.

All sides of a rectangle are shrunk in half. What happens to the area?

(A) Divided by two

(B) Divided by four

(C) Multiplied by two

(D) Multiplied by six

Answer (B), divided by 4, is the correct answer. The original area is evenly divided into four parts.

Circle Important Information and Key Words and Cross Out Information You Don't Need

This approach will draw your attention to the information needed to answer the question. A common mistake is to use from the question information that has nothing to do with the solution.
Example:

> In the morning, a train travels at a constant speed over an 800 kilometer distance. In the afternoon the train travels back over this same route. There is less traffic and the train travels four times as fast as it did that morning. However, there are more people on the train during the afternoon. Which of the following do you know about the train's afternoon trip?
>
> (A) The time is divided by four
>
> (B) The time is multiplied by four
>
> (C) The rate and time are divided by four
>
> (D) The distance is the same so the rate is the same

To solve the problem you just need to know that the speed is constant, four times as fast, and the same route was covered. Circle the information you need to solve the problem.

The distance traveled or that there were more people in the afternoon is extra information. Cross off this extra information, which may interfere with your ability to solve the problem.

> In the morning, a train travels at a constant speed over an 800 kilometer distance. In the afternoon the train travels back over this same route. There is less traffic and the train travels four times as fast as it did that morning. However, there are more people on the train during the afternoon. Which of the following do you know aobut the train's afternoon trip?

The correct answer is (A), the time is divided by four. The route is the same, but the train travels four times as fast. Therefore, the time to make the trip is divided by four. Rate means the same thing as speed, and we know that the speed has been multiplied by four.

OTHER STRATEGIES

Estimate to Be Sure Your Answer Is Reasonable

You can use estimation and common sense to be sure that the answer is reasonable. You may make a multiplication error or misalign decimal points. You may be so engrossed in a problem that you miss the big picture because of the details. These difficulties can be headed off by making sure your answer is reasonable.
A few examples follow.

A question involves dividing or multiplying. Multiply: 28×72.

Estimate first: $30 \times 70 = 2{,}100$. Your answer should be close to 2,100. If not, then your answer is not reasonable. A mistake was probably made in multiplication.

A question involves subtracting or adding. Add: $12.9 + 0.63 + 10.29 + 4.3$

Estimate first: $13 + 1 + 10 + 4 = 28$. Your answer should be close to 28. If not, then your answer is not reasonable. The decimal points may not have been aligned.

A question asks you to compare fractions to $^{11}/_{10}$.

Think: $^{11}/_{10}$ is more than 1. Any number 1 or less will be less than $^{11}/_{10}$. Any number $1^{1}/_{8}$ or larger will be more than $^{11}/_{10}$. You have to look closely only at numbers between 1 and $1^{1}/_{8}$.

A question asks you to multiply two fractions or decimals.

The fractions or decimals are less than 1. The product of two fractions or decimals less than 1 is less than either of the two fractions or decimals. If not, you know that your answer is not reasonable.

Stand back for a second after you answer each question and ask, "Is this reasonable? Is this at least approximately correct? Does this make sense?"

Check answers to computation, particularly division and subtraction. When you have completed a division or subtraction example, do a quick, approximate check. Your check should confirm your answer. If not, your answer is probably not reasonable.

Work from the Answers

If you don't know how to solve a formula or relation, try out each answer choice until you get the correct answer. Look at this example.

What percent times $^{1}/_{4}$ is $^{1}/_{5}$?

(A) 25%

(B) 40%

(C) 80%

(D) 120%

Just take each answer in turn and try it out.

$$0.25 \times \frac{1}{4} = \frac{1}{4} \times \frac{1}{4} = \frac{1}{16} \qquad \text{That's not it.}$$

$$0.40 \times \frac{1}{4} = \frac{4}{10} \times \frac{1}{4} = \frac{4}{40} = \frac{1}{10} \qquad \text{That's not it either.}$$

$$0.8 \times \frac{1}{4} = \frac{4}{5} \times \frac{1}{4} = \frac{4}{20} = \frac{1}{5}$$

You know that 0.8 is the correct answer, so choice (C) is correct.

Try Out Numbers

Look at the preceding question.

> Work with fractions at first. Ask: What number times $\frac{1}{4}$ equals $\frac{1}{5}$?
>
> Through trial and error you find out that $\frac{4}{5} \times \frac{1}{4} = \frac{1}{5}$.
>
> The answer in fractions is $\frac{4}{5}$.

$$\frac{4}{5} = 0.8 = 80\%$$

> The correct choice is (C).

In this example, we found the answer without ever solving an equation. We just tried out numbers until we found the one that works.

Eliminate and Guess

Use this approach when all else has failed. Begin by eliminating the answers you know are wrong. Sometimes you know with certainty that an answer is incorrect. Other times, an answer looks so unreasonable that you can be fairly sure that it is not correct.

Once you have eliminated incorrect answers, a few will probably be left. Just guess among these choices. There is no method that will increase your chances of guessing correctly.

MATHEMATICS PRACTICE ITEMS

These items will help you practice the concepts in this chapter. The items you encounter on the real LAST may have a different emphasis and may be more complete.

Instructions

Mark your answers on the sheet provided below. Complete the items in 20 minutes or less. Correct your answer sheet using the answers on page 139.

1 Ⓐ Ⓑ Ⓒ Ⓓ	5 Ⓐ Ⓑ Ⓒ Ⓓ	9 Ⓐ Ⓑ Ⓒ Ⓓ	13 Ⓐ Ⓑ Ⓒ Ⓓ	17 Ⓐ Ⓑ Ⓒ Ⓓ
2 Ⓐ Ⓑ Ⓒ Ⓓ	6 Ⓐ Ⓑ Ⓒ Ⓓ	10 Ⓐ Ⓑ Ⓒ Ⓓ	14 Ⓐ Ⓑ Ⓒ Ⓓ	18 Ⓐ Ⓑ Ⓒ Ⓓ
3 Ⓐ Ⓑ Ⓒ Ⓓ	7 Ⓐ Ⓑ Ⓒ Ⓓ	11 Ⓐ Ⓑ Ⓒ Ⓓ	15 Ⓐ Ⓑ Ⓒ Ⓓ	19 Ⓐ Ⓑ Ⓒ Ⓓ
4 Ⓐ Ⓑ Ⓒ Ⓓ	8 Ⓐ Ⓑ Ⓒ Ⓓ	12 Ⓐ Ⓑ Ⓒ Ⓓ	16 Ⓐ Ⓑ Ⓒ Ⓓ	20 Ⓐ Ⓑ Ⓒ Ⓓ

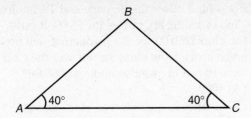

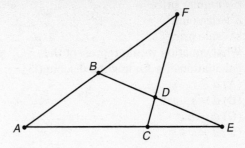

1. What is the measure of angle *B*?
   (A) 10
   (B) 40
   (C) 80
   (D) 100

2. After a discount of 25%, the savings on a pair of roller blades was $12.00. What was the sale price?
   (A) $48.00
   (B) $36.00
   (C) $24.00
   (D) $25.00

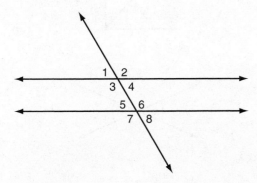

3. Which two angles are supplementary?
   (A) 6 & 7
   (B) 1 & 4
   (C) 3 & 6
   (D) 2 & 4

4. Chad rolls a fair die. The sides of the die are numbered from 1 to 6. Ten times in a row, he rolls a 5. What is the probability that he will roll a 5 on his next roll?
   (A) $\frac{1}{5}$
   (B) $\frac{1}{6}$
   (C) $\frac{1}{50}$
   (D) $\frac{1}{11}$

5. Which of the following set of points do not form an angle in the diagram?
   (A) *ABF*
   (B) *ABE*
   (C) *AFC*
   (D) *ABC*

6. An apple costs (*C*). You have (*D*) dollars. What equation would represent the amount of apples you could buy for the money you have?
   (A) *C/D*
   (B) *CD*
   (C) *C + D*
   (D) *D/C*

7. If a worker gets $144.00 for 18 hours' work, how much would that worker get for 32 hours' work?
   (A) $200.00
   (B) $288.00
   (C) $256.00
   (D) $432.00

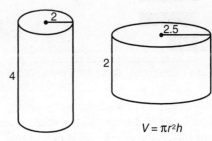

$V = \pi r^2 h$

8. What is the combined volume of these two cylinders?
   (A) 12.5π
   (B) 16π
   (C) 26.5π
   (D) 28.5π

9. r = regular price
   d = discount
   s = sale price
   What equation would represent the calculations for finding the discount?
   (A) $d = r - s$
   (B) $d = s - r$
   (C) $d = sr$
   (D) $d = s + r$

10. A printing company makes pamphlets that cost $.75 per copy plus $5.00 as a setter's fee. If $80 were spent printing a pamphlet, how many pamphlets were ordered?
    (A) 50
    (B) 75
    (C) 100
    (D) 150

11. Which is furthest from $\frac{1}{2}$ on a number line?
    (A) $\frac{1}{12}$
    (B) $\frac{7}{8}$
    (C) $\frac{3}{4}$
    (D) $\frac{2}{3}$

12. Which of the following could be about 25 centimeters long?
    (A) a human thumb
    (B) a doorway
    (C) a car
    (D) a notebook

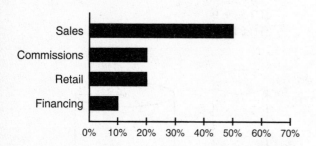

13. The sales department staff draws its salary from four areas of the company's income, as shown in the above graph. What percentage is drawn from the retail fund?
    (A) 10%
    (B) 20%
    (C) 25%
    (D) 30%

14. What percentage of 250 is 25?
    (A) 5%
    (B) 10%
    (C) 20%
    (D) 25%

15. For a fund raiser the Science and Technology Club is selling six raffles for $5.00. It costs the club $250.00 for the prizes that will be given away. How many raffles will the club have to sell in order to make $1,000.00?
    (A) 1500
    (B) 1200
    (C) 600
    (D) 300

16. $5.3 \times 10^4 =$
    (A) 0.0053
    (B) 0.00053
    (C) 5,300
    (D) 53,000

17. Which of the following represents supplementary angles?

(A)

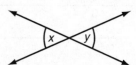

(B)

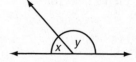

(C)

(D)

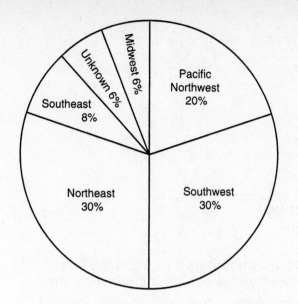

18. The above graph shows the percentage of students that attend a college according to the area of the United States that they come from. How many more college students come from the Northeast than come from the Midwest?
    (A) twice as many
    (B) three times as many
    (C) half as many
    (D) five times as many

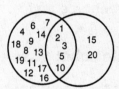

19. Each of these rectangles has a total area of 1 square unit. What number represents the area of the shaded regions?
    (A) ⁵/₆ square units
    (B) ⁷/₈ square units
    (C) 1³/₄ square units
    (D) 1⁵/₂₄ square units

20. Which diagram shows that the set of whole numbers between 1 and 20 contains multiples of 5?

(A)
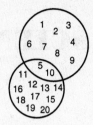

(B)

(C)
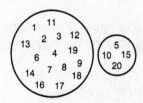

(D)

Answers

1. **D**	5. **D**	9. **A**	13. **B**	17. **D**
2. **A**	6. **D**	10. **C**	14. **B**	18. **D**
3. **D**	7. **C**	11. **A**	15. **A**	19. **D**
4. **B**	8. **D**	12. **D**	16. **D**	20. **B**

SCIENCE

This chapter helps you prepare for the Science items on the LAST. It includes a comprehensive subject review of the topics included on the LAST.

A diagnostic quiz helps you decide which parts of the chapter to review.

Use the review material in this chapter to learn how to read about science, not to learn about science.

This chapter includes a section that shows you how to read and interpret graphs.

Practice items at the end of the chapter help you prepare for the multiple-choice test.

MULTIPLE-CHOICE TEST
There are about 12 science items on the LAST.

Many of the items are reading comprehension items.

Other items are about reading and interpreting charts and graphs.

USING THIS CHAPTER

This chapter prepares you to take the Science part of the LAST. Choose one of these approaches.

I want all the Science review I can get.

❏ Skip the Science Review Quiz on page 142 and read the entire review section.
❏ Take the Science Review Quiz on page 142.
❏ Correct the Review Quiz and reread the indicated parts of the review.
❏ Review the Reading and Interpreting Graphs section on page 170.
❏ Complete the Science Practice Items on page 175.

I want a thorough Science review.

❏ Take the Science Review Quiz on page 142.
❏ Correct the Review Quiz and read the indicated parts of the review.
❏ Review the Reading and Interpreting Graphs section on page 170.
❏ Complete the Science Practice Items on page 175.

I want a quick Science review.

❏ Take and correct the Science Review Quiz on page 142.
❏ Review the Reading and Interpreting Graphs section on page 170.
❏ Complete the Science Practice Items on page 175.

I want to practice Science Items.

❏ Complete the Science Practice Items on page 175.

SCIENCE REVIEW QUIZ

This quiz uses a short answer format to help you find out what you know about the Science topics reviewed in this chapter. The quiz results direct you to the portions of the chapter you should read.

This quiz will also help focus your thinking about Science, and these questions and answers are a good review in themselves. It's not important to answer all these questions correctly, and don't be concerned if you miss many of them.

The answers are found immediately after the quiz. It's to your advantage not to look at them until you have completed the quiz. Once you have completed and corrected this review quiz, use the answer checklist to decide which sections of the review to study.

Write the answers in the space provided or on a separate sheet of paper.

1. What name is given to the cells that make up most living things?

2. Name the two methods of cell reproduction.

3. What does photosynthesis create?

4. What do cells create when they respire?

5. Where are genes located?

6. What type of life could have developed spontaneously in earth's early atmosphere?

7. What is the name of the very first cells to develop?

8. What is the dominant invertebrate animal species?

9. Which animal has the most striking genetic similarity to humans?

10. What types of organisms make up the Protistae kingdom?

11. What three main functions do bacteria perform?

12. How many pairs of chromosomes do humans usually have?

13. How is AIDS transmitted?

14. What part of the circulatory system carries blood back to the heart?

15. What part of a cell transmits signals?

16. What does the endocrine system consist of?

17. What function do granulocytes perform in the immune system?

_____

_____

18. What do ecologists study?

_____

_____

19. What survival options do subdominant individuals have?

_____

_____

20. How do plants and animals balance the carbon cycle?

_____

_____

21. What do cosmologists study?

_____

_____

22. About how long does it take for light to travel from the North Star to the earth?

_____

_____

23. What causes seasons on earth?

_____

_____

24. What percent of earth's atmosphere is nitrogen? _____ oxygen? _____

25. About what percent of the earth's surface is covered by water?

_____

_____

26. What is the temperature in the earth's inner core?

_____

_____

27. In which direction does Coriolis force pull air in the Southern Hemisphere?

_____

_____

28. About what percent of sea water is salt?

_____

_____

29. How were the earth's continents arranged during the Permian period about 280,000,000 years ago?

_____

_____

30. How are metamorphic rocks formed?

_____

_____

31. What subatomic particles do atoms consist of?

_____

_____

32. How can matter be destroyed?

_____

_____

33. When do chemical reactions occur?

_____

_____

34. Does a body's mass vary?

_____

_____

35. What two factors determine a body's velocity?

_____

_____

36. How does Newton's Second Law describe the relationship between mass and acceleration?

_____

_____

37. What type of energy does fuel in a car's gas tank represent?

_____

_____

38. What must happen for work to occur?

_____

_____

39. What method of transfer moves heat from a heating pad to a person's back?

_____

_____

40. What determines a wave's frequency?

_____

_____

41. What three things may happen when light strikes a surface?

_____

_____

42. Through which medium does sound travel most quickly?

_____

_____

43. What charges may an object possess?

_____

_____

44. What does an ampere measure?

_____

_____

45. Where is the magnetic North Pole?

_____

_____

46. Name the three types of energy radioactive material can release.

_____

_____

47. What is the advantage of nuclear fusion over nuclear fission?

_____

_____

ANSWER CHECKLIST

The answers are organized by review sections. Check your answers. If you miss any question in a section, check the box and review that section.

Biology

Cellular Biology

❏ *Cells, page 147*
1. eukaryotes

❏ *Reproduction, page 147*
2. mitosis and meiosis

❏ *Photosynthesis, page 148*
3. carbohydrates, water, and oxygen

❏ *Cell Activities, page 148*
4. energy

❏ *Genes, page 148*
5. Genes are located on chromosomes.

Biology of Organisms and Evolution

❏ *Evolution, page 149*
6. molecule
7. prokaryotes
8. insects
9. African apes

❏ *Cell Classification, page 150*
10. single-celled eukaryotes including algae and protozoa
11. Bacteria live on dead material, are helpful in human bodies, and function as parasites.

❏ *Human Biology, page 151*
12. 23
13. blood and bodily fluids
14. veins
15. dendrites
16. glands that secrete hormones
17. They ingest antigens already killed by cell enzymes.

❏ *Ecology, page 154*
18. the relationship between organisms and their ecosystems
19. They accept a poorer habitat, give up resources, immigrate, or perish.

❏ *Life Cycles, page 155*
20. Plants use carbon dioxide and give off oxygen. Animals use oxygen and give off carbon dioxide.

Geosciences

❏ *Astronomy, page 156*
21. the universe
22. 300 years
23. the tilt of the Earth's axis

❏ *Meteorology, page 160*
27. Southeast

❏ *Oceanography, page 161*
28. 3.5 percent (0.035)

❏ *Geology, page 162*
29. Earth's land mass consisted of a single continent.
30. Existing rocks are subjected to enormous pressure.

❏ *The Earth's Parts, page 162*
24. 78 percent nitrogen, 21 percent oxygen
25. about 75 percent
26. 10,000° F

Physical Sciences

Chemistry

❏ *Atoms, page 164*
31. protons, neutrons, and electrons

❏ *Matter, page 165*
32. Matter cannot be destroyed; it can only be converted.

❏ *Chemical Reactions, page 165*
33. when bonds between atoms form or break

Physics

❏ *Matter and Mass, page 165*
34. A body's mass is constant.

❏ *Motion, page 166*
35. magnitude and direction
36. The more the mass, the less the acceleration.

❑ *Energy, page 166*
  37. potential

❑ *Work, page 167*
  38. There must be some movement.

❑ *Heat, page 167*
  39. conduction

❑ *Wave Phenomena, page 168*
  40. vibrations per second

❑ *Light, page 168*
  41. Light can be reflected, absorbed, or
  scattered.

❑ *Sound, page 168*
  42. solid

Electricity and Magnetism

❑ *Electricity, page 168*
  43. positive, negative, neutral
  44. rate of current flow

❑ *Magnetism, page 169*
  45. northeastern Canada

❑ *Modern Physics and Radioactivity, page 170*
  46. alpha, beta, and gamma
  47. Fusion is much safer because it releases
  less radioactivity.

SCIENCE REVIEW

BIOLOGY

CELLULAR BIOLOGY

Cells

The cell is the basic unit of all living things. A cell may be an organism by itself or the basic building block of a multicell living organism. Animal and plant cells are different.

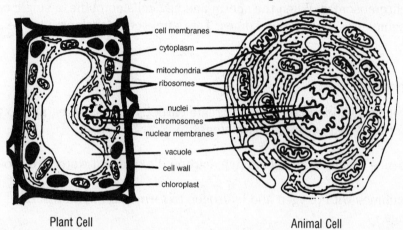

cell membranes
cytoplasm
mitochondria
ribosomes
nuclei
chromosomes
nuclear membranes
vacuole
cell wall
chloroplast

Plant Cell   Animal Cell

Most cells that make up living things are eukaryotes. The second type of cells are called prokaryotes. Most prokaryotes are bacteria or blue-green algae.

All cells have a cell membrane at the outer edge of the cell. A gel-like cytoplasm throughout the interior of the cell protects the different organelles (cell organs) inside the cell. A nucleus, the cell's brain, inside the cytoplasm is protected by a nuclear membrane. The nucleus contains chromosomes. The golgi apparatus make, store, and distribute hormone and enzyme materials. The mitochondria process food into energy.

Plant cells have a thicker cell wall outside the membrane. Plant cells also contain chloroplasts where photosynthesis takes place.

Reproduction

Cells must reproduce to survive. There are two methods of cell reproduction—mitosis and meiosis.

the cell divides

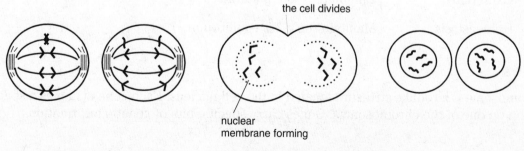

nuclear
membrane forming

Mitosis

In mitosis, cells make a carbon copy of themselves and create duplicate chromosomes. The chromosomes migrate to opposite sides of the cell; then the cell splits, making an exact copy of itself.

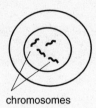  

spindle fibers

chromosomes

Meiosis

Higher multicell organisms reproduce sexually. In these organisms, the sperm and egg cells combine in a process called meiosis. Meiosis begins with egg and sperm cells, each with half the number of chromosomes. When the sperm and egg cells combine, a single cell, zygote, is created with a complete set of chromosomes. This single cell develops into the advanced organism.

Photosynthesis

Photosynthesis occurs within plant cells to create carbohydrates, water, and oxygen needed by the plant. Photosynthesis occurs in two stages.

1. In the presence of light and chlorophyll, carbon dioxide and water are broken down.

2. Carbon combines with oxygen and hydrogen to form carbohydrates. Light is not needed for this stage.

Cell Activities

Respiration

Cells create energy through respiration. This process, which occurs in the mitochondria, can be either aerobic or anaerobic. Aerobic respiration is the oxidation of food, which takes place in the presence of oxygen. Anaerobic respiration is fermentation, which takes place without oxygen.

Other Cell Activities

Ingestion	Take in food
Digestion	Break down food to usable forms
Secretion	Create and release useful substances
Excretion	Eliminate waste material
Homeostasis	Maintain the cell's equilibrium

Genes

A chromosome is a rodlike structure located in the cell nucleus. Each gene occupies a specific location on one of the chromosomes. Genes carry specific bits of genetic information.

Deoxyribonucleic acid (DNA) is the genetic material found tightly coiled in a gene. DNA provides the genetic codes that determine many traits of an organism. The gene also contains very large quantities of noncoding DNA, which does not affect the makeup of an organism.

The DNA creates ribonucleic acid (RNA). The DNA cannot leave the nucleus; RNA serves as the messenger that carries the genetic code throughout the cell.

BIOLOGY OF ORGANISMS AND EVOLUTION

Early Life

There was very little oxygen in the earth's atmosphere about 3.5 billion years ago. Research has shown that atoms can combine spontaneously in this type of environment to form molecules. This is how life may have begun on earth about 3.4 billion years ago.

Eventually these molecules linked together in complex groupings to form organisms. These earliest organisms must have been able to ingest and live on nonórganic material. Over a period of time, these organisms adapted and began using the sun's energy. When photosynthesis released oxygen into the oceans and the atmosphere, the stage was set for more advanced life forms.

First Cells

The first cells were prokaryotes (bacteria), which created energy (respired) without oxygen (anaerobic). The next cells to develop were blue-green algae prokaryotes, which were aerobic (created energy with oxygen) and used photosynthesis. Advanced eukaryotes developed from these primitive cells.

It took about 2.7 billion years for algae to develop. When this simple cell appeared 950 million years ago, it contained an enormous amount of DNA. This very slow process moved somewhat faster in the millennia that followed as animal and plant forms slowly emerged.

Animals

Animals developed into vertebrate (backbone) and invertebrate (no backbone) species. Mammals became the dominant vertebrate species, and insects became the dominant invertebrate species. As animals developed, they adapted to their environment. Those species that adapted best survived. This process is called natural selection. Entire species have vanished from the earth.

Mammals and dinosaurs coexisted for over 100 million years. During that time, dinosaurs were the dominant species. When dinosaurs became extinct 65 million years ago, mammals survived. Freed of dinosaurian dominance, mammals evolved into the dominant creatures they are today. Despite many years of study, it is not known what caused the dinosaurs to become extinct or why mammals survived.

Humans

Humans are in the primate (upright) family of mammals. Very primitive primates, along with other mammals, were found on earth before the dinosaurs became extinct. Modern humans demonstrate striking genetic similarities to other members of the primate group, particularly to African apes.

Tools are a mark of the advanced adaptation of a species. Stone tools found in association with early humanoids date back about 2 million years. Sites dated 1 million years old show marks caused by humanlike use of tools.

Scientists believe that early sapiens developed about 250,000 years ago and that modern *Homo sapiens* developed about 75,000 years ago.

The ability to communicate is a sign of advanced development. Many forms of nonverbal communication have probably existed since the appearance of *Homo sapiens*. Scientists speculate that speech distinct from animal sounds probably occurred about 30,000 years ago. Writing first appeared about 5,500 years ago.

Era	Period		Epoch	Approximate Beginning Date	Life Forms Originating
Cenozoic	Quaternary		Recent	10,000	Humans
			Pleistocene	2,500,000	
	Tertiary		Pilocene	12,000,000	Grazing and Meat-eating Mammals
			Miocene	26,000,000	
			Oligocene	38,000,000	
			Eocene	54,000,000	
			Paleocene	65,000,000	
Mesozoic	Cretaceous			136,000,000	Primates-Flowering Plants
	Jurassic			195,000,000	Birds
	Triassic			225,000,000	Dinosaurs-Mammals
Paleozoic	Permian			280,000,000	
	Carbonifurous	Pennsylvanian		320,000,000	Reptiles
		Mississippian		345,000,000	Ferns
	Devonian			395,000,000	Amphibians-insects
	Silurian			430,000,000	Vascular Land Plants
	Ordovician			500,000,000	Fish-Chordates
	Cambrian			570,000,000	Shellfish-Trilobites
Precambrian				(700,000,000)	Algae
				(1,500,000,000)	Eukaryotic Cells
				(3,500,000,000)	Prokaryotic Cells

The History of Life

Cell Classification

Living things are generally classified into five kingdoms. Two kingdoms are dedicated to one-celled living things (prokaryote or eukaryote). There are three kingdoms of multicelled eukaryotes based on whether nutrition is obtained through absorption, photosynthesis, or ingestion.

Single Cells

The Moneran kingdom includes all prokaryotes. The organisms include bacteria and blue-green algae. These microscopic organisms are limited to respiration and reproduction.

The Protistae kingdom includes all single-celled eukaryotes. These organisms include algae and protozoa. These cells have a fully functional organ system and get their nutrition through photosynthesis.

Multi Cells

The Fungi kingdom includes multicelled eukaryotes that gain their nutrition through absorption. These organisms include mushrooms and are rootlike with caps and filaments.

The Plantae kingdom includes multicelled eukaryotes that gain their nutrition through photosynthesis. These organisms have thicker cellulose cell walls.

The Animalae kingdom includes multicelled eukaryotes that gain their nutrition through ingestion. Most of these organisms are mobile at some time in their existence.

Bacteria

Bacteria are small, single-celled organisms (prokaryotes) found everywhere in the environment. As noted already, bacteria were among the earliest organisms to develop. Bacteria are classified as bacilli (rod-shaped), cocci (circular or spherical), and spirilla (coiled). Bacteria that can move "swim" with flagella.

One type of bacteria live on dead animal and vegetable material. Without the decomposition these bacteria bring, the earth would quickly be covered with dead organic material. A second type of bacteria is a normal part of living tissues and is often needed for regular physiological processes. The third type, parasites, destroy the organisms in which they live. About 200 types of bacteria cause diseases in humans.

Viruses

A virus is a bit of genetic material surrounded by a protective coat of protein. The virus itself is lifeless, lacks the ability to reproduce, and is not classified in one of the five kingdoms. Viruses cannot be seen in even the most powerful regular microscope. The smallest virus is about one millionth of a centimeter long.

Viruses are parasitic and remain a major challenge in battling infectious diseases. Once in a living cell, a virus can send its own genetic material into the cell, reproduce, and do significant damage to the host cell and the host organism.

Human Biology

Humans have 23 pairs of chromosomes. Females typically have 23 similar pairs including a pair of X chromosomes. Males typically have 22 similar pairs and one X and one Y chromosome.

Genes carry specific bits of genetic information. Each gene occupies a specific location on one of the chromosomes. Researchers today have identified and mapped the exact location of more than 200 genes. Scientists can even identify whether or not a person has certain hereditary traits. For example, scientists have identified a gene linked to hereditary breast cancer.

Disease

Diseases compromise the body's defense system. Most diseases can be recognized by symptoms that may include fever, aches and pains, fatigue, growths, changes in blood cell composition, and high blood pressure.

Many infectious diseases, including pneumonia and infections in cuts, are caused by bacteria. Other infectious diseases, including measles and influenza (flu), are caused by viruses. Environmental causes of disease include smoking, a high-fat diet, and pollution. Other diseases may result from genetic or occupational causes and abnormal cell growth. Many diseases are related to mental disorders or stress.

Acquired Immune Deficiency Syndrome (AIDS) is a disease caused by the HIV virus that attacks the body's immune system. Current research indicates that all those with AIDS will die as a result of this virus. The HIV virus is transmitted through blood and bodily fluids, including those fluids associated with intimate sexual contact. Intravenous drug users who share needles may become infected with the virus by injecting small amounts of contaminated blood.

The Human Body

Parts of the human body are made up of highly specialized cells. These cells combine to make tissue. Some tissues combine to form organs. Various organs combine in systems that enable the body to function.

Cells → Tissue → Organ → Organ System → Body

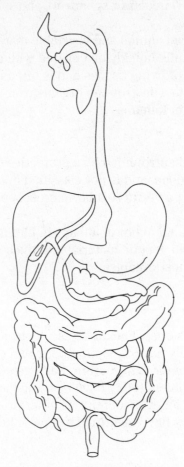

The Human Digestive System

Digestive System

Food is usually taken in through the mouth. The teeth and tongue break the food down mechanically, and the saliva begins the digestive process. When food reaches the stomach, the stomach churns to mix the food while digestive enzymes break down the proteins. The semiliquid, digested food moves into the small intestine.

Nutrients are absorbed through the small intestine into the bloodstream. Waste and undigested food move into the large intestine. The large intestine carries the waste and undigested food to the rectum.

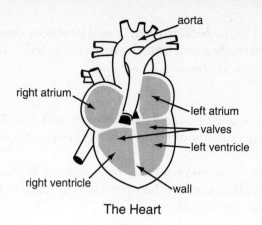

The Heart

Circulatory System

The circulatory system carries oxygen and nutrients throughout the body. A four-chambered heart (see above) pumps blood through the circulatory system. Oxygenated blood is pumped through the left side of the heart, through arteries to capillaries and then to cells. The right side of the heart pumps oxygen-poor blood back to the lungs.

Skeletal System

The bones (about 200) and cartilage that make up the skeletal system provide form and rigidity to the human body. A series of joints throughout the skeleton provide flexibility. Bone is living, rigid tissue. Cartilage is found at bone joints, such as the knee, and makes up the nose and other rigid parts of the body.

Muscular System

The muscular system consists of skeletal (striated), smooth, and cardiac muscles. Most skeletal muscles are attached to the skeleton by tendons. These muscles are called voluntary muscles because they can be controlled consciously and make up most of human flesh. Smooth muscle is involuntary and is found in large blood vessels, internal organs, and the skin. Cardiac muscles are an involuntary muscle found only in the heart.

Nervous System

The nervous system receives stimuli, transmits electrochemical signals, and activates muscles. Receptors in the skin and elsewhere in the body receive stimuli. Nerve cells, called neurons, send signals to the central nervous system. Dendrites in the cell transmit signals, while axons receive stimuli.

The central and peripheral nervous systems form a single operating system. The central nervous system includes the brain and spinal cord. The peripheral nervous system connects the central nervous system to the rest of the body. The autonomic nervous system is connected to the central nervous system and controls circulation, respiration, digestion, and elimination.

Excretory System

The excretory system consists of the kidney, bladder, and connecting tubes. Nephrons in the kidney collect liquid wastes. The liquid wastes are transferred to the bladder and leave the body as urine through the urethra.

Respiratory System

Respiration delivers oxygen to the bloodstream. Nasal passages clean and warm the air on its way to the lungs through the trachea and bronchi. Air is collected in the alveoli, which transfers oxygen and other gases to the bloodstream.

Endocrine System

The endocrine system is a complex system that produces and distributes hormones through the bloodstream. The system consists of glands that secrete hormones and other substances.

The **pituitary gland** is located near the brain and is the primary gland in the body. Hormones from this gland control the operation of other endocrine glands, sex glands, milk production, and pigmentation.

The **adrenal glands** are found near the kidney. Hormones from these glands effect heart rate, blood pressure, blood vessels, and blood sugar.

The **thyroid** is found in the neck. It regulates mental and physical alertness. The parathyroid glands are found near or inside the thyroid and regulate calcium in the blood.

Ovaries are located near the uterus. These glands produce eggs, control the development of secondary sex characteristics, and maintain pregnancy.

Testes produce sperm and control the development of secondary sex characteristics.

The **pancreas** secretes insulin and facilitates digestion.

Immune System

The immune system resists the spread of disease by destroying disease-causing agents (antigens). This system is exceptionally complex and not fully understood. Normally, a combination of the following immune responses is needed to defeat an antigen.

The lymphatic system produces lymphocytes in bean-sized lymph glands located throughout the body. The lymphocytes are transported throughout bodily tissue by lymphatic capillaries. Lymphocytes control the immune system and kill antigens directly.

Granulocytes are very numerous. They ingest antigens already killed by cell enzymes. Monocytes exist in small numbers. They ingest and kill antigens and more importantly alter antigens in a way that makes it easier for lymphocytes to destroy them.

Immunoglobins (antibodies) combine with antigens to remove them from the body. There are thousands of antibodies, each targeted for a specific antigen. Other proteins called cytokines complement proteins and aid the immune response.

ECOLOGY

Ecology refers to the relationship between organisms and their ecosystem (habitat). An ecosystem includes interdependent life forms and supports life through food, atmosphere, energy, and water. Organisms, including plants and animals, interact with and adapt to their ecosystem.

Earth is surrounded by a thin layer of atmosphere. Within that atmosphere lies earth's biosphere where life exists. The biosphere contains a number of biomes or living areas. Aquatic biomes include ocean, shallow water, and tidal marshes. Land biomes are classified by the predominant form of plant life and include forest, grassland, and desert.

Each organism in a biome occupies a place in the food web. Each organism, at some point in its life or death, is food for some other organism. In this way, energy is transferred among organisms in the biome.

A community refers to the interdependent populations of plants and animals. The dominance of one species in a community can affect the diversity (number of species and specie members). The community includes the habitat where a particular plant or animal lives and its niche (role).

Within a community, the primary interactions are predation (including parasitism) and cooperation. Predators and prey adapt and develop more effective ways of hunting or defense. Cooperation may develop due to the dependence of one organism on another.

Organisms may compete within their species or with other species for resources. Successful competitors survive and become dominant. Subdominant individuals either accept poorer habitats, give up the resources, migrate, or perish.

Life Cycles

A number of essential life cycles take place on earth.

Water Cycle

Most of the earth's water is salty, but humans need fresh water to survive. Fresh water is renewed through the water cycle. The cycle consists of three phases: evaporation, condensation, and precipitation.

Evaporation occurs when heat from the sun changes ocean water, and some water from other sources, into water vapor. Condensation follows when water vapor turns into water droplets, which form clouds. Precipitation occurs when the droplets become too heavy and water falls as rain, snow, sleet, or hail.

Oxygen Cycle

Humans and other animal organisms need oxygen to survive. Plants give off oxygen. An appropriate balance between plant photosynthesis and animal respiration ensures that enough oxygen is available.

Carbon Cycle

Carbon is used by all living things. Plants need carbon dioxide for photosynthesis. Animals get the carbon from the plant tissues they eat and exhale carbon dioxide as a by product of respiration. Here again, the balance between animal respiration and plant photosynthesis ensures that enough carbon will be available. In recent times, however, industrialization has added extra carbon to the atmosphere, jeopardizing the balance of this cycle.

Pollution

Air, water, and soil pollution are serious environmental problems. Some lakes, rivers, and streams are so polluted they can not be used by humans. Fish from many of these waters cannot be eaten. Air in some areas has been very polluted by factories and power plants, which use sulfur based fuels such as oil and coal. Land has been polluted by dumping hazardous wastes, including radioactive wastes. All forms of pollution lead to disease and premature death.

GEOSCIENCES

ASTRONOMY

Astronomy is the study of space and the relationship of objects in space. Astronomers use optical telescopes and radio telescopes, including the orbiting Hubble Telescope, to study space and objects in space.

Solar System

Our solar system has one star (the sun), nine planets, some comets, and lots of satellites (moons), asteroids, and meteors. A diagram of the solar system is shown below. Only the planets are shown to rough scale in this diagram.

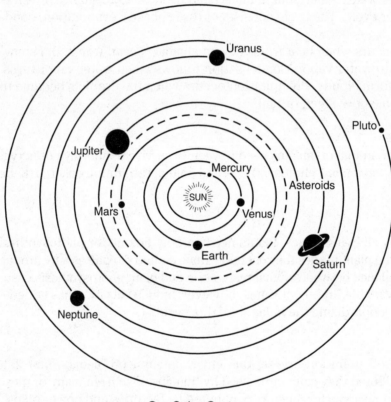

Our Solar System

The Sun

Our sun is a star, a turbulent mass of incredibly hot gases exploding with repeated nuclear fusion reactions. Without the heat and light from the sun, our universe would not exist as we know it. About 1,000,000 earths could fit inside the sun. The sun's diameter is about 864,000 miles, and the surface temperature is over 10,000° Fahrenheit. Still, the sun is just average size by galactic standards.

The sun is at the center of our solar system, although this was not realized until the time of Copernicus in the 1500s. The most noticeable features of the sun's surface are the sunspots, cooler areas that move across the sun's surface. Sunspots appear in somewhat predictable cycles and are associated with interruptions in radio and television transmissions.

The Earth and the Moon

Earth is the name of our planet. The earth is the third planet from the sun. The earth's distance from the sun ranges from about 91,000,000 to 95,000,000 miles. It takes light about eight minutes to travel from the sun to earth. The earth's diameter is about 7,900 miles. The earth's rotation and revolution have a tremendous impact on life here.

Rotation. The earth *rotates* around its axis, which roughly runs through the geographic north and south poles. This rotation creates day and night as parts of the earth are turned toward and then away from the sun.

Revolution. The earth *revolves* in an orbit (path) around the sun. The earth's axis is tilted about 23° from perpendicular with the orbit around the sun. The tilting and revolving creates seasons as regions of the earth are tilted toward the sun and away from the sun.

The diagram here shows the earth's tilt and earth's relation to the sun at the beginning of each season in the Northern Hemisphere. Seasons are opposite in the Southern Hemisphere.

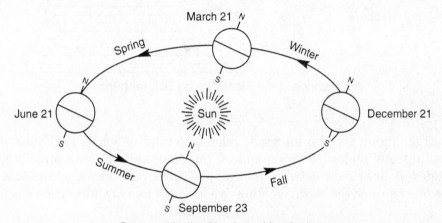

Seasons in the Northern Hemisphere

Moon is the name for the satellite that revolves around earth. The moon also rotates around its axis. The moon's diameter is about 2,100 miles and it is about 240,000 miles from the earth to the moon. The moon has no atmosphere and its surface is covered with craters from meteorites and from volcanoes.

The moon's rotation and revolution each take about 27 ½ days. These equal periods of rotation and revolution mean that the same part of the moon always faces the earth. It was not until lunar exploration in the 1970s that the other side of the moon was viewed and photographed.

The Moon's Phases

Different parts of the moon's surface reflect light to the earth, creating the different phases of the moons as shown on the next page.

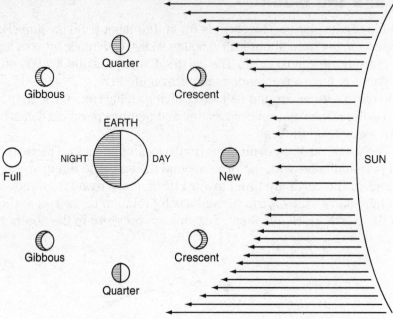

Appearance of the Moon During Different Phases

Tides

The phases of the moon are also integrally related to tides on earth. High tides occur on the parts of earth directly under the moon and on the other side of earth directly opposite this point. Low tides occur halfway between the two high tides. The tides move around the earth as the moon revolves around the earth, creating two high and two low tides each day at each place on earth.

The lowest and highest tides occur when the sun and the moon are in a straight line. These tides are called spring tides. The moon is either new or full during this direct alignment.

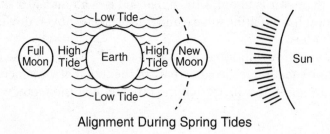

Alignment During Spring Tides

Eclipses

The position of the sun, earth, and moon can create eclipses. A lunar eclipse occurs when the moon is in the earth's shadow. A solar eclipse occurs when the sun is "hidden" behind the moon. Look at the diagrams below.

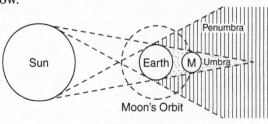

Lunar Eclipse

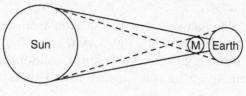

Solar Eclipse

Planets and Asteroids

The word planet comes from the Latin word meaning traveler. Ancient observers were taken by the "lights" they saw traveling around the sky against a background of other "lights" that seemed stationary.

Today we know that nine planets including earth travel in orbits around the sun. Also in orbit around the sun are a belt of asteroids from 1 to 500 miles in diameter that may be the remains of an exploded planet. The table below gives some information about the planets and asteroids.

BODIES IN SOLAR ORBIT

Name	Approximate diameter in miles	Approximate distance from sun in miles	Revolution Period
Mercury	3,100	36,000,000	88 days
Venus	7,700	67,000,000	225 days
Earth	7,900	93,000,000	$365\frac{1}{4}$ days
Mars	4,200	142,000,000	687 days
Asteroids		161,000,000	
Jupiter	88,700	483,000,000	12 years
Saturn	75,000	886,000,000	$29\frac{1}{2}$ years
Uranus	32,000	1,783,000,000	84 years
Neptune	28,000	2,794,000,000	165 years
Pluto	1,420 (?)	3,670,000,000	248 years

Unmanned spacecraft and other observations reveal more about the planets each year. Recent discoveries of meteorites on earth thought to have come from Mars have fueled speculation that some life forms might exist, or might have existed, on Mars.

Cosmology

Cosmology is the study of the universe. Cosmological theories are about the origin, development, and ultimate fate of the universe.

The universe consists of a large number of galaxies that contain an enormous number of stars and other material. Our solar system is located on the outer edge of the Milky Way galaxy. All the stars you can see from earth without a telescope are in the Milky Way galaxy.

Intergalactic distances are so huge that they are measured in light years. Light travels about 6 trillion miles in a year. It takes light 300 years to travel from Polaris, the North Star, to earth. It would take about 100,000 years for light to travel across the Milky Way galaxy.

Scientists have discovered a great many other galaxies. The Andromeda galaxy is over 2 million light years away from earth. The most distant detectable galaxies are about 10 to 15 billion light years from earth.

Scientists have discovered that galaxies are moving away from each other. This, among other factors, has led most scientists to embrace the Big Bang theory. This theory proposes that helium and hydrogen combined to create a gigantic explosion 15 billion to 20 billion years ago. This explosion led to the development of the stars, galaxies, and eventually planets.

METEOROLOGY

Meteorology is the study of the earth's atmosphere. We are most attentive to meteorologist's predictions about weather.

Weather observations are taken on the ground, in the upper atmosphere, and from satellites in space. All these observations inform us about likely weather events and add to our knowledge about the atmosphere.

The complex movement of air masses creates our weather. This movement begins because air around the equator is heated and air at the poles is cool. Air in the lower atmosphere moves toward the equator, while upper air moves toward the poles. Added to this is the effect of Coriolis force, caused by the rotation of the planet. Coriolis force pulls air to the right in the Northern Hemisphere and to the left in the Southern Hemisphere.

Weather fronts move from west to east in the United States. High pressure systems are usually associated with good weather. Wind circulates to the right (left in the Southern Hemisphere) around a high pressure system. Low pressure systems are usually associated with bad weather. Wind circulates to the left (right in the Southern Hemisphere) around a low pressure system.

Humidity

Humidity refers to the percent of water vapor in the air. Dew point is the temperature below which the air will become so humid that it is saturated with water. Humidity above 60 or 65 percent makes us more uncomfortable because perspiration evaporates slowly.

Fog and Clouds

When the temperature is below the dew point, the air is saturated with water droplets or ice crystals, and fog or clouds are formed. Fog is a cloud that touches the ground. Clouds are formed well above the ground.

Stratus clouds refer to low-hanging clouds. Rain or snow may fall from nimbostratus clouds. Other stratus clouds can appear after rain has fallen. Stratus clouds may be just a few thousand feet above the ground.

Cumulus can be puffy cotton-like clouds that appear in the afternoon. The base of these clouds is about a mile above the ground. Cumulonimbus clouds are huge dark cumulus clouds that produce thunderstorms and hail. All cumulus clouds have strong convective, upward wind currents.

Cirrus clouds are high wispy clouds made up of ice crystals. Cirrus clouds are frequently three to five miles above the ground.

Precipitation

When condensed water or ice crystals become too dense for the air to support the precipitate, they fall toward the ground. *Rain* is water droplets that fall to the ground. *Snow* crystallizes from water droplets in clouds and falls to the earth. *Sleet* begins as rain and freezes or partially freezes as it falls to the earth. *Freezing rain* is rain that freezes when it strikes the surface. *Hail* is rain that freezes in cumulonimbus clouds and is blown up and falls only to be blown up again. This cycle is repeated many times, forming noticeable layers of ice in a hailstone.

Lightning

Lightning is an instantaneous, high energy electrical discharge in the atmosphere. Lightning occurs when positive and negative charges are separated in the atmosphere. While this occurs most often in violent thunderstorms it can occur also in sandstorms or in clouds above volcanoes. Lightning can be from cloud to cloud, or from cloud to ground.

Weather Maps

Weather maps show the position of pressure systems and fronts. A *warm front* signals that the air behind the front is warmer than the air in front. A *cold front* signals that the air behind the front is colder. The map below shows the symbols for fronts and pressure systems.

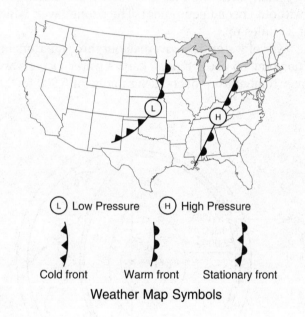

L Low Pressure   H High Pressure

Cold front   Warm front   Stationary front

Weather Map Symbols

OCEANOGRAPHY

Oceanography is the study of the world's oceans and ocean beds. Oceanographers are concerned with 71 percent of the earth's surface. The ocean floor is covered by sediment, which reveals information about life on earth. Midocean ridges are the source of many volcanic eruptions.

Seawater itself is about 3.5 percent salt. Ocean currents, such as the Gulf Stream, are like rivers of water within the ocean. The sea provides over one-quarter of the protein needed in the world. Off-shore wells provide about 15 percent of the world's petroleum. Pollution by petroleum spills and other factors has had a noticeable impact on the oceans and on marine life.

GEOLOGY

Geology is the study of the earth, its development and origin. The History of Life table on page 150 shows the different periods in earth's development and when living organisms appeared on earth.

Using this time scale, geologists are fairly certain that, during the Permian period, earth's land mass consisted of a single continent called Pangea. During the Triassic period, Pangea split into two continents. During the Jurassic period, the Atlantic Ocean was formed. During the Cretaceous period, the Rocky Mountains rose. During the Tertiary period, the land bridge between North America and Europe disappeared. During the Quaternary period, glaciers covered most of North America.

The Earth's Parts

The earth has five parts—atmosphere, crust, mantle, outer core, and inner core.

The atmosphere is the gaseous region that surrounds the earth; it consists of 78 percent nitrogen and 21 percent oxygen. The remaining 1 percent consists of carbon dioxide, argon, water vapor, and other gases. The atmosphere extends out about 650 miles. But air becomes thinner as you travel away from earth and only the bottom 3 $\frac{1}{2}$ miles or so of the atmosphere is habitable by humans without special equipment. The ozone layer, which protects earth from ultraviolet rays, is about 20 miles up.

The hydrosphere is the layer of water that covers about three-quarters of earth's surface. Ocean water, salt water, makes up about 95 percent of all earth's water. Oceans average about 12,400 feet deep. Below 100 feet, water temperature decreases rapidly. At 5,000 feet, the ocean temperature is near freezing.

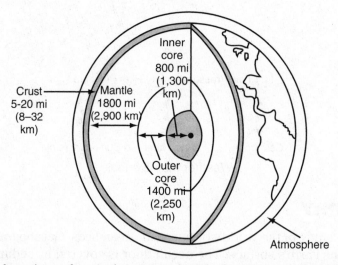

It is about 4,000 miles from the surface to the center of earth. Pressure and density increase with depth.

The lithosphere includes the rigid crust (20 miles thick) and upper mantle (40 miles thick) of the earth. The lithosphere is divided into a number of tectonic plates, which drift across earth's surface on the partially molten asthenosphere. The asthenosphere separates the lithosphere from the mantle.

The rigid mantle reaches to a depth of about 1,800 miles. The outer core is about 1,400 miles thick and consists of dense rigid materials. The inner core has a radius of about 800 miles and is very dense and hot with temperatures over 10,000° F. The heat generated in the inner core is transferred to the surface and provides the energy for continental drift and for molten rock, which erupts on land and in the ocean.

Rocks

Geologists study rocks. Three types of rocks are found in the earth's crust—sedimentary, igneous, and metamorphic. Sedimentary rocks form in water when sediments and remains of dead organisms harden. Igneous rocks form when molten rock, magma, crystallizes. Metamorphic rocks form when other rocks are subjected to extreme pressure. Sedimentary rocks are found near the surface of the earth while igneous and metamorphic rocks are usually found beneath the surface.

Fossils

Fossils are evidence of living organisms. Geologists and other scientists use fossils to learn about earth's history. Fossils usually form when organisms die and are buried in the sediment that forms sedimentary rocks. Other fossils include footprints or tracks of animals. Fossils of animals help us date rocks and other layers of the earth.

Geologic Processes

External Processes

As new rocks are being created, old ones are being destroyed, and earth's surface is being worn away. This process is called erosion.

Most erosion begins with weathering. Weathering disintegrates rocks physically and chemically. Physical weathering breaks up rocks and may be caused by intense heat or cold, by frost, or by the action of vines or the roots of plants. Chemical weathering changes the composition of the rocks. Rain water combines with small amounts of carbon dioxide in the atmosphere to form carbonic acid, which can dissolve or decompose minerals.

Streams, rivers, and wind erode rocks and carry away soil, while glaciers can gouge out huge grooves in rocks and in the soil. Beaches are the result of erosion from the pounding surf or oceans. Humans cause erosion. The dust bowl in the midwestern United States was caused by careless plowing, planting, and grazing.

Internal Processes

The earth's interior is very hot. Holes drilled one mile into the earth can be 85° to 90° warmer at the bottom than on the surface. This is why geologists believe that the interior of the earth, which extends down almost 4,000 feet, is exceptionally hot. This belief is bolstered by the molten rock that erupts from volcanoes and by the boiling water in springs at the earth's surface.

New Land Masses

New mountains and land are constantly being created. Hot magma comes to the surface, seeps out, and is cooled. Land masses also rise as the land is eroded and pushed up from below.

PHYSICAL SCIENCES

CHEMISTRY

Chemistry refers to the composition, properties, and interactions of matter. Organic chemistry is about living things. Inorganic chemistry deals with all other substances.

Atoms

Matter consists of atoms, which are so small they have never been seen—not even with the most powerful microscope. Atoms contain three subatomic particles—protons, neutrons, and electrons. The nucleus contains positively charged protons and neutrons with a neutral charge. Negatively charged electrons revolve around the nucleus.

Elements

Elements are the building blocks of chemistry. They cannot be broken by chemical means into other elements. Over 100 chemical elements are known today. Some have been produced artificially and have not been found in nature. Atoms are the smallest piece of an element.

Each element is classified by its atomic number, which is the total number of protons in the nucleus. Every element has its own symbol. Therefore, every substance can be represented by symbols that show how many atoms of each element it contains.

PERIODIC TABLE OF THE ELEMENTS

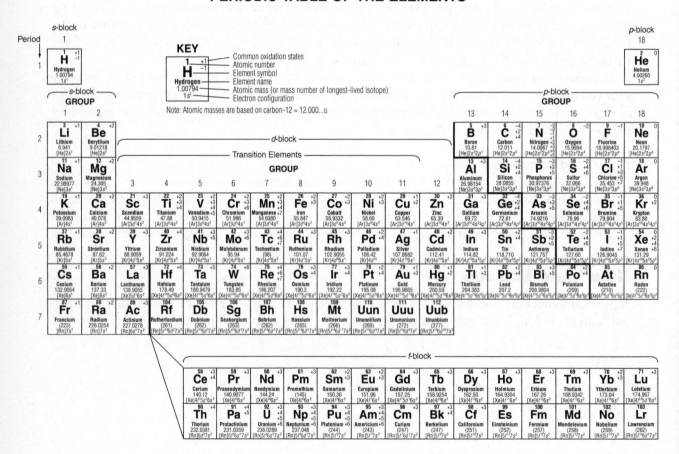

Matter

Matter is anything that has mass and takes up space. Matter can exist as a solid, liquid, or gas. The form of matter may change. For example, water becomes solid below freezing, and lead can be heated to a liquid.

All matter is made up of atoms. The weight of matter is a measure of the force that gravity places on its mass. Matter is conserved. That is, it cannot be created or destroyed, but it can be converted into energy.

Compound

A compound is formed when two or more elements unite chemically. A molecule is the smallest part of a compound with the properties of that compound.

There are three important types of chemical compounds—acids, bases, and salt. Acids dissolved in water produce hydrogen. Bases dissolved in water produce hydroxide. When acids and bases are combined chemically, they form salt.

Solution

A solution is formed when element(s) or compound(s) are dissolved in another substance. Club soda is a solution with carbon dioxide dissolved in water. Lemonade is a solution of lemon juice and sugar dissolved in water.

Chemical Reactions

Chemical reactions occur when bonds between atoms form or break. Energy, usually as heat, is absorbed when bonds are formed and released when bonds are broken. Water cooled below freezing forms bonds—energy is absorbed and ice forms. Water heated above boiling releases bonds—energy is released and steam is formed.

PHYSICS

Physics began at the earliest time with an attempt to understand matter and forces. This study has progressed through relativity and atomic physics to today when physicists are concerned with elementary particles. Physics seeks to describe nature through a number of general statements or laws. These laws are often stated in mathematical form.

Matter and Mass

Mass is the amount of matter in a body and is a measure of the body's inertia (resistance to change of motion). Weight is a measure of the force of gravity on a body. Weight and mass are different. Mass at rest is the same everywhere, but mass increases as it approaches the speed of light. Weight varies depending on its location in a gravitational field.

The density (specific gravity) of matter describes how compact the matter is. Archimedes discovered density and is reputed to have shouted "Eureka" in the process. He found that, in similar weights of lead and gold, the gold displaced less water, showing that it was more dense.

Motion

Physics is concerned with an object's response to force and the resulting movement. Force is energy that causes a change in an object's motion or shape. To explain force completely, you must describe both the magnitude and the direction. For example, two forces of the same magnitude pushing in the same direction are different from these same forces pushing at one another.

Velocity is described as magnitude (e.g., miles per hour) and direction (e.g., from 220 degrees). The magnitude portion of velocity is speed. The following formula describes the distance traveled for a constant velocity and a known time. For a time t and a constant velocity v the distance traveled d is:

$$d = vt$$

Newton's three laws of motion are still most important in everyday life. We must remember, though, that recent theories have shown that these laws do not apply to objects traveling near the speed of light or for very small subatomic particles.

Newton's First Law (Inertia). A body maintains its state of rest or uniform motion unless acted upon by an outside force.

Newton's Second Law (Constant Acceleration). As force is applied to an object, the object accelerates in the direction of the force. Both the mass and the force affect how the object accelerates. The more the mass the less the acceleration. The formula for this law follows:

$$F(\text{orce}) = M(\text{ass}) \times A(\text{cceleration}) \text{ or } A(\text{cceleration}) = \frac{F(\text{orce})}{M(\text{ass})}$$

Newton's Third Law (Conservation of Momentum). This law states that for every action there is an equal and opposite reaction. If two objects bump into each other, they are pushed away from each other with an equal force. The net effect of this event is 0, and the momentum is conserved.

ENERGY

Energy is the ability to do work. Energy can be mechanical, solar, thermal, chemical, electrical, or nuclear. Potential energy is stored energy or energy ready to be released. Kinetic energy is energy resulting from motion. Activation energy converts potential energy into kinetic energy.

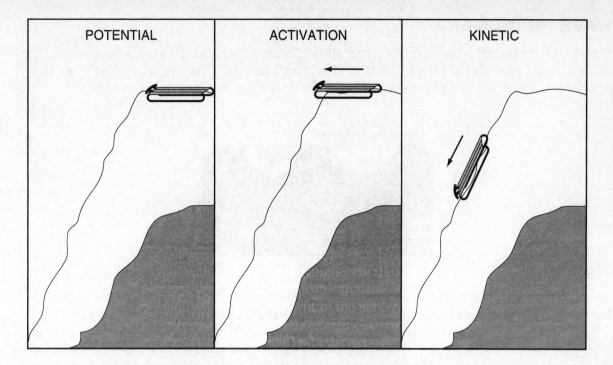

In one simple example, a sled at the top of a hill possesses potential energy. The push of the sledder is the activation energy needed to set the sled in motion. While in motion, the sled possesses kinetic energy.

In another example, the fuel in a rocket car has potential energy. This potential energy is activated by energy from a flame and transformed into the kinetic energy of the moving car.

Work

Work is the movement of a body by a force. If there is no movement, there is no work. Work occurs when you pick up an object. Trying without success to move a heavy object or holding an object steady involves no work. It does not matter that a lot of effort was involved. The rate of work is power. Power is measured in foot-pounds. A foot-pound is the amount of work it takes to raise one pound, one foot at sea level.

Heat

In physics, heat is energy in motion. Heat transfers energy within a body or from one body to the other when there is a temperature difference. Heat moves from higher temperature to lower temperature, lowering the former and raising the latter. Heat is measured in calories.

Temperature measures how fast the molecules in a substance are moving. The faster the molecules move, the hotter the substance. Temperature is commonly measured on two scales, Fahrenheit (freezing 32 degrees, boiling [water] 212 degrees) and Celsius (freezing 0 degrees and boiling [water] 100 degrees). The Kelvin scale is used in science. Zero on the Kelvin scale is absolute zero—molecules are not moving at all—and is equal to –273°C or –460°F.

Heat is transferred by conduction (physical contact), convection (from moving liquid or gas), and radiation (no physical contact). A heating pad *conducts* heat to your back. Moving hot water transfers heat to the radiator by *convection*. The sun *radiates* heat to the earth.

WAVE PHENOMENA

Waves transfer energy without transferring matter. Microwaves, radio waves, sound waves, and x-rays are examples of waves in action. Most waves resemble the one below. The frequency of a wave is the vibrations per second. The wavelength is the distance between crests.

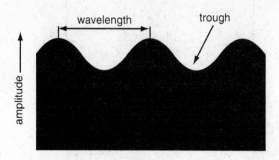

Light

Most light is produced by heated electrons vibrating at high frequencies. Light makes it possible for us to see things and to observe colors. Plants need light to carry out photosynthesis.

Light travels in straight lines and spreads out as it travels. When light strikes a rough surface it may be absorbed or scattered. When light strikes a highly polished surface it is reflected away at the angle of the original ray (angle of incidence equals the angle of reflection). Black surfaces absorb all light, while white surfaces scatter all light. This is why white clothes are recommended for sunny, warm days.

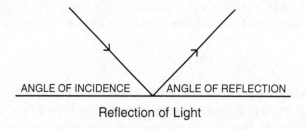

Reflection of Light

Sound

Sounds are waves. For the human ear to hear a sound it must travel through a medium—a gas, a solid, or a liquid. As the sound waves travel through the medium, molecules in the medium vibrate.

Sound travels more quickly through solid media because the molecules are more closely packed together. Sound travels through air at about 1,100 feet per second, through water at about 5,000 feet per second, and through stone at about 20,000 feet per second.

ELECTRICITY AND MAGNETISM

Atoms are composed of protons (positive charge), electrons (negative charge), and neutrons (neutral charge). All things have either a positive (more protons), negative (more electrons), or neutral (balance of protons and electrons) charge.

Electricity

Electricity is based on these charges and follows these rules. Like charges repel, unlike charge attract. Neutral charges are attracted by both positive and negative charges, but not as strongly as opposite charges.

In a static electricity experiment, the experimenter shows that the glass rod does not attract bits of paper. Then the glass rod is rubbed with a piece of silk. This process removes electrons from the rod, creating a negative charge. Then the rod attracts the neutral bits of paper.

Electricity speeds through conductors such as copper. Electricity moves slower through semiconductors such as ceramics. Electricity does not move through nonconductors or insulators such as rubber and glass.

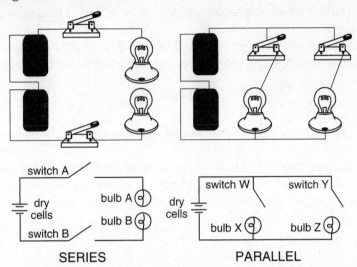

SERIES   PARALLEL

Electricity moves through wires to form circuits. Most circuits in this country use alternating current (AC). Circuits in other countries may use direct current (DC). Most circuits are wired parallel—if a light burns out, or a switch is off, all other switches or lights work. Some circuits are wired in series—if a switch is off or a light is missing or burned out, all lights go out.

Three units are used to measure electricity as it flows through wires. The volt measures the force of the current. The ampere (amp) measures the rate of current flow. The ohm tells the resistance in the wire to the flow of electricity.

Batteries are used to produce, store, and release electricity. Batteries used in a toy or flashlight are dry cell batteries. Car batteries are wet cell batteries.

Magnetism

Magnets occur naturally in magnetite, although most magnets are manufactured from iron. Magnetism is very similar to electricity, and electromagnets can be made from coils of wire. Magnets have a north and south pole—like poles repel, while opposite poles attract. The magnetic field is strongest around the poles.

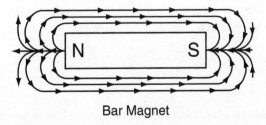

Bar Magnet

Earth has a magnetic field that aids navigation. Magnetic north is located in northeastern Canada. It is not located at the North Pole. Compass needles point to magnetic north, not to the geographic North Pole.

MODERN PHYSICS AND RADIOACTIVITY

Modern Physics

Modern physics studies very small particles of energy. Energy as very small, discrete quantities gives scientists a different view than energy as a continuous flow. Particle physics is particularly useful as scientists study atomic energy. For example, scientists study light as the transmission of tiny particles called photons. In fact, it is believed that energy is transmitted as both particles and waves.

Modern physics also studies the conversion of matter into energy and energy into matter. Einstein's famous equation quantifies the conversion between mass to energy.

$$E = mc^2$$

(E is energy, m is mass, and c is the speed of light, 186,000 miles per second.)

Calculations with this equation reveal that very small amounts of mass can create huge amounts of energy. Similarly, calculations reveal it would take huge amounts of energy to create a very small amount of mass.

Radioactivity

Materials are radioactive when they have unstable nuclei. Uranium is an example of a naturally occurring radioactive substance. Radioactive materials decay, losing their radioactivity at a certain rate. The decay of radioactive materials is very useful for dating rocks and other materials.

Other radioactive material is created through nuclear fission in nuclear power plants. The energy from the reaction can be used as a power source.

Radioactive materials release energy including alpha, beta, and usually gamma radiation. Gamma rays penetrate living organisms very deeply and can destroy living cells and lead to the death of humans.

Fusion

The sun creates energy through fusion. Attempts are underway to create energy through nuclear fusion. Fusion creates much less radioactivity and could be fueled by deuterium, which is found in limitless quantities throughout the ocean.

READING AND INTERPRETING GRAPHS

You will certainly encounter graphs on the tests. Examples of the four main types of graphs are shown below. Answer the questions that accompany the graphs and review the answers on page 173.

The Pictograph

The pictograph uses symbols to stand for numbers. In the following graph, each picture represents 1,000 phones.

Alpine
Bergenfield
Closter
Dumont
Emerson

Number of Phones in Five Towns
(in thousands)

Try these questions:

1. According to this graph, about how many more phones are there in Bergenfield than in Emerson?
   (A) 10,000
   (B) 15,000
   (C) 1,000
   (D) 1.5 thousand

2. This graph *best* demonstrates which of the following?
   (A) More people live in Bergenfield.
   (B) People in Alpine make the fewest calls.
   (C) There are about twice as many phones in Emerson as in Alpine.
   (D) There are about four times as many phones in Bergenfield as in Alpine.

The Bar Graph

The bar graph represents information by the length of a bar. The graph below shows the rainfall during two months in each of five towns.

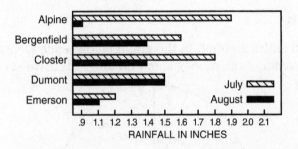

Alpine
Bergenfield
Closter
Dumont
Emerson

July
August

.9 1.1 1.2 1.3 1.4 1.5 1.6 1.7 1.8 1.9 2.0 2.1
RAINFALL IN INCHES

Rainfall in July and August for Five Towns

Try these questions:

3. You wanted to get the least rainfall. Based on this graph, which town would you go to in July and which town would you go to in August?
   (A) Closter, Bergenfield
   (B) Alpine, Dumont
   (C) Closter, Alpine
   (D) None of the above

4. This graph *best* demonstrates which of the following?
   (A) The rainiest town yearly is Closter.
   (B) Alpine has the largest rainfall difference between July and August.
   (C) The driest town yearly is Emerson.
   (D) In August, Alpine has more rain than Emerson.

The Line Graph

The line graph plots information against two axes. The graph below shows monthly sales for two corporations.

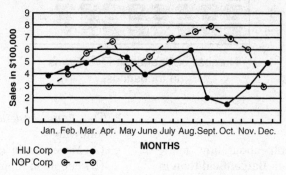

Sales for Two Companies During the Year

You might be asked two types of questions.

5. What was the approximate difference in sales between the HIJ and the NOP Corporations in June?
   (A) $15,000
   (B) $150,000
   (C) $400,000
   (D) $4.5 million

6. This graph *best* demonstrates which of the following?
   (A) NOP has more employees.
   (B) From August to September, the differences in sales grew by 400%.
   (C) In October, NOP had over $600,000 more in sales than HIJ.
   (D) In total, HIJ had more sales this year than NOP.

The Circle Graph

The circle represents an entire amount. In the graph below, each wedge-shaped piece of the graph represents the percent of tax money spent on different town services.

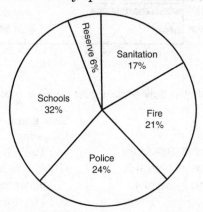

Percent of Tax Money Spent for Town Services

Use the circle graph to answer these questions.

7. The town collects $1,400,000 in taxes. How much will the town spend on schools?
   (A) $320,000
   (B) $60,000
   (C) $600,000
   (D) $448,000

8. The town collects $1,400,000 in taxes. The town needs to spend $392,000 for police. Any needed money will come from sanitation. The percents in the pie chart are recalculated. What percent is left for sanitation?
   (A) 21%
   (B) 17%
   (C) 13%
   (D) 10%

EXPLAINED ANSWERS

1. The correct answer is (D). Writing answers in a different format (1.5 thousand instead of 1,500) is common.

2. The correct answer is (D). You can't draw any valid conclusions about the populations or calls made. Some towns might have more businesses, own fewer phones, or make more calls per household.

3. The correct answer is (D). Emerson, Alpine are the towns you would choose. No need to compute. Find the smallest bar for each month.

4. The correct answer is (B). That fact is clear. We only have information about July and August, so we can't be sure about (A) or (C). Choice (D) is not true.

5. The correct answer is (B). Each space represents $100,000 and there are 1.5 spaces between the sales figures in June.

6. The correct answer is (B). You can't predict the number of employees from this information. Choices (C) and (D) are false.

7. The correct answer is (D). Multiply $0.32 \times \$1,400,000$.

8. The correct answer is (C). It takes 28 percent of the taxes to get $392,000. That's 4 percent more than the police get now. Sanitation loses 4 percent, leaving 13 percent.

SCIENCE PRACTICE ITEMS

These items will help you practice the concepts in this chapter. The items you encounter on the real LAST may have a different emphasis and may be more complete.

Instructions

Mark your answers on the sheet provided below. Complete the items in 20 minutes or less. Correct your answer sheet using the answers on page 178.

1 Ⓐ Ⓑ Ⓒ Ⓓ	5 Ⓐ Ⓑ Ⓒ Ⓓ	9 Ⓐ Ⓑ Ⓒ Ⓓ	13 Ⓐ Ⓑ Ⓒ Ⓓ	17 Ⓐ Ⓑ Ⓒ Ⓓ
2 Ⓐ Ⓑ Ⓒ Ⓓ	6 Ⓐ Ⓑ Ⓒ Ⓓ	10 Ⓐ Ⓑ Ⓒ Ⓓ	14 Ⓐ Ⓑ Ⓒ Ⓓ	18 Ⓐ Ⓑ Ⓒ Ⓓ
3 Ⓐ Ⓑ Ⓒ Ⓓ	7 Ⓐ Ⓑ Ⓒ Ⓓ	11 Ⓐ Ⓑ Ⓒ Ⓓ	15 Ⓐ Ⓑ Ⓒ Ⓓ	19 Ⓐ Ⓑ Ⓒ Ⓓ
4 Ⓐ Ⓑ Ⓒ Ⓓ	8 Ⓐ Ⓑ Ⓒ Ⓓ	12 Ⓐ Ⓑ Ⓒ Ⓓ	16 Ⓐ Ⓑ Ⓒ Ⓓ	20 Ⓐ Ⓑ Ⓒ Ⓓ

1. The following are parts of all cells EXCEPT:
   (A) chloroplasts
   (B) cytoplasm
   (C) nucleus
   (D) cell membrane

2. Cells may reproduce through
   (A) photosynthesis.
   (B) mitochondria.
   (C) mitosis.
   (D) eukaryotes.

3. All the following are cell activities EXCEPT:
   (A) homeostasis
   (B) respiration
   (C) ingestion
   (D) chromosome

4. The genetic material termed DNA has the following function:
   (A) It divides the nucleus acid in genes.
   (B) It provides the genetic codes that determine many traits of an organism.
   (C) It carries the genetic code throughout the cell.
   (D) It arranges rodlike structures located in the cell nucleus.

5. All the following belong to the class called mammals EXCEPT:
   (A) moles
   (B) humans
   (C) monkeys
   (D) carp

6. Which of the following is not one of the five kingdoms living things are generally classified into?
   (A) Moneran
   (B) Fungi
   (C) Plantae
   (D) Reptilae

7. Find the statement about bacteria that is not true.
   (A) Bacteria help decompose dead matter.
   (B) Bacteria cause disease.
   (C) Bacteria help regular physiological processes.
   (D) Bacteria are lifeless and lack the ability to reproduce.

8. Which is the correct hierarchy of the body makeup:
   (A) tissues-cells-organs-systems-body
   (B) cells-tissues-organs-systems-body
   (C) cells-tissues-systems-organs-body
   (D) tissues-cells-systems-organs-body

9. Which of the following is considered to be the primary gland in the male body?
   (A) testes
   (B) thyroid
   (C) pituitary
   (D) pancreas

10. Which of the following definitions best describes the meaning of ecology?
    (A) Recycling to keep the human habitat as pure as possible.
    (B) The relationship between organisms and their habitat.
    (C) Making use of natural materials from our habitat.
    (D) Keeping the biosphere free of toxic materials.

11. When the elements of hydrogen and oxygen combine they form
    (A) coal
    (B) diamond
    (C) carbon dioxide
    (D) water

12. Which is a false statement about matter?
    (A) Matter is anything that has mass and takes up space.
    (B) Matter is made up of atoms.
    (C) Matter cannot be changed, created, or destroyed.
    (D) The weight of matter depends on gravitational force.

13. Which of the following is not a planet of our solar system?
    (A) Pluto
    (B) Uranus
    (C) Neptune
    (D) Polaris

14. Which is not part of the gaseous make-up of our atmosphere?
    (A) nitrogen
    (B) water vapor
    (C) argon
    (D) ozone

15. Approximately what percent of the earth's surface is covered with water?
    (A) 90 percent
    (B) 75 percent
    (C) 60 percent
    (D) 45 percent

16. Which of the following is a stage in the water cycle?
    (A) photosynthesis
    (B) respiration
    (C) condensation
    (D) accumulation

17. Magnitude and direction together are needed to describe
    (A) work.
    (B) motion.
    (C) mass.
    (D) force.

18. A person is driving a car; what types of energy are represented respectively by the gas in the tank and the motion of the car?
    (A) kinetic, potential
    (B) activation, kinetic
    (C) potential, activation
    (D) potential, kinetic

19. Which of the following is the description of heat?
    (A) temperature
    (B) energy in motion
    (C) radiation
    (D) a temperature measurement

20. Which of the following would be the best conductor of electricity?
    (A) paper
    (B) copper
    (C) hair
    (D) rubber

Answers

1. A	5. D	9. C	13. D	17. D
2. C	6. D	10. B	14. D	18. D
3. D	7. D	11. D	15. B	19. B
4. B	8. B	12. C	16. C	20. B

7 HISTORY, HUMANITIES, AND SOCIAL SCIENCE

USING THIS CHAPTER

This chapter prepares you for the History, Humanities, and Social Science items on the LAST. Choose one of these approaches.

I want all the History, Humanities, and Social Science review I can get.

❏ Skip the History, Humanities, and Social Science Review Quizzes and read the entire review section.
❏ Take the History, Humanities, and Social Science Review Quizzes on page 181.
❏ Correct the Review Quizzes and reread the indicated parts of the review.
❏ Go over Reading and Interpreting Maps on page 230.
❏ Complete the History, Humanities, and Social Science Practice Items on page 231.

I want a thorough History, Humanities, and Social Science review.

❏ Take the History, Humanities and Social Studies Review Quiz on page 181.
❏ Correct the Review Quiz and reread the indicated parts of the review.
❏ Go over Reading and Interpreting Maps on page 230.
❏ Complete the History, Humanities, and Social Studies Practice Items on page 231.

I want a quick History, Humanities, and Social Science review.

❏ Take and correct the History, Humanities, and Social Science Review Quizzes on page 181.
❏ Go over Reading and Interpreting Maps on page 230.
❏ Complete the History, Humanities, and Social Science Practice Items on page 231.

I want to practice History and Social Science questions.

❏ Go over Reading and Interpreting Maps on page 230.
❏ Complete the History, Humanities, and Social Science Practice Items on page 231.

HISTORY, HUMANITIES, AND SOCIAL SCIENCE REVIEW QUIZZES

These three quizzes use a short answer format to help you find out what you know about the History, Humanities, and Social Science topics reviewed in this chapter. The quiz results direct you to the portions of the chapter you should read.

These quizzes will also help focus your thinking about History, Humanities, and Social Science, and these questions and answers are a good review in themselves. It's not important to answer all these questions correctly, and don't be concerned if you miss many of them.

The answers are found immediately after the quiz. It's to your advantage not to look at them until you have completed the quiz. Once you have completed and corrected the review quizzes, use the answer checklist to decide which sections of the review to study.

UNITED STATES HISTORY AND HUMANITIES REVIEW QUIZ

Write the answers in the space provided or on a separate sheet of paper.

1. Which Indian group established a culture off southern Alaska about 7,000 years ago?
   _____
   _____

2. In what structure did plains Indians live?
   _____
   _____

3. Name a nonindigenous group that established North American settlements before Columbus.
   _____
   _____

4. In what year did Columbus reach the mainland of North America?
   _____
   _____

5. Where were African slaves first brought to America?
   _____
   _____

6. What did Spanish explorers bring that caused great devastation to Native Americans?
   _____
   _____

7. Which nation established the first settlement in Manhattan?
   _____
   _____

8. How many English colonies were there in the 1740s?
   _____
   _____

9. Which things frequently used by colonists were taxed by the original Townsend Acts?
   _____
   _____

10. What was the Boston Tea Party and why was it held?
    _____
    _____
    _____
    _____

11. Which riders spread the word about the English march on Concord?
    _____
    _____

12. Name two of the self-evident truths found in the Declaration of Independence.

_____
_____
_____

13. Where did the Colonial army winter in 1777?

_____
_____

14. Which two main forces trapped Cornwallis at Yorktown, Virginia?

_____
_____

15. What was the first governing document for the United States?

_____
_____

16. Describe the effect of three of the first ten amendments to the Constitution.

_____
_____
_____
_____
_____

17. Briefly describe the theory of nullification.

_____
_____
_____
_____

18. What tract of land did Jefferson purchase from France?

_____
_____

19. What action started the War of 1812?

_____
_____

20. What famous national song was written during the War of 1812?

_____
_____

21. What impact did the Missouri Compromise have on the state of Missouri?

_____
_____
_____

22. What governmental group did Jackson ignore when he moved Native Americans onto reservations?

_____
_____

23. What was the status of Texas after it gained independence from Mexico?

_____
_____

24. What did the Underground Railroad transport?

_____
_____

25. What states seceded from the Union before hostilities began?

_____
_____
_____

26. What action began the Civil War?

_____
_____

27. What was the effect of the Emancipation Proclamation?

_____
_____
_____

28. What type of government did Lincoln call for in his Gettysburg Address?

_____
_____

29. Describe one of the three civil rights amendments adopted from 1865 and 1870.

_____
_____
_____

30. Until what year were Northern troops in the South following the Civil War?

_____
_____

31. Who was the only president to be elected and re-elected during this period?

_____
_____

32. What was the goal of the Dawes Severalty Act?

_____

_____

33. What inventions drew women to the workplace?

_____

_____

34. Name a territory the United States gained in the treaty ending the Spanish American War.

_____

_____

35. Teddy Roosevelt was awarded the Nobel Prize for helping to end what war?

_____

_____

36. Who did the United States army pursue in Mexico following the Mexican Revolution?

_____

_____

37. What act led to the beginning of World War I?

_____

_____

38. What occurred during World War I to remove an Ally from the conflict?

_____

_____

39. What German war policy brought the United States into the war?

_____

_____

40. Exactly when did World War I officially end?

_____

_____

41. What was the highest unemployment rate during the Depression?

_____

_____

_____

42. Name and describe two of FDR's New Deal programs.

_____

_____

_____

_____

_____

_____

43. What main factor led to Hitler's rise to power in Germany?

_____

_____

44. What conflict provided a proving ground for World War II?

_____

_____

45. What were Russia's first actions when World War II began?

_____

_____

46. What power did Roosevelt gain from the Lend-Lease Act?

_____

_____

47. What was the outcome of Operation Barbarosa?

_____

_____

48. Why was Roosevelt criticized for his actions at Yalta?

_____

_____

_____

49. What was the effect of the war on unemployment?

_____

_____

50. How did Truman use the Smith Act following World War II?

_____

_____

51. What led to China's involvement in the Korean War?

_____

_____

52. Describe the essence of the Supreme Court ruling in *Brown v. Board of Education.*

_____
_____
_____
_____
_____

53. Describe the effectiveness of Presidents Kennedy and Johnson in passing War on Poverty legislation.

_____
_____
_____
_____
_____

54. What happened after World War II to foster an alliance between Ho Chi Minh and Mao Tse-tung?

_____
_____

55. Through what process did Gerald Ford become president?

_____
_____

56. What major new programs did Carter introduce?

_____
_____
_____
_____
_____

57. What is supply-side economics?

_____
_____
_____
_____

58. What "read my lips" promise led to Bush's defeat in 1992?

_____
_____

59. What type of question dogged the Clinton presidency?

_____
_____

WORLD HISTORY AND HUMANITIES REVIEW QUIZ

Write the answers in the space provided or on a separate sheet of paper.

1. Give the approximate population of the world in 1 A.D._____ 1992 A.D._____

2. Approximately when was writing invented?

_____
_____

3. What is the name of the justice codes formulated in ancient Mesopotamia?

_____
_____

4. Approximately when were most Egyptian pyramids built?

_____

5. Who fought in the Peloponesian Wars?

_____
_____

6. Name two of the three greatest thinkers of the Greek Classic age.

_____
_____

7. What event marked the beginning of the Greek Hellenistic age?

_____
_____

8. What was the outcome of the Punic wars?

_____
_____

9. Which leaders were defeated at the Battle of Acton?

_____

_____

10. Approximately when was Christianity declared the national religion of Rome?

_____

_____

11. Who was the original founder of Islam and approximately when was he born?

_____

_____

_____

12. What was the original Japanese religion?

_____

_____

13. Why did the Samurai revolt in 1876?

_____

_____

14. Who was named emperor of the Holy Roman Empire in the late 700s A.D.?

_____

_____

15. What were the stated reasons for the Crusades?

_____

_____

16. Joan of Arc fought for which country in what war?

_____

_____

17. About what percent of the European population was killed by the bubonic plague?

_____

_____

18. Approximately when was Confucius born?

_____

_____

19. During what centuries did the Mongol Kahns rule China?

_____

_____

20. What was the cause of the Chinese-British Opium War?

_____

_____

21. What name was given to the earliest inhabitants of the Indus Valley in India?

_____

_____

22. What ideal did Buddha preach?

_____

_____

23. What was the beginning of Muslim and Hindu strife in India?

_____

_____

24. Where did the first towns in Africa appear?

_____

_____

25. During what century was Northern Africa predominately Islamic?

_____

_____

26. What role did African kingdoms play in the slave trade?

_____

_____

27. What was the dominant civilization of the Yucatan peninsula until about 900 A.D.?

_____

_____

28. What was the dominant civilization in South America in 1500 A.D.?

_____

_____

29. The ideas of which ancient civilization were dominant during the Renaissance?

_____

_____

30. Which practice of the Catholic church was particularly repugnant to Protestants?

_____

_____

31. What was the significant difference between the English queens Mary I and her successor Elizabeth I?

_____

_____

32. What was the main effect of European exploration on American Indians?

_____

_____

33. What major trade was begun during the Age of Exploration?

_____

_____

34. What major discovery did Copernicus make?

_____

_____

35. What was the average life expectancy in the early 1700s?

_____

_____

36. Who was the most famous Baroque painter?

_____

_____

37. Which Romanov leader began the modernization of Russia?

_____

_____

38. Which action began the French Revolution?

_____

_____

39. Which leader oversaw the reign of terror following the French Revolution?

_____

_____

40. Where was Napoleon exiled?

_____

_____

41. Which industries were the first to develop after the Industrial Revolution?

_____

_____

42. Which ideals were stressed by the Romantic Movement?

_____

_____

43. With which country were Great Britain and France allied during the Crimean War?

_____

_____

44. What do anarchists believe?

_____

_____

45. What continent drew the most attention from European countries during the period of New Imperialism?

_____

_____

_____

OTHER SOCIAL SCIENCE TOPICS REVIEW QUIZ

Write the answers in the space provided or on a separate sheet of paper.

1. What do physical anthropologists study?
   _____
   _____

2. What are the three primary determinants of culture?
   _____
   _____
   _____

3. What is the relationship of the legislative and executive branches in a parliamentary government?
   _____
   _____
   _____
   _____
   _____

4. What percentage of United States Representatives are elected every two years?
   _____
   _____

5. What percent of the popular vote is required to elect the president of the United States?
   _____
   _____

ANSWER CHECKLIST

The answers are organized by review sections. Check your answers. If you miss any question in a section, check the box and review that section. Everyone should review the section on Interpreting Graphs and Maps.

United States History and Humanities

Native American Civilizations
❏ *Primitive Cultures, page 192*
   1. Aleuts

❏ *Recent Cultures, page 192*
   2. tepees

European Exploration and Colonization
❏ *Visitors Before Columbus, page 193*
   3. Celtic/Norse (Vikings)

❏ *Columbus, page 193*
   4. never

❏ *English Colonization, page 193*
   5. Jamestown in 1619

❏ *Spanish Exploration, page 193*
   6. disease

❏ *Other Explorers, page 193*
   7. Holland (Dutch)

❏ *Colonies in the 1700s, page 194*
   8. thirteen

The American Revolution and the Founding of America
❏ *Road to the Revolutionary War, page 194*
   9. just about everything
   10. Tea was dumped in Boston harbor to protest the British tax on tea.

❏ *War's Beginnings, page 195*
   11. Revere and Dawes
   12. (1) equality of all persons; (2) inalienable rights of life, liberty, and the pursuit of happiness; (3) rights of government come from the governed; (4) the right of the people to alter or abolish a destructive government

❏ *Revolutionary War, page 195*
   13. Morristown, N.J.
   14. American army and the French fleet

Growth of the New Republic
❏ *The New Nation, page 197*
   15. Articles of Confederation

❏ *First Constitutional Government, page 197*
   16. I. Freedom of religion, speech, press, assembly, and petition
   II. Right to bear arms
   III No troops can be quartered in homes without permission
   IV. Warrants and probable cause needed for search and seizure
   V. Rights of the accused are assured
   VI. Right to a speedy public trial and the right to a lawyer
   VII. Right to a jury trial
   VIII. Excessive bail, excessive fines, and cruel and unusual punishment are forbidden
   IX. Rights not spelled out are retained by the people
   X. Powers not specifically federal are retained by the states

❏ *Adams to Madison, page 198*
   17. States can nullify federal laws in that state.
   18. Louisiana Purchase

❏ *War of 1812, page 198*
   19. American invasion of Canada
   20. "The Star Spangled Banner"

❏ *1830–1850, page 198*
   21. Missouri was admitted as a slave state.
   22. Supreme Court
   23. sovereign nation, then a state

❏ *Movements and Accomplishments 1800–1850, page 199*
   24. It moved slaves from the South to the North.

The Civil War and Reconstruction: Causes and Consequences

❑ *Road to Civil War, page 200*
25. South Carolina, Alabama, Georgia, Florida, Louisiana, Mississippi, and Texas seceded before hostilities began. Other states seceded once hostilities had begun.

❑ *Civil War, page 200*
26. Confederate attack on Fort Sumter, S.C.
27. It freed slaves in Confederate states.
28. "A government of the people, by the people, for the people"

❑ *Reconstruction, page 201*
29. XIII. Prohibits slavery
    XIV. Former slaves given citizenship
    XV. Voting rights for former slaves
30. 1877

Industrialization of America

❑ *1877–1897, page 202*
31. McKinley
32. to move Indians from reservations into society
33. sewing machine, typewriter

❑ *Spanish-American War, page 203*
34. Puerto Rico, Guam, and the Philippines

❑ *1900–1916, page 203*
35. Russo-Japanese War
36. Pancho Villa

World War I: Causes and Consequences

❑ *War Begins, page 204*
37. assassination of Archduke Ferdinand
38. Russian Revolution

❑ *American Involvement, page 204*
39. unrestricted submarine warfare
40. 11/11/1918, 11:00 A.M.

Post-World War I America

Prohibition, Depression, FDR, page 205
41. 25 percent
42. The Civilian Conservation Corps (CCC) put unemployed young men to work building roads, stopping erosion, and reforesting the country.
    The Works Project Administration (WPA) gave other public service jobs.
    The Agricultural Adjustment Act paid farmers for not growing crops.

The Federal Deposit Insurance Company (FDIC) insured bank deposits.
The Securities and Exchange Commission (SEC) oversaw the stock market.
The Tennessee Valley Authority (TVA) built hydroelectric plants and dams.

World War II: Causes and Consequences

❑ *Road to World War II, page 206*
43. The Depression
44. Spanish Civil War

❑ *World War II, page 206*
45. to occupy Estonia, Latvia, and Lithuania
46. power to lend or transfer arms to friendly countries
47. Germany occupied suburbs of Moscow but was defeated by the Russians.
48. He gave too much to Stalin.

❑ *The Home Front, page 208*
49. Unemployment was eliminated.

Post-World War II America

❑ *The Cold War, page 208*
50. He jailed Communist leaders.

❑ *Korean War, page 209*
51. UN troops reached the Yalu River border between North Korea and China.

❑ *Civil Rights, page 210*
52. Separate but equal schools are unconstitutional.

❑ *Kennedy and Johnson, page 210*
53. Kennedy was ineffective; Johnson was very effective.

❑ *Vietnam War, page 211*
54. The United States supported France in its effort to regain control of Indochina.

❑ *Nixon, Ford, Carter and Reagan, page 212*
55. Vice President Spiro Agnew resigned; Nixon appointed Ford vice president, and he was confirmed by Congress; Nixon resigned, and Ford became president.

❑ *Bush and Clinton, page 213*
56. none
57. Tax cuts lead to investments, which lead to jobs.
58. "No new taxes."
59. questions about his personal integrity.

World History and Humanities

Prehistory and Early Civilizations
❏ *World Population, page 213*
1. 1 A.D., 200 million; 1992 A.D., 5.7 billion

❏ *Early Civilizations, page 213*
2. 3500 B.C.

❏ *Mesopotamia (4000–500 B.C.), page 213*
3. Codes of Hammurabi

Classical Civilizations
❏ *Egypt (5000–30 B.C.), page 214*
4. 2600–2100 B.C.

❏ *Greece, page 214*
5. Athens and Sparta
6. There were three: Plato, Aristotle and Socrates.
7. the death of Alexander the Great

❏ *Rome, page 214*
8. Rome gained control of both sides of the Mediterranean.
9. Antony and Cleopatra

Development of World Religions
❏ *Judaism and Christianity, page 215*
10. 300s A.D.

❏ *Islam, Buddhism, Hinduism, page 216*
11. Mohammed, 570 A.D.

Feudalism in Japan and Europe
❏ *Japan, page 216*
12. Shinto
13. They had lost power and were forbidden to wear their swords.

❏ *Europe, page 217*
14. Charlemagne
15. to force Muslims from the Holy Land

The Middle and Late Ages
❏ *The Middle and Late Ages (1300–1500), page 218*
16. She fought for France in the Hundred Years War.
17. About 50 percent.

Chinese and Indian Empires
❏ *China to 1900, page 218*
18. 550 B.C.

19. 1200–1400 A.D.
20. The Chinese resisted importation of opium.

❏ *India to 1900, page 219*
21. Dravidians
22. Nirvana
23. the invasion of India about 1200 A.D. by Turk and Afghan Muslims

Sub-Saharan Kingdoms and Cultures
❏ *Early Africa, page 221*
24. around the Nile River

❏ *Sub-Saharan Africa, page 221*
25. 1000–1100 A.D.
26. They captured and sold African slaves.

Civilizations of the Americas
❏ *Mayan Culture, page 222*
27. Mayans

❏ *Aztec, Incan Culture, page 222*
28. Incas

Rise and Expansion of Europe
❏ *Renaissance (1300–1600), page 223*
29. Greece

❏ *Luther and the Reformation (1500–1600), page 223*
30. selling indulgences
31. Mary killed Protestants; Elizabeth was a Protestant.

❏ *Age of Exploration (1500–1650), page 223*
32. death from disease
33. slaves

❏ *Scientific Revolution (1550–1650), page 224*
34. The sun is at the center of the solar system.

❏ *Enlightenment (c. 1650–1790), page 224*
35. about 30
36. Michelangelo

❏ *Romanov Russia, page 225*
37. Peter the Great

❏ *French Revolution, page 225*
38. storming of the Bastille
39. Robspierre

❑ *Napoleon, page 225*
　　40. to Elba and then to St. Helena

❑ *Industrial Revolution (1750–1850), page 226*
　　41. textiles and metal

❑ *Romanticism (1790–1850), page 226*
　　42. personal freedom and humanitarianism

European Developments

❑ *Crimean War, page 226*
　　43. Turkey

❑ *Capitalism, Marxism, and Anarchism, page 226*
　　44. There should be no authority.

❑ *New Imperialism, page 227*
　　45. Africa

Other Social Science Topics

❑ *Anthropology, page 227*
　　1. the evolution of primates including humans
　　2. material aspects of life—food, energy, and technology

❑ *Government and Political Science, page 228*
　　3. The executive branch is subordinate to the legislative branch.

❑ *United States Government, page 228*
　　4. 100 percent
　　5. There is no set percent. Presidents are not elected by popular vote.

HISTORY, HUMANITIES, AND SOCIAL SCIENCE REVIEW

There is a lot of information here. Don't try to memorize it.

UNITED STATES HISTORY AND HUMANITIES

NATIVE AMERICAN CIVILIZATIONS

Immigration

Current scholarship indicates that Native Americans, "Indians," came to this continent about 30,000 years ago. They passed over a land bridge near what is now the Bering Strait between Siberia and Alaska. These Native Americans eventually spread throughout all of North, Central, and South America.

Primitive Cultures

Even with a glacier covering Alaska, the Aleuts had established a culture on the Aleutian islands off southern Alaska by 5000 B.C. This hunting/fishing society has retained much of its ancient character.

Primitive northern woodland cultures developed in the northeastern United States about 3000 B.C. These cultures included the Algonquin-speaking tribes, such as the Shawnee, and the Iroquois Federation. There is evidence that northern woodland Indians may have been exposed to outside contact hundred of years before the arrival of Columbus.

Also at about 3000 B.C., civilizations developed in southeast North America, in and around what is now Florida and Georgia. These sophisticated cultures built cities with central plazas. The tribes of this area included the Cherokee, Choctaw, and Seminole. These tribes had highly organized governments and economic systems.

Once glaciers melted in the area, the Eskimo and Inuit Indians established a culture in northern Alaska about 1800 B.C. Their use of igloos, kayaks, and dogsleds in harsh conditions was a remarkable adaptation to their environment.

Recent Cultures

In the Southwest United States the Anasazi (Pueblo) culture developed by about 500 A.D. Pueblo and Hopi Indians built walled towns, some on the sides of inaccessible mountains or on mesas.

Around 600 A.D. a mound-building culture developed from the Mississippi River into Ohio. This culture probably built a town with a population of over 30,000 on the east side of the Mississippi River near St. Louis.

Starting about 750 A.D., a nomadic culture was established on the great plains of the United States. These Native American nomads lived in tepees as they followed and hunted herds of bison. These are probably the most popularized of Native Americans. Original tribes of this area include the Blackfoot.

Around 1400 A.D., Native Americans who became the Navajos and the Apaches migrated from Canada to the southwestern United States.

Other western tribes included the Ute and Shoshone. The Nez Pierce and Walla Walla tribes inhabited the northwestern United States. Each had advanced agricultural and cultural traditions.

By 1500 advanced Native American cultures existed across North America. However, these cultures did not rival the Aztec, Inca, and Mayan cultures of Central and South America. They were nonetheless sophisticated, organized cultures that lacked only the technological developments of Europe and Asia.

EUROPEAN EXPLORATION AND COLONIZATION

Visitors Before Columbus

A number of groups visited what is now the United States before Columbus sailed. Whether by accident or design, sailors from Iceland, Europe, and Africa came to this continent before 1000 A.D. It appears that Celtic and Norse settlements were established in North America between 1000 and 1300 A.D. These settlements were not maintained.

Columbus

Notoriety greeted Columbus as he returned to Spain from the first of his four voyages. Columbus never reached the mainland of North America, but he landed throughout the Caribbean and established a settlement in what is now the Dominican Republic.

English Colonization

John Cabot reached the mainland in 1497 and claimed the land for England. In 1584 Sir Walter Raleigh established the "lost colony" on Roanoke Island just off the North Carolina coast. The settlement failed when all the settlers disappeared, leaving a cryptic message carved in a tree.

In 1607 the English established Jamestown, Virginia, under John Smith. Tobacco exports sustained the colony, and slaves from Africa were brought to Jamestown in 1619. In that same year, the House of Burgesses was formed as the first elected governing body in America.

In 1620 Pilgrims left England on the Mayflower to escape religious persecution. The Pilgrims established a colony at Provincetown and then a second colony at Plymouth in December 1620. The Pilgrims drafted and received popular approval for the Mayflower Compact as a way of governing their colony.

Spanish Exploration

Cortez conquered Mexico around 1520, and Pizarro conquered Peru around 1530. The Spaniards imported slaves from Africa at this time. Records of the native civilizations were destroyed, and natives were forced to convert to Catholicism. The Spanish also imported diseases, which effectively wiped out whole populations of natives. In North America the Spanish established a fort in St. Augustine, Florida, around 1565 and in Santa Fe, New Mexico, around 1610.

Other Explorers

In the 1500s the French through Cartier explored the Great Lakes. The French city of Quebec was founded about 1609.

Henry Hudson, under Dutch contract, explored the East Coast and the Hudson River in the 1600s. The Dutch established settlements under Peter Minuit in Manhattan about 1624. The Dutch built the first road for wheeled vehicles in America around 1650.

Colonies in the 1700s

By 1740 there were 13 English colonies, all located along the eastern seaboard. These colonies grew in size and prosperity and developed diversified populations by the time of the Revolutionary War. The colonists were in an almost constant state of conflict with Native Americans, with Spanish colonists, and with the French in the French and Indian wars.

THE AMERICAN REVOLUTION AND THE FOUNDING OF AMERICA

Road to the Revolutionary War

This chronology details the causes up to the Revolutionary War. Note how cumulative the causes are and how a change in English policy might have averted the conflict.

1763 Proclamation of 1763

After the English won the French and Indian War they signed the Proclamation of 1763, which forbade colonial expansion west of the current colonies. The proclamation was designed to avoid unnecessary expenditures and to appease France. It angered many colonists.

1764 Sugar Act

The English government was in serious financial debt after the French and Indian War. The English government levied a sugar tax on the colonies to help pay for the war. Colonists protested this tax saying it was "taxation without representation."

1765

In 1765 England passed a law called the Quartering Act. The act required colonial governments to pay for quarters and supplies for English troops and to quarter these troops in barracks and inns and taverns.

The Stamp Act required every legal piece of paper (college degrees, policies, licenses, etc.) to carry a tax stamp. The act was protested vehemently and eventually repealed by England.

These acts led to many colonial reactions. Patrick Henry spoke against the acts in the Virginia House of Burgesses. Revolutionary groups called Sons of Liberty were formed.

1767 Townsend Acts

The Townsend Acts were import duties on most things used by colonists. Colonists objected, and some tax officials in Boston were attacked. British troops were sent to Boston. Three years later, the British repealed all the Townsend duties except for the duties on tea!

1770 Boston Massacre

British troops fired on colonial protesters, killing five including Crispus Attucks in the Boston Massacre. The English soldiers were defended by patriots including John Adams. Other tensions continued for the next three years.

1773 Boston Tea Party

To protest the remaining import tax on tea, men dressed as Indians boarded English ships in Boston Harbor. They dumped hundreds of chests of tea into Boston Harbor in what has come to be known as the Boston Tea Party. In retaliation Britain closed Boston Harbor and took more direct control of the colony.

1774 First Continental Congress

In September, representatives from each colony except Georgia met at the First Continental Congress in Philadelphia. The congress called on the colonies to boycott goods from England until the English repealed the tax on tea and opened Boston Harbor. Massachusetts minutemen armed themselves and were declared in rebellion by Parliament.

War's Beginnings

1775

On April 18, 1775, English General Gage left Boston to commandeer arms at Concord. Revere and Dawes rode out to alert the minutemen. The English troops first encountered minutemen in Lexington. The first shot was fired, but no one knows by whom. There were American and English dead. British troops destroyed supplies at Concord but were decimated by minuteman attacks on the march back to Boston. Hostilities had begun.

The Second Continental Congress named George Washington commander-in-chief. The Congress asked England for negotiations but was rebuked.

Gage attacked colonists on the top of Breeds Hill (Bunker Hill because of the bunker on top). The British won the battle but at a tremendous loss, establishing the fighting ability of colonial forces.

1776

In this year Thomas Paine wrote his pamphlet *Common Sense*, which favored American independence. On July 4, 1776, the Continental Congress approved the Declaration of Independence authored by Jefferson.

The Declaration included four self-evident truths:

1. Equality of all persons.
2. Inalienable rights of life, liberty, and the pursuit of happiness.
3. Rights of the government come from the governed.
4. The right of the people to alter or abolish a destructive government.

Revolutionary War

1775

The battles of Bunker Hill and Concord and Lexington took place in 1775. Fighting also broke out in Virginia.

1776

In March, Washington laid siege to Boston. The British sent forces to New York. Washington failed in his attempt to drive the British out of New York and withdrew across New Jersey to Pennsylvania. Washington led a successful surprise attack against the British in Trenton, New Jersey, in December.

1777

In January, Washington followed up his Trenton victory with a successful attack at Princeton. Washington spent the remainder of the winter in camp at Morristown, New Jersey. The British, under Howe, attacked and occupied the American capital at Philadelphia. The fighting delayed Howe's planned move to Saratoga, New York. This action enabled American militia under Gates to defeat British troops from Canada at Saratoga.

The American victory at Saratoga and the British occupation of Philadelphia moved the French to recognize America. The French joined the war as allies in 1778. This action by France was the decisive moment in the Revolutionary War. Washington's forces spent the winter in Valley Forge, Pennsylvania.

1778

American forces suffered through a harsh winter in Valley Forge, while British forces were much better accommodated in New York and Philadelphia. The forces from Philadelphia marched to New York under the new British general, Clinton. They narrowly avoided defeat at the Battle of Monmouth in June. Late that year, British forces conquered Georgia.

1779

Fighting took place primarily around the British main headquarters in New York. Late in the year Clinton took the British army south.

1780

When Clinton captured Charleston, South Carolina, Cornwallis took over the southern army, while Clinton returned to New York. Cornwallis defeated American forces under Gates. Things were looking bleak for American forces, and American General Benedict Arnold became a traitor.

Then American forces under George Rogers Clark won a battle in the northwest while frontiersmen defeated Cornwallis in North Carolina.

1781

Cornwallis was beset by American guerrillas including Francis Marion, the swamp fox. Cornwallis moved into Virginia and maneuvered himself into a trap at Yorktown. Surrounded by American forces on the land and the French fleet in Chesapeake Bay, Cornwallis surrendered on October 17, 1781.

1782–1783

England decided to withdraw from the colonies. In 1783 Britain and the United States signed the Treaty of Paris, which gave the United States lands east of the Mississippi.

GROWTH OF THE NEW REPUBLIC

The New Nation

In 1781 the Articles of Confederation, drawn up in 1777, were approved. The Land Ordinance of 1785 established surveys of the Northwest Territories. (These territories became states such as Ohio and Illinois.) The Northwest Ordinance detailed the way in which states would be carved out of these territories.

The Articles of Confederation proved too weak and a Constitutional Convention convened during 1787 in Philadelphia. A compromise Constitution was written with special efforts by James Madison. The Constitution was sent to Congress, which approved it and in turn submitted it to the states for ratification.

The state ratification process fostered a brisk debate. Alexander Hamilton, John Jay, and James Madison authored *The Federalist Papers* to support ratification. Anti-Federalists were concerned that the Constitution did not sufficiently protect individual rights.

Delaware was the first state to ratify the Constitution in 1787 and Rhode Island was the last to ratify in 1790. Many of the ratification votes were very close. Strict versus loose construction of the Constitution has been a contentious issue since its ratification.

First Constitutional Government

New York was chosen as the temporary capital. Once the required nine states had ratified the Constitution, George Washington was sworn in as the first president on April 30, 1789. John Adams was sworn in as vice president.

The concern of the Anti-Federalists was partially answered in 1791 when the first ten amendments to the Constitution were ratified. A summary of the Bill of Rights follows.

I. Freedom of religion, speech, press, assembly, and petition
II. Right to bear arms
III. No troops can be quartered in homes without permission
IV. Warrants and probable cause needed for search and seizure
V. Rights of the accused are assured
VI. Right to a speedy public trial and the right to a lawyer
VII. Right to a jury trial
VIII. Excessive bail, excessive fines, and cruel and unusual punishment are forbidden
IX. Rights not spelled out are retained by the people
X. Powers not specifically federal are retained by the states.

The issue of a stronger versus a weaker central government was an active debate then as it is now. Washington was elected without opposition for his second term, the differences between Jeffersonians (less government, Democrat-Republicans) and Hamiltonians (more government, Federalists) led to a two party system.

In 1796 Washington bade farewell as president with three gems of advice for the country:

1. Avoid political parties based on geographic boundaries.
2. Avoid permanent alliances with foreign powers.
3. Safeguard the ability of America to pay its national debts.

Adams to Madison

In the 1796 presidential election, John Adams eked out a victory over Jefferson. In the controversial XYZ affair, France sought bribes from America. Concern about France led to the Alien and Sedition Acts. These acts put pressure on noncitizens and forbade writing that criticized the government.

Some western states opposed these acts and wanted to nullify the acts for their state. This Theory of Nullification, and the states' rights mentioned in the tenth amendment to the Constitution, raised issues still important today.

In 1800 Aaron Burr and Jefferson were tied for the presidency. Alexander Hamilton supported Jefferson. Jefferson won the vote in Congress and served a second term. Four years later, Burr killed Hamilton in a duel.

Jefferson resisted the demands of Barbary pirates for tribute. In 1801 Tripoli declared war on the United States, and Jefferson successfully blockaded the Tripoli coast. Tribute continued to be paid to other Barbary states.

Jefferson also purchased the Louisiana Territory from France, doubling the size of the country. In 1804 Jefferson sent Lewis and Clark to explore the territory and open it for settlement.

Madison was elected president in 1808 and again in 1812. For a number of years, British ships had been impressing American sailors at sea. In response to this practice, the war hawks pressed for war with Britain in 1811.

War of 1812

The War of 1812 began with a failed American invasion of Canada. The U.S.S. *Constitution* (Old Ironsides) and "Don't Give Up the Ship" Admiral Perry were active in this conflict. The British sacked and burned Washington and unsuccessfully attacked Fort McHenry. Francis Scott Key wrote "The Star Spangled Banner" while a prisoner on a British ship off Fort McHenry. After the war had been declared officially over, Andrew Jackson fought and defeated the British at the Battle of New Orleans.

Federalists had opposed the war and ceased to exist as a viable political party. In the wake of the Federalist collapse, Monroe was elected president in 1816 and again in 1820. In treaties with Spain and England, under the leadership of John Quincy Adams, the United States established borders with Canada, acquired Florida from Spain, and gave up any claims to Texas.

1830–1850

Missouri Compromise
The Missouri Compromise of 1820 was a response to rapid westward expansion and the slavery issue. It admitted Maine as a free state and Missouri as a slave state and excluded slavery in the northern part of the Louisiana Purchase. The compromise maintained the balance of free and slave states.

Monroe
James Monroe and John Quincy Adams established the Monroe Doctrine in 1823. The doctrine said: (1) the Americas were off limits for further colonization, (2) the political system in the United States was different from Europe, (3) the United States would see danger if European states meddled in the United States, and (4) the United States would not interfere in the internal affairs of other states or their established colonies.

Jackson

In 1824 Andrew Jackson entered the electoral college with a plurality of votes. He still lost in the House of Representatives to J.Q. Adams.

In 1828 Jackson was elected president. In this year, people voted directly for electors in all but 2 of 24 states. Jackson used a "kitchen cabinet" of friends to advise him on important issues. Jackson favored the removal of Native Americans to reservations and ignored Supreme Court decisions in favor of the Native Americans. This "trail of tears" is an uncomfortable American story. The age of Jackson marks a time of increased democracy in the United States.

Van Buren

Martin Van Buren was elected president in 1836. On the heels of the financial panic of 1837, Van Buren lost the presidency to William Harrison in 1840. Harrison died less than a month after his inauguration. John Tyler, the vice president, succeeded to the presidency.

Polk

James K. Polk was elected president in 1844. There had been conflict in Texas since 1836. Despite a loss at the Alamo, Texas became a sovereign country. After years of debate and in-fighting, Polk was able to get congressional approval, and Texas was admitted as a slave state in 1844.

Mexican-American War

Mexico objected, and the Mexican-American War started in 1846. U.S. generals, including Robert E. Lee, advanced into Mexico and captured Mexico City. The Treaty of Guadeloupe Hidalgo ended the war, and the United States acquired Texas south to the Rio Grande as well as the California and New Mexico Territories. Much of the manifest destiny of the United States to stretch from sea to sea had been achieved under Polk.

Taylor

Zachary Taylor, a general in the Mexican-American War, was elected president in 1848. Slavery remained a significant and contentious issue. In 1849 gold was discovered near Sutters Mill in California. The gold rush brought thousands of prospectors and settlers to California.

The Compromise of 1850 specified whether territories would be granted statehood as a free or slave state and contained a strict fugitive slave law. *Uncle Tom's Cabin* by Harriet Beecher Stowe was published in 1852.

Movements and Accomplishments 1800–1850

Horace Mann and others established public schools and training schools for teachers. The women's movement, featuring an 1848 meeting in Seneca Falls, New York, did not achieve much success. Abolitionists were active. The Underground Railroad helped slaves escape to the North. The temperance movement reduced the consumption of alcohol. Transcendentalist writers, who believed in the sanctity and importance of individual experience, were active during this period. These writers included James Fenimore Cooper, Ralph Waldo Emerson, Henry David Thoreau, and Herman Melville.

Large groups of non-English, Catholic immigrants arrived in New York. In the 1840s there was regular steamship travel between Liverpool, England, and New York City.

THE CIVIL WAR AND RECONSTRUCTION: CAUSES AND CONSEQUENCES

Road to Civil War

Pierce

Franklin Pierce was elected president in 1852. There was bloody warfare in Kansas over whether Kansas should enter the union as a free or slave state. Another significant event was Commodore Perry's visit to Japan, opening Japan to the West.

Buchanan

James Buchanan was elected president in 1856. In 1857 the Supreme Court decided the *Dred Scott* case. They found that Dred Scott, a slave, was property, not a citizen, and had no standing in the court.

John Brown

In 1859 an erratic John Brown launched an ill-prepared raid on the arsenal in Harpers Ferry, Virginia. Brown was tried, executed, and became a martyr in the abolitionist movement.

Lincoln

In 1860, and again in 1864, Abraham Lincoln was elected president. Southern states sought assurances about their right to hold slaves. Slaves were too important to the southern economy, and attempts at compromise failed. South Carolina seceded in December 1860. Alabama, Georgia, Florida, Louisiana, Mississippi, and Texas soon followed. In February 1861 the Confederate States of America (CSA) was formed with Jefferson Davis as its president.

Civil War

On April 12, 1861, Confederate forces attacked Fort Sumter in South Carolina. Arkansas, North Carolina, Tennessee, and Virginia seceded once hostilities began.

The war pitted brother against brother, and one in every 30 Americans was killed or wounded. The North had a larger population and an industrialized economy. The South had an agrarian economy.

Neither the English nor the French (who tried to conquer Mexico) supported the South. The English did build some Confederate ships.

While Northern troops performed poorly in initial battles, the North was too strong and too populous for the South. Lee's generalship during the early war years sustained the South.

Monitor *and* Merrimack

Northern ships blockaded Southern ports. This blockade effectively denied foreign goods to the South. The Confederate ironclad *Monitor* sailed out to challenge blockading ships in 1862, sinking several Union ships. The *Monitor* was challenged and repulsed by the Union ironclad *Merrimack* in March 1862.

Emancipation Proclamation

In 1862 Lincoln issued the Emancipation Proclamation. The proclamation freed all the slaves in Confederate states.

Sherman's March

The Union launched a successful attack on the South through Tennessee. New Orleans was captured in 1862. A final wedge was driven through the South with the capture of Vicksburg,

Mississippi, in 1863. Atlanta fell in 1864. Sherman then launched his infamous march to the sea, which cut a 20-mile wide swath of destruction through the South. Sherman reached the Gulf of Mexico in December 1864.

Gettysburg

Confederate forces did much better in and around Virginia, and there were draft riots in New York City during 1863. Lee brilliantly led his army and invaded Pennsylvania in 1863. The advance ended with Lee's questionable decision to launch Pickett's charge against the massed Union forces at Gettysburg.

Four months after the battle, Lincoln delivered the Gettysburg Address at the dedication of the Union Cemetery near Gettysburg. The brief transcendent address ends "...government of the people, by the people, for the people shall not perish from the earth."

War's End

In 1864 Grant took command of the Union Army of the Potomac. He waged a war of attrition against Lee. Richmond fell on April 2, 1865. On April 9, 1865, Lee surrendered at Appomattox Court House, Virginia.

Lincoln was assassinated five days later on April 15, 1865.

Homestead Act

In 1862 the Homestead Act made public lands available to Western settlers. Public lands were granted to the Union Pacific and Central Pacific companies to build rail lines from Omaha to California. After the war, farmers and settlers moved west.

Reconstruction

Three civil rights amendments were adopted between 1865 and 1870.

> XIII. Prohibited slavery (1865)
> XIV. Slaves given citizenship and rights (1868)
> XV. Voting rights for former slaves (1870)

Johnson

Andrew Johnson became president after Lincoln was assassinated. During his administration, William Seward acquired Alaska (Seward's Folly) and occupied Midway Island. Johnson's dismissal of Secretary of War Stanton led to Johnson's impeachment (legislative indictment). Johnson survived the impeachment ballot by one vote.

Southern states slowly returned to the Union, but troops stayed in the South until 1877. During Reconstruction, former slaves gained some power in the South. This power did not last beyond 1877. Carpetbaggers from the North collaborated with white scalawags and former slaves to keep Confederates out of power. In turn, the Black Codes and the KKK emerged as ways to subjugate and terrorize former slaves. Grandfather clauses, which stated that you couldn't vote if your grandfather didn't, were used to deny former slaves the vote.

Grant

In 1868 and again in 1872, Ulysses S. Grant was elected president. Corruption was widespread in Grant's government. The "Whiskey Ring" involved members of Grant's administration in fraud. Boss Tweed and the Tweed Ring were looting the New York City treasury.

The Indian Wars continued. In 1876 Sioux chiefs Sitting Bull and Crazy Horse defeated Custer and his cavalry at the Little Big Horn River in Montana.

INDUSTRIALIZATION OF AMERICA
1877–1897

Individual presidents in the late 1800s were not notable, and this was the era of caretaker presidents. The highlights of this era were the growth of business, economic conditions, and other national events and issues. The presidents in this period were:

Rutherford B. Hayes	1876	Wins a close disputed election
James A. Garfield	1880	Shot and killed in 1881
Chester Arthur	1881	Succeeds Garfield
Grover Cleveland	1884, 1892	
William Henry Harrison	1888	
William McKinley	1896, 1900	Shot and killed in 1901

In 1877 Hayes directed the removal of troops from the South and southern whites reestablished their control over the South. Reconstruction was over.

Indian Wars

During this period most of the Indian Wars were concluded. Until now the government moved Indians onto reserved areas (reservations). But in 1887, under the Dawes Severalty Act, the federal government tried to move Indians from reservations into society. The act failed, and Indians continued to be treated poorly.

Railroads

The unfenced frontier, which had produced most of American western folklore, was shrinking. By 1890 railroads, settlers, and farmers had brought it to a final end.

The railroads brought other changes to American life. Chinese immigrants who came to work on the railroads were banned from immigration by 1890. Huge herds of buffalo were killed so that they could not interfere with train travel. Railroads stimulated the economy and created a unified United States.

Business and Commerce

Inventions during this period included the telephone (Alexander Graham Bell) and the light bulb (Thomas Alva Edison).

But it was business and profits that ruled the time. John D. Rockefeller formed the Standard Oil Trust. A trust could control many companies and monopolize business. Business owners cut wages and hired new workers if there was a strike. Social Darwinism, popular during this time, stressed the survival of the fittest. Trusts grew so rapidly that the Sherman Anti-Trust Act was passed in 1890. Any trust "in restraint of trade" was illegal.

Sewing machines and typewriters drew many women to the workforce. Clara Barton founded the Red Cross in 1881.

Unions
Unions tried to respond. In 1878 the Knights of Labor started to organize workers successfully. The union collapsed after the Chicago Haymarket Riot in 1888. The American Federation of Labor, under Samuel Gompers, successfully organized workers in 1886.

The government intervened in several strike situations. In 1894 Grover Cleveland used troops to break the Pullman Strike. In 1902 Teddy Roosevelt sided with coal miners in the Anthracite Coal Strike.

Another issue was hard versus cheap money. Hard money meant that currency was linked to something valuable (gold), limiting inflation. Cheap money removes the linkage, hastening inflation.

Immigration
Immigration increased dramatically after 1880. The new immigrants to the United States now came from eastern and southern Europe. Many immigrants settled in urban areas in the eastern United States. Living conditions were difficult in tenements. Urban gangs and crime were common during this period.

Literature
Horatio Alger's rags to riches stories were very popular. Mark Twain (Samuel Clemens) wrote *The Adventures of Tom Sawyer* (1876) and *The Adventures of Huckleberry Finn* (1884). Joseph Pulitzer (Pulitzer Prize) introduced a yellow comic page in his newspaper. "Yellow journalism" came to mean sensationalized journalism.

Temperance
The temperance movement was making steady progress to prohibition (enacted in 1919). Carrie Nation was famous for smashing liquor bottles with a hatchet. Elizabeth Cady Stanton and Susan B. Anthony led the women's suffrage movement. (Suffrage for women came with the Nineteenth Amendment in 1920, nearly 125 years after the U.S. Constitution was adopted.)

Spanish-American War

During Spanish suppression of a Cuban revolt in 1898, the battleship *Maine* was sunk in Havana Harbor. Popular reaction led to the Spanish-American War in Cuba and the Philippines. The war lasted eight months with most casualties coming from disease. The treaty ending the war gave the United States Puerto Rico, Guam, and the Philippines. In unrelated actions, the United States also annexed Wake Island and Hawaii.

1900–1916

Teddy Roosevelt
In 1901 Teddy Roosevelt succeeded McKinley. Roosevelt was re-elected in 1904. Roosevelt was a progressive opposed to monopolies. Roosevelt was particularly moved by the novel *The Jungle* (Upton Sinclair), which exposed abuses in the meat-packing industry. Roosevelt championed conservation. Roosevelt used "big stick diplomacy," and the United States started to become policeman of the world. Roosevelt earned the Nobel Peace Prize for arranging a cessation to the Russo-Japanese War.

Taft
William Howard Taft was elected president in 1908. Taft continued Roosevelt's campaign against monopolies and established the Bureau of Mines. Some of Taft's policies on conservation offended Teddy Roosevelt. Roosevelt established the Bull Moose Party for the 1912 election.

Wilson

In 1912 Woodrow Wilson was elected president with about 40 percent of the vote in a three way race with Roosevelt and Taft. Wilson was a scholarly man who hated war. Wilson established the Federal Reserve Banking System in 1913. His Federal Trade Commission Act helped unions and forbade monopolies. The Mexican Revolution in 1910 led to the U.S. army's pursuit of Pancho Villa in Mexico in 1916.

WORLD WAR I: CAUSES AND CONSEQUENCES

War Begins

Europe was ripe for war. The balance of power had been destroyed, and Germany had a military advantage. There was tremendous tension in and around the Slavic, Balkan area of southeastern Europe that was controlled by the German Austro-Hungarian Empire.

Then a single act occurred. Archduke Ferdinand of Austria was assassinated on June 28, 1914. The unrest that followed led to Germany declaring war on Russia on August 1, 1914. Woodrow Wilson declared U.S. neutrality. By 1915 the Central powers of Germany, Austria-Hungary, Bulgaria, and Turkey were at war with the Allies of England, France, Japan, and Russia. (The United States joined the Allies in 1917.)

So began the war that was to claim over 12,000,000 lives and decimate Europe. The war consisted of two fronts—Western (France, etc.) and Eastern (Russia, etc.). The war soon deteriorated into trench warfare, which led to a virtual stalemate for four destructive years. Airplanes, tanks, poison gas, and machine guns were all introduced during this conflict.

The Russian Revolution occurred in 1917 as World War I was underway. The Bolsheviks gained power. As they had promised, the Bolsheviks withdrew from the war, even though Russia gave up over 1,000,000 square miles of land with over 50,000,000 people in the peace settlement.

American Involvement

The sinking of the cruise liner *Lusitania* in 1915 with 139 Americans on board marked the beginning of American involvement in the war. Wilson was outraged when Germany started to use submarines and protested when the *Lusitania* was sunk. The Germans agreed to stop unrestricted submarine warfare. In 1917 the Germans resumed unrestricted submarine warfare, and the United States declared war on Germany. The American Expeditionary Force (AEF) arrived in France on June 25, 1917. The Allies fought back German attacks and launched their own offensive in 1918. Germany signed a very demanding armistice, and the war ended on the eleventh hour of the eleventh day of the eleventh month in 1918.

The Germans were forced to sign the Treaty of Versailles on June 28, 1919, which officially ended World War I. Japan and Italy (Allies) were not pleased with some of the terms of the Treaty of Versailles.

League of Nations

As the war was drawing to a close, Wilson presented his Fourteen Points. These points form a basis for the Treaty of Versailles, which ended the war, and for the League of Nations. The league was formed in 1919 and lasted until the 1940s. The forerunner of the United Nations was built on President Wilson's Fourteen Points. The United States' seat was never filled because the Senate did not ratify the Treaty of Versailles. The League of Nations sought to provide mechanisms for worldwide monetary control, conflict resolution, and humanitarian assistance.

POST-WORLD WAR I AMERICA

Prohibition

Warren G. Harding was elected president in 1920. Calvin Coolidge became president in 1923 when Harding died. Coolidge was elected in 1924. Herbert Hoover was elected president in 1928.

Prohibition dominated this period, and America entered the roaring twenties. Speakeasys had liquor for those who wanted in, and distilling became a huge underground industry. Gangsters such as Al Capone were prominent on the American scene.

Sigmund Freud's views of sexuality had become well known, and the country entered the sexual revolution. In the "Monkey Trial," John Scopes was tried and convicted of teaching evolution in a Tennessee school.

Depression

In October 1929 the stock market crashed. People lost their investments and often their homes. Banks failed, and people lost their deposits. Excessive borrowing, greed, and ineffective regulations were all factors in the collapse. The Depression began and spread throughout the world.

During the Depression, unemployment reached 25 percent. Some workers had no employment for years. Hoover took an ineffective hands-off approach. He did support the Reconstruction Finance Corporation, which lent money to employers in the hope that it would "trickle down" to the unemployed.

Franklin Delano Roosevelt

In 1932 Franklin Delano Roosevelt (FDR) was elected president in a landslide victory. He was reelected in 1936, 1940, and 1944. Roosevelt's Democratic Party enjoyed an enormous margin in the Congress during this time.

FDR offered the country a New Deal. He said, "the only thing we have to fear is fear itself," and held radio fireside chats that reassured the country. A summary of the New Deal actions follow in a sort of governmental alphabet soup.

- The Civilian Conservation Corps (CCC) put unemployed young men to work building roads, stopping erosion, and reforesting the country.

- The Works Project Administration (WPA) gave other public service jobs.

- The Agricultural Adjustment Act provided subsidies to farmers for not growing crops.

- The Federal Deposit Insurance Company (FDIC) insured bank deposits.

- The Securities and Exchange Commission (SEC) oversaw the stock market.

- The Tennessee Valley Authority (TVA) built hydroelectric plants and controlled floods.

The Second New Deal started in 1934 and included the following acts.

- The Social Security Act gave unemployment insurance and other humanitarian relief.

- The National Labor Relations Board (Wagner Act) gave the right of collective bargaining.

- The Fair Labor Standards Act set a minimum wage.

WORLD WAR II: CAUSES AND CONSEQUENCES
Road to World War II

Germany and Hitler

The Depression of the late 1920s ruined the German economy. Imports and exports fell while unemployment soared. Germany was also frustrated by what they saw as the harsh Treaty of Versailles.

Out of all this emerged Adolf Hitler, a would-be artist who had emerged from World War I as a decorated corporal. In 1920 he had founded the Nazi Party and put together a group of "brown shirts" to exert his will forcefully. With 50,000 or so followers he tried to take power in 1923 in the Beer Hall Putsch. He was arrested and jailed, where he dictated *Mein Kampf* to Rudolf Hess.

Between 1930 and 1932 Hitler's Nazi Party got increasing vote counts. Hitler was made Chancellor, and then his party gained control of the legislature. In 1933 all political parties were outlawed except the Nazi Party. In that same year the Gestapo was established, and Hitler became Fuhrer on August 2, 1934.

Anti-Semitism

Anti-Semitism was rampant in Germany, and Jews were declined civil service employment. The regime became a harsh dictatorship in which no dissent was tolerated. However, economic conditions improved dramatically under Hitler, and military manufacturing just about erased unemployment. Hitler was supported by the German people, and the world was moving toward war.

Spanish Civil War

The United States proclaimed neutrality in 1935, 1936, and 1937. No belligerents were permitted to purchase arms from America. The United States also stayed neutral in the Spanish Civil War.

The Spanish Civil War (1936–1939) provided a testing ground for Hitler and his military leaders. The German Air Force fought on the side of the Fascist leader Franco, and the war united Hitler and the Italian dictator Mussolini. In 1938 Hitler bullied and then captured Austria, and later annexed Czechoslovakia.

Japan

The Depression also caused great economic hardship in Japan, and military leaders gained more power. In 1931 Japan occupied Manchuria, and in 1937 war broke out between Japan and China. In 1938 Japan announced its intentions to establish a new order in Asia. In 1940 Japan signed a formal alliance with Germany and Italy.

World War II

On September 1, 1939, Hitler invaded Poland without provocation. England and France declared war on Germany a few days later, and World War II began.

World War II began with the Soviet Union on the sidelines. In fact, the Soviets used this time to occupy Estonia, Latvia, and Lithuania and to force concessions from Finland. The Allies included England, France, and eventually the United States. The Axis powers included Germany, Japan, and Italy.

German forces launched a major offensive against Belgium, France, and the Netherlands and attacked Denmark and Norway. The Germans by-passed the fortified Maginot line armament by attacking through Luxembourg. About 400,000 British and French troops were trapped but managed to escape without their equipment from around Dunkirk.

Germany tried to conquer Britain from the air in the Battle of Britain. While devastating, this tactic was unsuccessful. The Germans considered and then abandoned a plan to invade England.

Churchill

Just before this time, British Prime Minister Chamberlain was replaced by Winston Churchill. Churchill had long warned of German intentions. Once the war began, the United States began to cooperate with England. The Lend-Lease Act of 1941 allowed the president to sell, lend, or transfer arms to countries vital to American defense. Roosevelt used this act to aid England.

France

Paris fell in June 1940, and France surrendered. The Vichy government of France followed a policy of collaboration. Only a few Frenchmen joined the Free French movement led by Charles DeGaulle from London.

United States

In 1940 Charles Lindbergh, the first person to fly solo across the Atlantic (1927), supported Hitler's call for an expanded Germany. Roosevelt said the United States would not enter the war, and he was re-elected.

In 1941 Roosevelt met with Churchill off Newfoundland and signed the Atlantic Charter. The charter's postwar goals roughly incorporated Roosevelt's Four Freedoms: Freedom of Speech and Expression; Freedom of Religion; Freedom from Want; Freedom from Fear.

Second Front

Hitler turned his attention to Russia in June, 1941. He began Operation Barbarosa, an invasion of Russia with 3,000,000 Axis troops. The invasion was initially successful, and Axis troops actually entered the suburbs of Moscow in November 1941. A combination of the Russian winter, very long supply lines, and a Russian counterattack drove the Axis forces away from Moscow during the winter of 1941–1942.

The German army attacked Russia again and was stopped literally in the streets of Stalingrad. Hitler forbade a retreat, and German forces were surrounded and decimated. The German forces at Stalingrad surrendered in January 1943, and the Russians moved to the offensive.

Pearl Harbor

On December 7, 1941, Japan attacked the United States at Pearl Harbor. The attack brought the United States into war against Japan, Germany, and Italy. American involvement in the war ultimately led to the defeat of Axis forces.

North Africa

The Italians and the Afrika Corps under German General Rommel controlled North Africa. Combined British and American forces launched a combined offensive that trapped Axis forces and led to their surrender in 1943.

Battle of the Atlantic

During the early years of the war, German U-boats were winning the Battle of the Atlantic. Adequate supplies could not reach England and Europe. Improved ships, planes, and sonar reversed this trend, and by 1943 the Atlantic was an unsafe place for German submarines.

Invasion

In January 1943 Churchill and Roosevelt met at Casablanca and planned the future conduct of the war. On June 6, 1944, after the successful invasion of Italy, the Allied forces under Dwight

Eisenhower launched Operation Overlord, an invasion of France from England. It was the largest amphibious operation ever undertaken. The invasion was successful and by the end of 1944 all France had been recaptured and Allied forces were poised at German borders. Soviet forces had also been successful in their operations in Poland.

Resistance to Hitler's leadership developed in Germany. On July 20, 1944, Hitler survived a bomb blast designed to kill him. His survival meant that there would be no truce.

American, British, Russian, and other Allied forces attacked Germany simultaneously. Hitler committed suicide in his bunker, and the German army surrendered. Already, American and British leaders were questioning the results of their alliance with Stalin and the Soviet Union.

Yalta

In February 1945, Churchill, Roosevelt, and Stalin met at Yalta and agreements were reached about postwar political subdivisions. Many have criticized Roosevelt's participation in this meeting. In their view, Roosevelt made agreements too favorable to Stalin.

Potsdam

In July 1945 Stalin and Churchill met at Potsdam with newly inaugurated President Truman (Roosevelt had died after the Yalta meeting). While at the conference, Churchill was defeated for prime minister.

The Bomb and VJ Day

Truman learned of the successful test of the atomic bomb (Manhattan Project) while at Potsdam. After deciding that there was no practical way to demonstrate the bomb's force, it was dropped twice on Japan. The cities of Hiroshima and Nagasaki were obliterated. A new era of warfare had begun and the Japanese surrendered immediately. The surrender was taken on the battleship *Missouri* in Tokyo Bay under the leadership of General Douglas MacArthur.

The Home Front

With about 12,000,000 Americans in the armed forces during World War II, unemployment was eliminated. New businesses were created, and many new workers, particularly women, entered the work force. "Rosie the Riveter" became the symbol of these new workers. The Office of Price Administration (OPA) issued ration books and set prices. Other government boards regulated business and labor.

The only documented attack on the United States occurred when a Japanese submarine shelled a refinery in California. However, fear of Japanese Americans reached hysterical proportions. All Japanese Americans, most of them American citizens, were sent to internment camps. None were accused of wrongdoing. They were not released until the end of the war.

POST-WORLD WAR II AMERICA
The Cold War

The Cold War broke out immediately after WW II. Immediate divisions appeared between Russia and the other Allies. Speaking in Fulton, Missouri in 1946, Churchill said that an Iron Curtain had descended across the Continent, describing Soviet isolation from the rest of the world.

Occupation

Germany and Berlin were divided into four Occupation Zones—American, British, French, and Russian. Berlin was inside the Russian zone. The Russians blockaded land access to Berlin, but the blockade was overcome by the Berlin Airlift.

Truman

After succeeding Roosevelt, Harry Truman won an upset victory over New York Governor Thomas Dewey in 1948 and served as president until 1952.

Truman reacted to the Cold War and fear of communism by issuing the Truman Doctrine. The doctrine stipulated that the United States would help any free countries resisting armed minorities. The United States entered a period of Soviet containment designed to counter worldwide Soviet pressure.

At home, Truman used the Smith Act, designed for use against World War II subversives, to jail domestic Communist leaders. A Loyalty Board and the House UnAmerican Activities Committee also investigated Communist infiltration into government.

Marshall Plan

The Marshall Plan helped rebuild Europe with West Germany reaping the greatest benefits. The United Nations was established with a Security Council consisting mainly of Allied countries. Stalin pushed for recovery at home while taking further control of Eastern Europe. Germany remained under Allied occupation.

Israel

The mass killings of Jews in concentration camps during Hitler's regime gained support for a Jewish State in Palestine. In 1948 Israel was established and a series of conflicts with Egypt and other Arab states began.

NATO

Following the Berlin Airlift, the North Atlantic Treaty Organization was formed, which united the European allies in a military alliance. NATO was strengthened in the aftermath of the Korean War. The Cold War between the Western powers and Russia became a nuclear arms race.

Soviet Union

Brooding and paranoid, Stalin died in 1953. Khrushchev and his successors Brezhnev, Andropov, and Gorbachev attacked his ruthlessness and relaxed the political climate. Gradually, countries occupied or controlled by the Soviet Union sought freedom or autonomy. These freedom movements, such as in Hungary, were usually thwarted by a Soviet military reaction.

Later Developments

Britain and Western Europe formed a Common Market designed to create a free trade zone and to stimulate commerce. Soviet Communist influence decreased markedly in the 1980s. Countries occupied by Russia sought and gained freedom. East and West Germany were reunited at a great cost to West Germany. Satellites of Russia, such as Cuba, stopped receiving aid. Provinces of Russia were in revolt and there was open warfare between the Russian President Yeltsin and the Russian parliament. Some have concluded that the Cold War is over and that communism has fallen.

There are still tensions throughout the world, and open warfare raged during the 1990s in what was Yugoslavia, Albania, and African states.

Korean War

The undeclared war in Korea broke out with an invasion by North Korea in 1950. American troops were sent to fight on South Korea's side. Later the defense of South Korea was under United Nation auspices. As UN troops approached the Yalu River border with China, China entered the war and forced UN forces back to the 38th parallel, the original boundary between North and

South Korea. In a notable act of the war, Truman dismissed Douglas MacArthur as Commander-in-Chief of American forces because MacArthur advocated the nuclear bombing of North Korea and mainland China.

Eisenhower

In 1952 Dwight Eisenhower, former Allied supreme commander in Europe, was elected president. He was re-elected in 1956. After his election, Eisenhower went to Korea. Shortly thereafter, an armistice was established at the 38th parallel. Under Secretary of State John Foster Dulles, the United States embarked on a campaign of "brinkmanship." The policy was designed to show American resolve and toughness. In 1957 Congress approved the Eisenhower Doctrine, which gave the president the right to use force against aggressive acts by any country under the control of communism.

Concurrent with the beginning of the Korean War, Senator Joseph McCarthy used the red scare to propel himself to national prominence (McCarthyism). He accused many Americans of anti-American activities, and needlessly ruined many lives. Accusations against the army led to Army-McCarthy hearings and McCarthy's censure by the Congress.

Civil Rights

In 1954 the Supreme Court decided the landmark case of *Brown v. Board of Education*. The Court found that "separate but equal" schools were unconstitutional. In 1955 the Supreme Court ordered an end to school segregation.

In Little Rock, Arkansas, the governor ordered the National Guard to prevent minority students from entering the high school. President Eisenhower sent troops, nationalized the Guard, and the Little Rock nine entered school. In subsequent years, many public schools were closed in the South and replaced by private academies to escape desegregation laws.

In 1955 Dr. Martin Luther King, Jr., led the Montgomery bus boycott. In 1956 the Supreme Court found that segregation on local buses was unconstitutional. Civil disobedience and nonviolent protest were used throughout the South to gain civil rights victories.

Kennedy and Johnson

John F. Kennedy was elected president in 1960. After his assassination in 1963, Lyndon Johnson succeeded him, and Johnson was elected in 1964.

John Kennedy proclaimed the "New Frontier" but was unsuccessful in moving legislation through Congress. He also began the vigorous exploration of space and established the Peace Corps.

Kennedy eventually ordered troops to ensure that James Meredith was enrolled as a student in the University of Alabama. During his term, there were civil rights sit-ins in Birmingham, Alabama, and a civil rights march of 250,000 on Washington, D.C. It was at this march that Dr. King made his "I have a dream" speech.

In 1961 Kennedy supported the Bay of Pigs invasion of Cuba. The invasion was disastrous. Some months later, Soviet missiles were located in Cuba. Kennedy established a blockade of Cuba and entered into a confrontation with Soviet leader Khrushev. Eventually, the missiles were withdrawn, and Cuba maintained its sovereignty.

John Kennedy is the president best known for his assassination. On November 22, 1963, John Kennedy was killed while visiting Dallas, Texas. The Warren Commission was formed to investigate the assassination and found that Lee Harvey Oswald was the lone assassin. Many disagree with this finding.

Lyndon Johnson succeeded Kennedy. Johnson was very effective in getting Kennedy's, and his own, legislative proposals through Congress. He supported a number of laws designed to create the Great Society and to launch a War on Poverty.

The War on Poverty included the Job Corps and Project Head Start, Upward Bound for bright but poor high school students, and VISTA, the domestic version of the Peace Corps.

Other Great Society programs included:

- The Water Quality and Air Quality Acts

- The Elementary and Secondary Education Act

- The National Foundation for Arts and Humanities

- The Omnibus Housing Bill

- Highway Safety Act

- Medicare

- Cabinet-level departments Housing and Urban Development (HUD)

- Transportation

Vietnam War

The Vietnam War stretched across the 12 years of the Kennedy and Johnson presidencies and into the presidency of Richard Nixon. While the war officially began with Kennedy as president, its actual beginnings stretched back many years.

Causes

Before the war, Vietnam was called French Indochina. During World War II the United States supported Ho Chi Minh in Vietnam as he fought Japan. After the war, the United States supported the French over Ho Chi Minh as France sought to regain control of its former colony.

Fighting broke out between the French and Ho Chi Minh with support from Mao Tse-tung, the leader of mainland China. Even with substantial material aid from the United States, France could not defeat Vietnam. In 1950 the French were defeated at Dien Bien Phu.

Subsequent negotiations in Geneva divided Vietnam into North and South with Ho Chi Minh in control of the North. Ngo Dinh Diem was installed by the United States as a leader in the South. Diem never gained popular support in the South. Following a harsh crackdown by Diem, the Viet Cong organized to fight against him. During the Eisenhower administration, 2,000 American "advisors" were sent to South Vietnam.

War Begins

When Kennedy came to office, he approved a CIA coup to overthrow Diem. When Johnson took office, he was not interested in compromise. In 1964 Johnson started a massive buildup of forces in Vietnam until the number reached more than 500,000. The Gulf of Tonkin Resolution, passed by Congress, gave Johnson discretion to pursue the war.

Living and fighting conditions were terrible. Although American forces had many successes, neither that nor the massive bombing of North Vietnam led to victory. In 1968 the Vietcong launched the Tet Offensive. While ground gained in the offensive was ultimately recaptured, the offensive shook the confidence of military leaders.

The war cost 350,000 American casualties. The $175 billion spent on the war could have been used for Great Society programs.

Home Front

At home, there were deep divisions. War protests sprung up all over the United States. Half a million people protested in New York during 1967 and the tension between hawks and doves increased throughout the country.

Nixon

Richard Nixon was elected in 1968 in the midst of this turmoil. While vigorously pursuing the war, he and Secretary of State Henry Kissinger were holding secret negotiations with North Vietnam. In 1973 an agreement was finally drawn up to end the war. American prisoners were repatriated although there were still a number Mission in Action (MIA), and U.S. troops withdrew from Vietnam.

Nixon was elected again in 1972, only to resign on August 8, 1974, during the Watergate investigation. Richard Nixon was the only U.S. president in history to resign. Spiro Agnew, Nixon's vice president, had resigned before him in 1973, and Gerald Ford took Agnew's place as vice president. When Nixon resigned, Ford became president.

The economy deteriorated during Nixon's administration. The expensive Great Society programs and the Vietnam War had increased the federal deficit. The OPEC oil embargo forced inflation up and worsened the economic situation.

Nixon's greatest diplomatic contributions were in China and the Middle East. He opened a dialogue with China and, through Henry Kissinger, arranged a peace settlement to the 1973 Yom Kippur War between Egypt/Syria and Israel.

Watergate

Nixon is best known for the Watergate scandal and his resignation. The resignation was caused initially by an unnecessary break-in by Republican operatives into the Democratic campaign headquarters in the Watergate office complex. Nixon was later taped in his office as he ordered the FBI to call off their Watergate investigation. When the Supreme Court ordered that these tapes be made public, Nixon resigned.

Ford

Gerald Ford was the first American president not elected through the electoral college. Unemployment and interest rates grew dramatically under Ford. Responses to these problems were inadequate, and the country started to enter a recession.

Carter

In 1976 Jimmy Carter was elected president. Carter introduced no major programs. The economy worsened under Carter with interest rates over 21 percent and double-digit inflation. The federal deficit continued to grow, and domestic programs became more expensive.

Reagan

Ronald Reagan was elected president in 1980 and again in 1984. Reagan was a conservative ideologue who believed in supply-side economics. Supply-side theory held that tax cuts would result in more investment, and, in turn, these investments would create more jobs.

Under Reagan, tax rates were cut drastically. The economy emerged from recession, and the interest rates were reduced. However, government revenues did not increase, and the federal deficit sky-rocketed. Homelessness grew to significant proportions and became a major urban problem.

Deregulation of the savings and loans organizations during Reagan's presidency led to abuses with a multibillion dollar bankruptcy of these groups. The cost of the bankruptcies was borne by taxpayers.

Bush

In 1988 George Bush was elected president. Bush continued Reagan's economic programs but was forced to raise taxes in 1990. This reversal of his promise "read my lips, no new taxes" probably led to his defeat in the 1992 election. S & Ls continued to fail, and the national debt continued to grow dramatically. The Communist bloc was disintegrating, and the Cold War was coming to a close.

Clinton

Bill Clinton was elected president in 1992 and again in 1996. He was the first president impeached (legislative indictment) since Andrew Johnson. He was acquitted by the Senate. Health reform, deficit reduction, and crime were three major issues of his administration. Inflation was low and the stock market soared during Clinton's presidency.

WORLD HISTORY AND HUMANITIES

PREHISTORY AND THE DEVELOPMENT OF EARLY CIVILIZATIONS

World Population

World population grew steadily from 1 A.D. through 1650 A.D. After 1650 A.D., world population exploded. Rapid population growth has made it more difficult to provide for everyone. A table showing population growth follows.

1 A.D.	500	1000	1650	1850	1930	1975	1992
200 million	220 million	300 million	500 million	1 billion	2 billion	4 billion	5.7 billion

Early Civilizations

Current knowledge of human history stretches back about 8,000 years to 6000 B.C. The earliest established date is around 4200 B.C. Most historians agree that civilization began when writing was invented about 3500 B.C. This date separates prehistoric from historic times.

In prehistoric time, humans used calendars, invented and used the wheel, played flutes and harps, and alloyed copper. These humans also created pottery and colored ceramics. There was an active trade in the Mediterranean Sea with Cretan shipping most prominent. What follows is a brief summary of historic times.

Mesopotamia (4000–500 B.C.)

The earliest recorded civilizations were in Mesopotamia. This region was centered near the Tigris and Euphrates Rivers in what is now Iraq and extended from the western Mediterranean to Palestine to the Persian Gulf. The Sumerians inhabited Mesopotamia from 4000 B.C. to 2000 B.C. and probably invented the first writing—wedge-shaped symbols called cuneiform.

The Old Babylonians (2000–1550 B.C.) inhabited this area and established a capital at Babylonia (hanging gardens). King Hammurabi, known for the justice code named after him, ruled during the middle of this period. The militaristic Assyrians ruled from 1000 to about 600 B.C. The Assyrians were followed by the New Babylonians under King Nebuchadnezzar from about 600 to 500 B.C. A defeat by the Persians in the fifth century B.C. led to a dissolution of Mesopotamia.

CLASSICAL CIVILIZATIONS

Egypt (5000–30 B.C.)

Egyptian history is usually divided into seven periods. Pharaohs became deities during the Old Kingdom (2685–2180 B.C.). Most pyramids were built during the Fourth Dynasty of the Old Kingdom (about 2600–2500 B.C.) Our common vision of Egyptians in horse-drawn chariots marked the Second Intermediate Period (1785–1560 B.C.). The Egyptians invaded Palestine and enslaved the Jews during the New Kingdom (1560–1085 B.C.). King Tutankhamen reigned during this period. In the first millennium B.C. Egypt was controlled by many groups and leaders, including Alexander the Great. In about 30 B.C., Egypt came under control of the Roman Empire.

Greece

Greece has always been linked to its nearby islands. One of these islands, Crete, was inhabited by the Minoans (about 2600–1250 B.C.). During this time the ancient city of Troy was built. The mainland, inhabited by the Myceneans since about 2000 B.C., eventually incorporated Crete and the Minoan Civilization about 1200 B.C.

Dorian invasions from the north around 1200 B.C. led to the defeat of the Myceneans and the Greek Dark Ages from 1200 to 750 B.C. The Trojan War, which occurred during this period, was described by Homer in the *Iliad*.

Athens (founded 1000 B.C.) and Sparta (founded 750 B.C.) were famous Greek city-states. Draco was a harsh Athenian leader and democracy was established only in 527 B.C. During this period, the Parthenon was built in Athens. In Sparta, each male citizen became a lifetime soldier at the age of 7.

Classic Age

The Classic Age of Greece began about 500 B.C. when Athens defeated Persia Marathon and declined with the Peloponnesian War (430–404 B.C.) between Athens and Sparta.

The Classic Age was a time for the development of great literature and great thought. During this period, Socrates, Plato, and Aristotle taught and wrote in Greece. (Aristotle tutored Alexander the Great after Alexander conquered Greece. Alexander spread Greek culture during his subsequent conquests.) In this relatively brief period, Aeschylus wrote his *Orestia Tiology* and Sophocles wrote *Oedipus Rex*. Also writing during this period were Aristophanes, Euripides, Herodotus, and Thucydides.

Hellenistic Age

This age begins with the death of Alexander the Great. Alexander lived for only 33 years (356–323 B.C.) but during his brief life he carved out a huge empire. His conquests led to the spread of Greek culture and thought to most of that region of the world. This age ended about 30 B.C. when Greece, like Egypt, was incorporated in the Roman Empire.

Epicurus and Zeno wrote during this time. The Hellenistic Age was a time of great scientific and mathematical development. Euclid wrote his *Elements* in the third century B.C. while Archimedes, and Erasthotenes made important discoveries later in the period.

Rome

Some say that Rome was founded between 700 and 800 B.C. The real founding of Rome may be closer to 500 B.C. The Roman Senate consisting of landowners was eventually replaced by the plebeian Assembly about 300 B.C. as the governing body of Rome.

Rome acquired all of Italy by about 300 B.C., defeated Carthage (in North Africa) during a series of Punic Wars, and controlled both sides of the Mediterranean by about 150 B.C. The Roman victories were marked by one defeat at the hands of the Carthaginian general Hannibal. Julius Caesar and Pompeii were leaders in the first century B.C. and Spartacus led a rebellion by slaves. Caesar was assassinated on the Ides of March, 44 B.C. in a conspiracy led by Brutus ("et tu Brute") and Cassius. Octavius defeated Antony and Cleopatra at the Battle of Acton around 38 B.C. Following this, Octavius was crowned the first "God-Emperor." The 500 years of peace that followed, called the Pax Romana, is the longest period of peace in the Western World.

Roman Empire

The birth of the Roman Empire coincided roughly with the beginning of the A.D. era. During the first century A.D., the Emperor Nero committed suicide. Jewish zealots also committed suicide at Masada following the destruction of their temple by the Romans. The empire reached its greatest size during this century. A code of law was established. Scientists Ptomely and Pliny the Elder were active, and the Colosseum was constructed.

Following the death of Emperor Marcus Aurelius, the Roman Empire began its decline. Civil war raged in the 200s A.D. and there were defeats of provinces by the Persians and the Goths. Constantine's attempts to stop the empire's decline were ultimately fruitless, and the Visigoths looted Rome in about 400 A.D.

DEVELOPMENT OF WORLD RELIGIONS

Major World Religions

Most of the world's religions emerged in Africa and Asia. There are about six billion people alive today. About two billion follow some Christian religion, and one billion Christians are Roman Catholics. There are about one billion Muslims, 800 million Hindus and 350 million Buddhists. There are fewer who follow tribal religions or who are Sikhs, Jews, Shamanists, Confucians, and followers of other religions. About one billion people are nonreligious and about 250 million people are atheists.

Judaism

Judaism developed from the beliefs of the Hebrew tribes located in and around Israel before 1300 B.C. From about 1000 B.C. to 150 B.C. a number of different authors wrote a series of books describing the religion, laws, and customs which are now known as the Old Testament of the Bible. The Old Testament describes a single just God. Judaism is an important world religion because elements of Judaism can be found in both Islam and Christianity.

Hebrews trace their ancestry to Abraham and his grandson Jacob, whose 12 sons are said to have founded the 12 tribes of Israel. About 1000 B.C. David is believed to have united these 12 tribes into a single religious state. Modern Jews refer to the Talmud, a book of Jewish law and tradition written around 400 A.D.

Christianity

Jesus was probably born about 5 B.C. He acquired a small following of Jews who believed he was the Messiah. Later this belief was developed into a worldwide religion known as Christianity. Christianity was generally tolerated in Rome, although there were periods of persecution. The Emperor Constantine converted to Christianity about 300 A.D. In the mid 300s Christianity was decreed the state religion of Rome. Augustine (St. Augustine) converted to Christianity in the late 300s.

In the Byzantine Era, starting after the Visigoths looted Rome, there was an Eastern and Western emperor. Constantinople was the capital in the East. This division led in 1054 to the great schism of the Catholic church, which survives to this day. The Crusaders captured Constantinople and defeated the Eastern Byzantines in 1204. In 1453 Constantinople was captured by the Turks and renamed Istanbul.

Islam

Mohammed was born in 570 A.D. and went into Mecca in 630 and founded Islam. The Koran contains the 114 chapters of Islamic religion and law. Around 640 A.D. the Omar, religious leader, established an Islamic empire with Damascus as the capital. The capital was eventually moved to Baghdad. The Muslims enjoyed a prosperous economy, and in the late days of the empire Omar Khayyam wrote the *Rubaiyat*.

Muslim armies conquered Spain and much of France by about 730. A series of Caliphs ruled from 750 until 1250 when an army originally led by Ghengis Kahn sacked Baghdad and killed the last caliph.

Buddhism

Buddhism was founded around 525 B.C. in India. The religion was founded by Buddha, Gautama Siddhartha, who lived from about 560 B.C. to about 480 B.C. The Triptika contains Buddha's teachings. A large number of *Sutras* contains a great body of Buddhist beliefs and teachings. Monastic life provides the main organizational and administrative structure for modern-day Buddhism.

It is said that Buddha achieved his enlightenment through meditation, and meditation is an important Buddhist practice. Buddhism holds that life is essentially meaningless and without reality. Buddhists seek to achieve Nirvana, a great void of perfection, through meditation and just acts.

Hinduism

Hinduism emerged in India about 25 years after Buddhism. Hindu beliefs are a mixture of the religious beliefs of invaders of India and the religious beliefs of native Indians. Hinduism embraces a caste system with religious services conducted by members of the priestly caste. Most Hindus worship one of the gods Vishnu and Shiva, and the goddess Shakti.

Hindus believe that a person's *karma*, the purity or impurity of past deeds, determines a person's ultimate fate. A karma can be improved through pure acts, deeds, and devotion.

FEUDALISM IN JAPAN AND EUROPE

Japan

The Japanese Islands had an early civilization by 3000 B.C. Throughout the whole B.C. period Japan remained a primitive society overrun by successive invasions by Mongols and Malays. Around the beginning of the A.D. period, Chinese writers referred to Japan as a backward nation.

The first religion in Japan was Shinto, a cult of nature and ancestor worship. Around 550 A.D., Buddhism was introduced in Japan and quickly spread throughout the country. Throughout this period Japan existed in the shadow of China. Chinese words are still found today in the Japanese language.

Shoguns

Japanese emperors had always been powerful, godlike figures. But around 1150 A.D., Shoguns were installed as the permanent leaders of Japan, leaving the emperor with only ceremonial duties. Until that time Shoguns had been only military leaders. In the following years a succession of Shoguns were ultimately unsuccessful in unifying Japan. Japan was reduced to a group of warring states.

Around 1600 the strong Tokugawa Shogunate was formed. This Shogunate ruled Japan until 1868. Japan was at peace for most of this period. Under this Shogunate, Christians were persecuted, and in 1639 foreign ships were forbidden in Japanese waters. This period of isolation lasted until American Commodore Perry forced Japan to sign a treaty in 1853, opening limited trade with the West.

Menji Period

The Menji period of Japan lasted from 1868 until 1912. Feudalism established under the Shogunates was outlawed, and Japan started to develop an industrial economy. As lords lost their feudal manors, the importance of the samurai (a lord's private soldiers) declined. In 1876 samurai were forbidden to wear their swords. Some 250,000 samurai rebelled in 1876 but were easily defeated by soldiers bearing modern weapons.

Buddhism declined, and Shintoism enjoyed a rebirth during this period. Japan actively sought contact with Western nations and adopted a number of Western customs and institutions. In 1889 the first Diet or parliament was established.

Wars

In 1894 Japan entered into war with China (Sino-Japanese War) over a dispute about Korea. Japan defeated China, establishing Japan as a military power. In 1904 Japan entered into war with Russia (The Russo-Japanese War). Japan also emerged victorious in this war and established a new balance of power between East and West. This new balance of power set the stage for conflicts yet to come.

Europe

Charlemagne

Charles Martel, a Frankish palace mayor who became known as Charlemagne, halted the Muslims in what is now France. Later he ruled the Frankish kingdom from about 770–815 A.D. He was named emperor of the Holy Roman Empire in 800 A.D. by Pope Leo III. Charlemagne's authority was also accepted in the East. After much fighting in Europe, the Normans, under William the Conqueror, defeated England at the Battle of Hastings in 1066.

The High Middle Ages lasted from the Battle of Hastings until about 1300. During this time the Roman road system was rebuilt, and Europe grew larger than the Muslim and Byzantine Empires.

In England a long series of battles with the Danes and Danish occupation preceded the Battle of Hastings. Henry II arranged for Archbishop Thomas Becket's murder in the late 1100s followed by the reign of Richard the Lionhearted and the signing of the Magna Carta in 1215.

Crusades

There were at least seven crusades from 1100 and 1300 to dislodge "infidels" from the Holy Land. The third crusade was led by Richard the Lionhearted. Ultimately, these crusades were unsuccessful, and many Muslims and Jews were massacred. Jews were persecuted throughout Europe beginning with the first crusade. Hundreds of Jewish communities were destroyed in the area of present-day Germany alone.

Scholasticism, an attempt to bring together the Christian faith and logic, was active during this period with leaders such as St. Anselm, Thomas Aquinas, Albertus Magnus, and Peter Abelard.

THE MIDDLE AND LATE AGES (1300–1500)

Hundred Years War

For much of this period, England and France were engaged in the Hundred Years War (actually about 120 years long). Most of the war was fought in France. Joan of Arc led the French army to a number of victories. She was burned at the stake at age 19. England was ultimately defeated. During this time, Chaucer wrote the *Canterbury Tales*.

Black Death

The bubonic plague, carried by rats' fleas, was epidemic in Europe by 1350. According to some estimates, almost half of the European population was killed by the plague.

CHINESE AND INDIAN EMPIRES

China to 1900

Early civilization developed near the Yellow River in ancient times. It appears that cities developed in China after they appeared in Egypt. The Shang Dynasty emerged in China about 1500 B.C. and lasted until about 1100 B.C. This dynasty is known for its works of art, particularly its fine bronze castings and walled cities. Life in this dynasty did not emphasize religion, a trait noted also in modern China.

The Chou Dynasty ruled from about 1100 to 250 B.C. Jade carvings and Chinese calligraphy were developed during this time.

Confucius

Confucius was born near the end of this dynasty around 550 B.C. He was a philosopher who was concerned with the way people acted. He emphasized regard for authority, self-control, conformity, and respectful behavior. Confucius had little impact during his lifetime. His disciples carried his thoughts and ideas throughout China. Eventually he came to be revered, and his ideas and sayings give a distinct shape and form to Chinese thought.

250 B.C.–220 A.D.

Following the Chou Dynasty were the Ch'in rulers, including the first emperor of China. During this time the Great Wall of China was expanded and built along the northern Chinese border. Confucian writings were destroyed by these leaders.

A successor in this period founded the Han Dynasty, which ruled China from about 200 B.C. to 220 A.D. During this period Confucius became a revered figure, and his writings were the objects of careful study.

Invaders

Invaders from the north attacked China around 315 A.D. and controlled north China until about 560 A.D. The Chinese maintained their independence in the south, but China was divided into a number of states. Influence from India established Buddhism in China during this time.

580 A.D.–1279 A.D.

China was reunited under the Sui Dynasty about 580 A.D. In 618 the Sui Dynasty was overthrown. The T'ang Dynasty that followed lasted until about 906 A.D. During this time Turkish incursions were halted, and Chinese influence grew to include Korea and northern Indochina. The T'angs developed a civil service testing apparatus, and the Chinese economy improved during this time.

During the Sung Dynasty (960–1279 A.D.) gunpowder was used for weapons. The nation prospered during this time, and the standard of living rose to new heights.

Mongols

The Mongols, under Genghis Kahn, invaded and controlled much of northern China by 1215. Kublai Khan followed, and his successors ruled China until 1368. During this time the Chinese launched a fleet to attack Japan. The fleet was destroyed in a typhoon. The Japanese refer to this typhoon as the divine wind—*kamikaze*.

Ming Dynasty

In 1368 Peking was captured, the Khan was overthrown, and the Ming Dynasty was born. The Mings reigned until 1644. Rulers of the Ming Dynasty launched a campaign to stamp out any remnants of the Mongol occupation. Even though there were some contacts with the West, the rulers of this dynasty forbade sea travel to foreign lands. Beginning in 1433 Chinese isolation and suspicion of foreigners grew.

Western Contacts

Contacts with the West increased under the Manchu Dynasty. However, in 1757 the Chinese government became offended by some Western traders. They allowed trade only through the port of Canton and under very strict regulations. At that time, opium was one of the few Chinese imports. The Chinese government objected to these imports, and this led to the Opium War of 1839, won by the British. Western intervention in China continued through 1900.

India to 1900

Early, advanced civilizations developed in the Indus Valley. The inhabitants were called Dravidians. Around 2500 B.C., a series of floods and foreign invasions appears to have all but destroyed these civilizations. Between 2500 and 1500 B.C. the Dravidians were forced into southern India by a nomadic band with Greek and Persian roots.

The conquerors brought a less sophisticated civilization to India. It was this latter group that formed the Indian civilization. An early caste system was established with the Dravidians serving as slaves.

After a time the society developed around religious, nonsecular concerns. The Mahabarata became a verbal tradition around 1000 B.C. It describes a war hero Krishna. The Mahabarata's most significant impact was the frequent descriptions of correct conduct and belief. The Mahabarata also describes how the soul remains immortal through transmigration—the successive occupation of many bodies.

Castes

From about 1000 to 500 B.C. the caste system became fixed and it was almost impossible for people to move out of their caste. The priests, or Brahmans, were at the top of the caste system. Next were rulers and warriors and then farmers and tradesmen. Near the bottom were workers. Finally, there were those who had no caste at all—outcastes—who could not participate in society.

Buddha

Buddha was born in India about 580 B.C. His teachings developed the Buddhist religion. Buddha preached nirvana—a rejection of worldly and material concerns and a surrender of individual consciousness. During his lifetime his ideas spread throughout India.

Maurya Empire

The Maurya Empire ruled India from about 320 to 185 B.C. During this time Buddhism was spread throughout Asia, China, and Southeast Asia. The Andrhan Dynasty ruled India proper to 220 A.D. Buddhism became less popular in India during this period while Brahmans gained more prominence.

Gupta Dynasty

After disorder following the collapse of the Andhran Dynasty, the Gupta Dynasty ruled from about 320 to 500 A.D. Arts, literature, and mathematics flourished during this period. Indian mathematicians used the decimal system and probably introduced the concept of zero. Hinduism developed from earlier religions and became the dominant religion in India. Most people in India worshipped many gods including Brahma (creator), Vishnu (preserver), and Shiva (destroyer).

The Gupta Dynasty declined with the invasion of the Huns in the fifth century A.D. Successors of these invaders, called Rajputs, intermarried, joined Hindu society, and dominated northern India until 1200 A.D. Other kingdoms were established in central and southern India.

By this time the caste system and the power of Brahman priests were dominant throughout India.

Muslims

Around 1200 A.D. Muslims (Turks and Afghans) invaded India from the north. The invaders controlled all but the southern part of India by about 1320. The Delhi Sultanate lasted in a state of intrigue until about 1530. Muslim sultans oppressed Hindus while their supporters killed or converted many Hindus. Remnants of this strife between Muslims and Hindus can be seen to this day.

In 1530 the Mongols, also Muslims, invaded India and by 1600 controlled most of India. The Mongol leader Akbar assumed the throne about 1560. His reign featured religious tolerance, the development of arts and literature, and a massive building campaign. In 1756 the Mongol Dynasty was overthrown by internal strife and Hindu resistance. India became a divided state.

Britain

Into this void stepped the European powers, particularly England. The East India Company of England virtually ruled India through 1857. In 1857, sepoys, Indian soldiers in the British army, mutinied. The British government began to rule Indian directly. This form of British rule was superior to that provided by the East India Company. Indian troops fought with Britain in World War I.

SUB-SAHARAN KINGDOMS AND CULTURES

Early Africa

Humans (*Homo sapiens*) are believed to have developed in Africa about 250,000 years ago. Humans formed nomadic bands that spread throughout Africa about 30,000 years ago. The first "towns" were founded in the Nile River Valley about 4500 B.C.

By about 3000 B.C. sophisticated civilizations developed throughout Egypt, which occupied a swath of land along the Nile River and extending to the Mediterranean. Pharaohs ruled with godlike powers, and there was a sophisticated bureaucracy. The Egyptians had writing (hieroglyphics) and invented a calendar still in use today. Pyramids were built during the Old Kingdom of Egypt from 2700 to 2150 B.C.

Pharaohs

Beginning around 2150 B.C., a century of weak pharaohs, civil wars, and famines weakened and fragmented Egypt. From about 2050 to 1650 B.C., Egypt came together in the Middle Kingdom. In 1650 B.C., foreign armies invaded and conquered Egypt. In about 1550 B.C. the Egyptians overthrew the foreign leaders and the New Kingdom (1550–1100 B.C.).

In the beginning of the New Kingdom, Egypt stretched along the Nile and occupied the coast of the Mediterranean out of Africa and in Palestine and Syria. By 1250 B.C., the Egyptian Empire was in decline. Egypt ceased to be the dominant force in the area about 750 B.C.

Sub-Saharan Africa

The Sudan, south of Egypt, developed a culture patterned after Egypt in about 1000 B.C. The Cush civilization of Sudan flourished in middle Africa and was dominant until about 250 A.D. The A.D. period marks the conquest of North Africa by the Roman Empire. Christian European influence was dominant until about 640 A.D.

Islam

Islam spread throughout Africa in the seventh century A.D. During this time Muslims conquered the area occupied by Egypt and the rest of North Africa, including Morocco and Libya. By about 1050 A.D. most of northern Africa was an Islamic land.

West Africa

The earliest state in West Africa was probably Ghana (established about 700 A.D.). By 1050 Ghana was also a Muslim state. In about 1100 A.D., the Mali evolved from tribes near the headwaters of the Senegal and Niger Rivers. Around 1300 Mali became a Muslim state. Songhai emerged as the dominant state in West Africa about 1400 A.D. Islam became the dominant faith in Songhai around 1500 and the capital, Timbuktu, became a major center for trade and learning. Songhai was overrun by Morocco in 1591.

East Africa

East African civilizations had an early exposure to Asian peoples. Most towns were established by Arab and Indonesian settlers. There was a great deal of intermarriage among natives and settlers. Mogadishu and Mombassa were among a number of smaller states, which emerged around 1250 A.D.

Central Africa

Civilizations in central Africa are shrouded in mystery. Bantu-speaking people apparently settled there around 700 A.D. In the fourteenth century the Kongo Kingdom was formed. The area around Lake Tanganyika was formed in the Luba Empire about the time Columbus made his first voyage. South Africa is best known for the Zulu people. They conquered most of South Africa between 1816 and 1850.

Slaves

European conquest and domination of Africa began in the late fifteenth century. Slave trade began at this time. Most slaves were supplied by African kingdoms, which grew rich on the slave trade.

CIVILIZATIONS OF THE AMERICAS

Early Cultures

Before 1500 the inhabitants of the Americas were related to the Native Americans. This group had migrated over the land bridge from Siberia about 30,000 years before. About 90 percent of the tens of millions of ancestors of this migratory tribe were found in Latin America in 1500.

By 7000 B.C., primitive cultures existed throughout the Americas. Cultures developed more slowly in the jungle areas of South America. Primitive cultures still exist there today. Agriculture seems to have been widespread by about 2500 B.C.

Mayan Culture

The dominant civilization in Mexico until about 900 A.D. were the Mayans. They began to occupy the Yucatan peninsula of Mexico and surrounding areas about 1700 B.C. The Mayans probably developed the most sophisticated indigenous American culture. The Mayan civilization ended suddenly with the mysterious desertion of Mayan cities and migration of the Mayan population.

Striking Mayan cities, plazas, and pyramids survive to this day. Mayans had a written language and wrote books about astronomy. Their calendar was the most accurate in the world at that time. Many Mayan descendants live as peasants in Mexico and speak dialects of their ancient language.

From about 1500 to 500 B.C., the Olmec civilization was a sophisticated culture in northern Mexico. About this time a culture centered in Teotihuacan also grew in prominence. This culture was to dominate northern Mexico until about 900 A.D.

Aztec Culture

In about 900 A.D. the Aztecs began their rise to power in northern Mexico. Aztecs referred to themselves as Mexica. Aztecs were warlike and sacrificed humans. By about 1300 A.D. they established a capital city in a marsh, which is now the site of Mexico City.

The Spaniards, under Cortez, duped the Aztec Emperor Montezuma II and easily defeated the Aztec confederation in 1521. Over a million descendants of the Aztecs still live in Mexico, mainly living a subsistence existence and speaking their ancient language.

Incan Culture

The Incas were the dominant pre-Columbian civilization in South America. This culture existed in Peru by about 500 A.D. From about 1100 to about 1500 A.D. the Incas expanded their empire to most of the western coast of South America including parts of Argentina.

The Incas had the best developed system of government in the Americas. They built extensive systems of stone roads and huge stone structures such as the Temple of the Sun. The Incas also built the fortress Machu Picchu high in the Andes. Machu Picchu may have been the last stronghold of the Incas after the Spaniard Pizzaro overcame the Incan empire in 1532 with about 200 troops and palace intrigue.

RISE AND EXPANSION OF EUROPE

Renaissance (1300–1600)

The Renaissance, which means the rebirth, arose in Italy and particularly in Florence. It was a time for the discovery and rediscovery of literature and art. Humanism, reading, and the ideas of Classical Greece were dominant during this period. Dante wrote the *Inferno* and the *Divine Comedy* early in the Renaissance and Machiavelli wrote *The Prince* near the end of the period. Leonardo DiVinci painted the Mona Lisa and designed many workable mechanical devices. Michelangelo painted the ceiling of the Sistine Chapel, among other accomplishments.

Luther and the Reformation (1500–1600)

The abuses of the Catholic church, then monolithic in Europe, drew much criticism. The practice of selling indulgences (relief from punishment in purgatory) was considered particularly repugnant. Martin Luther drew particular attention these abuses when, on October 31, 1517, he nailed his *95 Theses* to the Wittenburg Church door. Luther authored many books and wrote the most popular hymn of the time, *A Mighty Fortress Is Our God*. Since Luther's teachings *protested* church practice, his followers were called Protestants.

The reform movement spread beyond Luther in Germany to England and other parts of Europe. Henry VIII in England broke with the pope and formed the Church of England. Protestantism was effectively blocked in Spain and Italy and was the subject of warfare in France.

Religious Warfare

Most national boundaries were fixed at the end of the Reformation in 1560. The 90 years that followed were marked by religious strife. Gunpowder, available since the 1300s, was now used in cannons. Warfare became more regimented and more deadly. There were no fewer than seven civil wars in France. The St. Bartholomew's Day Massacre occurred in 1572, when Catherine DeMedici arranged the death of about 20,000 French Huguenots (Calvinist Protestants).

Mary I (Bloody Mary) of England killed many Protestants in her brief five-year reign (1553–1558). Her successor, Elizabeth I, was a Protestant and achieved some degree of religious peace in England. Later attempts were made to force England back to Catholicism.

By 1575 governments were in shambles, and many religious groups were discriminated against. In England the Puritans objected to what they saw as a pro-Catholic shift in the Church of England. Many Puritans escaped to the New World.

Age of Exploration (1500–1650)

Countries sponsored exploration throughout the world toward the end of the Renaissance. These countries were seeking new trade and easily accessible trade routes.

The New World had already been visited when Columbus sailed from Spain in 1492. His voyage followed on other explorations by Prince Henry the Navigator and Vasco Da Gama.

Many other explorers traveled to the New World and circumnavigated the world during this period. Cortes conquered the Aztecs, in Mexico, and Pizarro, in Peru, conquered the Incas.

The effect of exploration on the Native Indian population of the Americas was disastrous. Some estimates indicate that 80 percent of the native population was wiped out by disease in one of the greatest epidemics on earth. Gold and food were shipped back to Europe. A large number of English settled in North America. Small numbers of Spanish settlers went to South and Central America. Still smaller numbers of French settled in Canada following the explorations of Champlain.

Europeans, with the complicity of some African kingdoms, began transporting slaves from Africa to the Americas. The first African slaves arrived in Jamestown, Virginia, about 1620. By the early 1800s there were about 1 million slaves in the United States. By 1860 there were more than four million slaves in the United States.

We will return later to the development of the New World following this period of exploration.

Scientific Revolution (1550–1650)

The scientific revolution took place toward the end of the Renaissance and spilled over into the age of exploration. Copernicus showed that the sun was at the center of the solar system. Kepler discovered the orbits of the planets. Galileo made significant discoveries in astronomy, mechanics, and surveying. He proved that all falling bodies fall at the same rate.

Francis Bacon championed inductive investigations in which data are gathered and used to form hypotheses. Rene Decartes (Cartesian coordinates) provided leadership in mathematics and championed the deductive, step-by-step method of proof.

Enlightenment (C. 1650–1790)

In 1650 Europe consisted of 300–500 smaller states and a Germany devastated by the Thirty Years War. A series of treaties and wars brought a kind of order out of this chaos.

Peace of Westphalia (1648)—Holland and Switzerland officially formed.

First Dutch War (1667–1668)—Warfare between France and Spain led to the Triple Alliance (England, Holland, and Sweden).

War of the League of Augsburg (1688–1697)—France fought England and Holland. The conflict between England and France continued on and off for about 125 years.

The Grand Alliance (1701)—A coalition of Spain and France against England led to the formation of the Grand Coalition (Holy Roman Empire, England, Holland, and Prussia).

Treaty of Utrecht (1742)—The Spanish Empire was partitioned. England received Gibraltar, Newfoundland, Hudson Bay, and Nova Scotia.

King William's War (1744–1748)—Prussia emerged as a world power.

Seven Years War (1756–1763)—Prussia fought Austria, France, and Russia. With help from England and the withdrawal of Russia from the conflict, Prussia held onto its lands.

Treaty of Paris (1763)—France, which had already given Spain all its western American lands, lost the rest of its North American possessions to England. England traded Cuba to Spain for the Floridas.

Treaty of Paris (1783)—Britain recognized the United States following the Revolutionary War, but no lands were given to France, even though France (Lafayette, Rochambeau) had aided the United States in the Revolutionary War.

Life was still difficult in the 1700s. In the early 1700s the average life expectancy was 30, and almost no one lived to see their grandchildren. Famine and disease (including smallpox, bubonic plague, and typhus) were rampant. But, slowly, the economies and social institutions of Europe began to change for the better.

Mercantilism, an emphasis on material wealth, became a leading force in Europe. In Holland and England productivity became important. As a result, these countries became leading economic powers.

Technology, Art, and Literature

In the early 18th century, technology provided a means for further economic development. Watt refined and developed the steam engine, while other inventors devised power-driven textile equipment.

The Enlightenment established intellect as distinct from God and sought to establish a rational basis for life. Descartes paused in his scientific work to proclaim, "I think; therefore, I am."

This period included the Baroque art movement. Baroque art featured grandeur and included the works of Michelangelo. Rubens, Bach, and Handel were great Baroque artists and composers.

The impact of the Enlightenment can be seen in the theories of Jean Jacques Rousseau who believed that common people should have a wider role in their own government. The centralized mercantilist theory was attacked by economist Adam Smith and others, who believed in free trade and the law of supply and demand.

Romanov Russia

The Romanovs ruled Russia from about 1613 until 1917. From 1682 until 1725 the giant (7 feet tall), driven, and cruel Peter the Great ruled Russia. He used secret police to identify and punish those who opposed him. Despite his bizarre behavior, he spent time among the common people. He modernized and westernized Russia. He built St. Petersburg as a modern western city. Many of the companies begun during his reign were controlled by the state. After six short-lived emperors, Catherine the Great (1762–1796) continued the modernization of Russia.

French Revolution

King Louis XVI was on the throne as France became bankrupt in the late 1780s. Food was in short supply and food prices were inflated as the Third Estate (commoners) asserted themselves and took over the national assembly. They forced recognition by the king.

Galvanized by food shortages, repression, and unemployment, Parisian workers armed themselves and stormed the fortress Bastille on July 14, 1789. The French Revolution was born. After two years of fighting and intrigue, the newly formed national assembly condemned and executed Louis XVI and Marie "let them eat cake" Antoinette in 1792.

Robespierre emerged to direct a Committee of Public Safety, which conducted the Reign of Terror from 1793–1794. The Reign led to the deaths of over 20,000 who were summarily found guilty of real or imagined wrongs. Robespierre was executed under orders from the National Convention on July 27, 1794.

Napoleon

Napoleon was born in 1769, and while in Paris in 1795, he helped put down a royalist uprising. He was also there to lead the overthrow of the government in 1799 and soon become the dictator (Consul for Life in 1801) of France. Napoleon was a brilliant, charismatic man and a true military genius. He led France on a 10-year quest for an expanded empire from 1805 to 1815.

However, he was unable to complete his militaristic expansion successfully. He was deposed and exiled to Elba only to return to "meet his Waterloo" at the battle of that name. He was exiled again and died on the island of St. Helena in 1821.

The Quadruple Alliance (Austria, England, Prussia, and Russia), who had defeated Napoleon, reached a settlement that encircled France. This settlement maintained a balance of power in Europe until Germany was unified 60 years later.

Industrial Revolution (1750–1850)

Increased population, cheap labor, available capital, raw materials, and industrial skill led to the beginning of the Industrial Revolution in England about 1750. Textiles and metal industries were the first to develop. These industries were helped along by the steamboat and the locomotive. During the early 1800s this industrialism moved to the continent.

The Industrial Revolution produced a new class of factory workers. These workers did not benefit from the Industrial Revolution until late in the 1800s. Until then, work had centered around the family, but all that changed. Generally speaking, men worked outside the home, and women worked in the home.

Romanticism (1790–1850)

Romanticism had its biggest impact from the late 1700s through 1850. This movement stressed personal freedom and humanitarianism. The names of many Romantic writers, painters, and composers are familiar to us. Some writers were Balzac, Burns, Browning, Byron, Coleridge, Cooper, Dostoyevsky, Dumas, Emerson, Longfellow, Poe and Thoreau. Painters included Goya and Delacorte. Composers of the era were Brahms, Chopin, and Schubert.

Romanticism broadened thought and led to a number of different philosophies and approaches to living. Liberalism celebrated the individual and proclaimed that individuals have certain natural rights. Conservatism proposed that some people were better prepared to rule and lead than others. Nationalism stressed loyalty to a group or country rather than the individual. Socialism expressed the view that all should receive their share of a nation's wealth. Marxism developed by Marx and Engels was a popular form of socialism. Marxism is described in *Das Kapital* and *Communist Manifesto*.

A series of revolutions swept Europe in 1820, 1825, and 1830, culminating in 1848. Italy and Germany were unified as an aftermath of these revolutions.

EUROPEAN DEVELOPMENTS

Crimean War

The year 1854 found Great Britain and France allied with the Turks against Russia in the Crimean War. It was this war that sparked the writing of "The Charge of the Light Brigade" and featured the nursing work of Florence Nightingale and her disciples. The war ended in 1856 with the Peace of Paris.

Capitalism, Marxism, and Anarchism

Following the revolutions of 1848, capitalism and communism competed for economic supremacy in Europe. Anarchists believed that there should be no authority. They used violent means to further their ends.

New Imperialism

Beginning about 1870, Europe was producing more goods than it could consume. So European powers began to vie for colonies. Much of the early activity focused on Africa. By 1914 Belgium, Britain, France, Germany, Italy, Portugal, and Spain controlled about 90 percent of Africa, with Britain and then France controlling the most territory.

During this time the German Empire developed under Bismarck. Great Britain's move to democratic government ended in 1911 when the House of Commons usurped the power of the House of Lords. The Third French Republic survived infighting and socialist challenges and solidified support of the majority of the French populace.

This period also saw the emergence of new and revolutionary ideas. Freud established psychoanalytic psychology, Einstein presented his theory of relativity, and Darwin wrote the *Origin of the Species.*

OTHER SOCIAL SCIENCE TOPICS

Other social science topics are also the subject of test questions. These topics, which include anthropology, government/politics, geography, and graph interpretation, are discussed next.

ANTHROPOLOGY

Anthropology is a holistic study of humans. Anthropologists study the biology, culture, and development of human species and communities. Anthropologists rely on field work, fossils, and observation in their work.

Physical Anthropology

Physical anthropology is concerned with the evolution of primates and humans. Physical anthropologists are seeking to trace the evolution of humans through human fossils. Louis Leakey is probably the most famous physical anthropologist. He discovered the three-million-year-old remains of "Lucy" at the Olduvai gorge in Africa.

Biological Anthropologists

Human biology is another focus of anthropologists. Biological anthropologists study the genetic development of primates and humans. They seek to identify the cause of human diseases such as high blood pressure. Other biological anthropologists such as Jane Goodall study the behavior of apes and other primates. These anthropologists have found that primates can use tools and communicate.

Cultural Anthropologists

Cultural anthropology is concerned with the social systems, customs, languages, and religion of existing cultures. Cultural anthropologists classify cultures as patrilineal, matrilineal, or bilateral depending on whether the family roots are traced through the father, mother, or both father and mother.

Anthropological Development

The simplest cultures are associated with nomadic hunter-gatherers. About 13,000 years ago, humans began domesticating livestock and raising crops. More stable communities developed as cultures became more stationary. Then these communities became linked together to form tribes with a shared tradition (religion). Political systems developed, and leaders or chiefs of these tribes appeared. Some of these tribes developed unevenly into kingdoms with a shared language. Occasionally a kingdom would develop into a civilization with different hierarchies of individuals.

More advanced cultures featured complex religious systems, important priests, and codified religious rules. Early cultures typically had a single religious system. Until recently there was a close relationship between religion and government.

Most cultural anthropologists agree that the primary determinants of culture are the material conditions of life—food, energy sources, and technology. Geography and climate have a tremendous influence on these factors. Ideas, movements, and personalities also have a significant impact on a culture.

GOVERNMENT AND POLITICAL SCIENCE

Government and political science are studies of the ways governments are organized and how governments function.

There are a number of ways to classify governments. Aristotle placed governments in one of three categories:

Democracy—government by the populace

Aristocracy—government by a few

Monarchy—government by one

Current classifications of government include the following.

Parliamentary, or Cabinet (England)—The executive branch is subordinate to the legislative branch.

Presidential (United States)—The executive branch is independent of the legislative branch, although some executive actions require legislative action.

Federal States (United States)—The power of the central government is limited by rights of the states.

Unitary (England)—The states are subordinate to the central government.

Dictatorship (Nazi Germany)—Rule by a single individual or a small group in which the needs of the state are generally more important than the needs of the people.

Democracy (United States)—Rule through the will of the people within which the needs of the people are generally more important than the needs of the state.

UNITED STATES GOVERNMENT

The United States government is based on the Constitution of the United States. The Constitution can be amended by a two-thirds vote of Congress with concurrence of three-fourths of the state legislatures. The first ten amendments to the Constitution are called the Bill of Rights. Other important amendments provided protection by due process of law, abolished slavery, and gave women the right to vote.

The Constitution established a federal form of government. States have rights and hold all power not expressly granted to the federal government.

The federal government of the United States has three branches: legislative, executive, and judicial. The framers of the Constitution established these as three complementary, overlapping branches to provide checks and balances in the governmental process.

Legislative

The Congress of the United States consists of the Senate and the House of Representatives. The 100 senators, two from each state, serve for six years with one-third standing for election every two years. The 435 representatives in the House are partitioned among the states according to population. Every state must have at least one representative. All representatives stand for election every two years.

Measures passed by a majority of Congress present and voting are sent to the president as a bill. The president may sign the bill into law or veto it. If the bill is vetoed, the Congress may still make the bill law by a two-thirds vote of each body.

Executive

The president and the vice president are the elected heads of the federal government. Their election takes place through a cumbersome process in which electors are chosen from each state by popular vote. These electors then gather in an Electoral College to cast votes for the president and vice president.

The president is Commander-in-Chief of the Armed Forces, but only Congress has the power to declare war. The president also has the right to negotiate treaties. Two-thirds of the Senate must vote to ratify any treaties. Treaties are null and void without this ratification.

Judicial

The Constitution established the Supreme Court as the final arbiter of whether a law adhered to the Constitution. Other federal courts established by Congress can also rule on a law's constitutionality.

Supreme Court justices are nominated by the president. A majority of the Senate must consent to any Supreme Court nomination.

Checks and Balances

The three branches of government provide adequate checks and balances. There are ways to remove presidents, legislators, and judges from office.

Reading and Interpreting Charts, Graphs, and Maps

Review the reading and interpreting graphs section on page 230.

READING AND INTERPRETING MAPS

Read the map and answer the items.

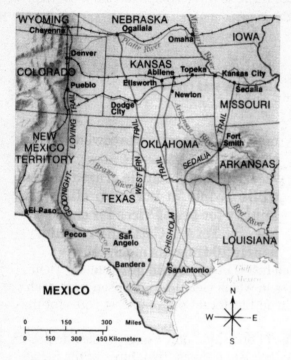

Western cattle trails and railroads about 1875

1. Which cattle trail goes from San Antonio to Abilene?
   (A) Chisholm
   (B) Sedalia
   (C) Goodnight-Loving
   (D) Western Trail

2. Which cattle trail crosses the Pecos River?
   (A) Chisholm
   (B) Sedalia
   (C) Goodnight-Loving
   (D) Western Trail

3. Which cattle trail passes through the fewest states?
   (A) Chisholm
   (B) Sedalia
   (C) Goodnight-Loving
   (D) Western Trail

4. About how far is it by train from Sedalia to Abilene?
   (A) 150 miles
   (B) 300 miles
   (C) 450 miles
   (D) 600 miles

5. The Goodnight-Loving trail turns north after Pecos because
   (A) that's the way to Denver
   (B) cattle drovers did not want to go into Mexico
   (C) of the mountains
   (D) of the Rio Grande River

6. Which state contains the final railhead for the largest number of cattle trails?
   (A) Texas
   (B) Kansas
   (C) Oklahoma
   (D) Nebraska

7. If drovers move a herd of cattle about 25 kilometers per day, about how many days would it take to move a herd from Fort Smith to Sedalia on the Sedalia Trail?
   (A) 8
   (B) 16
   (C) 24
   (D) 32

Answers

1. A	5. C
2. C	6. B
3. A	7. B
4. B	

HISTORY, HUMANITIES, AND SOCIAL SCIENCE PRACTICE ITEMS

These items will help you practice the topics in this chapter. The items you encounter on the LAST may have a different emphasis and may be more complete.

Instructions

Mark your answers on the sheet provided below. Complete the items in 20 minutes or less. Correct your answer sheet using the answers on page 234.

1 Ⓐ Ⓑ Ⓒ Ⓓ	5 Ⓐ Ⓑ Ⓒ Ⓓ	9 Ⓐ Ⓑ Ⓒ Ⓓ	13 Ⓐ Ⓑ Ⓒ Ⓓ	17 Ⓐ Ⓑ Ⓒ Ⓓ
2 Ⓐ Ⓑ Ⓒ Ⓓ	6 Ⓐ Ⓑ Ⓒ Ⓓ	10 Ⓐ Ⓑ Ⓒ Ⓓ	14 Ⓐ Ⓑ Ⓒ Ⓓ	18 Ⓐ Ⓑ Ⓒ Ⓓ
3 Ⓐ Ⓑ Ⓒ Ⓓ	7 Ⓐ Ⓑ Ⓒ Ⓓ	11 Ⓐ Ⓑ Ⓒ Ⓓ	15 Ⓐ Ⓑ Ⓒ Ⓓ	19 Ⓐ Ⓑ Ⓒ Ⓓ
4 Ⓐ Ⓑ Ⓒ Ⓓ	8 Ⓐ Ⓑ Ⓒ Ⓓ	12 Ⓐ Ⓑ Ⓒ Ⓓ	16 Ⓐ Ⓑ Ⓒ Ⓓ	20 Ⓐ Ⓑ Ⓒ Ⓓ

1. Which of the following has the least significant impact on the culture of a group?
   (A) material conditions of life
   (B) geography
   (C) climate
   (D) physical appearance

2. Which of the following forms of government is least used in the countries of today's world?
   (A) democracy
   (B) aristocracy
   (C) monarchy
   (D) federal states

3. In the United States, the power to declare war is given to the
   (A) president.
   (B) Congress.
   (C) Supreme Court.
   (D) Senate.

4. Which of the following limits the powers of the federal government?
   (A) judicial branch
   (B) the Bill of Rights
   (C) Constitution
   (D) executive branch

5. Social psychologists study
   (A) people as individuals.
   (B) animals in interactive settings.
   (C) children at play.
   (D) people's behavior in groups.

6. The Ming, Chou, Sung, and Manchu Dynasties were
   (A) Indian.
   (B) Taiwanese.
   (C) Japanese.
   (D) Chinese.

7. Sigmund Freud's psychosexual stages of development listed below are organized into which sequence?
   (A) oral, genital, anal, latency
   (B) genital, anal, oral, latency
   (C) oral, anal, genital, latency
   (D) oral, anal, latency, genital

8. All the following would be considered the job of an anthropologist EXCEPT:
   (A) studying the genetic make up of a fossil.
   (B) living with a community of Aborigines.
   (C) testing a rock sample with carbon 14.
   (D) organizing a dig at a burial site.

9. Who coined the term "iron curtain"?
   (A) Churchill
   (B) Truman
   (C) Lenin
   (D) Stalin

10. A U.S. Army officer describes any victory over Native American groups as a triumph, but any defeat as a massacre. What is this an example of?
    (A) authoritarianism
    (B) ethnocentrism
    (C) righteousness
    (D) an inferiority complex

11. Which invention revolutionized the South's economy and breathed new life into slavery?
    (A) the steam engine
    (B) the cotton gin
    (C) standard parts
    (D) the conveyor belt

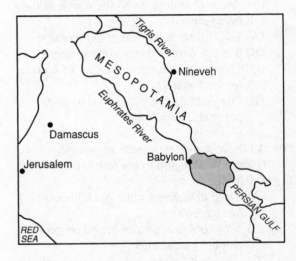

12. Which of the following is not a reason why early civilization began in these shaded areas?
    (A) comfortable climate
    (B) fertile land
    (C) fresh water supply
    (D) potential commerce opportunities

13. Why do multinational corporations produce goods in countries such as Mexico and the Philippines?
    (A) to increase cash flow in these countries
    (B) to widen the marketing area
    (C) to lower the cost of labor
    (D) to lower the price of the product

14. During one of the Lincoln-Douglas debates, Abraham Lincoln acknowledged that the Southern people were no more responsible for the existence of slavery than those in the North. He went on to say that he understood and appreciated the position of those in the South who said that it was very difficult to get rid of the institution of slavery in an acceptable way. He concluded, however, that these arguments were no more a basis for extending slavery into the free territories of the United States, than they were a basis for legalizing the importation of African slaves.

    During this debate, Lincoln conveyed the notion
    (A) existence doesn't justify expansion.
    (B) hate the sin but not the sinner.
    (C) do unto others as they would do unto you.
    (D) let sleeping dogs lie.

15. Those who validly criticize the workings of the electoral college do so for which of the following reasons?
    (A) The system is not direct democracy.
    (B) It is not a true representative democracy.
    (C) There is not an equal number of votes for each state.
    (D) The electors are influenced by their party affiliation only.

16. All these statements were advice given by George Washington in his farewell address EXCEPT:
    (A) Avoid permanent alliances with any foreign powers.
    (B) Avoid political parties based on geographic boundaries.
    (C) The ability of America to pay its national debts must be safeguarded.
    (D) Avoid supplying monetary aid to foreign countries.

17. Karl Marx's *Communist Manifesto* wished for what result for an economic revolution?
    (A) a society where the proletariat ruled
    (B) a democratic society
    (C) authoritarian society
    (D) a classless society

18. What reason was given to Japanese Americans when they were put in internment camps during World War II?
    (A) They were told that their lives were in danger.
    (B) They were thought to be plotting a sneak attack on home soil.
    (C) They were considered a threat to national security.
    (D) They were being shipped back to Japan as soon as possible.

Use this map to answer questions 19 and 20.

Military Districts During Reconstruction
Date State Readmitted to the Union

19. Which of the states listed below was under federal rule for the longest period of time?
    (A) Texas
    (B) Arkansas
    (C) Alabama
    (D) South Carolina

20. Florida was part of a military district with which two other states?
    (A) Mississippi and Arkansas
    (B) Texas and Louisiana
    (C) North Carolina and South Carolina
    (D) Georgia and Alabama

Answers

1. D	5. D	9. A	13. C	17. D
2. D	6. D	10. B	14. A	18. A
3. B	7. D	11. B	15. C	19. A
4. C	8. C	12. D	16. D	20. D

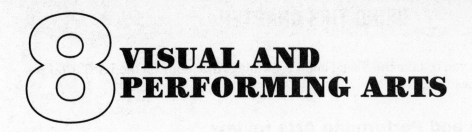

8 VISUAL AND PERFORMING ARTS

USING THIS CHAPTER

This chapter prepares you to take the Visual and Performing Arts items on the LAST. Choose one of these approaches.

I want a Visual and Performing Arts review.

❏ Read the Visual and Performing Arts Review.
❏ Complete the Visual and Performing Arts Practice Items on page 245.

I want to practice Visual and Performing Arts questions.

❏ Complete the Visual and Performing Arts Practice Items on page 245.

VISUAL AND PERFORMING ARTS REVIEW

VISUAL ARTS

Visual art includes paintings, photographs, prints, carvings, sculpture, and architecture. *Representational* art presents a recognizable representation of real people, places, or things. *Abstract* art presents nonrecognizable representations of real things or thoughts, perhaps using geometric shapes or designs. *Nonrepresentational* art is unrelated to real things or thoughts and represents only itself.

Visual arts are built around certain visual elements.

Points are represented by dots and are the simplest visual element. **Lines** are created when points move and may be horizontal, vertical, diagonal, straight, jagged, or wavy. Lines come in many thicknesses and lengths. Lines in a painting or drawing may suggest three-dimensional images or outline a shape.

Shapes are bounded forms in two-dimensional art. The boundary of a shape is usually a line, but it may also be created by color, shading, and texture. A shape may be geometric or fluid.

Space refers to the area occupied by the art. Paintings occupy two-dimensional space, while sculpture occupies three-dimensional space. Sculptors manipulate three-dimensional space and forms to create the desired effect, while painters often manipulate two-dimensional space to create the illusion of three-dimensional space.

Color: The colors of the spectrum are red, orange, yellow, green, blue, indigo, and violet. White is actually the combination of all the spectral colors, and black is an absence of color. Colors communicate mood (blue is cold, yellow is warm). Warm colors appear to expand a work's size while cold colors appear to contract its size. Color has three properties.

1. **Hue** is the color itself. It describes a color's placement in the color spectrum.
2. **Value** refers to the amount of lightness or darkness in a color. Low value shades are dark, while high value shades are light. You can raise the value of a color by adding white, and lower the value by adding black.
3. **Saturation** (also called chroma or intensity) describes the brightness or dullness of a color.

Perspective refers to methods of manipulating two-dimensional space to create the illusion of three-dimensional space. *Foreshortening* means exaggerating linear perspective by drawing the near parts of an object in close proximity to the far parts of the same object. *Linear perspective* means drawing objects smaller as they get further away. Still photographs naturally employ linear perspective.

Principles of Design

These elements of design are frequently used to analyze and describe an artwork.

Balance refers to the equilibrium of elements that create a work. Balance can be achieved through both symmetrical and asymmetrical arrangements.

Symmetry is achieved when one half of an artwork more or less reflects the other half. Symmetrical works tend to create a sense of formality.

Asymmetry is achieved when color and the lightness of different parts of a work create a sense of balance. For example, a lighter area may balance a darker area. Asymmetrical works tend to create a sense of informality.

Rhythm refers to the repetition of elements in an artwork. Effective repetition of design elements tends to create a more dynamic work.

Dominance means to use color or positioning to draw the attention of the viewer to the most important element or elements in a work.

Painting

Painting techniques include oil, watercolor, gouache, and fresco. The paint for all of these techniques consists of a pigment (color), binder (e.g., egg, oil, wax), which holds the pigment together, and solvents (water, turpentine), which permit the paint to spread on a surface.

Oil is the primary painting form. The oil can be applied as thinly or thickly as desired and dries slowly so that the artist can rework it until the desired result is obtained.

Watercolor presents a thin wispy appearance and is widely used for landscape painting. Gouache is an opaque watercolor that is often applied to a board. Acrylic paints combine most of the advantages of oil paint with easy clean up. Acrylics are often applied with an airbrush.

Analyzing Art Forms

Art appears in many incarnations, including paintings, photographs, prints, carvings, sculpture, and architecture. When asked to analyze any work of art, you can comment on the content, the form, the style, and the method used by the artist.

The *content* is what actually appears in a work of art. It is the subject matter of the art. Don't take the obvious subject matter for granted when considering your analysis. Choose descriptive words as you search for ways to capture the content of the image in front of you. For example, a landscape may contain peaceful blue skies, a raging river, cows and horses grazing, or seemingly endless grassy fields. A portrait may show a happy person or someone filled with concern or worry. A sculpture may show a smoothly muscled athlete. A building may have cascading stairs or a series of columns that thrust upward to the ceiling.

The *form* of a work of art is the order imposed by the artist. Form is the design of the work regardless of the content. A painting or photograph may show strong horizontal or vertical orientation. Perhaps the work is symmetrical, with one part a mirror image of the other. Some works may be tilted or asymmetrical.

The *style* refers to the artist's way of expressing ideas including formal styles such as gothic, high renaissance, baroque, or impressionist. In a painting or picture you can notice how the artist uses color. The colors may blend or clash. There may be an overall dark tone to the picture, or it may be light and airy. Perhaps the artist used dots of paint to produce the image.

The *method* is the medium used by the artist to create the work. It may be an oil painting or a watercolor. Perhaps the artist created prints or an etching. A three-dimensional work of art may have been sculpted, cast, carved, molded, or turned on a potter's wheel.

Keep these elements of content, form, style, and method in mind as you respond to the questions on the LAST.

GLOSSARY OF ART TERMS

allegory Art that represents or symbolizes some idea or quality.

amphora An egg-shaped Grecian urn.

ankh An Egyptian hieroglyph that represents life. See illustration.

Ankh

annealing Softening by heating glass or metal that has become hardened.

arebesque Very intricate designs based on plant forms.

arch A curved span. See illustration.

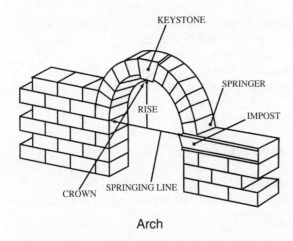

Arch

atrium An open rectangular-shaped court, often in front of a church.

avant-garde Art considered ahead of its time.

baluster A small curved post or pillar.

balustrade A railing usually supported by balusters.

batten Strips of wood used as a base for plastering or for attaching tile.

belfry The top floor of a tower usually containing bells.

bevel To round off a sharp edge.

biscuit Unglazed porcelain.

bust A sculpture showing the head and shoulders.

calligraphy Decorative writing.

canopy A fabric covering.

casement A vertically hinged window frame.

ceramics All porcelain and pottery.

chalice An ornamental cup often used in religious services.

chancel The part of a church reserved for clergy.

collage Art created by pasting together many media including newspaper, fabric, and wood. A collage may also include paintings or drawings.

colors Many colors can be created by combining the primary colors. See illustration.

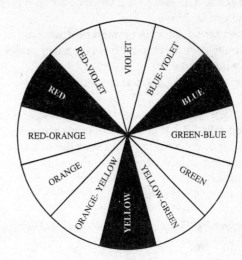

Color Wheel

column A free-standing, circular pillar. Several different styles exist. See illustration.

Corinthian   Doric   Ionic   Tuscan

course A row of bricks or stones.

cuneiform Wedge-shaped writing associated with Babylonians and Sumerians.

decoupage Cutting out designs to be used in a collage.

eclectic Drawing on many styles.

enamel Powdered glass bonded to a metal surface by firing.

engraving Inscribing a design on glass, metal, or some other hard surface.

etching Designs created on metal plates by applying acid to initial scratchings and the prints made from these plates.

filigree Gold or silver soldered to create elaborate, delicate patterns.

focal point The place on a work of art to which the eye is drawn.

foreshortened Objects painted or drawn as though they were seen from an angle projecting into space.

fresco A painting applied to wet plaster.

genre The type of painting—portrait, landscape, etc.

golden ratio The proportion of approximately 1.6 to 1, which is said to represent the most pleasing artistic proportion. For example, a window 3 feet wide would meet this proportion by being 4.8 feet high.

hieroglyphics Egyptian symbols representing letters or words.

illustration An idea or scene represented in art.

jamb The sides of a window or door.

kiosk A small booth with a roof and open sides.

linear A way of representing three-dimensional space in two dimensions.

louvers Shutter slats.

macrame Artwork made of knotted fabrics.

monolith A figure sculpted or carved from a single block of stone.

mural A painting made on or attached to a wall.

niche A wall recess.

obelisk A rectangular block of stone, often with a pyramidal top.

papier maché Paper (newspaper) soaked with water and flour and shaped into figures.

parquet A floor made of wooden tile.

perspective Representing three dimensions on a flat surface.

pigment The material used to color paint.

plaster Limestone and sand or gypsum mixed with water, which can be shaped and then hardened. Plaster can also be carved and is often used to finish walls and ceilings.

projection The techniques of representing buildings on a flat surface.

quarry tile Unglazed tile.

relief Carved or molded art in which the art projects from the background.

sarcophagus A stone coffin.

scale The relative size of an object, such as the scale was one inch to one foot.

sizing Gluelike material used to stiffen paper or to seal a wall or canvas.

stipple Dab on paint.

tapestry Fabric woven from silk by hand.

tempera A type of painting that binds the pigment with a mixture of egg and water or egg and oil.

uppercase Capital letters.

vihara A Buddhist monastery.

warp In weaving, the thick, fixed threads.

weft In weaving, the thin threads that are actually woven.

DANCE

Dance means an intentional movement designed to express a thought, image, feeling, or reality. *A dance* is a sequential, rhythmic movement in two or three dimensional space. A dance has a beginning, a middle, and an end.

Dance medium refers to the types of movement used during dance, including space, shape, force, and time. *Space* refers to the outer space or sphere immediately around the body, and inner space, the real or imaginary space inside the body. *Shape* is the deliberate positioning of the body to create a particular appearance. *Force* is release of energy. Force is the energy that produces a dance. *Time* refers to tempo, beat, and accent during a dance.

Creative movement refers to children's dance movement, which is more exploratory and less purposeful than adult dance. Body movements during a dance may be locomotor or non-locomotor.

Kinesthetic perception describes the body's ability to sense movement. It refers to the muscles' retention of the movement and effort required to produce a dance.

Dancing means to move in a dance-like way. *Choreography* refers to the art of composing dances. A dance style describes the kind of dance associated with a particular style, location, or time period.

There are several types of dance including ballet, tap, jazz, and modern. Improvisation refers to an unplanned dance.

DRAMA AND THEATER

Participation

As used here, *drama* means the reenactment of life situations. Drama emphasizes the participant and does not require an audience. *Theater* involves an audience. Theater is a more formal presentation that may include a script, sets, acting, directing, and producing.

A *script* is a written description of a play or other performance. The script tells actors what to say, where to stand, and how to enter and leave a stage. *Actors* are the participants in a play or presentation. *Playmaking* means creating an original story and structuring, performing, and evaluating the presentation without a formal audience.

Acting includes the skills of speaking, movement, and sensory awareness. Acting requires preparation and rehearsal before presentation to the audience. Acting may also involve *improvisation* in which actors create their own spontaneous presentation in response to a problem or some other stimulus.

Production means to arrange for a theater performance. Producers coordinate all the technical aspects of the theater presentation. Producers may be concerned with the overall presentation or with technical aspects within a presentation. *Direction* means to coordinate the on-stage activities. Directors help actors practice and are concerned with the actual on-stage presentation.

Evaluating Dramatic Works

Drama and theater provides a natural basis for reflection and evaluation. The following criteria can be used to reflect on and evaluate a dramatic work.

> **Intent** is the reason for a drama or theater work. The intent reflects the objective or purpose for presenting the work.

Structure is the relationship among the different components of a dramatic work. These components include, but are not limited to, balance, coherence, conflict, contrast, emphasis, harmony, rhythm, stress, and transition.

Effectiveness refers to the impact of the dramatic work on the audience. An audience may be affected in many ways by a work including being amused, elated, informed, interested, or moved.

Worth refers to the value of the work itself. That is, it refers to the amount of insight, knowledge, or wisdom found in a work.

MUSIC

Music can be thought of as organized sounds. Our culture has many different types of music, and there are various types of music from cultures all over the world. We usually classify our music in three categories.

1. Popular music is professionally composed, recorded, or performed live and represents the type of music of most current interest to the public.

2. Classical music was composed in the past and, while it is also recorded for sale, is usually performed by large orchestras in "symphony" halls.

3. Folk music usually has a rural origin, is usually not composed professionally, and is often transmitted by oral tradition.

Music consists of pitch, the actual frequency or sound of a note, and duration. A tone has a specific pitch and duration. Different tones occurring simultaneously are called chords.

Harmony is chords with a duration. A melody is the tones that produce the distinctive sound of the music.

Rhythm in our music refers primarily to the regularity of beats or meter. The most common meter in our music has four beats with an emphasis on the first beat.

Pitches separated by specific intervals are called a scale. Most music is based on the diatonic *scale* found on the piano white keys (C, D, E, F, G, A, B). The chromatic scale includes the seven notes of the diatonic scale with the five sharps and flats corresponding to the white and black keys on the piano.

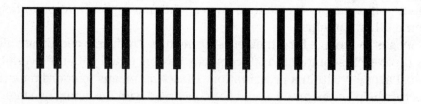

Think of the piano. The piano represents the chromatic scale with groups of seven white keys and five black keys. Music is played using tones from this scale for varying durations.

Usually the melody consists of one note at a time and is played with the right hand. Harmony usually consists of chords and is played with the left hand. The rhythm of the music reflects the meter, and the arrangements and duration of notes.

Form refers to the overall structure of music. Patterns or sections of a musical may repeat or all parts of the pieces may be unique. Phrases or sections in a musical piece may complement one another or they may contrast.

Dynamics describes how loud or how soft the music is. The dynamic aspects of a musical work add to its expressive qualities. Terms such as *pianissimo* (play very softly) are used to refer to musical dynamics.

Tempo refers to the speed of a musical work. The tempo of a piece may vary in different sections of the piece to provide contrast and alert the listener to the various meanings that sections are meant to convey.

Texture refers to the "feel" the musical work imparts. Terms such as *staccato* (choppy) are used to describe the texture of a musical work.

Timbre describes the unique sound produced by different instruments, instrumental combinations and by the human voice. Families of instruments such as woodwinds (clarinet, saxophone) and horns (trumpet, trombone) have similar timbres.

Musical Notation

Our musical notation uses a staff to represent notes. The clef placed at the beginning of the staff determines the pitches for each line and space on the staff.

Notes are written on the staff using the following notation. A flat (♭) lowers the note a half tone while a sharp (♯) raises the note a half tone. The natural (♮) cancels a flat or sharp. Rests indicate a time when no music is played. A note followed by a dot is increased in value by half.

o	Whole-note	♪.	Dotted quarter-note
♩	Half-note	–	Whole-rest
♩	Quarter-note	–	Half-rest
♪	Eighth-note	‏	Quarter-rest
♪	Sixteenth-note	‏	Eighth-rest

The staff is partitioned into measures. The sum of the values of the notes in any measure equals 1. A key signature of sharps and/or flats can be written at the beginning of a staff to change these notes throughout the piece.

A time signature is written at the beginning of each staff. The top number shows how many beats per measure and the bottom number shows which note gets a beat. A typical staff showing the G clef is shown here.

244 Subject Matter Preparation

Musical Instruments

Until recently, music was created by the human voice or by instruments. One typical classification of instruments follows.

Percussion instruments are played by being struck. Bell, drum, gong, piano, symbol, and xylophone are examples.

Brass instruments have traditionally been made from "brass" or some other metal and are played by vibrating the lips against the mouthpiece. French horn, trombone, trumpet, and tuba are examples.

Woodwinds are played by blowing. Most woodwinds have reeds while a few, such as the flute, do not. Bassoon, clarinet, flute, oboe, and saxophone are examples.

Stringed instruments are played by plucking or drawing a bow across the strings. Notes are formed by holding the strings down while plucking or bowing. Cello, guitar, viola, and violin are examples.

This century saw the development of electronically produced music. In the past few decades, computers and other devices have been able to replicate exactly the sounds of almost every instrument. Today, a person can compose a musical piece on a computer and have the computer play that music using a full array of musical sounds without ever picking up an instrument. The full impact of this electronic music is yet to be realized.

GLOSSARY OF MUSICAL TERMS

acoustics The science of sound or the sound property of a room or auditorium.

allegro Cheerful or happy music.

aria A song set off from the rest of the opera.

bass The lower notes in a musical piece; the lowest voice in a choir.

cadence Several notes that signal the ending of a musical piece or phrase.

chamber music Music played by a small group of eight or fewer musicians.

chorale German Protestant hymns.

concerto A musical piece that juxtaposes an orchestra with a soloist or small group of soloists.

movement One part of a piece of music consisting of several large parts.

orchestra A large group of musicians playing many different types of instruments.

overture A musical, orchestral introduction.

VISUAL AND PERFORMING ARTS PRACTICE ITEMS

These items will help you practice for the real LAST. These items have the same form and test the same material as the LAST items. The items you encounter on the real LAST may have a different emphasis and may be more complete.

Instructions
Mark your answers on the sheet provided below. Complete the items in 20 minutes or less. Correct your answer sheet using the answers on page 249.

1 Ⓐ Ⓑ Ⓒ Ⓓ   5 Ⓐ Ⓑ Ⓒ Ⓓ   9 Ⓐ Ⓑ Ⓒ Ⓓ   13 Ⓐ Ⓑ Ⓒ Ⓓ   17 Ⓐ Ⓑ Ⓒ Ⓓ
2 Ⓐ Ⓑ Ⓒ Ⓓ   6 Ⓐ Ⓑ Ⓒ Ⓓ   10 Ⓐ Ⓑ Ⓒ Ⓓ   14 Ⓐ Ⓑ Ⓒ Ⓓ   18 Ⓐ Ⓑ Ⓒ Ⓓ
3 Ⓐ Ⓑ Ⓒ Ⓓ   7 Ⓐ Ⓑ Ⓒ Ⓓ   11 Ⓐ Ⓑ Ⓒ Ⓓ   15 Ⓐ Ⓑ Ⓒ Ⓓ   19 Ⓐ Ⓑ Ⓒ Ⓓ
4 Ⓐ Ⓑ Ⓒ Ⓓ   8 Ⓐ Ⓑ Ⓒ Ⓓ   12 Ⓐ Ⓑ Ⓒ Ⓓ   16 Ⓐ Ⓑ Ⓒ Ⓓ   20 Ⓐ Ⓑ Ⓒ Ⓓ

A.

The Metropolitan Museum of Art, Gift of Mrs. Charles Stewart Smith, Charles Stewart Smith Jr. and Howard Casell Smith, in memory of Charles Stewart Smith, 1914. (14.76.37)

B.

The Metropolitan Museum of Art, Rogers & Fletcher Funds, Erving & Joyce Wolf Fund, Raymond J. Horowitz Gift, Bequest of Richard De Wolfe Brixey, by Exchange, & John Osgood & Elizabeth Amis Cameron Blanchard Memorial Fund, 1978. (1978.203)

C.

The Metropolitan Museum of Art, Gift of Mr. and Mrs. Joseph G. Blum, 1970. (1970.527.1)

1. Picture A expresses
   (A) anger.
   (B) pensiveness.
   (C) distraction.
   (D) assertiveness.

2. Picture A could be best described as
   (A) an abstract work whose primary meaning is the work itself.
   (B) a central figure surrounded by rectangular border.
   (C) an impressionistic work in which the figure represents an animal.
   (D) an 18th century American work.

3. Picture A is distinctive because
   (A) the border is decorated.
   (B) the figure is horned.
   (C) The sword has a carved, ornamental handle.
   (D) The figure is thrust forward.

4. Picture B depicts a
   (A) rocky shore.
   (B) seaport.
   (C) sloping shore.
   (D) turgid sea.

5. Picture B could be best described as
   (A) a bucolic scene.
   (B) an active scene.
   (C) a morning scene.
   (D) a languid scene.

6. Which of the following best describes Picture B?
   (A) A scene with people talking
   (B) A scene with children playing
   (C) A commercial scene
   (D) A scene dominated by the sky

7. Picture C primarily depicts
   (A) geometric contrasts.
   (B) a swirling sky.
   (C) a skyward needle.
   (D) a supported walkway.

8. Which of the following best describes Picture C?
   (A) A brick plaza sweeping by open latticed rectangles
   (B) A surreal world visited by real people
   (C) A visitors center at a spaceport
   (D) A central spire framed by sphere, semicircle, and sky

9. Picture C is most likely
   (A) an artist's rendering of buildings to be constructed.
   (B) a set for a futuristic movies.
   (C) a three-dimensional model of a NASA visitors center.
   (D) a picture of an actual structure.

10. Which picture best depicts determination?
    (A)
    (B)
    (C)

11. Which picture does not include a semicircular shape?
    (A)
    (B)
    (C)

12. Which picture shows multiple events?
    (A)
    (B)
    (C)

13. Which of the following is the name for the process of applying watercolors to a freshly plastered surface?
    (A) fresco
    (B) watercolor
    (C) mosaic
    (D) mural

14. When a mason refers to a course, he or she usually means
    (A) time spent as an apprentice.
    (B) a row of bricks.
    (C) a layer of plaster.
    (D) a stretch of lawn.

15. The songs "Frankie and Johnny," and "John Henry" are American examples of
    (A) blues.
    (B) jazz.
    (C) protest.
    (D) ballads.

16. The impressionist art movement, which included artists such as Monet and Renoir, was founded as a reaction against more classical styles and featured
    (A) abstract, linear works.
    (B) undetailed, but recognizable works.
    (C) blue and rose hues.
    (D) realistic, precise works.

17. Masks were worn regularly in Greek and Roman plays. A character wore the mask from the very beginning of the play
    (A) to conceal the actor's identity.
    (B) until the very last act, when it was removed.
    (C) enabling the actor to show a range of emotions.
    (D) removing any doubt about the characters eventual fate.

18. What form of dance do you associate with Alvin Ailey?
    (A) ballet
    (B) modern
    (C) rock
    (D) tap

19. In the key of C, which of these chords is a minor chord?
    (A) C E G
    (B) G B D
    (C) A C E
    (D) F A C

20. The Dutch artist Mondrian is best known for what art form?
    (A) abstract art
    (B) architecture
    (C) non-representational art
    (D) representational art

Answers

1. D	5. D	9. D	13. A	17. D
2. B	6. D	10. A	14. B	18. A
3. D	7. A	11. A	15. D	19. C
4. A	8. D	12. B	16. B	20. C

9 LITERATURE AND COMMUNICATION

USING THIS CHAPTER

This chapter prepares you for the Literature items on the LAST. Choose one of these approaches.

I want a Literature and Communication review.

❏ Read the Literature and Communication Review on page 252.
❏ Review Analyzing Literary Imagery on page 263.
❏ Complete the Literature and Communication Practice Items on page 267.

I want to practice Literature items.

❏ Complete the Literature and Communication Practice Items on page 267.

LITERATURE

Children's Literature

Children's literature, as we know it, did not exist until the late 1700s. Jean Rousseau, in his influential *Emile*, was among the first writers to popularize the view that children were not just small adults. A collection of age-old fairy tales, *The Tales of Mother Goose*, was published in France about 1700. The first illustrated book was probably *The Visible World in Pictures*, which was written in Latin about 1760 by John Comenius.

Before this time, most children's literature conveyed a religious or moral message or was designed for instruction. A few adult books appealed to children including *Robinson Crusoe* and the satirical *Gulliver's Travels*.

In the United States during the 1800s, James Fenimore Cooper wrote *The Last of the Mohicans*, Washington Irving wrote *The Legend of Sleepy Hollow*, and Nathaniel Hawthorne wrote *A Wonder Book for Boys and Girls*. Louisa May Alcott wrote *Little Women* and Samuel Clemens, writing as Mark Twain, wrote *The Adventures of Huckleberry Finn*. Horatio Alger wrote a series of "rags to riches" books at the end of the century.

On the European continent, the Brothers Grimm published *Grimm's Fairy Tales*, which included "Snow White and the Seven Dwarfs." Hans Christian Anderson published a number of stories including "The Ugly Duckling." *Heidi* and the *Adventures of Pinocchio* were also published about this time.

In England, Charles Dodgson, writing as Lewis Carroll, penned *Alice's Adventures in Wonderland*. John Tenniel provided the illustrations for this famous work. Robert Louis Stevenson wrote *Treasure Island*, Rudyard Kipling wrote *The Jungle Book*, and Edward Lear wrote the *Nonsense Book*.

At the beginning of this century, Frank Baum wrote the first *Wizard of Oz* book and Lucy Maud Montgomery wrote *Anne of Green Gables*. Also in this century, Hugh Loftig penned the famous Dr. Doolittle books, A. A. Milne published a series of Winnie-the-Pooh books and P. L.

Travers wrote the Mary Poppins books. Albert Payson Terhune wrote a series of dog stories, most notably *Lad a Dog*.

The Little Prince and *Charlotte's Web* were published in the mid 1900s. About this time, Theodore Geisel, writing as Dr. Seuss, began to write a popular series of books, including *Green Eggs and Ham*. Notable books of the past twenty years include *The Snowy Day*, and *Where the Wild Things Are*.

The Newbery Award and Caldecott Medal are given annually to the most notable American children's books. The Newbery Award is named after publisher John Newbery and is awarded to the best American children's book. The Caldecott Medal is named after illustrator Randolph Caldecott and is given to the best picture book.

Poetry

Poetry usually communicates through linguistic imagery, sounds of words, and a rhythmic quality. Poetry and poems are among the oldest forms of literature and date to ancient Greece. Ancient poems were originally sung, and poetry has been slowly emancipated from this reliance on music, replacing it with a linguistic cadence.

Poetry is often associated with rhyming. However, many poems do not rhyme. Some poems rely on their rhythmic patterns alone, others are composed of open verses, while still others, such as Japanese haiku, rely on special features such as the number of syllables in a line.

The epic, the lyric, and some romances are examples of early poetry.

Epic

The epic is a very long narrative poem, usually about a single heroic person. Epics have a monumental sweep, embrace the essence of an entire nation, and frequently include mythical forces that influence the inevitable battles and conflicts. Epics include the *Odyssey* and the *Illiad*, which were written by Homer and embrace Greek national themes, as well as the Scandinavian *Beowulf*.

Lyric

The lyric is related to the epic, but it is shorter and presents profound feelings or ideas. The terms elegy and ode both refer to lyric poems. Lyric poems were called rondeaus when sung by French troubadours and madrigals when sung by English balladeers. During the 1800s both Robert Browning and Tennyson wrote lyrics. Modern lyrics are still written but no longer occupy a central place in culture.

Romance

The romance and the epic are similar. However, the romance is concerned with love and chivalry and, originally, was written in one of the romance languages. This genre of literature dates from the 1100s and was most popular during the 1200s. Stories of *King Arthur and the Knights of the Round Table* are romances.

Satire

Satire exposes the frailty of the human condition through wit, irony, mockery, sarcasm, or ridicule. For example, the sentence, "The doctor looked down at the man sneaking away from the impending flu shot and said, 'At least he knows to avoid sharp objects,'" is an example of satire. Occasionally, entire works such as Jonathan Swift's *Gulliver's Travels* are satirical.

Short Story

The short story is a short fictional piece, usually with a single theme. The first short stories date from ancient Egypt. O. Henry and Mark Twain were famous writers who penned short stories in the early 1900s. Hemingway and Faulkner wrote short stories before mid-century with John Cheever and Eudora Welty noted as prominent short story writers in the latter half of the century.

Novel

The novel is a fictional story that depicts characters in a plot. The novel builds on the epic and the romance. The first novels were written during the Renaissance (1300–1600) and were developed more fully during the 1700s and 1800s in England.

The modern novel developed in the 1800s. Novels with strong historical and social themes, including dialogue, were written by the English authors Dickens, Thackeray, and Eliot. American novels written during this time tended to be allegorical.

American novels in the early 1900s focused on social ills. These novels include *The Jungle* by Sinclair Lewis, *Studs Lonigan* by James Farrell, and *The Grapes of Wrath* by John Steinbeck. In the late 1900s American novels of great strength appeared including *The Naked and the Dead* by Norman Mailer and *Catch-22* by Joseph Heller.

APPROACHES TO READING AND INTERPRETING LITERATURE

Recognize the Author's Purpose

The author's primary purpose explains why the author wrote the passage. The purpose is closely related to the main idea. You might think. "Fine, I know the main idea. But why did the author take the time to write about that main idea?" "What is the author trying to make me know or feel?"

The author's purpose will be in one of the following five categories.

Describe	Present an image of physical reality or a mental image.
Entertain	Amuse, Perform
Inform	Clarify, Explain, State
Narrate	Relate, Tell a story
Persuade	Argue, Convince, Prove

There is no hard and fast rule for identifying the author's purpose. Rely on your informed impression of the passage. Once in a while a passage may overtly state the author's purpose. But you must usually figure it out on your own. Remember, one of the answer choices will be correct. Your job is to decide which one it is.

Distinguish Between Fact and Opinion

Facts can be proven true *or* false by some objective means or method. *A fact refers to persons, things, or events that exist now or existed at some time in the past.* Note that a fact does not have to be true. For example, the statement "The tallest human being alive today is 86 inches tall" is false. This statement is a fact because it can be proven false.

Opinions, however, cannot be proved or disproved by some objective means or method. Opinions are subjective and include attitudes and probabilities. Some statements, which seem true, may still be opinions. For example, the statement "A car is easier to park than a bus" seems true. However, this statement is an opinion. There is no way to objectively prove this statement true or false.

Examples:

Fact: <u>Abraham Lincoln was President of the United States during the Civil War</u>. We can check historical records and find out if the statement is true. This statement of fact is true.

Fact: <u>Robert E. Lee went into exile in Canada after the Civil War</u>. We can check historical records. This factual statement is true. Lee later became president of Washington College, now called Washington and Lee University.

Fact: <u>It is more than 90°F. outside</u>. We can use a thermometer to prove or disprove this statement.

Fact: <u>More people were born in November than in any other month</u>. We can check statistical records to prove or disprove this statement.

Opinion: <u>If Lincoln had lived, Reconstruction would have been better</u>. This sounds true, but there is no way to prove or disprove this statement.

Opinion: <u>Lee was the Civil War's most brilliant general</u>. Sounds true, but there is no way to prove it.

Opinion: <u>It will always be colder in November than in July</u>. Sounds true! But we can't prove or disprove future events.

Detect Bias

Bias

A statement or passage reveals bias if the author has prejudged or has a predisposition to a doctrine, idea, or practice. Bias means the author is trying to convince or influence the reader through some emotional appeal or slanted writing.

Bias can be positive or negative.

Positive Bias: She is so lovely, she deserves the very best.
Negative Bias: She is so horrible, I hope she gets what's coming to her.

Forms of Bias

Biased writing can often be identified by the presence of one or more of the following forms of bias.

Emotional Language	Language that appeals to the reader's emotions, and not to common sense or logic.
	Positive: If I am elected, I will help your family get jobs.
	Negative: If my opponent is elected, your family will lose their jobs.

Inaccurate Information	Language that presents false, inaccurate, or unproved information as though it were factual.
	Positive: My polls indicate that I am very popular. Negative: My polls indicate that a lot of people disagree with my opponent.
Name Calling	Language that uses negative, disapproving terms without any factual basis.
	Negative: I'll tell you, my opponent is a real jerk.
Slanted Language	Language that slants the facts or evidence toward the writer's point of view.
	Positive: I am a positive person, looking for the good side of people. Negative: My opponent finds fault with everyone and everything.
Stereotyping	Language that indicates that a person is like all the members of a particular group.
	Positive: I belong to the Krepenkle party, the party known for its honesty. Negative: My opponent belongs to the Perplenkle party, the party of increased taxes.

Recognize the Author's Tone

Tone

The author's tone is the author's attitude as reflected in the passage. Answering this question means choosing the correct tone word. How do you think the author would sound while speaking? What impression would you form about the speaker's attitude or feeling? The answer to the latter question will usually lead you to the author's tone. A partial list of tone words is given below.

absurd	excited	outraged
amused	formal	outspoken
angry	gentle	pathetic
apathetic	hard	pessimistic
arrogant	impassioned	playful
bitter	indignant	prayerful
cheerful	intense	reverent
comic	intimate	righteous
compassionate	joyous	satirical
complex	loving	sentimental
concerned	malicious	serious
cruel	mocking	solemn
depressed	nostalgic	tragic
distressed	objective	uneasy
evasive	optimistic	vindictive

Recognize Valid Arguments

Valid arguments are reasonable. Valid arguments are objective and supported by evidence. Invalid arguments are *not* reasonable. They are not objective. Invalid arguments usually reflect one of the following fallacies.

Ad hominem	Arguing against a person to discredit their position, rather than an argument against the position itself
Ad populum	An argument that appeals to the emotions of the person
Bandwagon	Arguing for position because of its popularity
Begging the question	Assuming that an argument, or part of an argument, is true without providing proof
Circular logic	Using a statement of a position to argue in favor of that position
Either/or	Stating that the conclusion falls into one of two extremes, when there are more intermediate choices
Faulty analogy	Using an analogy as an argument when the analogy does not match the situation under discussion
Hasty generalization	Reaching a conclusion too quickly, before all the information is known
Non sequitur	A conclusion that does not logically follow from the facts
Post hoc, ergo propter hoc	Falsely stating that one event following another is caused by the first event (faulty cause and effect)
Red herring	An irrelevant point, diverting attention from the position under discussion

GLOSSARY OF LITERARY TERMS

allegory Expression in which the characters, story, and setting actually represent other people, settings, or abstract ideas. This symbolic meaning is more important than the literal meaning. For example, Jonathan Swift's *Gulliver's Travels* is allegorical when it uses horses and other creatures to represent people. *Aesop's Fables* use allegory to represent moral or ethical ideas. Parables such as the Prodigal Son use allegory to teach a lesson.

alliteration The repetition of an initial consonant in nearby words. For example, the selections "Neither rain, nor sleet nor dark of night," and "Peas?—Please. Peanuts?—Possibly. Potatoes?—Potentially. Pigs knuckles?—Please!" use alliteration.

anthropomorphism Attributing the human body or human qualities to nonhuman things or entities. Initially, anthropomorphism meant depicting a god or gods as humans with human qualities.

biography A full account of a person's life. An autobiography is a biography written by the person.

connotation The secondary meanings that the word represents.

couplet Two successive poetic lines that form a single unit because they rhyme.

denotation Actual meaning of the word

doggerel A work that features awkward or rough verbiage. Most often, this clumsy verse is the result of an inept writer, although it may occasionally be intended as humor.

essay A fairly brief work that tries to get across a particular point of view or to persuade the reader about the correctness of a point of view.

fable A short literary piece designed to present a moral or truth. Fables frequently involve animals. The most famous fables are attributed to a reputed Greek slave, Aesop, who lived in the sixth century.

figures of speech Figurative language that is not meant to be taken literally. Figures of speech are used to create some special meaning or imagery.

euphemism Figure of speech in which an inoffensive term is substituted for one that may be offensive or cause distress. For example, *pass away* may be substituted for *die*, and *indisposed* may be substituted for *ill*.

hyperbole Figure of speech in which a drastic overstatement or understatement is used. Hyperbole may be used to emphasize a point or for comic effect. For example, after an argument between friends one might exclaim, "You are the worst person who has ever lived." In another example, the winner of the Olympic decathlon may be referred to as "Not that bad an athlete."

metaphor Figure of speech in which one thing is discussed as though it were something else. The words *like* or *as* are not used. For example, "My life's a tennis match, but I never get to serve" and "The night crept through til dawn" are metaphors.

mixed metaphor Figure of speech in which two or more unrelated metaphors are combined. For example, "Running on empty, the soccer player plowed through the rest of the match" is a mixed metaphor.

onomatopoeia Figure of speech that refers to words that imitate natural sounds. Onomatopoeia appears in the words of a once popular song, "*Buzz, buzz, buzz* goes the bumble bee, *twiddely, diddely, dee* goes the bird."

simile Figure of speech that compares two different things, usually using the words *like* or *as*. For example, "Her eyes are like deep, quiet pools" or "Her nails are like tiger claws" are similes.

haiku Poetry of Japanese origin with three non-rhyming lines with a pattern of five-seven-five syllables.

legend A heroic story or collection of stories about a specific person or persons. Legends are presented as fact but are actually a combination of fact and fiction. Legends with differing degrees of factual content have been built around Davy Crockett, who "kilt him a bar when he was only three," and the gigantic logger Paul Bunyan and his blue ox Babe. Paul Bunyan reputedly cleared out entire Maine forests with one swing of the ax.

COMMUNICATION

INFORMATION SOURCES

Print

Information can be retrieved from books, magazines, and other print sources by simply picking up the reading materials and turning and flipping through the pages. The book, newspaper, or periodical remains one of the most efficient ways to access print information.

Print materials are also found in libraries or other repositories on microfilm and microfiche. Microfilms are 35mm films of books, while microfiche are flat and can contain hundreds of pages of text material. Microfilm and microfiche are read with specialized readers.

Technology

Other information can be retrieved on or through the computer. Written materials can be entered on a computer, usually with a word processor. This information can be accessed directly through the computer's hard disk. Special features of most word processors and other utilities permit the user to search electronically for words and phrases. Sound, graphics, and animation may also be stored on a computer's hard disk. These sounds and images may be accessed using specialized computer programs.

Print materials, images, sounds and animation may also be stored on CD-ROMs designed for computer use. Information on these CD-ROMs may be accessed through a CD-ROM player that is connected to the computer. Images and sounds on videotapes, audiotapes, music CD-ROMs, and videodisk may also be accessed through the computer.

Computers can be connected to telephone lines and television cables using a modem. Modems allow computers to upload and download data from other computers, usually via the Internet. "Going on line" has become a popular way to gather information.

The Internet is a vast collection of computers around the world. These computers are connected by cables and phone lines, forming a huge net. Once on the Internet, a person can have access to enormous amounts of information.

Browsers such as Microsoft Explorer and Netscape Navigator turn the Internet's electronic signals into viewable text and images. You can retrieve text, pictures, video, and sound with these browsers. Almost all periodical and newspaper information is available on line, and you can hold Internet conversations and Internet videoconferences.

The World Wide Web is the collection of sites on the Internet. Web addresses identify the different sites and the information contained at these sites. For example the Web address http://www.barronseduc.com connects you directly to the Barron's Web site.

Search engines such as Excite and Yahoo help you to find sites containing the information you want. If you entered "teacher testing," these search engines would return a list of WWW sites in their catalog containing these key words.

Rhetorical Conventions of Argumentation, Exposition, Narration, and Reflection

In **argumentation** the writer or speaker tries to convince the readers or listeners to accept a particular view or idea. There are several rules to follow to construct a well-ordered argument. Your presentation should appear moderate and reasoned, and you should acknowledge the reasonableness of those who differ with you.

The statements must be believable in form and in fact. That is, the statements must distinguish among fact, opinion, and the conclusions you have drawn. The presentation should clarify the meanings of key ideas and words. The presentation must also squarely address the question and not beg the question as described in the preceding example.

The presentation must support any views or conclusions with solid evidence and arguments. The arguments can be inductive or deductive. However, these arguments must avoid the invalid and fallacious arguments noted previously.

> **Expository** presentations simply explain. This book is essentially expository presentation. It explains about the LAST and how to pass it.

> **Narration** presents a factual or fictional story. A written fictional account or a spoken presentation about your life as a child is a narration.

> **Reflection** describes a scene, person, or emotion. A spoken description of your neighborhood or a written note describing how you felt when you graduated from high school are reflections.

LANGUAGE

We use language, including gestures and sounds, to communicate. Humans first used gestures, but it was spoken language that opened the vistas for human communication. Language consists of two things: the thoughts that language conveys and the physical sounds, writing, and structure of the language itself.

Human speech organs (mouth, tongue, lips, etc.) were not developed to make sounds but they uniquely determined the sounds and words humans could produce. Human speech gradually came to be loosely bound together by unique rules of grammar.

Many believe that humans developed their unique ability to speak with the development of a specialized area of the brain called Broca's area. If this is so, human speech and language probably developed in the past 100,000 years.

The appearance of written language about 3500 B.C. separates prehistoric from historic times. Written language often does not adequately represent the spoken language. For example, English uses the 26-letter Latin alphabet, which does not represent all the English sounds.

The English Language

The English language emerged 1500 years ago from Germanic languages on the European continent and developed primarily in England. American English is based on the English language and includes words from every major language including Latin, Greek, and French.

English is spoken throughout Australia, Canada, the United Kingdom, and the United States. It is the most universally accepted language in the world, and only Chinese is spoken by more people. In all likelihood, English will become even more prominent as the world's primary language.

Some experts estimate that there are over 1,000,000 English words, more than any other language in the world. Sounds and letters do not match in the English language. For example the word spelled t-o-u-g-h is pronounced *tuf*. The rock group Phish also reminds us of this variation, which often makes English words difficult to pronounce and spell.

Linguistics

Linguistics is the scientific study of language. Linguistics studies the development of languages and language groups, vocabulary and meaning, the structure of contemporary languages, and how speech and language is learned and taught. A list of the areas of language studied by linguistics follows.

Morphology studies morphemes, the building blocks of language. These building blocks include words and roots, word endings, prefixes and suffixes, case, number, and tense.

Phonetics studies all speech sounds in a language and the way speech sounds are produced. Phonetics is reflected in many school curricula.

Phonology studies the important sounds in a language.

Transformational grammar is an approach to understanding language developed by Noam Chomsky, an American linguist. He posited that a universal linguistic structure was present in all humans. He further said that this structure naturally leads people to "transform" their thoughts into sentences that follow natural grammatical rules. There are also grammatical rules for individual languages. Chomsky pointed out that many errors found in children's grammar follow these natural grammatical rules.

LANGUAGE DEVELOPMENT

Language has a structure and a function. The structure of a language refers to the way words and sentences are combined to create effective communication. The function of a language is the ability to use language to think and communicate. Understanding language development means understanding how each of these aspects develops.

Much of the recent work on structural language development is related to Chomsky's work. Chomsky says that the "old" explanations of language development, modeling and reinforcement, were incorrect. This is not to say that language cannot be learned through these methods because this task is accomplished every day as people learn a foreign language. Rather, Chomsky says that this model-repeat-reinforce approach is not the way that children actually learn language.

Chomsky holds that children possess an innate ability to learn language, both words and structure, merely through exposure. To bolster his argument, Chomsky points out that most grammatical mistakes made by children actually follow the general grammatical rules of the language and that the children's errors represent exceptions to these rules.

For example, a child may say "Lisa goed to the store" instead of "Lisa went to the store." Chomsky would say, *goed* is structurally sound and represents a good grasp of the English language. The child would certainly say *hopped* if Lisa had gotten to the store that way. The problem is created because the past tense for *go* is an exception to the past tense formation rule.

Vygotsky is a prominent psychologist who studied the relationship between thought and language. A contemporary of Piaget, he pointed out that thought and language are not coordinated during the sensorimotor and most of the preoperational stages. That is, from birth through about age 6 or 7, thought and language develop independently, with language being primarily functional.

As students move toward the concrete operational stage, their language also becomes operational. That is, thought and the structural and functional aspects of language become integrated, and students can use language to think and solve problems.

Teachers can foster language development most effectively by constantly encouraging and enabling students to express themselves by speaking and writing. Students should be encouraged to integrate writing and speaking with all subject matter, and writing and speaking should be the overarching classroom objectives to be developed in every lesson. In all cases, teachers should help children communicate in standard English while in school.

ANALYZING LITERARY IMAGERY

How to Analyze Literary Imagery

When you analyze a literary passage, you should consider both the literal meaning of the passage and the imagery it evokes. Consider this sentence: "The beggar pushed his way through the crowds in the squalid slum." We can tell from the sentence that the person is poor and is in a run-down area. However, what imagery does the passage evoke? That is, what sights, sounds, tactile experiences, smells, taste, and experiences of temperature and movement do you have?

The beggar pushed his way through the crowds in the squalid slum.

Sight. Try to visualize the beggar. Do you see a person on a street or sidewalk in an urban slum? Do you see a beggar with tattered clothes in the streets of India? Write what you visualize about the beggar.

_____
_____
_____
_____

Try to visualize the surroundings. Do you see apartment houses with boarded-up windows and crowds of people sitting on corners and outside doors? Do you see the crowded streets of India teeming with people? Write what you visualize.

_____
_____
_____
_____

Sound. Try to hear the sounds. Do you hear the honking of horns or do you hear the cries of hawkers? Write about the sounds you hear.

_____
_____
_____

Tactile. Try to feel the tactile experience. Can you feel the pavement beneath the beggar's feet or the press of the crowds? Write about the tactile experience.

_____
_____
_____

Smell. Explore your sense of smell. Do you smell exhaust fumes or can you smell the odor of decaying food left in the sun? Write about the odors you smell.

_____

_____

_____

Taste. Explore your sense of taste. Can you taste food cooking or a bit of food just eaten? Write about your taste experience.

_____

_____

_____

Temperature. Explore your sensation of temperature. Can you feel the cold of night or do you experience a hot day? Write about your experience of temperature.

_____

_____

_____

Movement. What movement do you experience? Can you sense the beggar's movement through the crowd? Write about your experience of movement.

_____

_____

_____

Write below the imagery you experience from the following passage.

The pilot swung the plane around in an attempt to make an emergency landing on the small field.

Sight. Write what you visualize.

_____

_____

_____

Sound. Write about the sounds you hear.

_____
_____
_____

Tactile. Write about the tactile experience.

_____
_____
_____

Smell. Write about the odors you smell.

_____
_____
_____

Taste. Write about your taste experience.

_____
_____
_____

Temperature. Write about your temperature experience.

_____
_____
_____

Movement. Write about your movement experience.

_____
_____
_____

LITERATURE AND COMMUNICATION PRACTICE ITEMS

These items will help you practice the concepts in this chapter. The items you encounter on the LAST may have a different emphasis and may be more complete.

Instructions

Mark your answers on the sheet provided below. Complete the items in 20 minutes or less. Correct your answer sheet using the answers on page 271.

1 Ⓐ Ⓑ Ⓒ Ⓓ	5 Ⓐ Ⓑ Ⓒ Ⓓ	9 Ⓐ Ⓑ Ⓒ Ⓓ	13 Ⓐ Ⓑ Ⓒ Ⓓ	17 Ⓐ Ⓑ Ⓒ Ⓓ
2 Ⓐ Ⓑ Ⓒ Ⓓ	6 Ⓐ Ⓑ Ⓒ Ⓓ	10 Ⓐ Ⓑ Ⓒ Ⓓ	14 Ⓐ Ⓑ Ⓒ Ⓓ	18 Ⓐ Ⓑ Ⓒ Ⓓ
3 Ⓐ Ⓑ Ⓒ Ⓓ	7 Ⓐ Ⓑ Ⓒ Ⓓ	11 Ⓐ Ⓑ Ⓒ Ⓓ	15 Ⓐ Ⓑ Ⓒ Ⓓ	19 Ⓐ Ⓑ Ⓒ Ⓓ
4 Ⓐ Ⓑ Ⓒ Ⓓ	8 Ⓐ Ⓑ Ⓒ Ⓓ	12 Ⓐ Ⓑ Ⓒ Ⓓ	16 Ⓐ Ⓑ Ⓒ Ⓓ	20 Ⓐ Ⓑ Ⓒ Ⓓ

Questions 1–5 are based on this passage

The United States National Park system is extensive, although most land dedicated to the park system is in the western states. This is no doubt the case because these lands are
(5) occupied by states most recently admitted to the union. I have some very happy personal memories about Yellowstone National Park, having visited there on several occasions. All of my visits came before the series of fires, which
(10) burned much of the park's forested areas. My most unusual recollection dates back a number of years when I was part of a group waiting for the Old Faithful geyser to erupt. A young child was standing about twenty yards away looking
(15) at something on the ground. The group gathered around where the child was standing. And while Old Faithful _____, we all watched a small, rusty water pipe leak onto the ground. I
(20) never understood what about the pipe drew everyone's interest. It must have to do with a child's wonder.

1. Which of the following best characterizes the preceding passage?
   (A) A person describes the American National Park System.
   (B) A person describes his childhood in Yellowstone National Park.
   (C) A person describes group behavior with an example from his or her own experience.
   (D) A person describes an unusual memory from Yellowstone Park.

2. Why does the writer discuss the Yellowstone fires in lines 9-11?
   (A) to discuss the destruction of the park
   (B) to give a time frame to the writer's visits
   (C) to warn against careless use of fire
   (D) to describe the burned areas

3. Which of the following words would be most appropriate to fill the blank space in line 18?
   (A) burned
   (B) gurgled
   (C) foamed
   (D) gushed

4. This passage is best characterized as
   (A) argumentation.
   (B) exposition.
   (C) narration.
   (D) reflection.

5. What is the subject of the sentence "My most unusual recollection dates back . . .," which begins at the end of line 10 and ends on line 13?
   (A) My
   (B) recollection
   (C) I
   (D) group

6. These are the first two lines from a haiku poem:

   The waves on the beach
   Are a-rhythmically crashing.

   Which of the following choices could be the third line in the poem?
   (A) Like the precarious fate
   (B) Like the sands of time
   (C) Like the love clinging
   (D) Like the deafening quiet

7. Which of the following examples would Chomsky (transformational grammar) identify as an error demonstrating children possess an innate grammatical sense?
   (A) "Jim told me I ain't going to no picnic."
   (B) "Lynne goed to the picnic already."
   (C) "Not right to make me stay home."
   (D) "I hollers and screams if I can't go to that picnic."

Questions 8–11 are based on the following passages.

   (A) The tires screeched, and the car spun uncontrollably. I gripped the wheel in fear as the car swung around again and again. My body was thrown against the side of the car—my heart pounded. A horn blared in my ear, and images of cars, buildings, and light poles went whizzing by. It seemed that I would careen into the car just ahead of me. Then everything stopped. I'm not going on that ride again.

(B) A soft and silent breeze swept across the field carrying with it the sweet smell of blooming flowers, the delightful chirping of circling birds, and small bits of pollen and newly cut grass. The breeze softly passed unfelt by all but the few standing at the field's edge. Life is like that breeze in that field for all who will but stop to experience it.

(C) The seat was hard, the room was crowded, and the perspiration flowed. All eyes were on the proctor who was handing out tests and on the air conditioner, which wasn't working. They all wanted to be teachers, and they were all ready to take the test, but they were not ready for the hottest day of the year and the stuffiest room imaginable. Someone sighed. What were they to do?

(D) "I object your honor," called out the lawyer. "I object to the way that my rights and my client's rights have been systematically, outrageously, and impermissibly denied by this court, by the incredibly irresponsible reporting of the tawdry tabloid shows, and by the second-rate journalists who control the newspapers in this town."
"I guess the evidence is against that lawyer," thought the judge.

8. Which passage includes a metaphor for life?

9. Which passage describes a person's reaction to an amusement park ride?

10. Which passage includes a rhetorical question?

11. Which of the following choices describes a common element of these passages?
    (A) Each passage draws a conclusion.
    (B) Each passage describes a feeling.
    (C) Each passage includes dialogue.
    (D) Each passage is descriptive.

Questions 12–14 are based on the following reading.

I remember my childhood vacations at a bungalow colony near a lake. Always barefoot, my friend and I spent endless hours playing and enjoying our fantasies. We were
(5) pirates, rocket pilots, and detectives. Everyday objects were transformed into swords, ray guns, and two-way wrist radios. With a lake at hand, we swam, floated on our crude rafts made of old lumber, fished, and fell in. The
(10) adult world seemed so meaningless while our world seemed so full. Returning years later I saw the colony for what it was—tattered and torn. The lake was shallow and

muddy. But the tree that had been our look-
(15) out was still there. And there was the house where the feared master spy hid from the FBI. There was the site of the launching pad for our imaginary rocket trips. The posts of the dock we had sailed from many times were
(20) still visible. But my fantasy play did not depend on this place. My child-mind would have been a buccaneer wherever it was.

12. Which of the following choices best characterizes this passage?
    (A) An adult describes disappointment at growing up.
    (B) A child describes the adult world through the child's eyes.
    (C) An adult discusses childhood viewed as a child and as an adult.
    (D) An adult discusses the meaning of fantasy play.

13. The sentence "The adult world seemed so meaningless while our world seemed so full" on lines 10 and 11 is used primarily to
    (A) emphasize the emptiness of most adult lives.
    (B) provide a transition from describing childhood to describing adulthood.
    (C) show how narcissistic children are.
    (D) describe the difficulty this child had relating to adults.

14. Which of the following best characterizes the last sentence in the passage?
    (A) The child would have been rebellious, no matter what.
    (B) Childhood is not a place but a state of mind.
    (C) We conform more as we grow older.
    (D) The writer will always feel rebellious.

Questions 15–18 are based on the following passages.
    (A) Swept along the gnarly road of life,
        Abounding with its traffic laden strife.
        Rest you now upon the yonder hill,
        Tis there that you'll finally be still.

I am about the richest man there is,
(B) 'Cause I was ever so great at biz.
The biz that I was great at though,
Was little more than blowing snow.
(C) Birds in the meadow—
chirp, chirp, chirp,
Too full a tummy—
burp, burp, burp,
Cats at the milk saucer—
slurp, slurp, slurp,
Don't have another rhyme—
gulp, gulp, gulp.
(D) They say that fame and fortune
comes,
From starring in some fil-e-ums.
But it seems to me that you end up,
Just taking lots of pill-e-ums.

15. Which passage provides a contrast between two possible outcomes?

16. Which passage appears to be a metaphor for the end of life?

17. Which passage relates a person's success to obscuring or hiding?

18. Which of the following best explains why the author of selection (C) chose the words that appear at the end of each line?
(A) For poetic effect
(B) To have a particular number of beats in each line
(C) To emphasize the *urp* sound
(D) To conform to the rules for haiku

Questions 19–20 are based on the passages preceding them.

Japanese students have always been considered to be well-prepared for life in the world's business and engineering communities. The mathematics and science curricula of Japanese schools are considered to be superior to those in American schools. With the daily advancement of Japanese technological prowess, how can American children ever hope to compete with their Japanese counterparts?

19. Which of the following is the best descriptor of the author's tone in this passage?
(A) disbelief
(B) anger
(C) pride
(D) concern

The retired basketball player said that, while modern players were better athletes because there was so much emphasis on youth basketball and increased focus on training, he still believed that the players of his day were better because they were more committed to the game, better understood its nuances, and were more dedicated to team play.

20. The retired basketball player attributes the increased athletic prowess of today's basketball players to
(A) better nutrition.
(B) youth basketball programs.
(C) salary caps.
(D) more athletic scholarships.

Answers

1. D	5. B	9. A	13. C	17. B
2. B	6. B	10. C	14. B	18. A
3. D	7. B	11. D	15. D	19. D
4. D	8. B	12. C	16. A	20. B

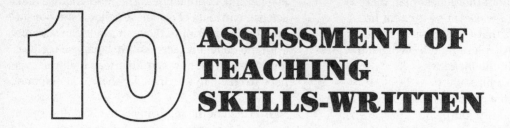

10 ASSESSMENT OF TEACHING SKILLS-WRITTEN

TEST INFO BOX

This chapter helps you prepare for the ATS-W. The chapter includes a comprehensive subject review of the topics included on the ATS-W and sample ATS-W written assignments.

Test takers agree that teaching experience is an important component of preparing for the ATS-W.

MULTIPLE-CHOICE TEST

The ATS-W has 80 multiple-choice items. The items are about the practical aspects of teaching and are partitioned approximately among the ATS-W subareas as shown below.

Knowledge of the Learner.............................20 multiple-choice items
Instructional Planning and Assessment.....15 multiple-choice items
Instructional Delivery....................................25 multiple-choice items
The Professional Environment ....20 multiple-choice items

WRITTEN ASSIGNMENT

The ATS-W includes a written assignment. This written assignment may not be an essay. For example, past written assignments have asked for the curricula and lesson plans. You may be asked to respond to a classroom situation, or some other education-related situation. The written assignment must be clear enough to be understood, but the readers do not evaluate your writing ability. However, a well-written assignment always makes the best impression. The written assignment is rated 0–3 by two readers based on the appropriateness of your response. The final written assignment score of 0–6 is the sum of these two scores.

USING THIS CHAPTER

This chapter prepares you to take the ATS-W. Choose one of these approaches.

I want all the ATS-W review I can get.

❑ Read the entire review section on page 279.
❑ Take the ATS-W Review Quiz on page 274.
❑ Correct the Review Quiz and reread the indicated parts of the review.
❑ Complete the ATS-W Practice Items on page 319.
❑ Complete the ATS-W Practice Written Assignment on pages 20–22.

I want a thorough ATS-W review.

❑ Take the ATS-W Review Quiz on page 274.
❑ Correct the Review Quiz and read the indicated parts of the review.
❑ Complete the ATS-W Practice Items on page 319.
❑ Complete the ATS-W Practice Written Assignment on pages 20–22.

I want a quick ATS-W review.

❑ Take and correct the ATS-W Review Quiz on page 274.
❑ Complete the ATS-W Practice Items on page 319.
❑ Complete the ATS-W Practice Written Assignment on pages 20–22.

I want to practice ATS-W Items.

❑ Complete the ATS-W Practice Items on page 319.
❑ Complete the ATS-W Practice Written Assignment on pages 20–22.

ATS-W REVIEW QUIZ

This Review Quiz tests your knowledge of topics included on the ATS-W. The quiz will help you refresh your memory about these topics.

This quiz is not like the ATS-W. It does not use a multiple-choice format. The idea here is to find out what you know and what you don't know. So don't guess answers on this Review Quiz.

This short-answer quiz will also be more difficult than the questions on the actual ATS-W. It is not important to answer all of these questions and don't be concerned if you miss many of them.

The answers are found immediately after the quiz. It is to your advantage not to look at them until you complete the quiz. Once you complete and score the quiz, you can use the checklist to decide which sections to study.

Write the answers in the space provided or on a separate sheet of paper.

---

1. At about what age do boys and girls enter adolescence? Boys _____ Girls _____

2. Who provided an experimental basis for behaviorism?

3. Give Piaget's four stages of cognitive development along with the approximate ages and one characteristic of each stage.

4. According to Eriksen, what is the primary emotional crisis experienced by children in grades 6–9?

5. Generally speaking, what moral behavior do children exhibit in Kohlberg's stage of Preconventional Morality?

6. What do social learning theorists mean when they talk about modeling?

7. Which has the most significant impact on human development, nature or nurture?

8. About what percent of American families have children, a mother at home, and a father at work?

9. About when would we expect the school population in America to be evenly divided between Caucasian and minority students?

10. To what country do most Hispanic Americans trace their origin?

11. Which ethnic group in America has the highest suicide rate and alcoholism rate?

_____

_____

12. About what percent of those who commit serious crimes are caught?

_____

_____

13. What is the most used and abused drug?

_____

_____

14. How is the HIV virus transmitted?

_____

_____

15. The New York Learning Standards are presented in which six categories?

_____

_____

16. Planning for instruction begins with what first step?

_____

_____

17. What is the highest order of thinking in cognitive domain?

_____

_____

18. What types of diversity might require modification of objectives?

_____

_____

19. What should an objective describe?

_____

_____

20. What are prerequisite competencies?

_____

_____

21. According to Madeline Hunter, what is an anticipatory set?

_____

_____

22. Describe formative evaluation.

_____

_____

23. What is the most common error made when reading standardized test reports?

_____

_____

24. What is content validity?

_____

_____

25. What is authentic assessment?

_____

26. What factor correlates most highly with normed scores?

_____

_____

27. What is extrinsic motivation?

_____

_____

28. Do students learn more when they are being taught or when they are working independently?

_____

_____

29. Lectures and explanations are most effective when they begin with what first step?

_____

_____

30. Using Bloom's Taxonomy, what level of questions should be asked in classrooms?

_____

_____

31. About how long should a teacher wait for a student to respond to a question?

_____

_____

32. What types of questions do teachers ask in a student-centered classroom?

_____

_____

33. What important aspects characterize active learning?

_____

_____

34. What is the last step in inquiry learning?

_____
_____

35. How would you adapt instruction for learning disabled students?

_____
_____

36. Overall, what factor correlates most highly with school achievement?

_____
_____

37. Where do most seventh and eighth graders typically turn for leadership?

_____
_____

38. List three characteristics of successful teachers.

_____
_____

39. Initially, how should the teacher arrange classroom seating?

_____
_____

40. Kounin's approach of with-it-ness has been shown to be an effective disciplinary technique. What is with-it-ness?

_____
_____

41. Under the approach recommended by Canter and Canter, how should a teacher respond when students break rules during class?

_____
_____

42. What are nonverbal cues?

_____
_____

43. How can modeling change student behavior?

_____
_____

44. How can negative reinforcement change student behavior?

_____
_____

45. Which groups or entities in the United States are legally responsible for education?

_____
_____

46. What New York regional organization provides services to local school districts?

_____
_____

47. How has the acculturation of ethnic groups changed during the last 40 years?

_____
_____

48. What federal document establishes responsibility for education?

_____
_____

49. When in the process of hiring and dismissing teachers may "reverse discrimination" be legal?

_____
_____

50. What limits have the courts placed on the free speech rights of teachers?

_____
_____

51. How may students publish a paper not subject to review and editing by school officials?

_____
_____

52. About when and where did formal education begin?

_____
_____

53. What educator is credited with establishing the kindergarten?

_____
_____

54. Where did dame schools offer classes?

_____
_____

55. What was the primary teaching device during the American colonial period?

_____

_____

56. What was the main feature of Dewey's progressive schools?

_____

_____

57. How did PL 94-142 impact American education?

_____

_____

ANSWER CHECKLIST

The answers are organized by review section. Check your answers. If you miss any question in a section, check the box and review that section.

Knowledge of the Learner
❑ *Human Development, page 279*
1. Boys about 12, girls about 10

2. Pavlov with his experiments on dogs

3. *Sensorimotor* (Birth–18 months) Children develop the idea of object permanence, out of sight not out of mind, during this stage.
Preoperational (18 months–7 years) Children develop language and are able to solve some problems. Students' thinking is egocentric and they have difficulty developing concepts such as the conservation of number task.
Concrete Operational (7 years to 12 years) During this period, students' thinking becomes operational. This means that concepts become organized and logical, as long as they are working with or around concrete materials or images. Students master the conservation tasks.
Formal Operational (12 years–) Children develop and demonstrate concepts without concrete materials or images. Students think fully in symbolic terms about concepts. Children become able to reason effectively, abstractly, and theoretically.

4. Identity vs. Identity confusion

5. No conscience, no clear morality

6. Acting in a way you want others to act

7. The issue remains unresolved.

❑ *Diversity, page 284*
8. About 10 percent

9. By about 2020. (Count your answer correct if you were within 10 years.)

10. Mexico

11. Native Americans

12. About 30 percent

13. Alcohol

14. Exchange of blood and bodily fluids (Intravenous drug users can acquire AIDS when they share needles and inject small quantities of infected blood.)

Instructional Planning and Assessment
❑ *New York Learning Standards, page 288*
15. - The Arts
    - Mathematics, Science and Technology
    - English/Language Arts
    - Social Studies
    - Languages Other than English
    - Health, Physical Education/Home Economics

❏ *Objectives, page 293*
16. Write an objective

❏ *Taxonomy of Objectives, page 293*
17. Evaluation

❏ *Choosing and Modifying Objectives, page 293*
18. Academic, Cultural, Linguistic

❏ *Writing Objectives, page 294*
19. What a student should know or be able to do *after* instruction

❏ *Planning to Teach the Lesson, page 295*
20. What a student should know or be able to do *before* instruction

21. Anticipatory set—something that is said or done to focus students on the lesson.

❏ *Evaluating Instruction, page 303*
22. Formative is used to plan instruction.

23. Looking at a single score instead of a range of scores.

24. Content validity describes the extent to which a test measures the material being taught.

25. Students are evaluated as they demonstrate knowledge or a skill in a real life setting.

26. Socioeconomic status (SES)

❏ *Motivation, page 306*
27. External rewards to improve student performance

❏ *Successful Learning, page 306*
28. Students learn more when they are being taught.

❏ *Classroom Approaches, page 308*
29. Motivation

30. Questions should be asked at all levels.

31. 4 to 5 seconds

32. More open-ended questions

33. Group work, active learning, full participation, democratic structure

34. Metacognition—that is, students analyze their thought processes.

❏ *Adapting Instruction, page 311*

35. Provide structured brief assignments, manipulative activities, and auditory learning

❏ *Cultural and Linguistic Diversity, page 311*
36. Socioeconomic status (SES)

Instructional Delivery
❏ *Managing the Instructional Environment, page 313*
37. They turn to their peer group

38. Any three of the following:
- Accept children within a teacher-student relationship.
- Set firm and clear but flexible limits.
- Enforce rules clearly and consistently.
- Have positive, realistic expectations about student's achievement.
- Have clear reasons for expectations about students.
- Practice what they preach (model acceptable behavior).
- Don't take it personally. Students usually misbehave or act out because of who they are, not because of who you are.

39. So that they can see the faces of all the students

❏ *Specific Management Techniques, page 315*
40. With-it-ness means that the teacher is constantly monitoring and aware of what is happening in the classroom.

41. Write the names of the students on the board.
One violation—no action
Two violations—conference
Three violations—parental conference

42. A silent gesture or signal to alert students to a transition or to gain attention

❏ *Changing Behavior, page 316*

43. Students who observe a person behaving a particular way often emulate that person.

44. Negative reinforcement means showing students how to avoid undesirable consequences by doing acceptable work.

The Professional Environment

❏ *The Schools in Society, page 298*

45. Boards of Cooperative Educational Services (BOCES)

46. The states

47. Recent immigrants have been less acculturated and have maintained more of their cultural identity and language.

❏ *Legal, Legislative, and Political Influences, page 298*

48. Constitution of the United States

49. May be legal for hiring, but not for dismissal

50. Teachers cannot disrupt the curriculum or the schools.

51. Publish it with private funds off school property.

❏ *Historical and Philosophical Foundations, page 301*

52. About 2000 B.C. in Northern Africa and China. Formal education that led to our system began about 500 B.C. in Athens, Greece

53. Herbart

54. In the houses of the female teachers

55. The Horn Book

56. Student centered education

57. It mandated an appropriate education in the least restrictive environment for handicapped Americans aged 3–21.

ATS-W REVIEW

KNOWLEDGE OF THE LEARNER

Physical Development

Adequate nutrition in mothers is essential for proper fetal development. Adequate nutrition and exercise are essential for a child's physical growth. Inadequate nutrition can hamper growth and lead to inattentiveness and other problems that interfere with learning.

Alcohol and drug abuse by mothers can cause irreparable brain damage to unborn children. Children of drug-and-alcohol-abusing mothers tend to have lower birth weights. Low birth weight is associated with health, emotional, and learning problems. Alcohol and drug addiction, smoking, stress, and adverse environmental factors are among the other causes of abnormal physical and emotional development.

During the first 12 months after birth, the body weight of infants triples and brain size doubles. Infants crawl by about 7 months, eat with their hands at about 8 months, sit up by about 9 months, stand up by about 11 months, and walk by about 1 year.

From 12–15 months to 2.5 years, children are called toddlers. During this period, children become expert walkers, feed themselves, evidence self control, and spend a great deal of their time playing. This period is characterized by the word *no* and is also when children begin bowel training.

The preschool years span the time from the end of toddlerhood to entry into kindergarten. Children start to look more like adults with longer legs and a shorter torso. Play continues but becomes more sophisticated.

The elementary school years refer to ages 6–10 in girls but 6–12 in boys. During this period children enter a period of steady growth. Most children double their body weight and increase their height by one-half. Play continues but involves more sophisticated games and physical activities, often involving groups or teams of other children.

Adolescence begins at about age 10 for girls but at about age 12 for boys. The growth rate spurt begins during this time. Because this period begins earlier for girls than for boys, girls are more mature than boys for a number of years. Sexual and secondary sex characteristics appear during this time. Most adolescents rely heavily on peer group approval and respond to peer pressure.

Behavioral Development

Behaviorism was the first significant theory of development. Behaviorism is concerned with observable, measurable behavior and with those events that stimulate or reinforce the behavior.

Watson
John Watson originated the behaviorist movement during the early 1900s. His theoretical ideas centered around conditioned responses in children. Conditioned response means that a child was "taught" to respond in a particular way to a stimulus that would not naturally elicit that response. Watson's experiment to condition a child to fear a white rat that the child initially liked is most quoted in texts. Many claim that the success of the experiment was overstated.

Pavlov
Many trace the experimental basis for behaviorism to the Russian psychologist Pavlov who, in the 1920s, conducted classical conditioning experiments with dogs. Dogs naturally salivate in an unconditioned response to the unconditioned stimulus of food. Pavlov showed that dogs would salivate in response to any neutral stimulus. The neutral stimulus is called a conditioned stimulus, and the salivation that occurs is called a conditioned response.

Thorndike
Also in the early 1900s Edward Thorndike developed his own form of behaviorism called instrumental conditioning. Thorndike's work with animals led him to two significant conclusions:

- The law of exercise—a conditioned response can be strengthened by repeating the response (practice).
- The law of effect—rewarded responses are strengthened while punished responses are weakened.

Skinner
Skinner was the most influential behaviorist. Skinner referred to his approach as operant conditioning, which studied how voluntary behavior could be shaped. Operant conditioning relies on these basic mechanisms.

- Reward or positive reinforcement—Students are rewarded for repeating desired responses.

- Negative reinforcement—Students escape punishment by repeating desired responses.

- Extinction—Undesired responses are not reinforced.

- Punishment—Undesired responses are punished.

Skinner showed that he could condition very complex behaviors in animals. He believed that students learned when teachers gave immediate positive feedback for a desired behavior and used extinction or punishment for undesirable behaviors.

Cognitive Development

Jean Piaget

Jean Piaget is the most prominent of cognitive psychologists who believe that students develop concepts through a series of stages. Stage theory is currently the most popular form of child development.

According to Piaget, children proceed through a fixed but uneven series of stages of cognitive development. His stages help us understand the general way in which students learn and develop concepts.

Action and logic versus perception are at the center of Piaget's theory. He believed that children learn through an active involvement with their environment. He also believed that students have developed a concept when their logical understanding overcomes their perceptual misunderstanding of the concept.

His conservation experiments explain this last point. In conservation of number, students are shown two matched rows of checkers. The child confirms that there are the same number of checkers in each row. Then one row of checkers is spread out and the child is asked if there are still the same number of checkers. Children who believe there are more checkers in one of

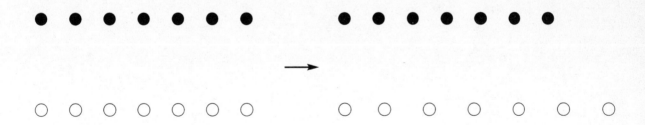

the rows do not understand the concept of number because their perception holds sway over their logic.

Piaget presents these four stages of cognitive development.

- Sensorimotor (birth to 18 months)—Children exhibit poor verbal and cognitive development. Children develop the idea of object permanence (out of sight not out of mind) during this stage.

- Preoperational (18 months to 7 years)—Children develop language and are able to solve some problems. Students' thinking is egocentric, and they have difficulty developing concepts. For example, students in this stage may not be able to complete the conservation of number task shown above.

- Concrete operational (7–12 years)—Students' thinking becomes operational. This means that concepts become organized and logical, as long as they are working with or around concrete materials or images. During this stage, students master the number conservation and other conservation tasks, but most students do not understand symbolic concepts.

- Formal operational (12+ years)—Children develop and demonstrate concepts without concrete materials or images. In this stage, students think fully in symbolic terms about concepts. Children become able to reason effectively, abstractly, and theoretically. Full development of this stage may depend on the extent to which children have had a full range of active manipulative experiences in the concrete operational stage.

Personality Development

Freud's psychoanalytic theories have profoundly affected modern thought about psychological and personality development. He believed that humans pass through four stages of psychosexual development: oral, anal, phallic, and genital. The personality itself consists of the id, ego, and superego. According to Freud, an integrated personality develops from the gratification experienced at each of these stages.

Psychosocial Development

Eriksen built on Freud's work and partitioned the life span into eight psychosocial stages. An emotional crisis at each stage can lead to a positive or negative result. The result achieved at each stage determines the development pattern for the next stage. Four of these stages fall within the school years.

Stage	Characteristic	Description
Kindergarten	Initiative vs. Guilt	Children accepted and treated warmly tend to feel more comfortable about trying out new ideas. Rejected children tend to become inhibited and guilty.
Elementary grades	Industry vs. Inferiority	Students who are accepted by their peer group and do well in school, and those who believe they are accepted and do well, are more successful than those who do not feel good about themselves.
Grades 6–9	Identity vs. Identity Confusion	Students who establish an identity and a sense of direction and who develop gender, social, and occupational roles experience an easier transition into adulthood than those students who do not establish these roles.
Grades 10–12	Intimacy vs. Isolation	Students who have passed successfully through the other stages will find it easier to establish a relationship with a member of the opposite sex. Those students who are unsuccessful at this stage may face an extremely difficult transition into adult life.

Moral Development

Kohlberg built on Piaget's original work to develop stages of moral development. Kohlberg proposed three levels of moral development with two stages at each level. His stages provide a reasonable approach to understanding moral development. Not everyone moves through all stages.

Preconventional Morality (preschool and primary grades)

Stage 1   Children do not demonstrate a conscience but do react to fear of punishment. Children are very egocentric.

Stage 2   Children still have no clear morality. Children concentrate on their own egocentric needs and let others do the same. Children may not be willing to help others meet their needs even though it would help them meet their own needs.

[Some children and antisocial adults may not pass this stage.]

Conventional Morality (middle grades through high school)

Stage 3   These children want to be good. They associate themselves with parents and other adult authority figures. They show concern for others and evidence a number of virtues and try to live up to expectations.

Stage 4   These children shift from wanting to please authority figures to a more generalized sense of respect for rules and expectations. These children see their responsibility to maintain society through a strict enforcement of society's laws.

[Many adults do not progress beyond this stage of development.]

Postconventional Morality (high school and beyond)

Stage 5   People at this stage differentiate between legality and morality. They have a more flexible view of right and wrong and realize that societal needs often take precedence over individual needs.

Stage 6   Very few people reach this stage. Those at stage six have pure, cosmic understanding of justice and dignity. These principles always take precedence when they conflict with what is considered legal or socially acceptable.

Social Learning Theory

Social learning theory is a fairly new field. Social learning theorists seek to combine behavioral and cognitive learning theories along with other types of learning.

Albert Bandura is the leading social learning theorist. He believes that a great deal of learning can take place through modeling. That is, students often act the way they see others act, or they learn vicariously by observing others. Bandura believes that verbal explanations and reinforcement are also important and that students become socialized through systematic modeling of appropriate behavior. Students can also develop cognitive skills by observing a problem-solving process and learn procedures by observing these procedures in action.

Nature Versus Nurture

The relative affects of nature (heredity and genes) and nurture (environment and experience) on growth and development is still not resolved. Certain traits, sex, eye color, some forms of mental retardation, and susceptibility to some mental illnesses such as schizophrenia are linked to genes and heredity. However, other developmental questions are not clear, and even studies of twins separated at birth has not yielded the kind of conclusive results needed to draw conclusions.

DIVERSITY

Society and Culture

America is a multiethnic and multicultural society. Consequently, the culture of the community and the culture of the school varies widely depending on the school's geographic location, socioeconomic setting, and local norms. To understand schools, we must understand society and culture.

Anthropology and sociology provide a scientific basis for studying society and culture. Anthropology is the formal study of culture and the development of society. Much of the early anthropological work dealt with primitive cultures. However, in recent years anthropologists have turned their attention to communities and schools. Sociology is the study of how people behave in a group. Sociology can help us understand how students behave in school, how teachers function on a faculty, and how citizens interact in the community.

Culture is directly affected by the ethnicity of the community. Each ethnic group brings its own culture, its own language, and its own customs to this country.

Until recently, most immigrant groups have been acculturated. That is, they have largely adopted the dominant language and culture of the United States. Lately there has been a shift toward cultural pluralism in which immigrants maintain their cultural, and occasionally linguistic, identity.

Under cultural pluralism, the challenge is to provide equal educational opportunity while also providing for these cultural differences among students. There is little prospect, however, that non-English speakers will realize their full potential in the United States.

Socioeconomic status has a direct affect on culture and on the schools. As noted earlier, there is a strong correlation between SES and academic achievement. In the United States, groups, communities, and schools are stratified by social class. Social stratification often occurs within schools. Unlike many other countries, individuals are able to move among social classes, usually in an upward direction.

The Family

The family remains the predominant influence in the early lives of children. However, the nature of the American family has changed, and for the worse.

Divorce rates are very high and some say that a majority of Americans under 40 will be divorced. American families are fragmented with about 30 percent of children living with a stepparent. About one-quarter of children are raised in one-parent families, and about two-thirds of these children live below the poverty level.

An increasing number of children, called latchkey children, return from school with no parents at home. School programs developed for these students cannot replace effective parenting.

In many respects, the school, social or religious institutions, peer groups, and gangs have replaced parents. This means that parents and families have less influence on children's values and beliefs.

The pressures of economic needs have drastically changed the American family. Less than 10 percent of American families have children, a mother at home, and a father at work. Over 30 percent of married couples have no children, and over 70 percent of mothers with children are working mothers.

Ethnicity

In 1990 the population of the United States was about 78 percent Caucasian, 12 percent African American, 9 percent Hispanic, 3 percent Asian, and 1 percent Indian or Eskimo. Hispanics are the fastest growing ethnic group. By the year 2000 we expect about 67 percent of the population to be white, 15 percent Hispanic, 12 percent African American, 5 percent Asian, and 1 percent Native American. By the year 2020 America's school population will be about evenly divided between white and minority students.

About 15 percent of the families in the United States live below the poverty level. Some 30 percent of African American and Hispanic families do so, and an astonishing 65 percent of Native American families also live below the poverty level.

Hispanics

Hispanics come predominantly from Mexico and from other countries in Central and South America and the Caribbean. Many Mexican American families have been in this country for more than 100 years. Puerto Ricans form another large Hispanic group.

Language is the primary difficulty faced by this ethnic group. About half of the Hispanics in this country speak Spanish as their first language.

The nature of the Hispanic population varies by region. Most Hispanics in California or their forbearers are from Mexico. Many Hispanics living in and around New York City are from Puerto Rico or the Dominican Republic, while many Hispanics in Florida trace their ancestry to Cuba.

Hispanic students have more school problems than white students. Hispanics are disproportionately poor and low achieving.

African Americans

African Americans have been in this country for centuries, but they began their lives here as slaves. There is not a recent history of large-scale African immigration to the United States.

Their status as slaves and second-class citizens denied African Americans the education, experience, and self-sufficiency needed for upward social mobility. Even when African Americans developed these qualities, they were frequently discriminated against just because of their race. It took almost 200 years from the founding of this country for the Supreme Court to rule that overt school segregation was unconstitutional. Of course, de facto segregation continues to exist.

Many African Americans have achieved middle class status. However, the overwhelming proportion of poor in urban areas are African Americans. The unemployment rate of young African Americans can be near 50 percent in some areas.

Native Americans

Groups of Eskimos and other Native Americans have lived on the North American continent for over 25,000 years. Most Native Americans living today are descendents of tribes conquered and put on reservations about 100 years ago.

During this time of conquest, treaties made with tribes were frequently broken. Native Americans lost their lands and their way of life. They were made dependent on the federal government for subsidies and were not able to develop the education, experience, or self-sufficiency needed for upward mobility.

Native Americans have the largest family size and fastest growth rate of any ethnic group. They also have among the highest suicide and alcoholism rates of any ethnic group.

Native Americans are disproportionally poor and disenfranchised. They live in poverty on reservations and are often alienated when they move off reservations to metropolitan areas.

Asian Americans

Asian Americans are predominately Chinese and Japanese together with recent immigrants from Korea and Southeast Asia. Asian Americans represent a countertrend among American minorities. Their achievement and success tend to be above the national average.

Many recent immigrants do not have the educational background of other Asian Americans. They tend to be more ghettoized and to attain a lower SES than other Asian Americans.

However, overall, Asian students perform better on American standardized tests than non-Asian students. This finding holds also for those Asian Americans who immigrated to this country unable to speak, read, or understand English.

Some researchers have said that a particular work ethic currently found in Asian countries together with a strong family structure are responsible for these trends.

Societal Problems

This decade finds our society beset with unprecedented problems of crime and violence, alcohol and drug abuse, sex, AIDS, high dropout rates, and child abuse. Many of these problems can be traced directly to poverty. Schools are a part of society so that they too are affected by these problems.

Crime and Violence

The number of serious crimes in the United States is at the highest level in memory. Students bring guns to school, and large urban areas report dozens of deaths each year from violent acts in school. Murder is the leading cause of death among African American teens. More than 70 percent of those who commit serious crimes are never caught. We live in a society where crime is rampant and crime pays.

Crime in school presents a particular problem for teachers. Some estimate that 3 to 7 percent of all students bring a gun with them to school. Students attack teachers every day in America. While this behavior is not defensible, attention to the principles of classroom management mentioned earlier can help in averting some of these incidents.

Alcohol and Drug Abuse

Alcohol is the most used and abused drug. Even though it is legal, there are serious short- and long-term consequences of alcohol use. Alcoholism is the most widespread drug addiction and untreated alcoholism can lead to death.

Tobacco is the next most widely used and abused substance. Some efforts are being made to declare tobacco a drug. Irrefutable evidence shows that tobacco use is a causative factor in hundreds of thousands of deaths each year.

Other drugs including marijuana, cocaine, heroin, and various drugs in pill form carry with them serious health, addiction, and emotional problems. The widespread illicit availability of these drugs creates additional problems. Many students engage in crimes to get money to pay for drugs. Others may commit crimes while under the influence of drugs. Still others may commit crimes by selling drugs to make money.

More than 90 percent of students have used alcohol by the time they leave high school. About 70 percent of high school graduates have used other illegal drugs. Awareness programs that focus on drug use can have some positive effects. However, most drug and alcohol abuse and addiction has other underlying causes. These causes must be addressed for any program to be effective.

Sex

Many teens, and preteens, are sexually active. While many of these children profess to know about sex, they do not. It is in this environment that we find increases in teenage pregnancies, abortions, dropouts, and ruined lives. Sex spreads disease. So we also note increases in syphilis, gonorrhea, and other sexually transmitted diseases.

About 10 percent of teenage girls will become pregnant. Teenage pregnancy is the primary reason why girls drop out of high school. These girls seldom receive appropriate help from the child's father and are often destined for a life of poverty and dependence.

AIDS

AIDS stands for Acquired Immune Deficiency Syndrome. AIDS is a breakdown in the body's immune system caused by a virus called HIV. This virus can be detected with blood tests. People with the HIV virus may take 10 years or longer to develop AIDS. Those who develop AIDS die.

The HIV virus is transmitted by infected blood and other bodily fluids. Sexual relations and contact with infected blood, including blood injected with shared hypodermic needles, are all examples of ways that AIDS can be transmitted. Some 2 to 5 percent of the teens in some urban areas may be HIV positive.

Students can try to avoid becoming HIV positive by reducing their risk factors. Abstinence from sex and never injecting drugs will virtually eliminate the likelihood that a teenager will become HIV positive. Less effective measures can be taken to help sexually active students reduce the likelihood of becoming HIV positive. Girls run a higher risk than boys of becoming HIV positive through sexual activity.

Acquiring the HIV virus is associated with drug and alcohol use. Even when students know the risks, and how to avoid them, alcohol and drug use can lower inhibitions and lead to unsafe practices.

Dropouts

About 10 percent of white students, 15 percent of African American students, and 30 percent of Hispanic students drop out of school. Dropout rates are worst in urban areas, with over half the students dropping out of some schools. High school dropouts are usually headed for a life of lower wages and poorer living conditions.

Many of these students feel alienated from society or school and need support or alternative learning environments. Intervention, counseling, and alternative programs such as therapeutic high schools, vocational high schools, and other special learning arrangements can help prevent a student from dropping out.

Child Abuse

Child abuse is the secret destroyer of children's lives. Some estimate that between two and three million children are abused each year. Child abuse is a primary cause of violent youth, runaways, and drug abusers.

Physical and sexual abuse are the most destructive of the abuses heaped upon children. Contrary to popular belief, most child abuse is perpetrated by family members, relatives, and friends. Younger children are often incapable of talking about their abuse and may not reveal it even when asked.

In many states, teachers are required to report suspected child abuse. When child abuse is suspected, a teacher should follow the guidelines given by the school, the district, or the state.

INSTRUCTIONAL PLANNING AND ASSESSMENT

New York Learning Standards

Those at the New York State Education Department recently developed 28 preliminary Learning Standards in broad curricular areas. These final standards will form the basis for instruction in New York State schools. Elementary school, middle school, and high school assessments will be based on these broad standards. The standards are summarized below.

The Arts—Dance, Music, Theater, and Visual Arts
1. **Creating, Performing, and Participating in the Arts**
   Students will actively engage in the processes that constitute creation and performance in the arts (dance, music, theater, and visual arts) and participate in various roles in the arts.

2. Knowing and Using Arts Materials and Resources

Students will be knowledgeable about and make use of the materials and resources available for participating in the arts in various roles.

3. Responding to and Analyzing Works of Art

Students will respond critically to a variety of works in the arts, connecting the individual work to many other works and to other aspects of human endeavor and thought.

4. Understanding the Cultural Dimensions and Contributions of the Arts

Students will develop an understanding of the personal and cultural forces that shape artistic communication and how the arts in turn shape the diverse cultures of past and present society.

Mathematics, Science, and Technology

1. Analysis, Inquiry, and Design

Students will use mathematical analysis, scientific inquiry, and engineering design, as appropriate, to pose questions, seek answers, and develop solutions.

2. Information Systems

Students will access, generate, process, and transfer information using appropriate technologies.

3. Mathematics

Students will understand mathematics and become mathematically confident by communicating and reasoning mathematically, by applying mathematics in real-world settings, and by solving problems through the integrated study of number systems, geometry, algebra, data analysis, probability and trigonometry.

4. Science

Students will understand and apply scientific concepts, principles, and theories pertaining to the physical setting and living environment and recognize the historical development of ideas in science.

5. Technology

Students will apply technological knowledge and skills to design, construct, use, and evaluate products and systems to satisfy human and environmental needs.

6. Interconnectedness: Common Themes

Students will understand the relationships and common themes that connect mathematics, science, and technology and apply the themes to these and other areas of learning.

7. Interdisciplinary Problem Solving

Students will apply the knowledge and thinking skills of mathematics, science, and technology to address real-life problems and make informed decisions.

English Language Arts

1. Language for Information and Understanding

Students will listen, speak, read, and write for information and understanding. As listeners and readers, students will collect data, facts, and ideas, discover relationships, concepts, and generalizations; and use knowledge generated from oral, written, and electronically produced texts. As speakers and writers they will use oral and written language to acquire, interpret, apply, and transmit information.

2. Language for Literary Response and Expression

Students will listen, speak, read, and write for literary response and expression. Students will listen to oral, written, and electronically produced texts and performances, relate texts and performances to their own lives, and develop an understanding of the diverse social, historical, and cultural dimensions the texts and performances represent. As speakers and writers, students will use oral and written language for self-expression and artistic creation.

3. Language for Critical Analysis and Evaluation

Students will listen, speak, read, and write for critical analysis and evaluation. As listeners and readers, students will collect and analyze experiences, ideas, information, and issues presented by others using a variety of established criteria. As speakers and writers, they will present, in oral and written language and form, a variety of perspectives and opinions.

4. Language for Social Interaction

Students will use oral and written language for effective social communication with a wide variety of people. As readers and listeners, they will use the social communications of others to enrich their understanding of people and their views.

Social Studies

1. History of the United States and New York

Students will use a variety of intellectual skills to demonstrate their understanding of major ideas, eras, themes, developments, and turning points in the history of the United States and New York.

2. World History

Students will use a variety of intellectual skills to demonstrate their understanding of major ideas, eras, themes, developments, and turning points in world history and examine the broad sweep of history from a variety of perspectives.

3. Geography

Students will use a variety of intellectual skills to demonstrate their understanding of the geography of the independent worlds in which we live—local, national, and global —including the distribution of people, places, and environments over the earth's surface.

4. Economic Systems

Students will use a variety of intellectual skills to demonstrate their understanding of how the United States and other societies develop economic systems and associated institutions to allocate scarce resources. Students will also use these skills to understand how major decision making units function in the United States and other national economies, and how an economy solves the scarcity problem through market and nonmarket mechanisms.

5. Civics, Citizenship, and Government

Students will use a variety of intellectual skills to demonstrate their understanding of the necessity for establishing governments; the governmental system of the United States and other nations, the United States Constitution, the basic civil values of American constitutional democracy; and the roles, rights, and responsibilities of citizenship, including avenues of participation.

Languages Other Than English

1. Communication Skills

Students will be able to use a language other than English for communication.

2. Cultural Understanding

Students will develop cross-cultural skills and understandings.

Health, Physical Education, and Home Economics

1. Personal Health and Fitness

Students will have the necessary knowledge and skills to establish and maintain physical fitness, participate in physical activity, and maintain personal health.

2. A Safe and Healthy Environment

Students will acquire the knowledge and ability necessary to create and maintain a healthy environment.

3. Resource Management

Students will understand and be able to manage their personal and community resources.

Career Development and Occupational Studies

1. Career Development

Students will be knowledgeable about the world of work, explore career options, and relate personal skills, aptitudes, and abilities to future career decisions.

2. Integrated Learning

Students will demonstrate how academic knowledge and skills are applied in the workplace and other settings.

3a. Universal Foundation Skills

Students will demonstrate mastery of the foundation skills and competencies essential for success in the workplace.

3b. Career Options

Students who choose a career major will acquire the career-specific technical knowledge/skills necessary to progress toward gainful employment, career advancement, and success in post-secondary programs.

Thematic Unit Plans and Interdisciplinary, Integrated Approaches to Instruction

Contemporary instructional units are built around themes. Within these themes many different subject areas are taught in an integrated way. For example:

Consider a thematic unit about weather. Weather seems to be a unit about science and yet this unit can be used to teach almost every subject area in an integrated way. Look at the following examples.

Art—Students draw or paint clouds and create weather maps.

Reading—Students read books and articles about weather.

Technology—Students gather information about weather, including weather forecasts on the Internet.

Writing/Language Arts—Students write reports about their research on weather. Students write original short stories or poems about weather.

Social Studies—Students learn about the effects of local climates on the lives and about the impact of climates worldwide.

Science—Students learn about the mechanics of cloud building, such as the forces that create cumulonimbus storm clouds.

Thematic units such as the one outlined here provide a basis for teaching needed skills and concepts in all subject areas while emphasizing the interrelatedness of these topics.

Objectives

All useful instruction has some purpose. Planning for instruction begins with choosing an objective that expresses this purpose. Objectives usually refer to outcomes, while goals usually refer to more general purposes of instruction. The terms *aim, competency, outcome,* and *behavioral objective* are also used to refer to an objective. Each New York Learning Standard is accompanied by an extensive set of objectives.

Objectives are also established by national or state organizations. The national or state English, mathematics, and science professional organizations may recommend objectives for their subject. The national or state organizations for speech, primary education, elementary education, preschool education, and special education may recommend objectives for specific grades or specialties.

Most school texts contain objectives, usually given for each text unit or lesson. These objectives are also reflected in national, state, and local achievement tests.

School districts usually have their own written objectives. There may be a scope and sequence chart that outlines the objectives for each subject and grade. The district may also have a comprehensive set of objectives for each subject and grade level.

Taxonomy of Objectives and Critical Thinking

Benjamin Bloom and others described three domains of learning: cognitive, affective, and psychomotor. The cognitive domain refers to knowledge, intellectual ability, and the other things we associate with school learning. The affective domain refers to values, interests, attitudes, and the other things we associate with feelings. The psychomotor domain refers to motor skills and other things we associate with movement.

Each domain describes various levels of objectives. The six levels on the cognitive domain, noted below, are most useful in classifying objectives. Students should be exposed to objectives at all levels of the taxonomy, particularly analysis, synthesis, and evaluation, which foster critical thinking.

1. Knowledge—Remembering specifics, recalling terms and theories.
2. Comprehension—Understanding or using an idea but not relating it to other ideas.
3. Application—Using concepts or abstractions in actual situations.
4. Analysis—Breaking down a statement to relate ideas in the statement.
5. Synthesis—Bringing or putting together parts to make a whole or find a pattern.
6. Evaluation—Judging value, comparing work or product to a criteria.

Choosing and Modifying Objectives

Initially, you will identify an objective from the Learning Standards or one of the sources noted previously. Consider these criteria when choosing and sequencing objectives.

- The objective should meet the intent of the New York Learning Standards and overall goals of the school district.
- The objective should be appropriate for the achievement and maturation level of students in the class.
- The objective should be generally accepted by appropriate national, regional, or state professional organizations.

The objective you select may not exactly describe the lesson or unit you are going to teach. Modify the objective to meet your needs. You also may need to select or modify objectives and other plans to meet the needs of diverse student populations.

Your class may be academically diverse. You may teach special-needs students or you may have special-needs students in your class under the inclusion model. When you select and modify objectives for academically diverse students, consider the different achievement levels or learning styles of these students.

Your class may be culturally diverse. When you select and modify objectives for a culturally diverse class, consider the range of experiences and backgrounds found among the class. Do not reduce the difficulty of the objective.

Your class may be linguistically diverse. You may have limited English proficiency (LEP) students in your class. For a linguistically diverse class, take into account the limits that language places on learning. You may have to select or modify objectives to help these students learn English.

Writing Objectives

An objective should answer the question: "What are students expected to do once instruction is complete?" Objectives should not describe what the teacher does during the lesson. Objectives should not be overly specific, involved, or complicated.

Whenever possible, objectives should begin with a verb. Here are some examples.

Not an objective:	I will teach students how to pronounce words with a silent *e*. [This is a statement of what the teacher will do.]
Not an objective:	While in the reading group, looking at the reading book, students will pronounce words with a silent *e*. [This statement is overly specific.]
Objective:	Sounds out words with a silent *e*. [This is an objective. It tells what the student is expected to do.]
Objective:	States what he or she liked about the trip to the zoo.
Objective:	Reads a book from the story shelf.
Objective:	Serves a tennis ball successfully twice in a row.

Do not limit objectives to skills or tiny bits of strictly observable behavior. Specific objectives are not limited objectives. Objectives can include statements that students will appreciate or participate in some activity. Objectives should include integrating subject matter, applying concepts, problem solving, decision making, writing essays, researching projects, preparing reports, exploring, observing, appreciating, experimenting, and constructing and making art work and other projects.

Special Education Classification and IEPs

Students are generally classified as special education students by the district Committee on Special Education (CSE) with the approval of the student's parents. The classification process includes thorough testing along with observations and reports by the social worker, the psychologist, the teacher, the occupational therapist, and other education evaluators.

Once students are classified, each receives an Individualized Education Plan (IEP). The IEP is a complete education plan for that student. The plan includes test scores and reports prepared as a part of the classification process.

The IEP prominently contains the goals and objectives for the student in all applicable academic and nonacademic areas and their placement in classes. This listing is extensive. Also included are the modifications to be made for this student. Some typical modifications are listed here.

- extra test time
- hearing aid
- preferential class seating
- extra homework help
- writing aid
- test exemptions
- sessions with a psychologist or a social worker

The final version of the IEP is discussed and agreed to at a CSE meeting with the teacher, psychologist, social worker, parent advocate, and child's parent(s) in attendance. Once enacted the district must provide the services and arrange for the modifications described in the IEP.

Planning to Teach the Lesson

Once you have decided what to teach, you must plan how to teach it. Consider these factors as you plan the lesson or unit.

- Determine the prerequisite competencies. This is the knowledge and skills students must possess before they can learn the objective. Draw up a plan that ensures students will demonstrate prerequisite competencies before you teach the lesson.

- Determine the resources you need to help students reach the objective. The resources could include books, manipulatives, overhead transparencies, and other materials for you or the students to use. The resources could also include technological resources including computers or computer software and human resources including teacher aides, students, or outside presenters.

- Devise a plan to help students reach the objective. In addition to the factors discussed previously, the plan will usually include motivation and procedures.

Madeline Hunter posited the following important stages for effective lessons.

- Anticipatory set—Something that is said or done to prepare students and focus the students on the lesson.

- Objective and purpose—The teacher should state the objective of the lesson, and the students should be aware of the objective.

- Input—New information is presented during this stage.

- Modeling—The skills or procedures being taught or demonstrated.

- Checking for understanding—Following the instructional components in the previous two stages, the teacher should ensure that students understand the concept before moving to the next phases of the lesson.

- Guided practice—Students are given the opportunity to practice or use the concept or skill with the teacher's guidance.

- Independent practice—Students practice or use the concept on their own.

A sample lesson plan format follows.

SAMPLE LESSON PLAN FORMAT

Name _____   Date _____

Class _____

Objective: The objective answers the question "What do I expect students to be able to do once instruction is complete?"

Integration: Indicate which, if any, topics are "integrated" in this lesson.

Resources: The materials and the technological and human resources needed to teach the lesson.

Motivation: An introduction that interests the students and focuses their attention on the lesson.

Procedures

Review (Warm-up)
Review the prerequisite competencies. Reteach these competencies if students have forgotten them.

Preview
Fully inform students about the lesson objective and the way they will learn the objective.

Teach
The actual procedures, approaches, and methods for teaching the lesson.

Assessment
Use interaction, observation of students, tests, or other means to determine if the objective has been reached.

Practice
Students practice the skill or concept embodied in the objective.

Independent Work (Seatwork-Homework)
Assign up to fifteen minutes of work for students to do on their own.

THE PROFESSIONAL ENVIRONMENT

The School in Society

The school is a part of society. It reflects the society and socializes students. To that end, the schools prepare students to function in society. Students are taught, directly and indirectly, acceptable social values and behavior.

The academic curriculum reflects society's expectations. Students are taught a generally accepted body of knowledge. Students are also prepared for society by being exposed to potential careers as a part of the school curriculum.

Every society has a culture. The culture combines the history of the society and the society's current norms. The culture includes customs, values, ethical and moral structures, religions and beliefs, laws, and a hierarchy of most valued contributions by members of society.

The School as a Society

The school is a society in itself. The school society consists of a complex interrelationship of teachers, students, administrators, parents, and others. Each school has its own character, practices, and informal hierarchy. Generally speaking, new teachers must find a niche in the school's society to be successful. The school has a formal decision-making hierarchy of teachers, supervisors, principals, superintendents, and school boards. The new teacher must usually gain acceptance at each level of this hierarchy to experience success.

Each state in the United States has its own system of education. States are legally responsible for education. Locally elected or appointed school boards usually have the most direct legal impact on the schools. Within state and federal laws, school boards pay for the schools from tax receipts and other funds, hire teachers and administrators, approve curricula, and set school policy.

Many of the decisions made by school boards are affected by the amount of money available to the schools. Generally speaking, wealthier districts have more money to spend on schools. The difference in the funds available may create a difference in the quality of schooling.

LEGAL, LEGISLATIVE, AND POLITICAL INFLUENCES

Structure and Organization of the New York Education System

The Constitution of the United States does not assign the responsibility for education to the federal government, leaving this responsibility to each state. The state government, including the governor, the legislature, and the courts have the ultimate responsibility for public education. The Board of Regents of the State University of New York (SUNY) has overall responsibility for all educational activities in New York State. The Board of Regents was established on May 1, 1784. The State University of New York includes all elementary, secondary, and postsecondary institutions, both public and private, offering education in New York. The board acts primarily as a policy making body.

The Board of Regents appoints the New York State Commissioner of Education who is also president of the State University of New York, chief executive officer for the board, and head of the New York State Education Department.

The New York State Education Department supervises all educational institutions in New York State. Among these responsibilities, the Education Department charters all schools in the state, develops and approves school curricula and assessments, and supervises teacher certification.

There are 38 Boards of Cooperative Educational Services (BOCES) located throughout New Y ork State. Each BOCES superintendent reports directly to the New York State Commissioner of Education and serves as the commissioner's local representative. Every public school system in New York is affiliated in some way with a BOCES that offers vocational and special education programs as well as administrative services to member districts.

Local or regional boards of education are directly responsible for operating schools in their district or town. In most cases, these boards are elected. A local or regional superintendent of schools reports to the board and, along with other administrators and support staff, has the daily responsibility for operating the schools.

Building principals report to the superintendent and are responsible for the daily operations of their school building. Teachers have the responsibility for teaching their students and carrying out district and state education policies.

It's the Law

A complex set of federal, state, and local laws govern education. Court cases are changing the interpretation of these laws each day. Here is a brief summary of legal rights they may apply to schools, teachers, and students. This summary should not be used to make any decisions related to school law. Any specific interest in legal issues should be referred to a competent attorney.

Schools

- Schools may not discriminate against students, teachers, or others because of their race, sex, ethnicity, or religion. "Reverse discrimination" *may* be legal when hiring teachers, but it is not legal when dismissing teachers.

- Prayer is not permitted in schools. In all other ways, schools may not embrace or support religion.

- Schools must make children's school records available to parents and legal guardians.

- Schools may remove books from the school library. However, a book may not be removed from the library just because a school board member or other school official does not agree with its content.

Teachers

- Teachers do not have to provide information unrelated to employment on an employment form or to an interviewer. You do not have to give your age, your marital status, sexual orientation, or any other unrelated information.

- Nontenured teachers usually have very limited rights to reappointment. Generally speaking, schools may not rehire a nontenured teacher for any reason. For example, the schools may simply say that they want to find someone better, that the teacher doesn't fit in, or that they just don't want to renew the contract.

- Teachers cannot be fired for behavior that does not disrupt or interfere with their effectiveness as teachers. However, even personal behavior away from school, which significantly reduces teaching effectiveness, might be grounds for dismissal.

- Pregnant teachers may not be forced to take a maternity leave. Decades ago, pregnant teachers were often forced to resign.

- Teachers may be dismissed or suspended for not doing their job. Any such action must follow a due process procedure.

- Teachers may be sued and be liable for negligence. Successful suits and actions against teachers have occurred when the evidence showed that the teacher could have reasonably foreseen what was going to happen or that the teacher acted differently than a reasonable teacher would have acted in that same situation.

- Teachers have the right to associate freely during off-school hours with whomever they wish. They may belong to any political party, religious group, or other group even if the group is not supported in the community or is disapproved of by board members, administrators, or others.

- Teachers have freedom of speech. Teachers have the same free speech rights as other citizens. They may comment publicly on all issues, including decisions of the school administrators or the school board. However, a teacher may not disclose confidential information or be malicious, and the statements can't interfere with teaching performance. Teachers do not have unlimited academic freedom or freedom of speech in the classroom or elsewhere in the school. Teachers are not permitted to disrupt the school or the school curriculum.

- Corporal punishment is not unconstitutional. However, corporal punishment is generally not permitted in New York. Teachers should never strike children in anger and should administer corporal punishment if permitted only as a part of a due process procedure.

Students

- Handicapped students from ages 3 to 21 are entitled to a free and appropriate public education as a matter of federal law. This education should take place in the least restrictive environment available.

- Students have limited freedom of the press. Student newspapers supported by school funds may be reviewed and edited by school officials. However, papers paid for and produced by students off school property may not be censored by school officials.

- Students are entitled to due process. In particular, students have a right to a hearing and an opportunity to present a defense before being suspended. Students who pose a threat to others in the school are not entitled to this due process.

- Students have freedom of speech unless it causes a significant disruption in the school. They may display messages or symbols on their persons, and refuse to participate in the pledge of allegiance. However, they may not use speech considered vulgar or offensive.

HISTORICAL AND PHILOSOPHICAL FOUNDATIONS OF EDUCATION

Development of Formal Education

Education is a fairly recent development. Formal education has existed for only a fraction of the time that humans have been on earth. Many events in the history of education led to the structure of our education system today.

The first formal education probably began about 2000 B.C. in northern Africa and China. It was about 500 B.C. when the formal education that led to our system was instituted in Athens, Greece. Boys were educated in schools, and girls were educated at home.

Three philosopher-intellects of this time—Socrates, Plato and Aristotle—left an indelible mark on education. Socrates developed the Socratic or inquiry method of teaching. Plato believed that an education should help a person fully develop body and soul. Aristotle introduced a scientific and practical approach to education. Plato and Aristotle both believed in the superiority of the ruling classes and the inferiority of women and slaves.

Formal Roman education began about 50 B.C., after Rome had conquered Greece. The grammiacticus schools, developed in Rome, taught such subjects as Latin, history, mathematics, and music and were like our high schools.

Around 70 A.D. Quintilian wrote a series of twelve books that described current and preferred Roman educational practices. These books may have been the first educational methods and psychology texts.

Education continued to develop and began to bring a unified language and thought throughout the known world. Then the Dark Ages (400 to 1000 A.D.) began. Enormous amounts of learning were lost during this period, and schooling was set back. The revival of learning following the Dark Ages was led by religious leaders such as St. Thomas Aquinas, who devised scholasticism (the formal study of knowledge).

During the Renaissance and the Reformation (1300–1700 A.D.), schooling was freed from control by the church. Church groups, particularly the Jesuits and the Christian Brothers, established religious schools.

Beginning around 1700, thought and schooling focused more on reason and logic. During this time, the "common man" in Europe sought a better life and better education. Great educators emerged from this period. Jean Jacques Rousseau, who wrote *Emile* in 1762, held a positive view of children and believed that education should be a natural process. Pestalozzi established schools that incorporated Rousseau's ideas. The schools featured understanding and patience for children and methods that enabled students to develop concepts through manipulative materials.

Herbart was Pestalozzi's student. In the early 1800s, Herbart formalized the approach to education. He presented some steps for teaching including presentation, generalization, and application. These steps bear a remarkable similarity to the stages from the taxonomy of educational objectives presented earlier.

Froebel was another educator influenced by Rousseau and Pestalozzi. Froebel established the first kindergarten with emphasis on social development and learning through experience. Kindergarten means child's garden.

American Education

In the 1600s American children were educated at home by their parents. Later that century, Dame schools began in the East. Classes were offered in a woman's home and often amounted to no more than child care. Secondary education consisted of Latin grammar schools, which provided a classical education.

In the mid-1600s laws were introduced in Massachusetts requiring education. Some localities provided schooling, and this form of local school lasted into the 1800s. Private schools also offered an education during this period. Admission to these schools was limited to those who could afford to pay.

In rural America there were not enough students in one locality to form a school. In these areas schooling was provided by tutors through the 1700s and by itinerant teachers through the 1900s.

English grammar schools and academies began operation as secondary schools during the 1700s. English grammar schools prepared students for careers while academies combined the features of Latin and English grammar schools.

Common schools provided free, public education for all students beginning in the 1800s. About that same time high schools were established to provide free, public secondary education. Junior high schools were introduced in the early 1900s, and middle schools were introduced in the 1950s.

Horn books, the alphabet covered by a transparent horn, were the predominant teaching device of the colonial period. The New England primer was the first substantial text and was used as a reading text until the late 1700s. The American spelling book, written by Noah Webster, contained stories and the alphabet along with lists of spelling words and was the most popular school book in the early 1800s. McGuffey's readers were reading books geared for different grade levels and were the main education materials for Americans from around 1840 to 1920.

American schools from the early 1800s through the early 1900s were based on the teachings of Pestalozzi and Herbart. These schools showed both the compassion suggested by Pestalozzi and the severe formalism based on Herbart's ideas.

Maria Montessori established her school, Casa Bambini, in 1908. She believed that students thrive in an environment that naturally holds their interest and that offers specially prepared materials. Schools following a modified version of her approach are found throughout the United States today.

Around 1900 John Dewey established the first "progressive" school. Progressive schools sought to build a curriculum around the child rather than around the subject matter. Progressive schools were very popular through the 1930s, and the progressive education movement continued into the 1950s.

The essentialist movement has a view opposite to progressivism. Educators associated with this movement favor a teacher-centered classroom. They believe in a more challenging, subject-oriented curriculum, and have a heavy reliance on achievement test results. Most school practices today primarily reflect the essentialist approach.

With the Depression of the 1930s, the federal government took a more active role in the schools. This active role increased through 1960 with programs designed to improve mathematics and science programs to bolster the national defense. In the 1960s and 1970s federal government focused on social issues as they relate to the schools, such as desegregation and equal educational opportunity.

Public Law 94-142 marked the federal government's first direct intervention in school instruction. This law and Public Law 99-457 mandate an appropriate public education in the least restrictive environment for handicapped Americans aged 3–21. Public Law 98-199 mandates transitional services for high school students. The federal government remains a vital force in American education today.

Jerome Bruner, B. F. Skinner, and Jean Piaget had an impact on American schools in the last half of this century.

In the *Process of Education*, Bruner urged the student's active involvement in the learning process. He called for more problem solving and believed that any topic could be taught in some significant way to children of any age.

B. F. Skinner took a different view than Bruner. He thought that material to be learned should be broken down into small manageable steps. Then students should be taught step by step and rewarded for success. Skinner's approach, behaviorism, built on the work of the Russian scientist Pavlov. Token reinforcement is an example of the behaviorist approach. Behaviorism is characterized by many as too limiting and controlling for regular classrooms.

Jean Piaget posited that students go though a series of stages—sensorimotor, preoperational, concrete operational, and formal operational—as they develop concepts. He believed that students need to work individually, based on their stage of development, and that movement through the stages for a concept could not be accelerated. Piaget's work indicates that more concrete and pictorial materials should be used in the schools and that students should be actively involved in the learning process.

ASSESSMENT

Evaluating Instruction

Every teacher evaluates instruction. The assessment program and the assessment instruments should measure mastery and understanding of important topics. The assessment program should also be used as a teaching tool. That is, the program should be used to help students learn and to improve instruction. The program should include authentic assessment of students' work as well as teacher-made and standardized tests.

Formative assessment information is usually gathered before or during teaching. Formative information is used to help you prepare appropriate lessons and assist students. Formative evaluations help teachers decide which objectives to teach, which instructional techniques to use, and which special help or services to provide to individual students.

Summative assessment information is usually gathered once instruction is complete. Summative evaluation is used to make judgments about student achievement and the effectiveness of the instructional programs. Summative evaluations lead to grades, to reports about a student's relative level of accomplishment, and to alterations of instructional programs.

Assessment information may be used for both purposes. For example, you may give a test to determine grades for a marking period or unit. You may then use the information from this test to plan further instruction and arrange individual help for students.

You may informally gather formative and summative information. Just walking around the room observing students' work can yield a lot of useful information. You can frequently discern the additional work that students need and identify different levels of student achievement.

Assessment Instruments

Tests have long been used to determine what students have learned and to compare students. Every test is imperfect. Many tests are so imperfect that they are useless. It is important to realize how this imperfection affects test results.

Some students are poor test takers. Every test assumes that the test taker has the opportunity to demonstrate what they know. A student may know something but be unable to demonstrate it on a particular test. We must also consider alternative assessment strategies for these students.

Familiarize yourself with these basic assessment concepts.

- Errors of Measurement—Every test contains errors of measurement. In other words, no one test accurately measures a student's achievement or ability. Carefully designed standardized tests may have measurement errors of 5 percent or 10 percent. Teacher-designed tests typically have large errors of measurement.

A test result shows that a student falls into a range of scores and not just the single reported score. Focusing on a single score and ignoring the score range is among the most serious of score-reporting errors.

- Reliability—A reliable test is consistent. That is, a reliable test will give similar results when given to the same person in a short time span. You can't count on unreliable tests to give you useful scores. Use only very reliable standardized tests and be very aware of how important reliability is when you make up your own tests.

- Validity—Valid tests measure what they are supposed to measure. There are two important types of validity: content validity and criterion validity.

  A test with high content validity measures the material covered in the curriculum or unit being tested. Tests that lack high content validity are unfair. When you make up a test it should have complete content validity. This does not mean that the test has to be unchallenging. It does mean that the questions should refer to the subject matter covered.

  A test with high criterion validity successfully predicts the ability to do other work. For example a test to be an automobile mechanic with high criterion validity will successfully predict who will be a good mechanic.

Norm-Referenced and Criterion-Referenced Tests

Norm-referenced tests are designed to compare students. Intelligence tests are probably the best-known norm-referenced tests. These tests yield a number that purports to show how one person's intelligence compares to everyone else's. The average IQ score is 100.

Standardized achievement tests yield grade-level equivalent scores. These tests purport to show how student achievement compares to the achievement of all other students of the same grade level.

A fifth grader who earns a grade level equivalent of 5.5 might be thought of as average. A second-grade student with the same grade equivalent score would be thought of as above average. About half of all the students taking these tests will be below average.

Standardized tests also yield percentile scores. Percentile scores are reported as a number from 0 through 100. A percentile of 50 indicates that the student did as well as or better than 50 percent of the students at that grade level who took the test. The higher the percentile, the better the relative performance.

Criterion-referenced tests are designed to determine the degree to which an objective has been reached. Teacher-made tests and tests found in teachers' editions of texts are usually criterion referenced tests. Criterion referenced tests have very high content validity.

Authentic Assessment

Standardized and teacher-made tests have significant drawbacks. These types of tests do not evaluate a student's ability to perform a task or demonstrate a skill in a real-life situation. These tests do not evaluate a student's ability to work cooperatively or consistently.

In authentic assessment, students are asked to demonstrate the skill or knowledge in a real-life setting. The teacher and students collaborate in the learning assessment process and discuss how learning is progressing and how to facilitate that learning. The idea is to get an authentic picture of the student's work and progress.

The student has an opportunity to demonstrate what they know or can do in a variety of settings. Students can also demonstrate their ability to work independently or as part of a group.

Portfolio assessment is another name for authentic assessment. Students evaluated through a system of authentic assessment frequently keep a portfolio of their work.

Authentic assessment might include the following approaches.

- The student might be observed by the teacher, or occasionally by other students. The observer takes notes and discusses the observation later with the students.

- Students establish portfolios that contain samples of their work. Students are told which work samples they must include in their portfolios. The students place their best work for each requirement in the portfolio. Portfolios are evaluated periodically during a conference between the teacher and the student.

- Students maintain journals and logs containing written descriptions, sketches, and other notes that chronicle their work and the process they went through while learning. The journals and logs are reviewed periodically during a conference between the teacher and the student.

Grading and Interpreting Test Scores

The grade level at which you are teaching determines the approach you will take to grading. In the primary grades, you are often asked to check off a list of criteria to show how a student is progressing. Starting in intermediate grades, you will usually issue letter grades.

You should develop a consistent, fair, and varied approach to grading. Students should understand the basis for their grades. You should give students an opportunity to demonstrate what they have learned in a variety of ways.

It is not necessary to adopt a rigid grading system in the elementary grades. Remember, the purpose of a grading system should be to help students learn better, not just to compare them to other students.

Beginning about sixth or seventh grade, the grade should reflect how students are doing relative to other students in the class. By this age, students need to be exposed to the grading system they will experience through high school and college. The grading system should always be fair, consistent, and offer students a variety of ways to demonstrate their mastery.

You will need to interpret normed scores. These scores may be reported as grade equivalents or as percentiles. You may receive these results normed for different groups. For example, one normed score may show performance relative to all students who took the test. Another normed score may show performance relative to students from school districts that have the same socioeconomic status (SES) as your school district.

When interpreting normed scores for parents, point out that the student's performance falls into a range of scores. A student's score that varies significantly from the average score from schools with a similar SES requires attention followed by remediation or enriched instruction.

When interpreting district-wide normed scores, remember that these scores correlate highly with SES.

INSTRUCTIONAL DELIVERY

Planning instruction and implementing instruction are intertwined. Many of the points discussed here will have been considered during the planning process.

Classrooms are dynamic places. Students and teachers interact to further a student's learning and development. Follow these guidelines to establish a successful classroom and teach successful lessons.

Motivation

Most good lessons begin with a motivation. The motivation interests the learner and focuses their attention on the lesson. It is also important to maintain students' motivation for the duration of the lesson.

The motivation for a lesson may be intrinsic or extrinsic. Intrinsic motivation refers to topics that students like or enjoy. Effective intrinsic motivations are based on a knowledge of what is popular or interesting to students of a particular age.

For example, you might introduce a lesson about the French and Indian War to older students by discussing the book and movie *Last of the Mohicans*. You might introduce a lesson on patterns to young children by picking out patterns in children's clothes. You might introduce a lesson on fractions to middle school students with a discussion about the stock market.

Extrinsic motivation focuses on external rewards for good work or goal attainment. Extrinsic rewards are most successful when used in conjunction with more routine work. Extrinsic motivations may offer an appropriate reward for completing an assignment or for other acceptable performance. Establish rewards for activities that most students can achieve and take care to eliminate unnecessary competition.

For example, you might grant a period of free time to students who successfully complete a routine but necessary assignment. You might offer the whole class a trip or a party when a class project is successfully completed. Special education programs feature token reinforcement in which students receive or lose points or small plastic tokens for appropriate or inappropriate activity.

Motivation needs to be maintained during the lesson itself. Follow these guidelines for teaching lessons in which the students remain motivated. Lessons will be more motivating if you have clear and unambiguous objectives, give the students stimulating tasks at an appropriate level, get and hold the students' attention, and allow students some choices. Students will be most motivated if they like the topic or activities, believe that the lesson has to do with them, believe that they will succeed, and have a positive reaction to your efforts to motivate them.

Individual work gives a further opportunity to use intrinsic motivation. Use the interests and likes of individual students to spark and maintain their motivation.

The extrinsic motivation of praise can be used effectively during a lesson. For praise to be successful, it must be given for a specific accomplishment, including effort, and focus on the student's own behavior. It does not compare behavior with other students nor establish competitive situations.

Successful Learning

Research indicates that the following factors are likely to lead to successful learning.

- Students who are engaged in the learning process tend to be more successful learners, particularly when they are engaged in activities at the appropriate level of difficulty.

- Students learn most successfully when they are being taught or supervised as opposed to working independently.

- Students who are exposed to more material at the appropriate level of difficulty are more successful learners.

- Students are successful learners when their teachers expect them to master the curriculum and use available instructional time for learning activities.

- Students who are in a positive, uncritical classroom environment are more successful learners than students who are in a negative, critical classroom environment. This does not mean that students cannot be corrected or criticized but that students learn best when the corrections are done positively and when the criticisms are constructive.

- Students generally develop positive attitudes to teachers who appear warm, have a student orientation, praise students, listen to students, accept student ideas, and interact with them.

Classroom Interaction

Flander's interaction analysis gives a way to understand how teachers teach. His scheme focuses on the kind of teacher talk and student talk in a classroom. In Flander's work, one of the codes below was assigned to every three seconds of classroom instruction. This kind of frequent coding and the numbers or precise names of the categories are not important. However, the coding system can help you understand how to structure successful learning experiences.

Indirect Teacher Talk

1. Accepts feelings—Teacher acknowledges and accepts students' feelings.

2. Praises and encourages—Teacher praises students' contributions and encourages students to continue their contributions.

3. Accepts or uses students' ideas—Teacher helps students develop their own ideas and uses students' own ideas in the lesson.

4. Asks questions—Teacher asks questions about lesson content or solicits students' opinions. Rhetorical questions and questions not related to the lesson content are not included in this category.

Direct Teacher Talk

5. Lectures, explains, or demonstrates—Teacher presents facts, opinions, or demonstrations related to the lesson topic.

6. Gives directions—Teacher gives directions to which students are expected to comply.

7. Criticizes or justifies authority—Teacher responds negatively to students, criticizes, or justifies authority.

Student Talk

8. Student talk (response)—Student responds to a teacher's question. The correct answer is predictable and anticipated by the teacher.

9. Student talk (initiation)—Student initiates response that is not predictable. The response may follow an open-ended or indirect question from the teacher.

10. Silence or confusion—The classroom is silent or you can't make out what is being said.

Classroom Approaches

Effective classrooms are characterized by a variety of teaching approaches. The approaches should be tailored to the ability of the learner and the lesson objectives.

Teacher-Centered Approaches

Teacher-centered approaches are characterized by teacher presentation, a factual question, and a knowledge-based response from the student.

Lecture or Explanation

You can present material through a lecture or an explanation. A lecture is a fairly long verbal presentation of material. Explanation refers to a shorter presentation. Lecture and explanation are efficient ways to present information that must be arranged and structured in a particular way. However, lecture and explanation may place learners in too passive a role.

Lecture and explanation work best under the following circumstances: (1) the lesson begins with a motivation, (2) the teacher maintains eye contact, (3) the teacher supplies accentuating gestures but without extraneous movements, (4) the presentation is limited to about 5–40 minutes depending on the age of the student, and (5) the objective is clear and the presentation is easy to follow and at an appropriate level.

Demonstrations

Demonstrations are lectures or explanations in which you model what you want students to learn. That is, you exhibit a behavior, show a technique, or demonstrate a skill to help students reach the objective. Demonstrations should follow the same general rules as lectures and the actual demonstration should be clear and easy to follow.

Teacher Questions

Teachers frequently ask questions during class. The following guidelines describe successful questions.

• Formulate questions so that they are clear, purposeful, brief, and at an appropriate level for the class.

• Address the vast majority of questions to the entire class. Individually addressed questions are appropriate to prepare "shy" students to answer the question.

• Avoid rhetorical questions.

• Use both higher and lower level questions on Bloom's taxonomy (knowledge, comprehension, application, analysis, synthesis, evaluation). All types of questions have their place.

- Avoid question-and-answer drills. A consistent pattern of teacher questions that call for responses at the first level of Bloom's taxonomy is too limiting for most classrooms.

- Pause before you call on a student to answer the question, giving students an opportunity to formulate their responses.

- Call on a wide range of students to answer. Do not pick students just because they are either likely or unlikely to respond correctly.

- Wait 4 or 5 seconds for an answer. Don't cut off students who are struggling with an answer.

- Rephrase a question if it seems unclear or vague.

- Set a target for about 70 percent or so of questions to be answered correctly.

Student-Centered Approaches—Active Learning

In a student-centered or active learning environment, the teacher ceases to be the prime presenter of information. The teacher's questions are more open-ended and indirect. Students will be encouraged to be more active participants in the class. This type of instruction is characterized by student-initiated comments, praise from the teacher, and the teacher's use of students' ideas.

Just because there is student involvement does not mean that the teacher is using a student-centered or active approach. For example, the pattern of questions and answers referred to as drill is not a student-centered approach.

Cooperative Learning

Students involved in cooperative learning work together in groups to learn a concept or skill or to complete a project. Students, in groups of two to six, are assigned or choose a specific learning task or project presented by the teacher. The group consults with the teacher and devises a plan for working together.

Students use many resources, including the teacher, to help and teach one another and to accept responsibilities for tasks as they complete their work. The students summarize their efforts and, typically, make a presentation to the entire class or the teacher.

Cooperative learning is characterized by active learning, full participation, and democracy within a clearly established structure. Cooperative learning also engages students in learning how to establish personal relationships and a cooperative working style.

Inquiry Learning

Inquiry learning uses students' own thought processes to help them learn a concept, solve a problem, or discover a relationship. This kind of instruction has also been referred to as Socratic. Inquiry learning often requires the most structure and preparation by the teacher. The teacher must know that the situation under study will yield useful results.

The teacher begins by explaining inquiry procedures to students, usually through examples. Next the teacher presents the problem to be solved or the situation that will lead to the concept or relationship. Students gather information and ask questions of the teacher to gain additional information. The teacher supports students as they make predictions and provide tentative solutions or results. Once the process is complete, the teacher asks students to think over and describe the process they used to arrive at the solution. This last step is referred to as a metacognition.

Resources for Instruction

You may have to assemble a number of resources for instruction. It often helps to jot down the resources you will need to teach a lesson or a unit. The materials you select should help the students meet the lesson objectives and match the teaching-learning approach you will use. The resources may include textual, manipulative, technological, and human resources.

Be sure to assemble in advance the materials you need to teach a lesson. The materials may include texts, workbooks, teacher-made handouts, or other printed materials. Check the materials to ensure that they are intact and in appropriate condition.

You may use manipulative materials to teach a lesson. Be sure that the materials are assembled and complete. Any laboratory materials should be tested and safe. Be sure that the materials are at an appropriate level for the students.

You may use technological resources, such as a computer, during your lesson. Be sure that the computer will be available during your lesson. Try the computer out and be sure that it is working. Be sure that any software you will use is at an appropriate grade and interest level and matches the objectives of the lesson.

You will frequently use human resources in your lesson. You may decide to cooperatively teach a lesson or unit with another teacher. This approach requires advanced planning and regular communication. You may need to arrange for a guest speaker to speak to the class about a particular topic.

Special education teachers frequently teach in consultative or collaborative roles. That is, they work in classrooms with regular education teachers. In this arrangement, teachers must coordinate their activities and agree on how they will interact during the lesson.

INCLUSION

Inclusion means that special needs students are included in a regular school setting and placed in more restrictive environments only when needed. This does not mean that every special education student will be in a regular classroom all day. It does mean that students will be given every opportunity to function in a regular environment.

For some students, inclusion means attending a local special education school instead of a residential school. For other students it may mean attending a neighborhood school instead of a special education school. For still other students it means spending the maximum amount of time in regular classrooms.

Inclusion may mean placing students in regular education class and then switching them to special education settings as needed during the day. Inclusion may mean that a special education teacher goes into a regular education classroom to work with special education students in the class during the regular class periods. Teams of regular education and special education teachers frequently work together with students moving easily from regular education to special education settings.

It is impossible to include all students. Some students with severe physical disabilities require a special setting. Other students with severe mental handicaps will not be able to function effectively in a regular setting. Other students with severe emotional disorders or who are extremely disruptive will have to be educated in a self-contained special education class.

Parental Involvement

The key to a successful special education program is parental involvement. Parents are naturally concerned about their child's special education classification. They need to be constructively involved in their child's program. Keep parents abreast of the child's progress on a regular basis. If there are issues or concerns about the child, notify the parents immediately. Help parents understand the academic gains their child is making.

ADAPTING INSTRUCTION

Adapt instruction for the following factors, types of learners, and students.

> Age—Primary students should have more structure, short lessons, less explanation, more public praise, more small group and individual instruction, and more experiences with manipulatives and pictures. Older students should have less structure, increasingly longer lessons, more explanation, less public praise, more whole-class instruction, more independent work, and less work with manipulatives.

Academically Diverse

> Aptitude—Students exhibit different abilities to learn. You can provide differentiated assignments to enable students at different aptitude levels to maximize their potential.

> Reading Level—Ensure that a student is capable of understanding the reading material. Do not ask students to learn from material that is too difficult. Identify materials at an appropriate reading level or with an alternative learning mode (tapes, material read to student). Remember that a low reading level does not mean that a student cannot learn a difficult concept.

> Learning Disabled—Learning-disabled students evidence at least a 2-year discrepancy between measures of ability and performance. Learning-disabled students should be given structured, brief assignments, manipulative experiences, and many opportunities for auditory learning.

> Visually Impaired—Place the visually impaired student where he or she can most easily see the instruction. Use large learning aids and large print books. Use a multisensory approach.

> Hearing Impaired—Ensure that students are wearing an appropriate hearing aid. Students with less than 50 percent hearing loss will probably be able to hear you if you stand about 3 to 5 feet away.

> Mildly Handicapped—Focus on a few, highly relevant skills, more learning time, and lots of practice. Provide students with concrete experiences. Do not do for students what they can do for themselves, even if it takes these students an extended time.

> Gifted—Gifted students have above average ability, creativity, and a high degree of task commitment. Provide these students with enriched or differentiated units. Permit them to test out of required units. Do not isolate these students from the rest of the class.

Cultural and Linguistic Diversity

> SES (Socioeconomic Status)—Socioeconomic status and school achievement are highly correlated. Overall, students with higher SES will have higher achievement scores. In America, SES differences are typically associated with differences in race and ethnicity. However, the achievement differences are not caused by and are not a function of these differences in race or ethnicity. Rather, achievement differences are

typically caused by differences in home environment, opportunity for enriched experiences, and parental expectations.

Teachers frequently have a higher SES than their students. These students often behave differently than teachers expect. The crushing problems of poor and homeless children may produce an overlay of acting out and attention problems. All this frequently leads the teacher to erroneously conclude that these students are less capable of learning. In turn, the teacher may erroneously lower learning expectations. This leads to lower school performance and a compounding of students' difficulty.

A teacher must consciously and forcibly remind herself or himself that lower SES students are capable learners. These teachers must also actively guard against reducing learning expectations for lower SES students.

There are appropriate ways of adapting instruction for students with different SES levels. For high SES students, minimize competitiveness, provide less structure, and present more material. For low SES students, be more encouraging, guard against feelings of failure or low self-esteem, and provide more structure. Do not lower learning expectations, but do present less material and emphasize mastery of the material.

Culturally Diverse—Almost every class will have students from diverse cultural backgrounds. Use the values embedded in these cultures to motivate individual learners.

Language Diverse—The first language for many students is not English. In addition, a number of American students speak local variants of the English language. Teachers frequently, and erroneously, lower their learning expectations for these students. There are a number of useful strategies for adapting instruction for these students.

A number of students are referred to as Limited English Proficiency (LEP) who need English as a second language (ESL) instruction. Teaching English as a second language can be accomplished in the classroom, but often requires a specialist who works with students in "pull-out programs." When teaching these students, use simpler words and expressions, use context clues to help students identify word meaning, clearly draw students' attention to your speech, and actively involve students in the learning process.

Multiple Intelligences and Learning Styles

Multiple intelligences means there are many different ways students can demonstrate their ability. It follows that students have different learning styles. This approach is in sharp contrast to the current approach of measuring ability on a single scale, usually with an IQ test.

Howard Gardner of Harvard is credited with originating this approach to understanding intelligence. According to Gardner, there are eight ways to be smart. These seven intelligences are listed below.

1- verbal/linguistic
2- logical/mathematical
3- visual/spatial
4- bodily/kinesthetic
5- musical/rhythmic
6- interpersonal
7- the naturalist

Gardner also says that if students are smart in different ways then they learn in different ways. Children will have a learning style that matches their particular intelligence or intelligences. The idea is to use instructional approaches that match the learner's style. For example, use art to teach visual learners and use music to reach musical learners.

MANAGING THE INSTRUCTIONAL ENVIRONMENT

Classroom management is a more encompassing idea than discipline or classroom control. Classroom management deals with all the things a classroom teacher can do to help students become productive learners. The best management system for any classroom will establish an effective learning environment with the least restrictions.

Teachers who are proactive and take charge stand the best chance of establishing an effective learning environment. Classroom management is designed to prevent problems, not react to them.

Classroom management begins with understanding the characteristics of students in your class.

Characteristics of Students

We can make some general statements about the students in a class. We know that 3–7 percent of girls and 12–18 percent of boys will have some substantial adjustment problems. Prepare yourself for these predictable sex differences.

Boys are more physically active and younger children have shorter attention spans. Respond to this situation by scheduling activities when students are most likely to be able to complete them.

A teacher's management role is different at different grade levels. Prepare for these predictable differences in student reaction to teacher authority.

In the primary grades, students see teachers as authority figures and respond well to instruction and directions about how they should act in school. In the middle grades, students have learned how to act in school and still react well to the teacher's instruction.

In seventh through tenth grade, students turn to their peer group for leadership and resist the teacher's authority. The teacher must spend more time fostering appropriate behavior among students. By the last two years of high school, students are somewhat less resistant and the teacher's role is more academic.

We know that many adolescents resent being touched and that teachers may anger adolescents by taking something from them. Avoid this problem by not confronting adolescent students.

We know that there will be cultural differences among students. Many minority students, and other students, may be accustomed to harsh, authoritarian treatment. Respond to these students with warmth, acceptance, and structure. Many minority students will feel completely out of place in school. These students also need to be treated warmly and also with the positive expectation that they will succeed in school.

Many other students may be too distracted to study effectively in school. These students may need quiet places to work and the opportunity to schedule some of their own work time.

Other factors, such as low self-esteem, anxiety, and tension, can also cause students to have difficulty in school.

Classroom Management Techniques

The following guidelines for effective classroom management include techniques for dealing with student misbehavior.

Teacher's Role

Teachers who are good classroom managers understand their dual role as an authority figure and as someone who helps children adapt to school and to life. Teachers are authority figures. Students expect the teacher to be an authority figure and expect teachers to establish a clear and consistent classroom structure.

Teachers must also help students learn how to fit into the classroom and how to get along with others. Teachers fare better in their role as authority figures than they do in this latter role. But teachers who have realistic expectations and know how to respond to problems can have some success.

Characteristics of Successful Teachers

In general effective teachers have these general characteristics.

- Accept children within a teacher-student relationship.
- Set firm and clear but flexible limits.
- Enforce rules clearly and consistently.
- Have positive, realistic expectations about students' achievements and adaptations.
- Have clear reasons for expectations about students.
- Practice what they preach (model acceptable behavior).
- Don't take students' actions personally. Students usually misbehave or act out because of who they are, not because of who the teacher is.

Establishing an Effective Climate for Management

Classroom Physical Layout

There are several general rules to follow for a successful classroom layout. Set up the initial layout of the room so that you can see the faces of all the students. Rearrange the desks for individual and group work. Ensure that heavily used areas are free of all obstacles. Arrange the room so students do not have to stand in line, by having books and supplies available at several locations.

Classroom Leadership

Research indicates that the following factors are most important in establishing effective classroom leadership. Develop a cohesive class by promoting cooperative experiences and minimizing competition among class members. Identify and gain the confidence of peer leaders, particularly in grades 7–10. Establish an authoritative, but not authoritarian, leadership style.

Depending on the grade level, set three to six reasonable, adaptable rules that describe the overall nature of acceptable and unacceptable behavior. The expectations that accompany these rules should be stated clearly. The rules should be posted for students to see.

Much of the first two weeks of school should be spent establishing these rules, which may be stated by the teacher and/or developed through class discussion. Once the rules are established and the expectations are understood, the teacher should follow through. Student misbehavior should be handled immediately and appropriately but without causing a confrontation or alienating the student from the class.

Effective classroom managers take steps to ensure that the majority of class time is spent on instruction. They also take steps to ensure that students use their seat work and other in-class study time to complete assignments.

Specific Management Techniques

There are some specific management techniques that a teacher can apply to all classes. These techniques are summarized here.

Kounin

Kounin is a well-known expert on classroom management. Research results show that a number of Kounin's management techniques are effective. The following techniques have the most research support:

Kounin noted that teacher with-it-ness is an important aspect of classroom management. In other words, teachers who are constantly monitoring and aware of what is happening in the classroom are better managers.

Kounin also showed that effective managers' lessons have smoothness and momentum. By this he meant that these lessons are free of teacher behavior that interrupts the flow of activities or slows down lesson pacing.

Finally, Kounin showed that group alerting was an effective technique. In group alerting, the teacher keeps bringing uninvolved students back into the lesson by calling their attention to what is happening and forewarning them of future events.

Canter and Canter

Canter and Canter developed an approach called assertive discipline. Their approach is popular but lacks the research support of the approach recommended by Kounin.

The Canters recommend a direct and assertive approach to problem children. They point out that passive and hostile reactions to student misbehavior are not effective. Among other approaches, they recommend that the teacher and students establish rules and post those rules in the classroom. During each class session, the teacher writes and then marks the names of students who have violated rules. One rule violation in a session requires no action. Two rule violations, and the student meets with the teacher after school. Three violations requires a parental visit to the school.

Cueing

Cues are words, gestures, or other signals that alert students to a coming transition or that gain their attention. A cue may be spoken, such as "We'll be leaving for art in about 5 minutes. Take this time to get ready." Another cue might be, "Your group has about 15 minutes to complete your project."

Other cues are nonverbal. You may glance at a student or make eye contact to re-engage them in the lesson. You may raise your arm or hold your hand in a particular way to gain attention. You may flick the classroom lights quickly to indicate that groups should stop working and return to whole-class instruction.

Other Effective Techniques for Maintaining Attention During a Lesson
The techniques listed below have proven effective in classrooms.

- Stand where you can scan and see the entire class.

- Ask questions of the whole class and then call on individuals for a response.

- Involve all students in the question-and-answer sessions and don't call on students just to catch them in a wrong answer or because they will give the correct answer.

- Gain attention through eye contact or a gesture.

- If a comment is required, make it very brief.

- Ensure that the material being taught is at an appropriate level.

- Base seat work or group work on an established system that is monitored closely and positively.

Changing Behavior

Students may act so unacceptably that their behavior must be changed. Here are some suggestions for changing behavior.

Modeling
Students learn how to behave from observing others. In the classroom the teacher is the authority figure and the one whom students may model their behaviors after. The following teacher behaviors can have a positive impact on student behaviors. In general, teachers should act as they expect their students to act.

- Listen carefully to what students say.

- Act after thoughtful consideration, not in anger or on an impulse.

- Treat students with respect.

- Do not be sarcastic or hostile with students.

- Respond to difficulty or criticism carefully. Don't take it personally.

Reinforcement
All teachers use positive reinforcement, whether through grades, praise, tokens, or other means. Teachers also use negative reinforcement by showing students how to avoid an undesirable consequence (poor grade) by doing acceptable work. Negative reinforcement is not punishment.

In the classroom you should increase the duration or quality of the desired behavior before reinforcing. Reach explicit agreements with students about the level of performance that will yield rewards (positive reinforcement). Praise is often an ineffective reinforcer.

Contracts and Logs

You may be able to help children change behavior by using contracts or by asking students to maintain logs. These approaches cause students to think about their behavior and both have been proven effective.

When writing a contract, work with a student to establish desired learning goals or classroom behavior. The contract, signed by the teacher and the student, sets short-term goals for classroom conduct and academic achievement. A teacher may also ask students to maintain a log of their classroom behavior. A brief daily review of the log may improve behavior.

Punishment

Punishment is a temporary measure. It should be administered to improve student performance, not to make the teacher feel better. Limited punishment given for a specific reason when students are emotionally stable can be effective. Other punishments, such as extra work, punishment of the entire class, and corporal punishment, are usually not effective.

Effective punishment should be reasonable, deliberate, and unemotional. The punishment should also be short and somewhat unpleasant. The reason for the punishment should be clear, and the punishment should be accompanied by examples of appropriate behavior.

ATS-W PRACTICE ITEMS

These practice items are designed to help you practice the concepts and skills presented in this chapter. For that reason, questions may have a different emphasis than the actual test and the actual test will certainly be more complete.

    Mark your choice, then check your answers. Review the test taking tips on pages 16–23.

1	Ⓐ Ⓑ Ⓒ Ⓓ	5	Ⓐ Ⓑ Ⓒ Ⓓ	9	Ⓐ Ⓑ Ⓒ Ⓓ	13	Ⓐ Ⓑ Ⓒ Ⓓ	17	Ⓐ Ⓑ Ⓒ Ⓓ
2	Ⓐ Ⓑ Ⓒ Ⓓ	6	Ⓐ Ⓑ Ⓒ Ⓓ	10	Ⓐ Ⓑ Ⓒ Ⓓ	14	Ⓐ Ⓑ Ⓒ Ⓓ	18	Ⓐ Ⓑ Ⓒ Ⓓ
3	Ⓐ Ⓑ Ⓒ Ⓓ	7	Ⓐ Ⓑ Ⓒ Ⓓ	11	Ⓐ Ⓑ Ⓒ Ⓓ	15	Ⓐ Ⓑ Ⓒ Ⓓ	19	Ⓐ Ⓑ Ⓒ Ⓓ
4	Ⓐ Ⓑ Ⓒ Ⓓ	8	Ⓐ Ⓑ Ⓒ Ⓓ	12	Ⓐ Ⓑ Ⓒ Ⓓ	16	Ⓐ Ⓑ Ⓒ Ⓓ	20	Ⓐ Ⓑ Ⓒ Ⓓ

1. In order to assess what a student learned in a mathematics class, a teacher would need to know
   (A) the student's standardized test score in mathematics.
   (B) the percent of correct answers on a test about the lesson.
   (C) the extent to which the teacher is satisfied with the lesson.
   (D) what the student knew before the lesson began.

2. Many students in your fifth grade class are hesitant to choose their own books because their interests are few. How could you devise a book list to promote reading about new topics?
   (A) List books by author
   (B) List books by number of pages
   (C) List books by topic
   (D) List books by topics and related topics

3. Because of a drought, the whole town has to sharply reduce water usage. Which of the following comments by a teacher is most likely to gain students' participation in this effort?
   (A) "Perhaps we can contact our local government and find out what we can do to help in our own way."
   (B) "Let the adults take responsibility for the water conservation. You are too young to be responsible for something so important."
   (C) "I'm sorry but we will no longer be getting water or using the rest rooms at school."
   (D) "Let's sit down and write letters to our legislature and ask them why they misuse our water supply."

4. During oral reading, a student sees "save" and reads "Sam." This student most likely requires work with
   (A) whole language.
   (B) comprehension.
   (C) context clues.
   (D) phonics.

5. A mentally retarded student will be moving from the middle school to the senior high school. Which of the following strategies would best prepare this student for the high school years and those that follow?
   (A) Formulate and update IEP.
   (B) Engage student in real-life situations.
   (C) Formulate an Individualized Family Support Plan.
   (D) Offer less challenging activities until the student becomes accustomed to the surroundings.

6. Auditory learners are more likely to learn about geography by which of the following methods?
   (A) Playing a geography card game
   (B) Listening to an audiocassette about geography
   (C) Reading a geography text
   (D) Using a map or a chart

7. Which of the following would be most helpful in assessing a young student who cannot name the number of elements in a set?
   (A) A conservation of number task
   (B) A counting task
   (C) An arithmetic task
   (D) A numeral-recognition test

8. Which of the following should NOT be considered when determining the most appropriate environment for students with disabilities?
   (A) The cost of augmentative apparatus
   (B) The opinions of the parents
   (C) The advice of pupil personal staff
   (D) The suggestions of the classroom teacher

9. Research indicates that cooperative learning is most effective in all of the following EXCEPT
   (A) comprehension.
   (B) psychomotor skills.
   (C) problem solving.
   (D) social skills.

10. Each of the following student assignments would encourage divergent thinking EXCEPT
    (A) list alternatives to capital punishment not currently legislated.
    (B) describe the effects of acid rain on the environment.
    (C) identify the country that had the largest gross national product in 1993.
    (D) design a device to turn on a light with just a towel, a rubber band, and a paper clip.

11. A criterion-referenced test is administered to a student. Questions about the validity of the test can be answered by showing that
    (A) the test has been standardized.
    (B) the test is consistent.
    (C) odd- and even-numbered questions yield about the same percent of correct and incorrect answers.
    (D) the test correctly predicts students' abilities.

12. Each of the following practices would help a learning-disabled student EXCEPT
    (A) manipulative activities.
    (B) short lessons.
    (C) auditory learning.
    (D) complex problem-solving.

13. Judicial decisions to allow the availability of condoms for high school students are largely based on
    (A) parents' right to know if their children are sexually active.
    (B) the likelihood of condom use will increase promiscuity among teens.
    (C) students' right to protect themselves from sexually transmitted diseases.
    (D) parents' right to be informed of the health of their child.

14. Which of the following is an appropriate way to modify instruction for LEP students?
    (A) Conduct classes in the native language.
    (B) Give additional homework.
    (C) Give students additional time for tests.
    (D) Avoid difficult topics.

15. Which of the following is LEAST likely to help the teacher learn about a student's interests outside of school?
    (A) Personal interview with the student
    (B) Attitude and interest survey
    (C) Discussions with other teachers
    (D) A student's daily journal

16. A teacher feels that her direct administrative superior is sexually harassing her or him during school hours. What action should the teacher take?
    (A) File a civil complaint with the local police.
    (B) Inform her co-workers of the administrator's behavior.
    (C) Avoid contact with the administrator and take no action.
    (D) Contact a union representative and have them alert the legal advisor of the union.

17. Which of the following best describes the current state of the American family?
    (A) The nuclear family no longer exists.
    (B) Most families today consist of two full-time working parents with children in day care.
    (C) Single parent families are headed by fathers.
    (D) Most families don't have a working father, a mother at home, and children in school.

18. The change in philosophy of special education has led to avoiding labeling students because
    (A) labeling is sometimes too specific for educational planning.
    (B) labeling caused discipline problems in the classroom.
    (C) incorrect labeling could lead to a lifelong stigma.
    (D) labeling could lead to discrimination during classroom planning.

19. Which of the following would NOT be an appropriate strategy for a teacher to employ to help a student who is hearing impaired?
    (A) Moving away from direct sunlight so that the student is not distracted by the glare
    (B) Seating a student in a well-lit section of the room
    (C) Talking very loudly
    (D) Clearly enunciating oral instructions

20. A teacher who interjects personal opinions into classroom discussions impairs the learning experiences of the students if
    (A) those opinions are presented as facts.
    (B) all participants' opinions in a discussion are not weighed equally.
    (C) the opinions do not personally threaten any student.
    (D) no other opinion is allowed.

Answers

1. D	5. A	9. B	13. C	17. D
2. D	6. B	10. C	14. C	18. D
3. A	7. A	11. D	15. C	19. C
4. D	8. A	12. D	16. D	20. A

PART III

Two Complete LASTs with Explained Answers

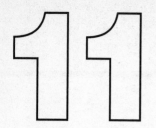 **PRACTICE LAST I**

This practice test contains the types of items you will encounter on the real test. The distribution of items varies from one test administration to another.

Take this test in a realistic, timed setting. You should not take this practice test until you have completed the appropriate review and practice questions.

The setting will be most realistic if another person times the test and ensures that the test rules are followed exactly. But remember that many people do better on a practice test than on the real test. If another person is acting as test supervisor, he or she should review these instructions with you and say "Start" when you should begin a section and "Stop" when time has expired.

You have 4 hours to complete the 80 multiple-choice questions and to complete the written assignment. Keep the time limit in mind as you work.

Each multiple-choice question or statement in the test has four answer choices. Exactly one of these choices is correct. Mark your choice on the answer sheet provided for this test.

Use a pencil to mark the answer sheet. The actual test will be machine scored so completely darken in the answer space.

Once the test is complete, review the answers and explanations for each item.

When instructed, turn the page and begin.

ANSWER SHEET PRACTICE LAST I

1 Ⓐ Ⓑ Ⓒ Ⓓ	21 Ⓐ Ⓑ Ⓒ Ⓓ	41 Ⓐ Ⓑ Ⓒ Ⓓ	61 Ⓐ Ⓑ Ⓒ Ⓓ
2 Ⓐ Ⓑ Ⓒ Ⓓ	22 Ⓐ Ⓑ Ⓒ Ⓓ	42 Ⓐ Ⓑ Ⓒ Ⓓ	62 Ⓐ Ⓑ Ⓒ Ⓓ
3 Ⓐ Ⓑ Ⓒ Ⓓ	23 Ⓐ Ⓑ Ⓒ Ⓓ	43 Ⓐ Ⓑ Ⓒ Ⓓ	63 Ⓐ Ⓑ Ⓒ Ⓓ
4 Ⓐ Ⓑ Ⓒ Ⓓ	24 Ⓐ Ⓑ Ⓒ Ⓓ	44 Ⓐ Ⓑ Ⓒ Ⓓ	64 Ⓐ Ⓑ Ⓒ Ⓓ
5 Ⓐ Ⓑ Ⓒ Ⓓ	25 Ⓐ Ⓑ Ⓒ Ⓓ	45 Ⓐ Ⓑ Ⓒ Ⓓ	65 Ⓐ Ⓑ Ⓒ Ⓓ

6 Ⓐ Ⓑ Ⓒ Ⓓ	26 Ⓐ Ⓑ Ⓒ Ⓓ	46 Ⓐ Ⓑ Ⓒ Ⓓ	66 Ⓐ Ⓑ Ⓒ Ⓓ
7 Ⓐ Ⓑ Ⓒ Ⓓ	27 Ⓐ Ⓑ Ⓒ Ⓓ	47 Ⓐ Ⓑ Ⓒ Ⓓ	67 Ⓐ Ⓑ Ⓒ Ⓓ
8 Ⓐ Ⓑ Ⓒ Ⓓ	28 Ⓐ Ⓑ Ⓒ Ⓓ	48 Ⓐ Ⓑ Ⓒ Ⓓ	68 Ⓐ Ⓑ Ⓒ Ⓓ
9 Ⓐ Ⓑ Ⓒ Ⓓ	29 Ⓐ Ⓑ Ⓒ Ⓓ	49 Ⓐ Ⓑ Ⓒ Ⓓ	69 Ⓐ Ⓑ Ⓒ Ⓓ
10 Ⓐ Ⓑ Ⓒ Ⓓ	30 Ⓐ Ⓑ Ⓒ Ⓓ	50 Ⓐ Ⓑ Ⓒ Ⓓ	70 Ⓐ Ⓑ Ⓒ Ⓓ

11 Ⓐ Ⓑ Ⓒ Ⓓ	31 Ⓐ Ⓑ Ⓒ Ⓓ	51 Ⓐ Ⓑ Ⓒ Ⓓ	71 Ⓐ Ⓑ Ⓒ Ⓓ
12 Ⓐ Ⓑ Ⓒ Ⓓ	32 Ⓐ Ⓑ Ⓒ Ⓓ	52 Ⓐ Ⓑ Ⓒ Ⓓ	72 Ⓐ Ⓑ Ⓒ Ⓓ
13 Ⓐ Ⓑ Ⓒ Ⓓ	33 Ⓐ Ⓑ Ⓒ Ⓓ	53 Ⓐ Ⓑ Ⓒ Ⓓ	73 Ⓐ Ⓑ Ⓒ Ⓓ
14 Ⓐ Ⓑ Ⓒ Ⓓ	34 Ⓐ Ⓑ Ⓒ Ⓓ	54 Ⓐ Ⓑ Ⓒ Ⓓ	74 Ⓐ Ⓑ Ⓒ Ⓓ
15 Ⓐ Ⓑ Ⓒ Ⓓ	35 Ⓐ Ⓑ Ⓒ Ⓓ	55 Ⓐ Ⓑ Ⓒ Ⓓ	75 Ⓐ Ⓑ Ⓒ Ⓓ

16 Ⓐ Ⓑ Ⓒ Ⓓ	36 Ⓐ Ⓑ Ⓒ Ⓓ	56 Ⓐ Ⓑ Ⓒ Ⓓ	76 Ⓐ Ⓑ Ⓒ Ⓓ
17 Ⓐ Ⓑ Ⓒ Ⓓ	37 Ⓐ Ⓑ Ⓒ Ⓓ	57 Ⓐ Ⓑ Ⓒ Ⓓ	77 Ⓐ Ⓑ Ⓒ Ⓓ
18 Ⓐ Ⓑ Ⓒ Ⓓ	38 Ⓐ Ⓑ Ⓒ Ⓓ	58 Ⓐ Ⓑ Ⓒ Ⓓ	78 Ⓐ Ⓑ Ⓒ Ⓓ
19 Ⓐ Ⓑ Ⓒ Ⓓ	39 Ⓐ Ⓑ Ⓒ Ⓓ	59 Ⓐ Ⓑ Ⓒ Ⓓ	79 Ⓐ Ⓑ Ⓒ Ⓓ
20 Ⓐ Ⓑ Ⓒ Ⓓ	40 Ⓐ Ⓑ Ⓒ Ⓓ	60 Ⓐ Ⓑ Ⓒ Ⓓ	80 Ⓐ Ⓑ Ⓒ Ⓓ

Each item on this test includes four answer choices. Select the best choice for each item and mark that letter on the answer sheet.

The space vehicle verification program is designed to show that the vehicle meets all design and performance specifications. The verification program also seeks to ensure that all hazards and sources of failure have been either eliminated or reduced to acceptable levels. The specific spacecraft verification is based on a series of carefully monitored testing protocols. The verification tests are conducted under the strictest controls including temperature and stress levels. Full-scale hull models are used to verify the drawn specifications.

To date, seven full-stress tests have been completed. The tests evaluated the redesigned hull and the hull-to-motor nozzle connectors. The temperature is closely controlled in these tests, as are the internal hull pressures. Both temperature and hull pressures are critical factors in hull integrity. These tests showed that the parts of the hull that were strongest had the most potential for being weak. The tests also revealed that the hull-to-motor nozzle connectors were stronger that the connectors found in earlier versions on the hull. Additional full-stress tests are expected to further clarify the full impact of redesign efforts on the strength of the hull and the hull-to-motor nozzle connectors.

There have been eight full-static tests of engine performance to evaluate the impact of engine motor thrust on hull integrity. Before the tests were begun, specific test objectives were established, including parameters for acceptable performance. The test included a thorough evaluation of all engine attitudes—engine up, engine down and engine nominal. The tests showed that the engines performed within acceptable parameters at each attitude. But further tests are planned to determine if engines need to be strengthened at the points at which they are most likely to show weakness.

There have been six tests of the hull strength where it interfaces with the payload. These portions of the hull are often subjected to additional stress during payload detachment. The tests involved dynamic models that included maximum payload weights combined with maximum thrust and maximum torque. The tests showed that a further evaluation is needed to determine the maximum payload weight that is appropriate for the hull strength and hull characteristics at the point of interface. This evaluation will be based on the tests conducted to date and the tests planned for the next phase.

Another phase of tests are planned to determine the effectiveness of hull integrity with a new version of rocket motor—the PL-12. The PL-12 has more thrust than previous engines and may subject the hull to more stress requiring that potential hull weakness be fully evaluated. These tests will begin after a formal report on previous tests is prepared and new test guidelines and outcome expectations have been established.

1. Which of the following can be inferred from the statement above?
   (A) The parts of the hull that are potentially strongest do not receive as much attention from engineers as those that are potentially weakest.
   (B) The potentially weaker parts of the hull appear stronger in models than the potentially stronger parts of the hull.
   (C) Being potentially weaker, these parts of the hull appear relatively stronger in a model.
   (D) Potentially weaker parts of the hull have the most potential for being stronger.

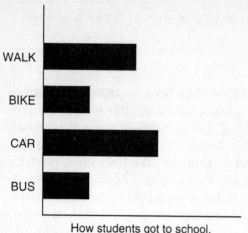

How students got to school.
MONDAY

School officials were trying to decide how students arrived to school each morning. This information was important because those at the school had to decide how many bike stands to have and how much space to set aside for parents to drop off their children at school.

At first they estimated the percent of students who walked to school and those who arrived by bike, car or bus. Their original estimates were that 60 percent of students walked to school or rode a bike to school, while 40 percent of students arrived by car or by bus. But then they realized that these estimates were not accurate enough. So they conducted a survey to gather this information directly from the students.

On Monday, the principal visited each class and found out how they arrived at school that morning. The principal tabulated the results and recorded them on the graph shown above. The principal also took the survey on each day that week. That was because the principal realized that students might not arrive the same way each day.

On Tuesday, the graph for walking shrank by half, while the graph for biking doubled. On Wednesday the results for walking and biking stayed the same, but the numbers for car and bus were reversed. On Thursday it rained and all but twenty percent of the students arrived by bus or by car. The results on Friday were almost the same as the results for Monday.

A committee reviewed the results and realized that the results were always going to be affected by the weather. So the committee decided to take another approach to plan for the different ways that students arrive at school. They posted a request for suggestions to answer this question.

2. Which of the following statements accurately describes the graph on that Wednesday
   (A) There were about twice as many walkers as bikers.
   (B) There were about three times as many car riders as bus riders.
   (C) There were about three times as many car riders as bikers.
   (D) There were about half as many car riders as bike riders.

We use language, including gestures and sounds, to communicate. Humans first used gestures but it was spoken language that opened the vistas for human communication. Language consists of two things. First we have the thoughts that language conveys and then the physical sounds, writing and structure of the language itself.

Human speech organs (mouth, tongue, lips, and the like) were not developed to make sounds, but they uniquely determined the sounds and words humans could produce. Human speech gradually came to be loosely bound together by unique rules for grammar.

Many believe that humans developed their unique ability to speak with the development of a specialized area of the brain called Broca's area. If this is so, human speech and language probably developed in the past 100,000 years.

3. What is the main idea of this passage?
   (A) Language consists of thoughts and physical sounds.
   (B) Human communication includes gestures.
   (C) Human speech and language slowly developed through the years.
   (D) Broca's area of the brain controls speech.

4. What is the first component of language development?
   (A) gestures
   (B) thoughts
   (C) sound
   (D) writing

5. What power of 10 would you multiply times 3.74 to get 374,000,000?
   (A) 10^6
   (B) 10^7
   (C) 10^8
   (D) 10^9

There was very little oxygen in the earth's atmosphere about 3.5 billion years ago. We know that molecules (much smaller than a cell) can develop spontaneously in this type of environment. This is how life probably began on earth about 3.4 billion years ago.

Eventually these molecules linked together to form complex groupings of molecules. These earliest organisms must have been able to ingest and live on nonorganic compounds. Over a period of time, these organisms adapted and began using the sun's energy. The organisms began to use photosynthesis, which released oxygen into the oceans and the atmosphere. The stage was set for more advanced life forms.

The first cells were prokaryotes (bacteria), which created energy (respired) without oxygen (anaerobic). Next these cells developed into blue-green algae prokaryotes, which were aerobic (creating energy with oxygen) and used photosynthesis. The advanced eukaryotes were developed from these primitive cells.

Algae developed about 750 million years ago. Even this simple cell contained an enormous amount of DNA and hereditary information. It took about 2.7 billion years to develop life to this primitive form. This very slow process moved somewhat faster in the millennia that followed as animal and plant forms slowly emerged.

Animals developed into vertebrate (backbone) and invertebrate (no back-bone) species. Mammals became the dominant vertebrate species and insects became the dominant invertebrate species. As animals developed, they adapted to their environment. The best adapted survived. This process is called natural selection. Entire species have vanished from earth.

Mammals and dinosaurs coexisted for more than 100 million years. During that time, dinosaurs were the dominant species. When dinosaurs became extinct 65 million years ago, mammals survived. Freed of dinosaurian dominance, mammals evolved into the dominant creatures they are today. Despite many years of study, it is not known what caused the dinosaurs to become extinct or why mammals survived.

6. This passage suggests
   (A) that mammals were the more intelligent species.
   (B) how life evolved on earth.
   (C) that mammals and dinosaurs were natural enemies.
   (D) the environment did not affect evolution.

7. The author's purpose for writing this passage is to
   (A) entertain.
   (B) narrate.
   (C) persuade.
   (D) inform.

8. The tone of this passage is best described as
   (A) objective.
   (B) depressed.
   (C) angry.
   (D) cheerful.

9. The main idea of the second paragraph is
   (A) Molecules can only ingest nonorganic compounds.
   (B) Evolution is based on adaptation.
   (C) Photosynthesis allowed organisms to exist without the need of sunlight.
   (D) Oxygen is more important to life than the sun's energy.

Many anthropologists believe the first inhabitants of South America crossed over the Bering Strait land bridge. These native South Americans traveled down the west coast of what is now Canada, the United States, Mexico, and Central America to South America.

The crossing may have begun 15,000 to 20,000 years ago, and continued for thousands of years. Some of these Native South Americans reached the Islands of Terra del Fuego off the tip of South America about 8,000 years ago. Two major native civilizations developed in South America. The Incan empire developed in the highlands near the Andes mountains, while the Chibcha empire became dominant in what is now Columbia. Other native civilizations developed throughout South America.

These native groups were the only human inhabitants of South America until Europeans arrived following the voyage of Columbus in 1492. At the beginning of the sixteenth century, there may have been 30,000,000 inhabitants of South America. But Europeans brought cruelty and disease that decimated the native population. At the beginning of the seventeenth century the native population in South America was most likely less than 7,500,000.

Official Languages of
South American Countries

European colonizing nations introduced African slaves into South America, primarily into northeastern Brazil and into the Caribbean Islands. Most slaves were forced into labor on sugar plantations. Historians believe that the number of slaves brought to these regions may be 25 times the 500,000 African slaves brought into the United States.

The importation of slaves stopped before 1850 and European immigration increased about this same time. Most Europeans came to the east coast of South America, primarily to southern Brazil and to Argentina. By 1950 about 8,000,000 Europeans had immigrated to South America.

Population experts estimate that there may by 300 million inhabitants in South America. About 7 percent of the inhabitants speak native languages, and pockets of native civilizations can still be found in the countryside. Most South Americans with European origins trace their roots to Portugal, Spain, and Italy.

10. The non-Spanish languages spoken in western South America result from
    (A) early Incan influence.
    (B) the primitive nature of the countries.
    (C) immigration by Mayan Indians.
    (D) proximity to Central America.

11. What accounts for the use of Italian as an official language in southeastern South America?
    (A) The voyages of Christopher Columbus
    (B) The exploration of the Americas by Amerigo Vespucci
    (C) Italian and German immigration following World War II
    (D) Italian and German immigration in the eighteenth century

12. The only French-speaking South American nation was the site of
    (A) the French Government in exile during World War II.
    (B) the "Jonestown Massacre" in the 1980s.
    (C) the revolt of the Foreign Legion during the Algerian crisis.
    (D) the French penal colony Devil's Island.

13. According to the map, about what percent of South American countries have Spanish as an official language?
    (A) 80 percent
    (B) 70 percent
    (C) 50 percent
    (D) 40 percent

Items 14–19.

The War of 1812 is one of the least understood conflicts in American history. However, many events associated with the war are among the best remembered from (5) American History. The war began when the United States invaded British colonies in Canada. The invasion failed, and the United States was quickly put on the defensive. Most Americans are not aware (10) of how the conflict began. During the war, the *USS Constitution* (Old Ironsides) was active against British ships in the Atlantic. Captain William Perry, sailing on Lake Erie, was famous for his yelling to his (15) shipmates, "Don't give up the ship." Most Americans remember Perry, and his famous plea but not where, or in which war, he was engaged.

Most notably, British troops sacked and (20) burned Washington, D.C. during this conflict. Subsequent British attacks on Fort McHenry near Baltimore were repulsed by American forces. It was during this battle that Francis Scott Key wrote the "Star (25) Spangled Banner" while a prisoner on a British ship. The "rockets red glare, bombs bursting in air" referred to ordinance used by the British to attack the fort. Many Americans mistakenly believe that the (30) "Star Spangled Banner" was written during or shortly after the Revolutionary War.

Uncle Sam is one of the most popular fictional representatives of the United States. Historians attribute the fictional (35) Uncle Sam to "Uncle Sam" Wilson, a meat packer who supplied meat to the American army during the War of 1812. Reports have it that he stamped U. S. on the sides of his packing cases. People (40) often assume that Uncle Sam was "born" during the first or second world war when "I Want You" recruiting posters featured an image of Uncle Sam.

Many are not aware that the War of (45) 1812 created a secessionist movement. In this case, it was the New England states that considered withdrawing from the Union. New England was threatened most by British troops in Canada, and (50) the war had devastated trade from New

England. Representatives of New England states met at the Hartford Convention in Connecticut to discuss creating their own country. In the end, the repre- (55) sentatives decided not to leave the Union.

The British defeat of Napoleon posed a further threat to the United States. The British were then able to transfer a large (60) number of troops and ships to the conflict. Most of these troops were sent to Canada and to New Orleans. It is not unusual to be unaware of the historical relationship between Britain's conflict (65) with France and the War of 1812.

The name Thomas MacDough is unfamiliar to most Americans, yet the forces under his command were likely responsible for preserving the United States of (70) America. In the fall of 1814, a large force of British troops entered the United States from Canada. The American force arrayed before them was almost certainly too weak to halt the British advance. (75) But on September 14, 1814 MacDough's naval forces destroyed the British fleet in the Battle of Lake Champlain, also called the battle of Plattsburg Bay. Almost inexplicably, the British were concerned (80) about the loss of a line of communication and the British forces withdrew into Canada.

American and British negotiators were in Europe discussing terms to end the (85) war. When word of the failed attack reached the British negotiators, they decided to end the war without any concessions from the United States. The treaty of Ghent was signed by both war- (90) ring powers on December 24, 1814 and that should have ended hostilities.

However, communication across the Atlantic was slow, and in January 1815 the British forces in New Orleans attacked as planned. But American forces (95) under the leadership of General Andrew Jackson won a complete victory over the British forces. Most Americans associate the ending of the War of 1812 with Jackson's success at New Orleans and were (100) convinced that the war ended in victory for the United States.

14. All the following statements can be implied from the passage EXCEPT
    (A) The British did not start the war.
    (B) Francis Scott Key was not at Fort McHenry when he wrote the "Star Spangled Banner."
    (C) The rockets referred to in the "Star Spangled Banner" were part of a celebration.
    (D) The British army entered Washington, D.C., during the war.

15. Which of the following words is the most appropriate replacement for "sacked" in line 19?
    (A) Entered
    (B) Ravished
    (C) Invaded
    (D) Enclosed

16. Which of the following statements best summarizes the difference referred to in the passage between Perry's involvement in the War of 1812 and the way many Americans remember his involvement.
    (A) Perry was a drafter of the Constitution and later served on the *Constitution* in the Atlantic, although many Americans don't remember that.
    (B) Perry served in the Great Lakes, but many Americans don't remember that.
    (C) Perry served in the Great Lakes, although many Americans don't remember that.
    (D) Perry served on the *Constitution* at Fort McHenry during the writing of the "Star Spangled Banner," although many Americans do not remember that.

17. What can be inferred about Francis Scott Key from lines 24–26 of the passage?
    (A) He was killed in the battle.
    (B) All his papers were confiscated by the British after the battle.
    (C) He was released by or escaped from the British after the battle.
    (D) He returned to Britain where he settled down.

18. Based on the passage, which of the following words best describes the United States' role in the War of 1812?
    (A) Colonizer
    (B) Neutral
    (C) Winner
    (D) Aggressor

19. What main point is the author making in this passage?
    (A) The Americans fought the British in the War of 1812.
    (B) The Revolutionary War continued into the 1800s.
    (C) The British renewed the Revolutionary War during the 1800s.
    (D) Many Americans are unaware of events associated with the War of 1812.

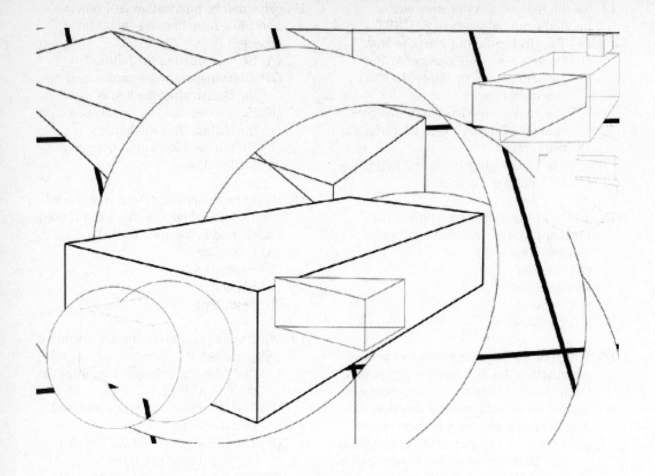

[Mercury Zone III. The Metropolitan Museum of Art, George A. Hearn Fund, 1976. (1976.21)]

20. This painting incorporates which of the following techniques?
(A) It uses three-dimensional space.
(B) It uses only regular geometric shapes.
(C) The curved lines of the three-dimensional figures contrast with the straight lines of the two-dimensional figures.
(D) It uses two-dimensional space to represent two- and three-dimensional figures.

21. A scientist cuts in half a just fallen hailstone and finds a series of rings much like tree rings. What could be found from counting the approximate number of rings?
(A) how long the hailstone was in the atmosphere before falling to earth
(B) how far from the surface the hailstone was before it started falling
(C) how much precipitation fell during the hailstorm
(D) how many times the hailstone was blown above the freezing level

$$(123 + 186 + 177) \div (3) =$$

22. Which of the following statements could result in the number sentence given above?
(A) The athlete wanted to find the median of the three jumps.
(B) The athlete wanted to find the average of the three jumps.
(C) The athlete wanted to find the quotient of the product of three jumps.
(D) The athlete wanted to find the sum of the quotients of the three jumps.

Use this graph to answer items 23 and 24.

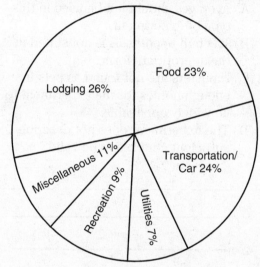

Jane's Monthly Budget

23. Jane spends $2,600 in the month of March. How much did she spend on food?
(A) $624
(B) $598
(C) $312
(D) $400

24. Jane spends $2,600 in May. She needs $858 that month for transportation/car expenses, which is more than the budget allows. Any needed money will come from miscellaneous. When she recalculates her budget chart, what percent is left for miscellaneous?
(A) 2 percent
(B) 6 percent
(C) 9 percent
(D) 11 percent

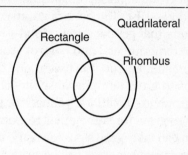

25. The above diagram shows the relationship among quadrilaterals, rectangles, and rhombuses. What conclusion can we draw from this diagram?
(A) All quadrilaterals are rhombuses.
(B) All quadrilaterals are rectangles.
(C) All rectangles are not rhombuses.
(D) Some rhombuses are not rectangles.

An experiment usually tries to test the effect of one thing on something else. The thing the experiment is testing the effect *of* is the independent variable. The thing the experiment is testing the effect *on* is the dependent variable. For example, the experimenter may test the effect of a particular hamster food. In that experiment, the independent variable is the type of food. The dependent variable is the growth of the hamster.

An experimental design should include both experimental and control groups. The experimental group consists of hamsters that get the new food—HF2. The control group consists of hamsters that get the current food—HF1

The experimental and control groups must be very similar. You don't want one of the groups to grow more because the hamsters in that group are healthier, younger or more likely to grow for some other reason.

You can take some steps to ensure that the two groups of hamsters will be as identical as possible. One way is to randomly assign hamsters to the two groups. Random assignment means that the experimenter has no role in assigning the hamsters, and ensures that hamsters are assigned to either the experimental group or the control group in an unbiased way.

Some experiments establish a correlation. Correlation is a way of showing how strongly two variables are related. But correlation does not mean cause and effect. For example, a correlation of 1 between two variables means they are perfectly related. However, this correlation does not mean that one necessarily causes the other. For example, economists report that there is a high positive correlation between the amount of snowfall in Colorado and the size of the state budget. The snowfall does not cause the higher state budget. But there is a strong correlation between the two.

AVERAGE OUNCES GAINED PER ANIMAL

Week #	HF1	HF2
1	4	9
2	3	4
3	2	3
4	1	2
5	1	2
6	1	1

26. An experiment is set up to determine the effects of a new hamster food HF2 as compared to the effects of a current hamster food HF1. Each group receives the same quantity of food and the same attention. From the above data choose the best conclusion for the experiment.
    (A) HF2 group gained more weight.
    (B) HF1 group lived longer.
    (C) HF2 group got more protein.
    (D) HF1 group got better nutrition.

27. What appropriate criticism might a scientist have of the experiment in the previous question?
    (A) Averages should not be used in this type of experiment.
    (B) The null hypothesis is not stated in the appropriate form.
    (C) Hamsters are not found as pets in enough homes for the experiment to be widely applicable.
    (D) The experiment does not describe sufficient controls to be valid.

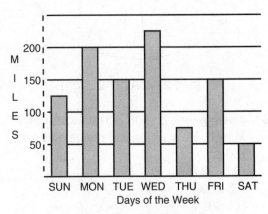

Miles Traveled Each Day
on a Family Camping Trip

28. In total, how many miles were traveled Wednesday through Friday?
    (A) 450 miles
    (B) 400 miles
    (C) 150 miles
    (D) 225 miles
    (E) 350 miles

Items 29 and 30 refer to this passage.

Good evening, my name is Max Drea. Before our host and our quartet come out, I want to talk to you a little bit about music.

Music can be thought of as organized sounds. Our culture has many different types of music and there are various types of music for cultures all over the world. We usually classify our music in three categories. (1) Popular music is professionally composed, recorded or performed live and represents the type of music of most current interest to the public. (2) Classical music was composed in the past and, while it is also recorded for sale, is usually performed by large orchestras in "symphony" halls (3) Folk music usually has a rural origin, is usually not composed professionally, and is often transmitted by oral tradition.

Music consists of pitch, the actual frequency or sound of a note, and duration. A tone has a specific pitch and duration. Different tones occurring simultaneously are called chords. A melody is the tones that produce the distinctive "sound" of the music. Harmony consists of chords with duration.

Pitches separated by specific intervals are called a scale. Most music is based on the diatonic scale found on the piano white keys (C, D, E, F, G, A, B). The chromatic scale includes the seven notes of the diatonic scale with the five sharps and flats corresponding to the white and black keys on the piano.

Rhythm in our music refers primarily to the regularity of beats or meter. The most common meter in our music has four beats with an emphasis on the first beat.

Think of the piano. The piano represents the chromatic scale with groups of seven white keys and five black keys. Music is played using tones from this scale for varying durations. Usually the melody consists of one note at a time and is played with the right hand. Harmony usually consists of chords and is played with the left hand. The rhythm of the music reflects the meter and the arrangements and duration of notes.

Our musical notation uses a staff to represent notes. A time signature is written at the beginning of each staff. The top number shows how many beats per measure and the bottom number shows which note gets a beat. A typical staff showing G and bass clefs is shown below. The clef placed at the beginning of the staff determines the pitches for each line and space on the staff. Notes are written on the staff using the notation shown below. A flat lowers the note a half-tone while a sharp raises the note a halftone. Rests indicate a time when no music is played. A note followed by a dot is increased in value by half. The staff is partitioned into measures. The sum of the values of the notes in a measure equals one. A key signature of sharps or flats can be written at the beginning of a staff to change these notes throughout the piece. The natural cancels a flat or sharp.

And now, on with the show.

Ladies and gentlemen, welcome to the Glow Room of the Rabrons Hotel. We are here tonight to bring you some enjoyable music for your listening pleasure. First let me introduce our musicians. On the piano, Mr. Ryan Bert. On the saxophone, Mr. Chad Ekred. That's Ms. Blaire Nan on the bass fiddle and Ms. Liz Mans on the drums. I'm your host Mr. Bob Mans. Take a bow everyone. Now we're going to play one of our favorites in three-quarter time.

29. What type of instrument is Mr. Ryan Bert playing?
(A) Percussion
(B) String
(C) Reed
(D) Woodwind

30. In the music the group is about to play,
(A) the quarter note gets two beats.
(B) there are four beats per measure.
(C) the dotted quarter note gets one beat.
(D) there are three beats per measure.

31.   ah autumn coolness
      hand in hand paring away

Which of the following could be the
third line in the haiku poem above?
(A) in the wetness
(B) branches and leaves
(C) eggplants cucumbers
(D) til the end of day

Items 32 and 33 refer to the following poem.

My love falls on silence nigh
I am alone in knowing the good-bye
For while a lost love has its day
A love unknown is a sadder way

32. The word *nigh* in line 1 means
(A) clear.
(B) complete.
(C) near.
(D) not.

33. This passage describes
(A) loving someone and being rebuffed.
(B) being loved by someone you do not
love.
(C) loving someone who loves another
person.
(D) loving someone without acknowl-
edgment.

An Internet advertising company renovat-
ed a deserted warehouse near the Canadian border to hold their offices. The offices
themselves occupied about 5,000 square
feet, and there was a lunchroom and other
common areas that took up about another
750 square feet. Just about everyone in the
company was a skier, so the location made
a lot of sense. Of course it did not make
any difference where the offices were—no
clients ever came to visit. All the work was
done over the Internet, or on the phone.

The advertising company placed advertisements on web pages. Most of their ads
were banner ads. That means when the
page came up the ad appeared. The number of pixels they occupied on a web page
identified the banner ad's size. There are
three banner ad sizes. Size A is 463 pixels
by 70 pixels. Size B is 130 pixels by 220
pixels. Size C is 130 by 145 pixels.

Advertising representatives like to sell the
largest ads because this size costs the most
and the representatives get a higher commission. The average representative sells
nine to ten size A banner ads each day. The
advertising company has a way to count
the number of times that a web page is
accessed. They base their advertising rates
on the number of times the ad appears in a
month. For example, an A banner ad costs
$85 per thousand appearances up to
100,000 appearances, and $75 per thousand
for each thousand over 100,000 appearances. The smallest banner is about half
the price of the largest banner ad, and the
average representative sells about fifteen to
twenty of these ads each day. This size ad
is good for a few high impact words.

Of course, the agency offers other types
of Internet ads as well. One type is where
the advertiser pays a fee each time the on
line user pushes a button that takes the
user to the advertiser's home page. This
type of ad costs more than other ads, but
it is used less frequently. The average representative sells six to ten of these ads
each day, while the average representative
sells twelve to fourteen middle-size banner ads. This advertising agency also has
contracts with Internet search engine
companies and the agency can arrange for
an ad to appear when a particular search
term is entered. These ads are the most
expensive, and the average representative
sells two to four of these ads each day.

34. What is the total maximum and mini-
mum of banner ads that the average
representative sells each day?
(A) 9 and 20
(B) 9 and 15
(C) 15 and 20
(D) 36 and 44

Items 35–40 refer to this passage.

Computer-based word processing programs
have spelling checkers and even a thesaurus
to find synonyms and antonyms for high-

lighted words. To use the thesaurus, the student just types in the word, and a series of synonyms and antonyms appears on the computer screen. The program can also show recommended spellings for misspelled words. I like having a computer program that performs these mechanical aspects of writing. However, these programs do not teach about spelling or word meanings. A person could type in a word, get a synonym and have not the slightest idea what either meant.

Relying on this mindless way of checking spelling and finding synonyms, students will be completely unfamiliar with the meanings of the words they use. In fact, one of the most common misuses is to include a word that is spelled correctly but used incorrectly in the sentence.

It may be true that a strictly mechanical approach to spelling is used by some teachers. There certainly is a place for students who already understand word meanings to use a computer program that relieves the drudgery of checking spelling and finding synonyms. But these computer programs should never and can never replace the teacher. Understanding words—their uses and meanings—should precede this more mechanistic approach.

35. What is the main idea of this passage?
 (A) Mechanical spell checking is one part of learning about spelling.
 (B) Programs are not effective for initially teaching about spelling and synonyms.
 (C) Teachers should use word processing programs as one part of instruction.
 (D) Students who use these programs won't learn about spelling.

36. Which of the following information is found in the passage?
 I. The type of computer that runs the word processor
 II. The two main outputs of spell-checking and thesaurus programs
 III. An explanation of how to use the word-processing program to teach about spelling and synonyms
 (A) I only
 (B) II only
 (C) I and II only
 (D) II and III only

37. Which aspect of spell-checking and thesaurus programs does the author like?
 (A) That you just have to type in the word
 (B) That the synonyms and alternative spellings are done very quickly
 (C) That the difficult mechanical aspects are performed
 (D) That you don't have to know how to spell to use them

38. Which of the following questions could be answered from the information in the passage?
 (A) When is it appropriate to use spell-checking and thesaurus programs?
 (B) How does the program come up with recommended spellings?
 (C) What type of spelling learning experiences should students have?
 (D) Why do schools buy these word processing programs?

39. Which of the following statements could be used in place of the first sentence of the last paragraph?
 (A) It may be true that some strict teachers use a mechanical approach.
 (B) It may be true that a stringently mechanical approach is used by some teachers.
 (C) It may be true that inflexible mechanical approaches are used by some teachers.
 (D) It may be true that some teachers use only a mechanical approach.

40. According to this passage, what could be the result of a student's unfamiliarity with the meanings of words or synonyms?
 (A) using a program to display the alternative spellings
 (B) relying on mindless ways of checking spelling and finding synonyms
 (C) strictly mechanical approaches
 (D) using microcomputers to find synonyms for highlighted words

Use this map to answer items 41 and 42.

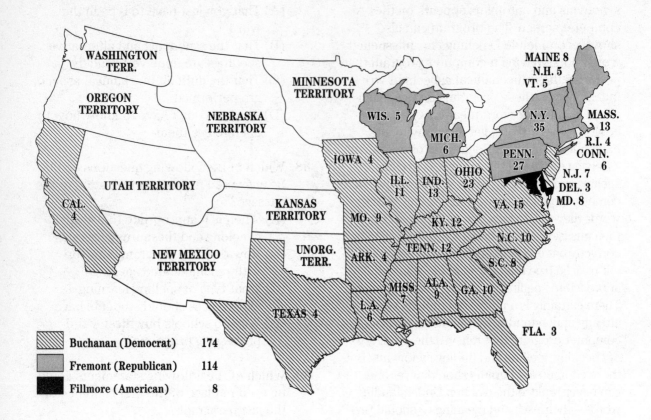

Presidential Election of 1856

41. The numbers in each state on this map show
  (A) the number of counties in each state.
  (B) the number of representatives from each state.
  (C) the electoral votes in each state.
  (D) the number of representatives won by the victorious party in each state.

42. What conclusion might you reasonably draw from this map?
  (A) Were it not for Texas and California, Fremont would have won the election.
  (B) Buchanan supported the rebel cause.
  (C) Fremont was favored by the north-ernmost states.
  (D) Fremont was favored by the states that fought on the Union side in the Civil War.

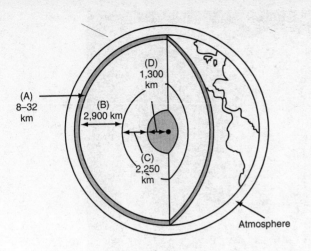

The Earth

44. Bob walked about 2,750 meters to school every day. About how many kilometers is that?
(A) 2.750
(B) 27.50
(C) 275
(D) 275,000

43. In the diagram, what letter labels the mantle?
(A) A
(B) B
(C) C
(D) D

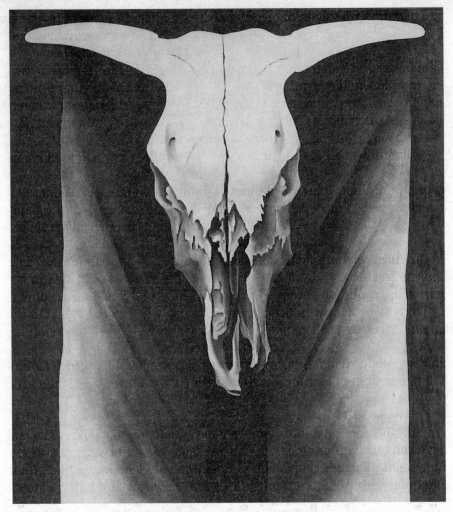

[The Metropolitan Museum of Art, The Alfred Stieglitz Collection, 1949. (52.203)]

45. This picture could be best described by saying
  (A) it is an abstract figure on a rectangular background.
  (B) the nearly symmetrical shape of the figure suggests that its completion is expected.
  (C) the Rorschach-like image suggests an underlying psychological theme.
  (D) the real life object has an abstract quality.

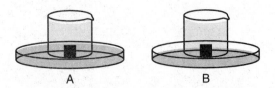

A   B

46. Identical beakers (above) were filled with water. Overflow was caused by the different solid objects placed in the beakers. The size of the objects cannot be determined. What is the most likely explanation of the differing amounts of overflow?
  (A) The object in beaker A is heavier.
  (B) The object in beaker B is heavier.
  (C) The object in beaker A has more mass.
  (D) The object in beaker B has more mass.

Cellular phones, once used by the very rich, are now available to almost everyone. With one of these phones, you can call just about anywhere from just about anywhere. Since the use of these phones will increase, we need to find legal and effective ways for law enforcement agencies to monitor calls.

47. Which of the following choices is the best summary of this passage?
(A) Criminals are taking advantage of cellular phones to avoid legal wire-taps.
(B) The ability to use a cellular phone to call from just about anywhere makes it harder to find people who are using the phones.
(C) The increase in cellular phone use means that we will have to find legal ways to monitor cellular calls.
(D) Cellular phones are like regular phones with a very long extension cord.

Occasionally, college students will confuse correlation with cause and effect. Correlation just describes the degree of relationship between two factors. For example, there is a positive correlation between poor handwriting and intelligence. However, writing more poorly will not make you more intelligent.

48. The authors main reason for writing this passage is to
(A) explain the difference between correlation and cause and effect.
(B) encourage improved penmanship.
(C) explain how college students can improve their intelligence.
(D) make those with poor penmanship feel more comfortable.

The way I look at it, Robert E. Lee was the worst general in the Civil War—he was the South's commanding general, and the South lost the war.

49. What assumption does the writer of this statement make?
(A) War is horrible and should not be glorified.
(B) Pickett's charge at Gettysburg was a terrible mistake.
(C) A general should be judged by whether he wins or loses.
(D) The South should have won the Civil War.

1	2	3	4	5	6	7	8	9	10
11	12	13	14	15	16	17	18	19	20
21	22	23	24	25	26	27	28	29	30
31	32	33	34	35	36	37	38	39	40
41	42	43	44	45	46	47	48	49	50
51	52	53	54	55	56	57	58	59	60
61	62	63	64	65	66	67	68	69	70
71	72	73	74	75	76	77	78	79	80
81	82	83	84	85	86	87	88	89	90
91	92	93	94	95	96	97	98	99	100

50. Cross off the multiples of 2, 3, 4, 5, 6, 7, and 8 in the above hundreds square. Which numbers in the 80s are not crossed off?
(A) 83, 87
(B) 81, 89
(C) 83, 89
(D) 81, 87

Use this graph to answer items 51 and 52.

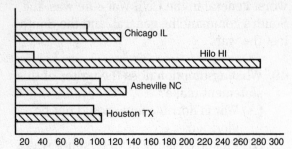

Clear Days
Days with Precipitation

51. A correct interpretation of this graph is, on average,
(A) most days in Houston have precipitation.
(B) less than 10 percent of the days in Hilo have no precipitation.
(C) most days in Asheville have no precipitation.
(D) most days in Chicago have precipitation.

52. A business may be moved to one of the four cities on the graph. What conclusion can be drawn from the graph to help make the final decision?
(A) On average, most precipitation in Hilo is from brief afternoon thundershowers.
(B) On average, Asheville, North Carolina, gets only a few inches of snow.
(C) On average, Asheville and Chicago receive about the same amount of precipitation.
(D) On average, Houston has the most days without precipitaton.

53. You add the first 5 odd numbers (1, 3, 5, 7, 9) and find that the answer is 25. What is the sum of the first 90 odd numbers?
(A) 450
(B) 8,100
(C) 179
(D) 4,500

54. The steplike appearance of the buildings in this photograph is created by
(A) the setbacks that occur every three or four stories.
(B) the photographer's position when the picture was taken.
(C) the proximity of the buildings to the street.
(D) the relationship between the symmetric appearance of the windows and the horizontal lines indicating new floors.

The computers in the college dormitories are actually more sophisticated than the computers in the college computer labs, and they cost less. It seems that the person who bought the dormitory computers looked around until she found powerful computers at a low price. The person who runs the labs just got the computers offered by the regular supplier.

55. The best statement of the main idea of this paragraph is
   (A) it is better to use the computers in the dorms.
   (B) it is better to avoid the computers in the labs.
   (C) the computers in the dorms are always in use so, for most purposes, it is better to use the computers in the labs.
   (D) it is better to shop around before you buy.

The college sororities are "interviewed" by students during rush week. Rush week is a time when students get to know about the different sororities and decide which ones they want to join. Each student can pledge only one sorority. Once students have chosen the three they are most interested in, the intrigue begins. The sororities then choose from among the students who have chosen them.

56. Which of the following strategies will help assure a student that she will be chosen for at least one sorority and preferably get into a sorority she likes?
   I Choose at least one sorority she is sure will choose her
   II Choose one sorority she wants to get into
   III Choose her three favorite sororities
   IV Choose three sororities she knows will choose her
   (A) I and II
   (B) I and III
   (C) I only
   (D) III only

In response to my opponent's question about my record on environmental issues, I want to say that the real problem in this election is not my record. Rather the problem is the influence of my opponent's rich friends in the record industry. I hope you will turn your back on his rich supporters and vote for me.

57. Which of the following statements best illustrates the author's primary purpose?
   (A) clearing the author's name
   (B) describing the problems of running for office
   (C) informing the public of wrongdoing
   (D) convincing the voting populous

58. A boat costs $5 more than half the price of a canoe. Which of the following expressions shows this relationship?
   (A) $B + \$5 = C/2$
   (B) $B = 1/2C + \$5$
   (C) $B + \$5 = 2C$
   (D) $B + \$5 > B/2$

["Reflection, Old St. Louis County Courthouse, 1976." © William Clift 1976 The Metropolitan Museum of Art, Purchase, Gift of Various donors and matching funds from NEA, 1981. 1981.1044.1]

59. The primary function of the central building in this photograph is to
(A) contrast with the cloudy sky.
(B) emphasize the symmetry of the roadways on either side.
(C) complete a collection of geometric shapes with the other structures shown to the left and right.
(D) serve as a reflective surface.

60. All the following items in this photograph suggest symmetry EXCEPT
(A) the clouds.
(B) the central building.
(C) the main building on the left part of the picture.
(D) the structure on the right part of the picture.

RECYCLING RATE BY CITY
(PER HUNDRED THOUSAND POUNDS PER YEAR FROM 1988–1993)

	1988	1989	1990	1991	1992	1993
Chicago, Illinois	*	52	67	120	302	485
St. Louis, Missouri	20	80	175	360	420	650
Seattle, Washington	15	70	98	136	243	358
San Francisco, California	*	23	75	124	285	402
New York, New York	*	10	56	250	370	590
Miami, Florida	*	25	98	145	290	370

* The recycling rate is less than one per hundred thousand pounds.

61. Which of the following statements is supported by the data given in the above table?
  (A) St. Louis increased the capabilities of its recycling plants by 50 percent during the years 1990 and 1991.
  (B) Since 1991 the recycling rate increased significantly in each city.
  (C) People living in Miami are not recycling as they should be.
  (D) The population of all these cities has increased significantly since 1988.

Items 62–66 refer to these three paragraphs.

I

(1) Of course, I have never gotten too involved in my children's sports. (2) I have never yelled at an umpire at any of my kid's games. (3) I have never even—_____, I didn't mean it.

II

(4) Before long, the umpire's mother was on the field. (5) There the two parents stood, toe to toe. (6) The players and the other umpires formed a ring around them and looked on in awe.

III

(7) Sometimes parents are more involved in little league games than their children. (8) I remember seeing a game in which a player's parent came on the field to argue with the umpire. (9) The umpire was not that much older than the player.

62. Which of the following shows the correct order for these three paragraphs?
  (A) I, II, III
  (B) I, III, II
  (C) II, I, III
  (D) III, II, I

63. Which of the following best fits in the blank in sentence 3?
  (A) Well
  (B) Being a parent
  (C) How come I
  (D) Repeat after me

64. Which primary form of rhetoric does the author use in this passage?
  (A) Argumentation
  (B) Exposition
  (C) Reflection
  (D) Narration

65. What other "sporting" event is the author trying to recreate in paragraph II?
  (A) Bullfight
  (B) Wrestling match
  (C) Boxing match
  (D) Football game

66. The author portrays herself as "innocent" of being too involved in her children's sports. How would you characterize this portrayal?
  (A) False
  (B) A lie
  (C) Tongue in cheek
  (D) Noble

Items 67–68.

I think women are discriminated against; however, I think men are discriminated against just as much as women. It's just a different type of discrimination. Consider these two facts: Men die about 6 years earlier than women, and men are the only people who can be drafted into the armed forces. That's discrimination!

67. What is the author's main point in writing this passage?
  (A) Men are discriminated against more than women are.
  (B) Both sexes are discriminated against.
  (C) Women are not discriminated against.
  (D) On average, men die earlier than women.

68. Which of the following could be substituted for the word *drafted* in the last sentence?
  (A) Inducted against their will
  (B) Signed up
  (C) Pushed in by society
  (D) Drawn in by peer pressure

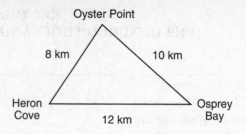

69. The diagram shows three towns, the roads connecting them, and the distance between each town. Which of the following is the shortest distance?
  (A) Osprey Bay to Heron Cove to Oyster Point and then halfway to Osprey Bay
  (B) Halfway between Oyster Point and Heron Cove, to Heron Cove to Osprey Bay to Oyster Point
  (C) Quarter-way from Heron Cove to Osprey Bay, to Osprey Bay to Oyster Point to Heron Cove
  (D) Heron Cove to Oyster Point to Osprey Bay, then halfway to Heron Cove

["The Veteran in a New Field" by Winslow Homer. The Metropolitan Museum of Art, Bequest of Miss Adelaide Milton de Groot (1876–1967), 1967]

70. Which of the following best describes how this picture shows the results of effort?
(A) The determination in the reaper's stance
(B) The fallen stalks of wheat
(C) The curved scythe handle
(D) The solitude of the reaper

The moon takes about 28 days to complete a cycle around the earth. Months, 28 days long, grew out of this cycle. Twelve of these months made up a year. But ancient astronomers realized that it took the earth about 365 days to make one revolution of the sun. Extra days were added to some months and the current calendar was born.

71. The passage indicates that the current calendar
(A) describes the moon's movement around the earth.
(B) is based on the sun's position.
(C) is based on the earth's rotation and position of the moon.
(D) combines features of the moons cycle and the earth's revolution.

Confederate Major General W. H. C. Whiting was recuperating in a prisoner-of-war camp in New York. Not long before, Whiting had been in charge of the Confederate forces in Wilmington, North Carolina. In the later years of the Civil War, Wilmington had become the gateway to the Confederacy. After Charleston, South Carolina, was captured by Union forces, Wilmington was the only southern port left open for blockade runners. These fast, sleek ships carried cotton to Bermuda, Nassau, and Nova Scotia and returned from these ports with arms, munitions, and commercial goods. Whiting knew that the capture of Wilmington closed the south's last supply pipeline. He said, "I do not know now that there is another place, excepting perhaps Richmond, we should not sooner see lost than this." Whiting died unexpectedly of his wounds in the prison camp.

Blockade runners coming to Wilmington traveled over the ocean, past Cape Fear into the Cape Fear River, and up the river to Wilmington. The most dangerous part of the journey was when ships entered the Cape Fear River. At the southern part of Cape Fear was Smith Island, now called Bald Head Island. This island and the barrier islands to the north form what looks like a huge check mark. The old inlet took ships one way around Smith Island into the Cape Fear River, while the new inlet took ships another way around the island and then into the river. Blockading Union ships waited outside the inlets. Some authorities report over a hundred blockade runners were captured or run aground in the Cape Fear region.

Whichever inlet that arriving blockade runners took, they passed by Fort Fisher. Fort Fisher was the key to protecting these ships, and the key to defending Wilmington. Blockade runners were just about immune from Union attack once they came under the fort's protection. No fewer than ten other fortifications protected the Cape Fear

River. Fort Holmes was on Smith Island, which was across the new inlet from Fort Fisher. Fort Caswell was west across the Old Inlet from Fort Holmes, and Fort Johnson was across the Cape Fear River from Fort Fisher. Fort Fisher had extensive fortifications, both on the sea face and on the land face. But on January 12, 1865, Union forces attacked the first with what may have been the fiercest naval bombardment of the Civil War. Federal ships bombarded the fort's land face and sea face. On January 15, more than 3,000 Union infantry troops assaulted the land face. After vicious hand-to-hand fighting, Union forces troops captured the fort. Union forces captured Wilmington, and the Civil War soon ended near Cape Fear.

72. A blockade runner approached Wilmington with goods from Nova Scotia. As the blockade runner passed through the new inlet, the Fort Fisher was generally to the
(A) north.
(B) south.
(C) east.
(D) west.

Items 73–76.

The Sullen Sky

I see the sullen sky;
Dark, foreboding sky.
Swept by dank and dripping clouds;
Like ominous shrouds.

A sky should be bright,
Or clear and crisp at night.
But it hasn't been that way;
Oh, a dungenous day.

That has been my life,
And that has been my strife.
I wish the clouds would leave;
Ah, a sweet reprieve.

73. Which of the following best describes the author's message?
    (A) The author doesn't like rainy, cloudy weather.
    (B) The author wants people to be free of worry.
    (C) The author is hoping his life will get better.
    (D) The author lives in an area where it is often cloudy and rainy.

74. The last two lines in the first stanza reflect which of the following?
    (A) simile
    (B) hyperbole
    (C) metaphor
    (D) euphemism

75. What main literary technique does the author use to convey the poem's message?
    (A) morphology
    (B) alliteration
    (C) allegory
    (D) personification

76. The author wants to use a line that reflects onomatopoeia. Which of the following lines could be used?
    (A) Soggy, slippery, sad
    (B) Drip, drip, drip
    (C) Like being at the bottom of a lake
    (D) The rain, the pain, explain

---

77. The school is planning a class trip. They will go by bus. There will be 328 people going on the trip, and each bus holds 31 people. How many buses will be needed for the trip?
    (A) 9
    (B) 10
    (C) 11
    (D) 18

Items 78–79.

Using percentages to report growth patterns can be deceptive. If there are 100 new users for a cereal currently used by 100 other people, the growth rate is 100 percent. However if there are 50,000 new users for a cereal currently used by 5,000,000 people, the growth rate is 1 percent. It seems obvious that the growth rate of 1 percent is preferable to the growth rate of 100 percent. So while percentages do provide a useful way to report growth patterns, we must know the initial number the growth percentage is based on before we make any conclusions.

78. According to this passage,
    (A) lower growth rates mean higher actual growth.
    (B) higher growth rates mean higher actual growth.
    (C) the growth rate depends on the starting point.
    (D) the growth rate does not depend on the starting point.

79. Which of the following can be implied from this passage?
    (A) Don't believe any advertisements.
    (B) Question any percentage growth rate.
    (C) Percentages should never be used.
    (D) Any growth rate over 50 percent is invalid.

---

80. Say that Company A and Company B try to raise money by selling bonds to the public. Which of the following could cause the interest rate for Company A's bonds to be much higher than the rates for Company B's bonds?
    (A) The bonds for Company A have a higher risk.
    (B) The bonds for Company B have a higher risk.
    (C) The management of Company A wants to reward its investors.
    (D) The management of Company B wants to reward its investors.

WRITTEN ASSIGNMENT

Write an essay on the topic below. Use the lined pages that follow. Write your essay on this topic only. An essay on another topic will be rated Unscorable (U).

Topic

For many years the highest allowable speed limit was 55 miles per hour. More recently this limit has been raised and you can travel on roads where the speed limit is 70 miles per hour.

Do you think having higher speed limits is a good idea or a bad idea?
Write an essay to support your position.

PRACTICE LAST I

Answer Key

1. A	11. D	21. D	31. C	41. C	51. C	61. B	71. D
2. B	12. D	22. B	32. C	42. C	52. D	62. D	72. A
3. C	13. B	23. B	33. D	43. B	53. B	63. A	73. C
4. B	14. C	24. A	34. D	44. A	54. A	64. D	74. A
5. C	15. B	25. D	35. B	45. D	55. D	65. C	75. C
6. B	16. B	26. A	36. B	46. C	56. A	66. C	76. B
7. D	17. C	27. D	37. C	47. C	57. D	67. B	77. C
8. A	18. D	28. A	38. A	48. A	58. B	68. A	78. C
9. B	19. D	29. A	39. D	49. C	59. D	69. D	79. B
10. A	20. D	30. D	40. B	50. C	60. A	70. B	80. A

PRACTICE LAST I

Explained Answers

1. **A** The item asks for an inference. Choices B, C, and D are true but they just restate the information in the paragraph. Only choice A draws an inference.

2. **B** The graphs for walkers and bikers remained unchanged from Monday to Wednesday, so this statement is true for both Monday's graph and Wednesday's graph. Choice A is true only for Monday's graph. The other statements are false.

3. **C** The author gradually traces the evolution of speech and language.

4. **B** The author clearly states in the first paragraph that thought precedes speech.

5. **C** You have to move the decimal point eight places to the right to get from 3.74 to 374,000,000. So multiply by 10^8 to achieve this result.

6. **B** The passage does not explicitly describe how life evolved, but it does suggest a chain of evolution. None of the other choices is supported by the passage.

7. **D** The passage states facts, clarifies, and explains. The author makes no particular attempt to persuade the reader.

8. **A** The author objectively states information and displays no particular emotion.

9. **B** The entire paragraph describes ways in which animals adapted to the environment.

10. **A** The Incas had an early culture in this region.

11. **D** This part of South America, particularly Argentina, experienced significant European immigration.

12. **D** The French penal colony of Devils' Island was located off the coast of French Guyana.

13. **B** Nine of 13 South American countries have Spanish as an official language.

14. **C** The passage states that rockets refer to ordinance or weapons used by the British.

15. **B** Ravished is the best choice and describes what happens when a town is sacked.

16. **B** The last sentence in the first paragraph says that most Americans remember Perry, but not where he served.

17. **C** Francis Scott Key must have been able to distribute his "Star Spangled Banner" in America, so he must have been released by or escaped from the British.

18. **D** Lines 5–7 show the United States as the aggressor.

19. **D** The author signals this main point in the first sentence of the passage.

20. **D** The painting uses only two dimensions, but it represents both two- and three-dimensions.

21. **D** A new layer of water is added below the freezing level of the atmosphere and then the layer is frozen when the hailstone is blown above the freezing level.

22. **B** The number sentence corresponds to finding an average. To find an average, you add the terms and divide by the number of terms.

23. **B** Multiply 0.23 and $2,600.

24. **A** Divide $858 by $2,600 to find the percent (33%) needed for transportation. Subtract the current transportation percentage from 33% to find the percent to be taken from miscellaneous (33% – 24% = 9%). Subtract 11% – 9% = 2% to find the percent left for miscellaneous.

25. **D** The overlap of the rhombus and the rectangle rings shows that some (not all) rhombuses are rectangles. This means that some rhombuses are not rectangles.

26. **A** The conclusion is clear and is the only conclusion supported by the data.

27. **D** The experiment does not describe how the experimenters ensured that group HF2 did not receive special attention, nor does it describe any other controls.

28. **A** Add 225, 75, and 150 to find the answer.

29. **A** The piano is a percussion instrument. Fingers strike the keys causing little "hammers" to strike strings.

30. **D** The 3 in ¾ time indicates that there are three beats per measure. The 4 indicates that the quarter note gets one beat.

31. **C** Haiku follows a 5-7-5 syllabic scheme with *no* rhyming. Choice C alone meets these criteria.
32. **C** The word *nigh* means near in space or time.
33. **D** The passage indicates that love falls on silence and that love unknown is sad. This leads to the conclusion that the passage is about loving without acknowledgment.
34. **D** Add the three smaller numbers, and then add the three larger numbers.
35. **B** The next to the last sentence in the first paragraph indicates that these programs do not teach about spelling or word processing.
36. **B** The types of computer used and teaching methods are not mentioned in the passage.
37. **C** The fourth sentence in the first paragraph explains that the author likes having a program to perform the mechanical aspects.
38. **A** This question can be answered from the information in the passage's last paragraph.
39. **D** This choice paraphrases the first sentence in the last paragraph.
40. **B** This information is found in the first sentence of the first paragraph.
41. **C** The map's caption reveals this information.
42. **C** Refer to the map, which shows that Fremont won most northern states.
43. **B** The earth's mantle is the first part of the earth beneath the earth's surface.
44. **A** There are 1,000 meters in a kilometer. So, divide 2,750 by 1,000 to find the answer.
45. **D** The title of this painting by Georgia O'Keeffe is "Cow's Skull."
46. **C** More mass means there is more of the object, that it takes up more space. A heavier object could be more dense, and therefore less mass, and would not necessarily take up more space.
47. **C** This choice paraphrases the conclusion found in the last sentence of the passage.
48. **A** The author explains the difference between correlation and cause and effect with an explanation and an example.

49. **C** The writer believes that generals should be judged by results. Even if you do not agree, that is the view of this writer.
50. **C** This process crosses all the numbers but the prime numbers. The numbers in answer C are all the prime numbers in the 80s.
51. **C** On average, Asheville has 235 days without precipitation. Note that the graph does not show days that are cloudy and have no precipitation.
52. **D** On average, Houston has 259 days without precipitation. Notice this item is different from the previous one because the correct choice is the one city that has the most days without precipitation.
53. **B** Investigate the pattern to find that the sum of the first n numbers is n^2. The sum of the first 90 odd numbers is 90^2 or 8,100.
54. **A** The setbacks create the steplike appearance.
55. **D** The paragraph describes how careful shopping can result in lower prices.
56. **A** Strategies I and II, together, assure the student that she will be chosen and gives her a chance to get into a sorority that she likes.
57. **D** The author is denying one accusation and making another and trying to convince others.
58. **B** This expression correctly shows the relationship.
Bus costs $5 more than half the price
B = $5 + 1/2
of a canoe
x c or B = 1/2 c + 5
59. **D** The central building serves as a reflective surface for the courthouse.
60. **A** The rectangular central building, the geometric buildings to the left and right, and the placement of the geometric buildings all suggest symmetry. The clouds do not.
61. **B** This choice is the only one supported by the data.
62. **D** The paragraphs are most naturally ordered as shown in choice D.
63. **A** The author is saying, "You caught me or I caught myself. I'm guilty, but I didn't mean it."
64. **D** A narration is a story. The author makes the point by telling a story.

65. **C** The description of going toe to toe inside a ring reminds us of a boxing match.

66. **C** The author is not lying, but the story is obviously not to be taken seriously.

67. **B** The author says, and gives an example to show, that men are discriminated against just as much as women.

68. **A** Drafted, in the sense used here, means to be inducted into the armed forces against your will.

69. **D** Add to find the distances. The totals for each answer choice are A: 25, B: 26, C: 27, D: 24. D is the shortest.

70. **B** The results of the farmer's effort can only be seen in the stalks of wheat already cut.

71. **D** The passage identifies both the moon's cycle and the earth's revolution as factors contributing to the development of the current calendar.

72. **A** The passage says that Smith Island was at the southern end of the Cape Fear. A cape juts out into the ocean, so the new inlet could not be in the ocean to the south or east. The new inlet must be west or north. But the passage says Fort Campbell is west across the Old Inlet from Smith Island. That leaves only north. The new inlet must be north of Smith Island, and Fort Fisher must be north across that inlet. Fort Fisher would be generally to the north of a ship traveling through the new inlet.

73. **C** This poem is not to be taken literally. The poet is describing his or her life and the author is hoping his or her life will improve.

74. **A** The last two lines in the first stanza compare clouds to shrouds. The comparison shows that the figure of speech must be a metaphor or a simile. The poem uses the word *like*, so the figure of speech must be a simile.

75. **C** Allegory means that a work represents some other idea and is not to be taken literally.

76. **B** Onomatopoeia uses words to represent sounds.

77. **C** Round the quotient (10) to 11 to ensure there will be enough room for everyone to go on the class trip.

78. **C** The rate, alone, does not provide enough information. You must know the starting point.

79. **B** You should question any growth rate when only the percentage is given.

80. **A** A company pays higher rates to attract investors. The main reason one company pays a higher rate than another company is because its bonds are riskier.

WRITTEN ASSIGNMENT

Show your essay to an English professor or a high school English teacher. Ask them to rate your essay 0–3 using this scale.

3 A well developed, complete written assignment.
Shows a thorough response to all parts of the topic.
Clear explanations that are well supported.
An assignment that is free of significant grammatical, punctuation, or spelling errors.

2 A fairly well developed, complete written assignment.
It may not thoroughly respond to all parts of the topic.
Fairly clear explanations that may not be well supported.
It may contain some significant grammatical, punctuation, or spelling errors.

1 A poorly developed, incomplete written assignment.
It does not thoroughly respond to most parts of the topic.
Contains many poor explanations that are not well supported.
It may contain some significant grammatical, punctuation, or spelling errors.

0 A very poorly developed, incomplete written assignment.
It does not thoroughly respond to the topic.
Contains only poor, unsupported explanations.
Contains numerous significant grammatical, punctuation, or spelling errors.

12 PRACTICE LAST II

This practice test contains the types of items you will encounter on the real test. The distribution of items varies from one test administration to another.

Take this test in a realistic, timed setting. You should not take this practice test until you have completed the appropriate review and practice questions.

The setting will be most realistic if another person times the test and ensures that the test rules are followed exactly. But remember that many people do better on a practice test than on the real test. If another person is acting as test supervisor, he or she should review these instructions with you and say "Start" when you should begin a section and "Stop" when time has expired.

You have 4 hours to complete the 80 multiple-choice questions and to complete the written assignment. Keep the time limit in mind as you work.

Each multiple-choice question or statement in the test has four answer choices. Exactly one of these choices is correct. Mark your choice on the answer sheet provided for this test.

Use a pencil to mark the answer sheet. The actual test will be machine scored so completely darken in the answer space.

Once the test is complete, review the answers and explanations for each item.

When instructed, turn the page and begin.

ANSWER SHEET PRACTICE LAST II

1 Ⓐ Ⓑ Ⓒ Ⓓ   21 Ⓐ Ⓑ Ⓒ Ⓓ   41 Ⓐ Ⓑ Ⓒ Ⓓ   61 Ⓐ Ⓑ Ⓒ Ⓓ
2 Ⓐ Ⓑ Ⓒ Ⓓ   22 Ⓐ Ⓑ Ⓒ Ⓓ   42 Ⓐ Ⓑ Ⓒ Ⓓ   62 Ⓐ Ⓑ Ⓒ Ⓓ
3 Ⓐ Ⓑ Ⓒ Ⓓ   23 Ⓐ Ⓑ Ⓒ Ⓓ   43 Ⓐ Ⓑ Ⓒ Ⓓ   63 Ⓐ Ⓑ Ⓒ Ⓓ
4 Ⓐ Ⓑ Ⓒ Ⓓ   24 Ⓐ Ⓑ Ⓒ Ⓓ   44 Ⓐ Ⓑ Ⓒ Ⓓ   64 Ⓐ Ⓑ Ⓒ Ⓓ
5 Ⓐ Ⓑ Ⓒ Ⓓ   25 Ⓐ Ⓑ Ⓒ Ⓓ   45 Ⓐ Ⓑ Ⓒ Ⓓ   65 Ⓐ Ⓑ Ⓒ Ⓓ

6 Ⓐ Ⓑ Ⓒ Ⓓ   26 Ⓐ Ⓑ Ⓒ Ⓓ   46 Ⓐ Ⓑ Ⓒ Ⓓ   66 Ⓐ Ⓑ Ⓒ Ⓓ
7 Ⓐ Ⓑ Ⓒ Ⓓ   27 Ⓐ Ⓑ Ⓒ Ⓓ   47 Ⓐ Ⓑ Ⓒ Ⓓ   67 Ⓐ Ⓑ Ⓒ Ⓓ
8 Ⓐ Ⓑ Ⓒ Ⓓ   28 Ⓐ Ⓑ Ⓒ Ⓓ   48 Ⓐ Ⓑ Ⓒ Ⓓ   68 Ⓐ Ⓑ Ⓒ Ⓓ
9 Ⓐ Ⓑ Ⓒ Ⓓ   29 Ⓐ Ⓑ Ⓒ Ⓓ   49 Ⓐ Ⓑ Ⓒ Ⓓ   69 Ⓐ Ⓑ Ⓒ Ⓓ
10 Ⓐ Ⓑ Ⓒ Ⓓ   30 Ⓐ Ⓑ Ⓒ Ⓓ   50 Ⓐ Ⓑ Ⓒ Ⓓ   70 Ⓐ Ⓑ Ⓒ Ⓓ

11 Ⓐ Ⓑ Ⓒ Ⓓ   31 Ⓐ Ⓑ Ⓒ Ⓓ   51 Ⓐ Ⓑ Ⓒ Ⓓ   71 Ⓐ Ⓑ Ⓒ Ⓓ
12 Ⓐ Ⓑ Ⓒ Ⓓ   32 Ⓐ Ⓑ Ⓒ Ⓓ   52 Ⓐ Ⓑ Ⓒ Ⓓ   72 Ⓐ Ⓑ Ⓒ Ⓓ
13 Ⓐ Ⓑ Ⓒ Ⓓ   33 Ⓐ Ⓑ Ⓒ Ⓓ   53 Ⓐ Ⓑ Ⓒ Ⓓ   73 Ⓐ Ⓑ Ⓒ Ⓓ
14 Ⓐ Ⓑ Ⓒ Ⓓ   34 Ⓐ Ⓑ Ⓒ Ⓓ   54 Ⓐ Ⓑ Ⓒ Ⓓ   74 Ⓐ Ⓑ Ⓒ Ⓓ
15 Ⓐ Ⓑ Ⓒ Ⓓ   35 Ⓐ Ⓑ Ⓒ Ⓓ   55 Ⓐ Ⓑ Ⓒ Ⓓ   75 Ⓐ Ⓑ Ⓒ Ⓓ

16 Ⓐ Ⓑ Ⓒ Ⓓ   36 Ⓐ Ⓑ Ⓒ Ⓓ   56 Ⓐ Ⓑ Ⓒ Ⓓ   76 Ⓐ Ⓑ Ⓒ Ⓓ
17 Ⓐ Ⓑ Ⓒ Ⓓ   37 Ⓐ Ⓑ Ⓒ Ⓓ   57 Ⓐ Ⓑ Ⓒ Ⓓ   77 Ⓐ Ⓑ Ⓒ Ⓓ
18 Ⓐ Ⓑ Ⓒ Ⓓ   38 Ⓐ Ⓑ Ⓒ Ⓓ   58 Ⓐ Ⓑ Ⓒ Ⓓ   78 Ⓐ Ⓑ Ⓒ Ⓓ
19 Ⓐ Ⓑ Ⓒ Ⓓ   39 Ⓐ Ⓑ Ⓒ Ⓓ   59 Ⓐ Ⓑ Ⓒ Ⓓ   79 Ⓐ Ⓑ Ⓒ Ⓓ
20 Ⓐ Ⓑ Ⓒ Ⓓ   40 Ⓐ Ⓑ Ⓒ Ⓓ   60 Ⓐ Ⓑ Ⓒ Ⓓ   80 Ⓐ Ⓑ Ⓒ Ⓓ

Each item on this test includes four answer choices. Select the best choice for each item and mark that letter on the answer sheet.

Lyndon Johnson was born in a farmhouse in central Texas in 1908. He grew up in poverty and had to work his way through college. He was elected to the U. S. House of Representatives in 1937, and served in the U. S. Navy during World War II. Following 12 years in the House of Representatives, he was elected to the U. S. Senate, where he became the youngest person chosen by any party to be their Senate leader.

In 1964, Johnson won the presidential election with 61 percent of the vote. He won the election by more than 15 million popular votes, the widest margin in the history of American presidential elections. But some historians report that the escalation of the Vietnam war made Johnson depressed almost to the point where he was unable to make decisions effectively. In 1968 Johnson announced that he would not be a candidate for president, even though he gained acceptance for programs suggested by his predecessor but never implemented. Robert Kennedy was assassinated before he had the chance to succeed Johnson as president. It appears that Johnson tried to reverse his decision to withdraw from the 1968 presidential campaign. His plans were thwarted when he did not get support from southern governors and because of the riots at the Chicago Democratic convention.

Johnson championed many Great Society programs including low-income housing; project Head Start, and Medicare. Historians suggest he supported Great Society programs because he experienced poverty as a child. To many, this made Johnson a better president than Kennedy.

But always it was the Vietnam war that preoccupied Johnson. He came to realize that American policy in Vietnam was a failed policy. He could scarcely accept that he had participated in a losing effort that cost 30,000 American lives during his presidency. Near the end of his presidency, he allegedly had wiretaps placed on the phones of friends and foes alike, including his party's standard bearer, Hubert Humphrey. He did not even try to help Hubert Humphrey in the 1968 campaign until he came to believe that Nixon had made a separate arrangement with the North Vietnamese not to negotiate so that Nixon would have a better chance of winning the election. Lyndon Baines Johnson died at his Texas ranch in 1973.

1. Based on this passage, Johnson
   (A) was a better president than Kennedy.
   (B) gained approval for programs proposed by Kennedy.
   (C) was a member of a Great Society.
   (D) was president before Kennedy.

2. Deena finished the school run in 52.8 seconds. Lisa's time was 1.3 seconds faster.

   What was Lisa's time?
   (A) 51.5 seconds
   (B) 54.1 seconds
   (C) 53.11 seconds
   (D) 65.8 seconds

[The Metropolitan Museum of Art, Purchase, 1975, Brandt-Edith Perry Chapman Fund. (1975.205)]

3. The pendant pictured above shows
   (A) evidence of pain.
   (B) evidence of ancient alien visitors.
   (C) a strange animal with legs attached to one another.
   (D) a close relationship between horse and rider.

Items 4–6.

The Black Plague—bubonic plague—was pandemic in Europe during a 200-year period in the middle of the twentieth century. The plague was a severe infection caused by bacteria that was untreatable until antibiotics were available. At its height, the plague killed two million people a year. AIDS has already claimed more than ten million lives, and AIDS in Africa is at the same pandemic levels as the Black Plague was in the Middle Ages. In some African nations more than 10 percent of the population, already infected with AIDS, will die from the disease. These deaths will create millions of orphans that will shatter the social fabric of the continent.

The AIDS rate may be highest in Zimbabwe where a culture of promiscuity fosters spread of the disease. In this country, women are victimized by a culture that virtually forces women to have sex with any man. In fact, women may be beaten or humiliated if they refuse a man's demand for sex. Other more subtle pressures present in the United States and other countries may compel both men and women to make unwise decisions about sexual partners. Freedom from pressure to engage in sex may be one of the most important tools for helping eradicate the AIDS epidemic.

Researchers were not sure at first what caused AIDS or how it was transmitted. They did know early on that everyone who developed AIDS died. Then researchers began to understand that the disease is caused by the HIV virus, which could be transmitted through blood and blood products. Even after knowing this, some blood companies resisted testing blood for the HIV virus. Today we know that the HIV virus is transmitted through blood and other bodily fluids. Women may be more susceptible than men, and the prognosis hasn't changed.

4. The main intent of this passage is to
   (A) show that blood companies can't be trusted.
   (B) detail the history of AIDS research.
   (C) detail the causes and consequences of AIDS.
   (D) raise awareness about AIDS.

5. Which of the following questions could be answered from this passage?
   (A) How do intravenous drug users acquire AIDS?
   (B) Is AIDS caused by blood transfusions?
   (C) Through what mediums is AIDS transmitted?
   (D) How do blood companies test for AIDS?

6. Which of the following would be the best concluding summary sentence for this passage?
   (A) AIDS research continues to be underfunded in the United States.
   (B) Sexual activity and intravenous drug use continue to be the two primary ways that AIDS is transmitted.
   (C) People develop AIDS after being HIV positive.
   (D) Our understanding of AIDS has increased significantly over the past several years, but we are no closer to a cure.

Items 7–9.

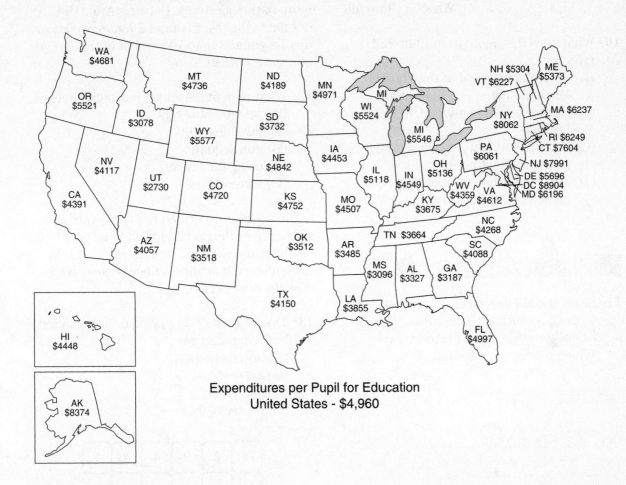

Expenditures per Pupil for Education
United States - $4,960

7. You can deduce from the map that
   teachers' salaries are probably lowest in
   (A) Georgia, Alabama, and Idaho.
   (B) South Dakota, Tennessee, and
   Oklahoma.
   (C) Kentucky, Louisiana, and New Mexico.
   (D) Florida, Hawaii, and Iowa.

8. You can deduce from the map that
   school taxes are probably highest in
   (A) the southeastern states.
   (B) the northeastern states.
   (C) the northwestern states.
   (D) the southwestern states.

9. Based on the information on this map,
   which of these states would be in the sec-
   ond quartile of per pupil expenditures?
   (A) Alaska
   (B) Alabama
   (C) Idaho
   (D) Arizona

An iron curtain has fallen across the continent.

Winston Churchill

10. What does this quote from Churchill refer to?
(A) The establishment of the French Maginot Line
(B) Germany's occupation of Western Europe
(C) Postwar Eastern Europe secretiveness and isolation
(D) The establishment of flying bomb launching ramps across Europe

11. Study the above shapes, and select A, B, C, or D, according to the rule:
(small or striped) and large.
Which pieces are selected?

(A)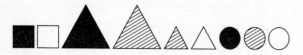

(B)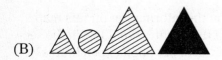

(C)

(D)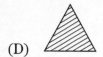

Everyone who finished a test in under 2 hours correctly answered 70 percent or more of the questions. Because Arum did not finish the test in under 2 hours, we know that he got less than 70 percent of the questions correct.

12. What type of fallacious reasoning does this statement reveal?
(A) false analogy
(B) non sequitur
(C) using the inverse
(D) stereotyping

The speaker described her teen years and spoke about the arguments she had with her brothers and sisters. Then the speaker told the audience that she and her siblings were now the best of friends.

13. This account of the speaker's presentation best characterizes
(A) argumentation.
(B) exposition.
(C) narration.
(D) propaganda.

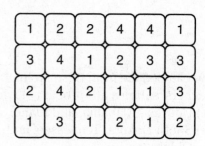

1	2	2	4	4	1
3	4	1	2	3	3
2	4	2	1	1	3
1	3	1	2	1	2

14. A ball is dropped randomly into the container shown above. What is the probability that the ball will land in a hole labeled "1"?
(A) 8/12
(B) 1/2
(C) 1/3
(D) 1/4

Items 15–16.

County highway officials have to submit all road construction plans to the state highway department for approval. The state highway department must approve all plans, but officials are most attentive to plans for new construction, and less concerned about plans for work on existing roads. A state highway inspector visits every site for a limited access highway. The department also uses a computer-simulation analysis to determine the traffic-flow impact of these roads. The state highway department may require a county to identify a similar road configuration elsewhere in the state to fully determine traffic-flow characteristics. The department is also very cautious about roads that may be used by school buses. The state highway department has found that there are more accidents on narrow, rural roads and they have taken planning steps to ensure that roads of this type are not built.

The state highway department has sets of regulations for the number of lanes a highway can have and how these lanes are to be used. A summary of these regulations follows.

- All highways must be five lanes wide and either three or four of these lanes must be set aside for passenger cars only.
- If four lanes are set aside for passenger cars, then one of these lanes must be set aside for cars with three or more passengers, with a second lane of the four passenger lanes also usable by school vehicles such as buses, vans, and cars.
- If three lanes are set aside for passenger cars, then one of these lanes must be set aside for cars with two or more passengers, except that school buses, vans, and cars may also use this lane.

15. Officials in one county submit a plan for a five-lane highway, with three lanes set aside for passenger cars and school buses able to use the lane set aside for cars with two or more passengers. Based on their regulations, which of the following is most likely to be the state highway department's response to this plan?
(A) Your plan is approved because you have five lanes with three set aside for passenger cars and one set aside for passenger cars with two or more passengers.
(B) Your plan is approved because you permitted school buses to use the passenger lanes.
(C) Your plan is disapproved because you don't include school vans and school cars among the vehicles that can use the lane for cars with two or more passengers.
(D) Your plan is disapproved because you include school buses in the lane for passenger cars with two or more passengers.

16. County officials send a list of three possible highway plans to the state highway department. Using their regulations, which of the following plans would the state highway department approve?
  I 5 lanes—3 for passenger cars, 1 passenger lane for cars with 3 or more passengers, school buses and vans can also use the passenger lane for 3 or more people
  II 5 lanes—4 for passenger cars, 1 passenger lane for cars with 3 or more passengers, 1 of the 4 passenger lanes can be used by school buses, vans, and cars
  III 5 lanes—3 for passenger cars, 1 passenger lane for cars with 2 or more passengers, school vehicles can also use the passenger lane for 2 or more passengers
(A) I only
(B) II only
(C) III only
(D) I and II only

Items 17–19.

(A)

["Photograph: After the San Francisco Earthquake" by Arnold Genther. The Metropolitan Museum of Art, The Alfred Stieglitz Collection, 1933. (33.43.223)]

(C)

["Near Union Square-Looking up Park Avenue" by Fairfield Porter. The Metropolitan Museum of Art, Gift of Mrs. Fairfield Porter, 1978. (1978.224)]

(B)

["The Plantation." The Metropolitan Museum of Art, Gift of Edgar William and Bernice Chrysler Garbisch, 1963. (63.210.3)]

(D)

["Illustration from 'Interesting Events in the History of the U.S.': New Hampshire-Stamp Master in Effigy," Wood Engraving. The Metropolitan Museum of Art, Bequest of Charles Allen Munn, 1924. (24.90.1566a)]

17. Which of these pictures most likely involves dissent?

18. Which picture appears to have the least realistic representation of dimensionality?

19. Which realistic picture does not portray people?

Remove the jack from the trunk. Set the jack under the car. Use the jack to raise the car. Remove the lug nuts. Remove the tire and replace it with the doughnut. Reset the lug nuts loosely and use the jack to lower the chassis to the ground. Tighten the lug nuts once the tire is touching the ground.

20. The organization pattern used by the author to develop this passage could be best described as
    (A) time order.
    (B) simple listing.
    (C) cause and effect.
    (D) definition.

21. Which of the following songs begins
with the four bars shown above?
(A) "My Country 'Tis of Thee"
(B) "Appalachian Spring"
(C) "I Fall to Pieces"
(D) "Star Spangled Banner"

22. Which diagram shows object • to have
the most potential energy?

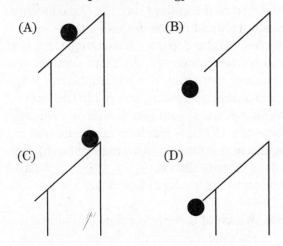

Items 23–24.

Archaeological techniques can be relatively
simple or very complex. One method of archae-
ology uses magnetic imaging to locate sites that
may yield useful archaeological artifacts. Topsoil magnetic mapping is used to identify patterns in the landscape and to identify these
resonance patterns that indicate where archaeological site work is indicated. The movement
of topsoil into ditches and other features often
leads to the development of pockets of material
that may later be transformed into the topsoil
by agricultural activity. It may be that the resulting patterns from agricultural activity will lead
to the discovery of even smaller prehistoric
ditches and other features. Magnetically, the
presence of prehistoric features is reflected in
the lower magnetic readings, particularly when
compared to the higher background readings.
These magnetic surveys can be combined with
results from other surveys to determine the effi-
cacy of further archaeological investigations.

Other techniques may just rely on the
examination of existing relics for sustained

patterns or relationships. Frequently,
advanced numeric methods are useful for a
full analysis of these patterns. In other cases,
informed observation alone may reveal striking cultural information. But still, the success
of these informed observations may presup-
pose a knowledge of mathematics or physics.

An archaeologist was investigating the
books of an old civilization. She found the
following table, which showed the number of
hunters on top and the number of people they
could feed on the bottom. For example, 3
hunters could feed 12 people. The archaeologist found a pattern in the table.

Hunters	1	2	3	4	5	6	7
Eaters	2	6	12	20	30		

23. Look for the pattern. How many eaters
can 6 hunters feed?
(A) 42
(B) 40
(C) 30
(D) 36

24. What is the formula for the pattern:
H stands for hunters and
E stands for eaters?
(A) $E = 3 \times H$
(B) $E = 4 \times H$
(C) $E = H^2 + H$
(D) $E = 3 \times (H + 1)$

Following a concert, a fan asked a
popular singer why the songs sounded
so different in person than on the
recording. The singer responded, "I
didn't record my emotions!"

25. Which of the following statements is
suggested by this passage?
(A) The singer was probably not in a
good mood during that performance.
(B) The fan was being intrusive, and the
performer was "brushing them off."
(C) The performance was outdoors
where sound quality is different.
(D) The performance may vary depending
on the mood of the performer.

26. Which of the following diagrams represents a situation that could result in a solar eclipse?

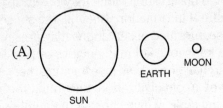

(A)

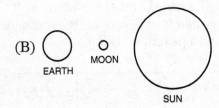

(B)

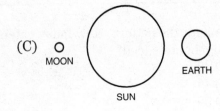

(C)

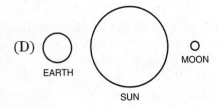

(D)

Items 27–28.

In response to my opponent's question about my record on environmental issues, I want to say that the real problem in this election is not my record. Rather the problem is the influence of my opponent's rich friends in the record industry. I hope you will turn your back on his rich supporters and vote for me.

27. What type of rhetorical argument does this passage reflect?
(A) narration
(B) reflection
(C) argumentation
(D) exposition

28. What type of fallacious reasoning is found in the passage?
(A) begging the question
(B) non sequitur
(C) false analogy
(D) bandwagon

Items 29–33.

(1) The choice of educational practices sometimes seems like choosing fashions. (2) Fashion is driven by the whims, tastes, and zeitgeist of the current day. (3) The education system should not be driven by these same forces. (4) But consider, for example, the way mathematics is taught. (5) Three decades ago, teachers were told to use manipulative materials to teach mathematics. (6) In the intervening years, the emphasis was on drill and practice. (7) Now teachers are being told again to use manipulative materials. (8) This cycle is more akin to _____ than to sound professional practice.

29. Which of these sentences contains a simile?
(A) (1)
(B) (2)
(C) (5)
(D) (6)

30. What does the author most likely mean by the word *zeitgeist* in sentence 2?
(A) Tenor
(B) Emotional feeling
(C) Fabric availability
(D) Teaching methods

31. Which of the following sentences contains an opinion?
(A) (4)
(B) (5)
(C) (6)
(D) (8)

32. For what reason did the author use the phrase *three decades* in sentence 5?
(A) To represent 30 years
(B) For emphasis
(C) To represent 10-year intervals
(D) To represent the passage of years

33. Which of the following choices best fits in the blank in sentence 8?
(A) Unsound practice
(B) A fashion designer's dream
(C) The movement of hemlines
(D) A fashion show

Items 34–39.

Computer graphing programs are capable of graphing almost any equations, including advanced equations from calculus. The student just types in the equation and the graph appears on the computer screen. The graphing program can also show the numerical solution for any entered equation. I like having a computer program that performs the mechanical aspects of these difficult calculations. However, these programs do not teach about graphing or mathematics because the computer does not "explain" what is going on. A person could type in an equation, get an answer, and have not the slightest idea what either meant.

Relying on this mindless kind of graphing and calculation, students will be completely unfamiliar with the meaning of the equations they write or the results they get. They will not be able to understand how to create a graph from an equation or to understand the basis for the more complicated calculations.

It may be true that a strictly mechanical approach is used by some teachers. There certainly is a place for students who already understand equations and graphing to have a computer program that relieves the drudgery. But these computer programs should never and can never replace the teacher. Mathematical competence assumes that understanding precedes rote calculation.

34. What is the main idea of this passage?
(A) Mechanical calculation is one part of learning about mathematics.
(B) Teachers should use graphing programs as one part of instruction.
(C) Graphing programs are not effective for initially teaching mathematics.
(D) Students who use these programs won't learn mathematics.

35. Which of the following questions could be answered from the information in the passage?
(A) How does the program do integration and differentiation?
(B) What type of mathematics learning experiences should students have?
(C) When is it appropriate to use graphing programs?
(D) Why do schools buy these graphing programs?

36. Which of the following information can be found in the passage?
 I The type of computer that graphs the equation
 II The graphing program's two main outputs
 III How to use the program to teach about mathematics
(A) I only
(B) II only
(C) I and II only
(D) II and III only

37. Which aspect of graphing programs does the author of the passage like?
(A) That you just have to type in the equation
(B) That the difficult mechanical operations are performed
(C) That the calculations and graphing are done very quickly
(D) That you don't have to know math to use them

38. Which of the following could be used in place of the first sentence of the last paragraph?
   (A) It may be true that some strict teachers use a mechanical approach.
   (B) It may be true that some teachers use only a mechanical approach.
   (C) It may be true that a stringently mechanical approach is used by some teachers.
   (D) It may be true that inflexible mechanical approaches are used by some teachers.

39. According to this passage, what could result in students' unfamiliarity with the meaning of equations or results?
   (A) Using a graphing program to display the graph of an equation
   (B) Relying on mindless graphing and calculation
   (C) Strictly mechanical approaches
   (D) Using microcomputers to graph equations and find solutions

Items 40–42.

The Vietnam war stretched across the twelve years of the Kennedy and Johnson administrations and into the presidency of Richard Nixon. While the war officially began with Kennedy as president, its actual beginnings stretch back many years.

Before the war, Vietnam was called French Indochina. During World War II, the United States supported Ho Chi Minh in Vietnam as he attacked Japan. After the war, the United States supported the French instead of Ho Chi Minh, as France sought to regain control of its former colony.

Fighting broke out between the French and Ho Chi Minh with support from Mao Zedong (Mao Tse-tung), the leader of mainland China. Even with substantial material aid from the United States, France could not defeat Vietnam. In 1950 the French were defeated at Dien Bien Phu.

Subsequent negotiations in Geneva divided Vietnam into North and South with Ho Chi Minh in control of the North. Ngo Dinh Diem was installed by the United States as a leader in the South. Diem never gained popular support in the South. Following a harsh crackdown by Diem, the Vietcong organized to fight against him. During the Eisenhower administration, 2000 American "advisors" were sent to South Vietnam.

When Kennedy came to office, he approved a CIA coup to overthrow Diem. When Johnson took office he was not interested in compromise. In 1964 Johnson started a massive buildup of forces in Vietnam until the number ultimately reached more than 500,000. The Gulf of Tonkin Resolution, passed by Congress, gave Johnson discretion in pursuing the war.

Living and fighting conditions were terrible. Although American forces had many victories, neither that nor the massive bombing of North Vietnam led to victory. In 1968, the Vietcong launched the Tet Offensive. While ground gained in the offensive was ultimately recaptured, the offensive shook the confidence of military leaders.

At home, there were deep divisions. War protests sprang up all over the United States. Half a million people protested in New York during 1967, while the tension between hawks and doves increased throughout the country.

Richard Nixon was elected in 1970 in the midst of this turmoil. While vigorously prosecuting the war, he and Secretary of State Henry Kissinger were holding secret negotiations with North Vietnam. In 1973 an agreement was finally drawn up to end the war. American prisoners were repatriated although there were still many missing in action (MIA), and U.S. troops withdrew from Vietnam.

The war cost 350,000 American casualties. The $175 billion spent on the war could have been used for Johnson's Great Society programs.

40. The tone of this passage is best described as
   (A) compassionate
   (B) reverent
   (C) serious
   (D) nostalgic

41. In this passage, the author expresses bias against
(A) the Eisenhower administration
(B) the French people
(C) the military
(D) hawks

42. The passage implies which of the following?
(A) The Vietnam War was a glorious war.
(B) Kennedy laid the foundation for this war.
(C) The United States paid a great price for this war.
(D) The United States people gave united support for the war effort.

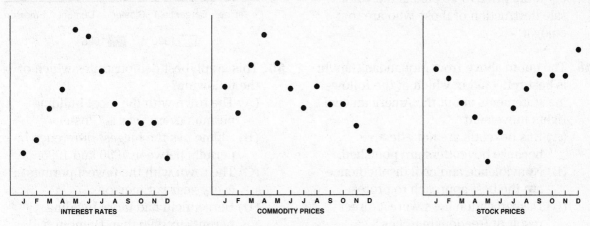

Graphs of Three Economic Indicators for the Same 12-month Period

43. Which of the following conclusions can be drawn from the information on the three graphs shown above?
(A) Higher interest rates cause lower stock prices.
(B) Interest rates and stock prices are inversely related.
(C) Commodity prices and interest rates are not related to one another.
(D) Commodity prices and stock prices are directly related.

Items 44–47.

As a child he read the *Hardy Boys* series of books and was in awe of the author Franklin Dixon. As an adult, he read a book entitled the *Ghost of the Hardy Boys*, which revealed that there was no Franklin Dixon and that ghost writers had authored the books. The authors were apparently working for a large publishing syndicate.

44. Which of the following is the likely intent of the author of this passage?
(A) To describe a book-publishing practice
(B) To contrast fiction and fact
(C) To contrast childhood and adulthood
(D) To correct the record

45. Which of the following does the word *syndicate* in the last sentence most likely refer to?
(A) A business group
(B) An illegal enterprise
(C) An illegal activity
(D) A large building

46. What does the word *Ghost* in the title of the second mentioned book refer to?
(A) A person who has died or was dead at the time the book was published
(B) A person who writes books without credit
(C) A person who influences the way a book is written
(D) The mystical images of the mind that affect the way any author writes

47. Which of the following would NOT be an acceptable replacement for the word *awe* in the first sentence?
(A) Wonder
(B) Admiration
(C) Esteem
(D) Aplomb

"The cause of liberty becomes a mockery if the price to be paid is the wholesale destruction of those who are to enjoy it."

48. The quote above from Mohandas Gandhi is best reflected in which of the following statements about the American civil rights movement?
(A) Bus boycotts are not effective because boycotters are punished.
(B) Nonviolence and civil disobedience are the best approach to protest.
(C) Desegregation laws were a direct result of freedom marches.
(D) America will never be free as long as minorities are oppressed.

Empty halls and silent walls greeted me. A summer day seemed like a good time for me to take a look at the school in which I would student teach. I tiptoed from classroom door to classroom door—looking. Suddenly the custodian appeared behind me and said, "Help you?" "No sir," I said. At that moment she may have been Plato or Homer for all I knew.

49. Which of the following best describes the main character in the paragraph above?
(A) timid and afraid
(C) confident and optimistic
(C) pessimistic and unsure
(D) curious and respectful

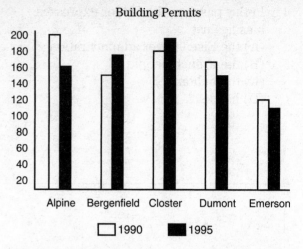

Building Permits

☐ 1990   ■ 1995

50. This graph best demonstrates which of the following?
(A) The town with the most building permits every year is Closter.
(B) Alpine has the biggest difference in permits between 1990 and 1995.
(C) The town with the fewest permits every year is Emerson.
(D) Bergenfield had more building permits in 1990 than Dumont had in 1995.

Items 51–56.

Europeans had started to devote significant resources to medicine when Louis Pasteur was born December 7, 1822. By the time he died in the fall of 1895, he had made enormous contributions to science and founded microbiology. At 32, he was named professor and dean at a French university dedicated to supporting the production of alcoholic beverages. Pasteur immediately began work on yeast and fermentation. He found that he could kill harmful bacteria in the initial brewing process by subjecting the liquid to high temperatures. This finding was extended to milk in the process called pasteurization. This work led him to the conclusion that human disease could be caused by germs. In Pasteur's time, there was a widely held belief that germs were spontaneously generated. Pasteur conducted experiments that proved germs were always introduced and never appeared spontaneously. This result was questioned by other scientists for over a decade. He proved his theory of vaccination and his theory of disease during his work with anthrax, a fatal animal disease. He vaccinated some sheep with weakened anthrax germs and left other sheep unvaccinated. Then he injected all the sheep with a potentially fatal dose of anthrax bacteria. The unvaccinated sheep died while the vaccinated sheep lived. He developed vaccines for many diseases and is best known for his vaccine for rabies. According to some accounts, the rabies vaccine was first tried on a human when a young boy, badly bitten by a rabid dog, arrived at Pasteur's laboratory. The treatment of the boy was successful.

51. What is the topic of this passage?
  (A) Microbiology
  (B) Pasteur's scientific discoveries
  (C) Germs and disease
  (D) Science in France

52. What does the process of pasteurization involve?
  (A) inoculating
  (B) experimenting
  (C) hydrating
  (D) heating

53. Which of the following statements could most reasonably be inferred from this passage?
  (A) The myth of spontaneous generation was dispelled immediately following Pasteur's experiments on the subject.
  (B) The pasteurization of milk can aid in the treatment of anthrax.
  (C) Pasteur's discoveries were mainly luck.
  (D) Even scientists don't think scientifically all the time.

54. Which of the following statements can be implied from this passage?
  (A) That germs do not develop spontaneously was already a widely accepted premise when Pasteur began his scientific work.
  (B) Scientists in European countries had made significant progress on the link between germs and disease when Pasteur was born.
  (C) Europe was ready for scientific research on germs when Pasteur conducted his experiments.
  (D) Most of Pasteur's work was the replication of other work done by French scientists.

55. Which of the following choices best characterizes the reason for Pasteur's early work?
  (A) to cure humans
  (B) to cure animals
  (C) to help the French economy
  (D) to study germs

56. According to this passage, the rabies vaccine
  (A) was developed after Pasteur had watched a young boy bitten by a rabid dog.
  (B) was developed from the blood of a rabid dog, which had bitten a young boy.
  (C) was developed from the blood of a young boy bitten by a rabid dog.
  (D) was developed in addition to the vaccines for other diseases.

Items 57–60.

The Iroquois were present in upstate New York about 500 years before the Europeans arrived. According to Iroquois oral history, this Indian nation was once a single tribe, subject to the rule of the Adirondack Indians. This tribe was located in the valley of the St. Lawrence River, but they left and moved south to be free from Adirondack control. According to reports from French explorers, there were still Iroquoian villages around the St. Lawrence between Quebec and Montreal in the early 1500s. But when explorers returned around 1600, these villages had disappeared. It was about this time that the Iroquois launched a fifty-year war against the Adirondacks. When the French reached Montreal around 1609, they found a vast deserted area along the St. Lawrence because Adirondack, and other Indian tribes avoided the river for fear of attacks from Iroquois raiding parties. The French sided with the local tribes and fought against the Iroquois, using firearms, which caused the Iroquois to give up mass formations and to replace wooden body armor with the tactic of falling to the ground just before the muskets were discharged. The Iroquois were engaged in many conflicts until the Revolutionary war, when the Iroquois sided with the British. The Iroquois were defeated and their lands were taken.

The Iroquois nation consisted of five main tribes—Cayuga, Mohawk, Oneida, Onondaga, and Seneca. Called the Five Nations or the League of Five Nations, these tribes occupied much of New York State. Since the tribes were arranged from east to west, the region they occupied was called the long house of the Iroquois.

The Iroquois economy was based mainly on agriculture. The main crop was corn, but they also grew pumpkins, beans, and fruit. The Iroquois used wampum (hollow beads) for money, and records were woven into wampum belts.

The Iroquois nation had a remarkable democratic structure, spoke a common Algonquin language, and were adept at fighting. These factors had made the Iroquois a dominant power by the early American Colonial period. In the period just before the Revolutionary War, Iroquoian conquest had overcome most other Indian tribes in the northeastern United States as far west as the Mississippi River.

During the Revolutionary War, most Iroquoian tribes sided with the British. At the end of the Revolutionary War the tribes scattered, with some migrating to Canada. Only remnants of the Seneca and Onondaga tribes remained in their tribal lands.

57. Which of these statements best explains why the Iroquois were so successful at conquest?
(A) The Iroquois had the support of the British.
(B) The Iroquois had a cohesive society and were good fighters.
(C) All the other tribes in the area were too weak.
(D) There were five tribes, more than the other Indian nations.

58. Which of the following best describes the geographic location of the five Iroquoian tribes?
(A) the northeastern United States as far west as the Mississippi River
(B) southern Canada
(C) Cayuga
(D) New York State

59. Which of the following best describes why the area occupied by the Iroquois was called the long house of the Iroquois?
(A) The tribes were arranged as though they occupied different sections of a long house.
(B) The Iroquois lived in structures called long houses.
(C) The close political ties among tribes made it seem that they were all living in one house.
(D) The Iroquois had expanded their original tribal lands through conquest.

60. According to the passage, which of the following best describes the economic basis for the Iroquoian economy?
(a) wampum
(B) corn
(C) agriculture
(D) conquest

Items 61–62.

I believe that there is extraterrestrial life—probably in some other galaxy. It is particularly human to believe that our solar system is the only one that can support intelligent life. But our solar system is only an infinitesimal dot in the infinity of the cosmos and it is just not believable that there is not life out there—somewhere.

61. What is the author of this passage proposing?
(A) There is other life in the universe.
(B) That there is no life on earth.
(C) That humans live on other planets.
(D) That the sun is a very small star.

62. The words *infinitesimal* and *infinite* are best characterized by which pair of words below?
(A) small and large
(B) very small and very large
(C) very small and limitless
(D) large and limitless

Items 63–65.

It is striking how uninformed today's youth are about Acquired Immune Deficiency Syndrome. Because of their youth and ignorance, many young adults engage in high-risk behavior. Many of these young people do not realize that the disease can be contracted through almost any contact with an infected person's blood and bodily fluids. Some do not realize that symptoms of the disease may not appear for ten years or more. Others do not realize that the danger in sharing needles to inject intravenous drugs comes from the small amounts of other's blood injected during this process. A massive education campaign is needed to fully inform today's youth about AIDS.

63. The main idea of this passage is
(A) previous education campaigns have failed.
(B) AIDS develops from the HIV virus.
(C) the general public is not fully informed about AIDS.
(D) young people are not adequately informed about AIDS.

64. Which of the following is the best summary of the statement about what young people don't realize about how AIDS can be contracted?
(A) The symptoms may not appear for ten years or more.
(B) AIDS is contracted because of ignorance.
(C) AIDS is contracted from intravenous needles.
(D) AIDS is contracted through contact with infected blood or bodily fluids.

65. Which of the following best describes how the author views young people and their knowledge of AIDS?
(A) Stupid
(B) Unaware
(C) Dumb
(D) Unintelligible

In humans, as in other higher organisms, a DNA molecule consists of two strands that wrap around each other to resemble a twisted ladder whose sides, made of sugar and rungs of nitrogen-containing chemicals called bases, connect phosphate molecules. Each strand is a linear arrangement of repeating similar units called nucleotides, which are each composed of one sugar, one phosphate, and a nitrogenous base. Four different bases are present in DNA: adenine (A), thymine (T), cytosine (C), and guanine (G). The particular order of the bases arranged along the sugar-phosphate backbone is called the DNA sequence; the sequence specifies the exact genetic instructions required to create a particular organism with its own unique traits.

The two DNA strands are held together by weak bonds between the bases on each strand, forming base pairs (bp). Genome size is usually stated as the total number of base pairs; the human genome contains roughly three billion bp. Each time a cell divides into two daughter cells, its full genome is duplicated; for humans and other complex organisms, this duplication occurs in the nucleus. During cell division the DNA molecule unwinds and the weak bonds between the base pairs break, allowing the strands to separate. Each strand directs the synthesis of a complementary new strand, with free nucleotides matching up with their complementary bases on each of the separated strands. Strict base-pairing rules are adhered to; adenine will pair only with thymine (an A-T pair) and cytosine with guanine (a C-G pair). Each daughter cell receives one old and one new DNA strand. The cells' adherence to these base-pairing rules ensures that the new strand is an exact copy of the old one. This minimizes the incidence of errors (mutations) that may greatly affect the resulting organism or its offspring.

Each DNA molecule contains many genes—the basic physical and functional units of heredity. A gene is a specific sequence of nucleotide bases whose sequences carry the information required for constructing proteins, which provide the structural components of cells and tissues as well as enzymes for essential biochemical reactions. The human genome is estimated to consist of approximately 80,000-100,000 genes. Human genes vary widely in length, often extending over thousands of bases, but only about 10 percent of the genome is known to include the protein-coding sequences (exons) of genes. Interspersed with many genes are intron sequences, which have no coding function. The balance of the genome is thought to consist of other noncoding regions (such as control sequences and intergenic regions), whose functions are obscure.

66. What is the guaranteed outcome of base pairing rules?
    (A) Adenine will pair only with thymine.
    (B) New strands exactly replicate old strands.
    (C) DNA strands are held together by weak bonds between the bases on each strand.
    (D) Sequences carry the information required for constructing proteins.

J O I N,   or   D I E.

67. This poster depicts
    (A) the horrors of animal cruelty in early U.S. history.
    (B) the break up of the United States leading to the Civil War.
    (C) the need for the colonies to ratify the Constitution.
    (D) the need for the colonies to unite against England.

Items 68–69.

Alice in Wonderland, written by Charles Dodgson under the pen name Lewis Carroll, is full of symbolism, so much so that a book titled *Understanding Alice* was written containing the original text with marginal notes explaining the symbolic meanings.

68. By symbolism, the author of the passage above meant that much of Alice in Wonderland
 (A) was written in a foreign language.
 (B) contained many mathematical symbols.
 (C) contained no pictures.
 (D) had a figurative meaning.

69. What does the author mean by the phrase "marginal notes" found in the last sentence?
 (A) Explanations of the musical meaning of the text
 (B) Notes that may not have been completely correct
 (C) Notes written next to the main text
 (D) Notes written by Carroll but not included in the original book

["A Connecticut Valley." The Metropolitan Museum of Art, Harris Brisbain Fund, 1940. (40.87.1)]

70. This picture best expresses
 (A) action and warmth.
 (B) isolation and cold.
 (C) fluctuation and flatness.
 (D) concern and denseness.

71. It is Monday at 6 P.M. near the coast of California when you call your friend who lives near the coast of New Jersey. It takes you 5 ½ hours to get through. What time is it in New Jersey when you get through?
 (A) 8:30 P.M. Monday
 (B) 9:30 P.M. Monday
 (C) 2:30 A.M. Tuesday
 (D) 3:30 A.M. Tuesday

During a Stage 4 alert, workers in an energy plant must wear protective pants, a protective shirt, and a helmet except that protective coveralls can be worn in place of protective pants and shirt. When there is a Stage 5 alert, workers must also wear filter masks in addition to the requirements for the Stage 4 alert.

Time	8 A.M.	9 A.M.	10 A.M.	11 A.M.	12 NOON
Temp	45°	55°	60°	60°	70°
Time	1 P.M.	2 P.M.	3 P.M.	4 P.M.	
Temp	75°	75°	70°	65°	
Time	5 P.M.	6 P.M.	7 P.M.	8 P.M.	
Temp	55°	50°	50°	45°	

72. During a Stage 5 alert, which of the following could be worn?
   I masks, pants, shirt
   II coveralls, helmet, mask
   III coveralls, mask
   (A) I only
   (B) II only
   (C) III only
   (D) I and II only

73. The accompanying table shows the temperature tracked for a 12-hour period of time. Which graph best illustrates this information?

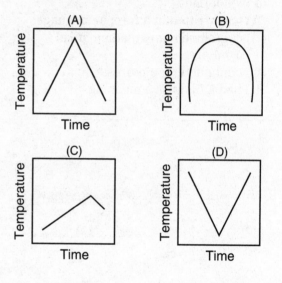

74. Which feature of this sculpture enables the viewer to perceive several different images?
   (A) The light color of the sculpture (against the dark background)
   (B) Mounting the sculpture at eye level
   (C) The sculpture's dimensionality
   (D) The alternating curvature of the sculpture's boundary

["Senil-Configurations" (Threshold Configuration) by Jean Arp. The Metropolitan Museum of Art, Gift of Arthur and Madelaine Lejwa to The Museum in honor of the citizens of New York, 1971. (1971.279)]

75. C is 5 more than half of B. Which of the following expressions states this relationship?

(A) $C + 5 = B/2$
(B) $C = \frac{1}{2}B + 5$
(C) $C + 5 = 2B$
(D) $C + 5 > B/2$

76. In which region of the United States did Algonquin-speaking people live?

---

77. A person throws a black cloth over a pile of snow to make the snow melt faster. Why is that?

(A) Cloth will make snow melt faster.
(B) The black material absorbs more sunlight and more heat.
(C) The black material holds the heat in.
(D) The black cloth reflects light better and so absorbs more heat.

Advances in astronomy and space exploration during the past twenty-five years have been significant, and we now know more answers to questions about the universe than ever before, but we still cannot answer the ultimate question, "How did our universe originate?"

78. Which of the following best characterizes the author's view of how the advances in astronomy and space exploration affect our eventual ability to answer the ultimate question?

(A) We now know more answers than ever before.
(B) All the questions have not been answered.
(C) Eventually we will probably find out.
(D) The question can't be answered.

The sunrise in the desert sky was accompanied by a strange and eerie glow. Normally the sun shone big and bright and yellow. Now all eyes squinted to see the cause. Suddently, as if out of the sun itself, horsemen thundered into our midst. They spared no one the wrath of the guns which they held in their hands. I hid as I could among some baskets and then, as fast as they had come, the horsemen galloped away. I looked out and saw that almost none were moving and listened as the sound of horses faded in the distance.

79. The glow in the sky was probably caused by

(A) an especially hot day.
(B) the sun shining through dust from the horses.
(C) the glint from the rider's guns.
(D) an emotional reaction on the part of the observers.

80. You flip a fair coin three times and it comes up heads each time. What is the probability that the fourth flip will be a head?

(A) 1/16
(B) 1/4
(C) 1/2
(D) 1/3

WRITTEN ASSIGNMENT

Write an essay on the topic below. Use the lined pages that follow. Write your essay on this topic only. An essay on another topic will be rated Unscorable (U).

Topic

In some schools, students are grouped homogeneously. That is, students with similar ability are grouped together. In other schools, students are grouped heterogeneously. That is, students with differing ability are grouped together.

Which grouping approach do you think is better? Write an essay to support your opinion.

PRACTICE LAST II

Answer Key

1. B	11. D	21. A	31. D	41. A	51. B	61. A	71. C
2. A	12. C	22. C	32. B	42. C	52. D	62. C	72. B
3. D	13. C	23. A	33. C	43. B	53. D	63. D	73. A
4. D	14. C	24. C	34. C	44. D	54. C	64. D	74. D
5. C	15. C	25. D	35. C	45. A	55. C	65. B	75. B
6. D	16. B	26. B	36. B	46. B	56. D	66. B	76. A
7. A	17. D	27. C	37. B	47. D	57. B	67. D	77. B
8. B	18. B	28. A	38. B	48. B	58. D	68. D	78. B
9. D	19. C	29. A	39. B	49. D	59. A	69. C	79. B
10. C	20. A	30. B	40. C	50. B	60. C	70. B	80. C

PRACTICE LAST II

Explained Answers

1. **B** This choice paraphrases the fourth sentence in paragraph 2.

2. **A** Faster times are represented by smaller numbers. Subtract 52.8 – 1.3 to find Lisa's time.

3. **D** This primitive African pendant clearly shows a close relationship between horse and rider.

4. **D** The author is trying to raise AIDS awareness and not to present any particular fact.

5. **C** The passage explains that AIDS is transmitted through blood and other bodily fluids.

6. **D** This sentence best sums up the passage.

7. **A** These states have the lowest per pupil expenditures.

8. **B** These states, as a group, have the highest per pupil expenditures.

9. **D** The second quartile is the second quarter of per pupil expenditures ranked from highest to lowest. Arizona is at the top of the second quartile.

10. **C** This famous quote from Churchill referred to the isolation of Communist Bloc countries.

11. **D** The process yields the one piece that is both (small or striped) and large.

12. **C** Using the inverse means reversing the premise (finished under 2 hours) and the conclusion (70 percent or more correct). Getting 70 percent or more correct does not mean that a person finished in under two hours.

13. **C** The speaker is telling a story about her life.

14. **C** There are 24 holes altogether, and 8 of them are labeled "1." So the probability of landing on a "1" is 8/24 or 1/3.

15. **C** If three lanes are set aside for passenger cars, then school buses, school vans, and school cars can all use the lane for cars with two or more passengers.

16. **B** Only this choice meets all the rules.

17. **D** This illustration represents stoning a tax agent in effigy.

18. **B** This painting from 1825 appears almost two-dimensional. Sizes are not represented proportionally.

19. **C** Only pictures A, C, and D are realistic. Of these, picture C does not portray people.

20. **A** Each of the steps must be followed in chronological order. Time order is the only logical answer.

21. **A** These notes show the distinctive beginning of "My Country 'Tis of Thee."

22. **C** The ball at the top of the ramp has the most potential to create energy.

23. **A** The correct answer is 42. The pattern increases by 4, 6, 8, 10, and then 12.

24. **C** This formula gives the correct formula: $H \times (H + 1)$ means the same as the formula shown in C.

25. **D** Music is more than just notes and varies with the mood of the performer.

26. **B** In a solar eclipse, the Moon blocks the Sun's light from reaching Earth. The Moon must be between the Sun and the Earth for a solar eclipse to occur.

27. **C** The speaker is clearly trying to convince the audience of his or her position and uses several rhetorical devices to that end.

28. **A** The speaker is begging the question because he or she does not respond to the original questions and raises other issues completely unrelated to the question asked.

29. **A** The first sentence contains the simile *choice of educational practices...like-choosing fashions.*

30. **B** The context tells us that the answer is the tenor (direction, tendency) of the times.

31. **D** Of the listed sentences, only sentence 8 contains an opinion.

32. **B** The author is being a little dramatic to emphasize the length of the time span.

33. **C** Hemlines move without apparent reason, which is the author's point about educational practices.

34. **C** The author objects to using these programs with students who don't know mathematics.

35. **C** This is the only question that can be answered from information in the passage. The answer is "It can be used when students already understand equations and graphing."

36. **B** Only the information listed next to II can be found in the passage.

37. **B** The passage mentions in the middle of the first paragraph that the author likes this aspect.

38. **B** This choice replicates the intent of the original sentence.

39. **B** The author presents this information in the first sentence of the second paragraph.

40. **C** The author's tone is serious, but the author does not reminisce, and the author is neither respectful nor sympathetic.

41. **A** In the last sentence of the fourth paragraph the quotes around the word *advisors* depict sarcasm.

42. **C** The author summarizes his or her thoughts in the last two sentences.

43. **B** The charts show that stock prices and interest rates go in opposite directions. A is false because the charts do not show a cause and effect relationship. C is false because the charts do show some relationship, but not the direct relationship implied in D.

44. **D** The author wants to share what he or she learned about the Hardy Boy's books.

45. **A** The word *syndicate* can have many meanings. The context reveals that here syndicate means a business group.

46. **B** A ghostwriter is someone who writes books but does not receive credit.

47. **D** Every other choice is an acceptable choice for the word *awe*.

48. **B** The quote supports the nonviolent, nondestructive approach to protest supported by Gandhi.

49. **D** The character visited the school and is certainly curious. The character's response to the custodian shows respect.

50. **B** Choices A and C cannot be inferred from the information given. Choice D is incorrect.

51. **B** This paragraph is about Pasteur's scientific discoveries and not about Pasteur the person.

52. **D** This answer can be found in lines 9–13 of the passage.

53. **D** The passage contains examples of scientists who opposed Pasteur's theories even though Pasteur had proven his theories scientifically.

54. **C** The first sentence indicates that Europeans had already started to devote resources to medicine when Pasteur was born, and theories about germs existed when Pasteur began his work.

55. **C** The passage mentions that his early work was at a university dedicated to supporting an important product of the French economy.

56. **D** The third from last sentence mentions that Pasteur developed vaccines for many diseases.

57. **B** The first sentence of the fourth paragraph supports this choice.

58. **D** This information is contained in the first sentence of the first paragraph.

59. **A** This choice is supported by the last sentence in the second paragraph.

60. **C** The first sentence in the third paragraph provides this information.

61. **A** This choice paraphrases the first sentence in the paragraph.

62. **C** Infinitesimal means very small, and infinite means without limit.

63. **D** The passage is about youth and constantly refers to what youths do and do not know about AIDS.

64. **D** This choice paraphrases the third sentence in the paragraph.

65. **B** The passage uses many synonyms of this word to describe young people's knowledge of AIDS.

66. **B** Choice A is a base pairing rule, not a guaranteed outcome of the rules. Choice B means the same as the next to the last sentence in the second paragraph. Choices C and D are taken directly from the passage, but are not related to this item.

67. **D** This famous poster reflects the sentiment "United we stand, divided we fall."

68. **D** *Alice in Wonderland*, a fanciful story about a young girl's adventures underground, has underlying figurative meanings.

69. **C** The context reveals that marginal means the area of a page to the left and the right of the text.

70. **B** The barren landscape and defoliated trees in this print show isolation and cold.

71. **C** There is a 3-hour time difference between coasts, and the time is later on the East Coast.

72. **B** List II is the only list that meets all the requirements.

73. **A** This graph best represents the steady movement up and then down of the temperatures.

74. **D** The curvature creates an illusion of several different images including a "three-eared rabbit" and a "running ghost." What images do you see?

75. **B** This equation correctly expresses the relationship.

76. **A** The Algonquin speaking tribes included the Iroquois Federation and other Northeast Native Americans.

77. **B** Dark material absorbs more heat than light material.

78. **B** The author writes that the question still cannot be answered. The author does not say that the question will eventually be answered.

79. **B** The dust from the horses is the most likely cause of the eerie glow that was seen that morning.

80. **C** The probability is always 1/2 regardless of what happens on previous flips.

WRITTEN ASSIGNMENT

Show your essay to an English professor or a high school English teacher. Ask them to rate your essay 0–3 using this scale.

3   A well developed, complete written assignment.
Shows a thorough response to all parts of the topic.
Clear explanations that are well supported.
An assignment that is free of significant grammatical, punctuation, or spelling errors.

2   A fairly well developed, complete written assignment.
It may not thoroughly respond to all parts of the topic.
Fairly clear explanations that may not be well supported.
It may contain some significant grammatical, punctuation, or spelling errors.

1   A poorly developed, incomplete written assignment.
It does not thoroughly respond to most parts of the topic.
Contains many poor explanations that are not well supported.
It may contain some significant grammatical, punctuation, or spelling errors.

0   A very poorly developed, incomplete written assignment.
It does not thoroughly respond to the topic.
Contains only poor, unsupported explanations.
Contains numerous significant grammatical, punctuation, or spelling errors.

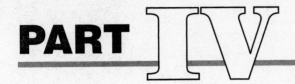

PART IV

Two Complete ATS-Ws with Explained Answers

13 PRACTICE ATS-W I (ELEMENTARY)

This practice test contains the types of items you will encounter on the real test. The distribution of items varies from one test administration to another.

Take this test in a realistic timed setting. You should not take this practice test until you have completed your subject matter review.

The setting will be most realistic if another person times the test and ensures that the test rules are followed. But remember that many people do better on a practice test than on the real test.

You have four hours to complete the multiple-choice items and the written assignment. Keep this time limit in mind as you work. Answer the easier questions first. Be sure you answer all the questions. There is no penalty for guessing. You may write in the test booklet and mark up the questions.

Each multiple-choice item has four answer choices. Exactly one of these choices is correct. Use a pencil to mark your choice on the answer sheet provided for this test.

The written assignment immediately follows the multiple-choice items. Once the test is complete, review the answers and explanations as you correct the answer sheet.

When instructed, turn the page and begin.

13 PRACTICE ARS-W I (ELEMENTARY)

ANSWER SHEET PRACTICE ATS-W I (ELEMENTARY)

1 Ⓐ Ⓑ Ⓒ Ⓓ   21 Ⓐ Ⓑ Ⓒ Ⓓ   41 Ⓐ Ⓑ Ⓒ Ⓓ   61 Ⓐ Ⓑ Ⓒ Ⓓ
2 Ⓐ Ⓑ Ⓒ Ⓓ   22 Ⓐ Ⓑ Ⓒ Ⓓ   42 Ⓐ Ⓑ Ⓒ Ⓓ   62 Ⓐ Ⓑ Ⓒ Ⓓ
3 Ⓐ Ⓑ Ⓒ Ⓓ   23 Ⓐ Ⓑ Ⓒ Ⓓ   43 Ⓐ Ⓑ Ⓒ Ⓓ   63 Ⓐ Ⓑ Ⓒ Ⓓ
4 Ⓐ Ⓑ Ⓒ Ⓓ   24 Ⓐ Ⓑ Ⓒ Ⓓ   44 Ⓐ Ⓑ Ⓒ Ⓓ   64 Ⓐ Ⓑ Ⓒ Ⓓ
5 Ⓐ Ⓑ Ⓒ Ⓓ   25 Ⓐ Ⓑ Ⓒ Ⓓ   45 Ⓐ Ⓑ Ⓒ Ⓓ   65 Ⓐ Ⓑ Ⓒ Ⓓ

6 Ⓐ Ⓑ Ⓒ Ⓓ   26 Ⓐ Ⓑ Ⓒ Ⓓ   46 Ⓐ Ⓑ Ⓒ Ⓓ   66 Ⓐ Ⓑ Ⓒ Ⓓ
7 Ⓐ Ⓑ Ⓒ Ⓓ   27 Ⓐ Ⓑ Ⓒ Ⓓ   47 Ⓐ Ⓑ Ⓒ Ⓓ   67 Ⓐ Ⓑ Ⓒ Ⓓ
8 Ⓐ Ⓑ Ⓒ Ⓓ   28 Ⓐ Ⓑ Ⓒ Ⓓ   48 Ⓐ Ⓑ Ⓒ Ⓓ   68 Ⓐ Ⓑ Ⓒ Ⓓ
9 Ⓐ Ⓑ Ⓒ Ⓓ   29 Ⓐ Ⓑ Ⓒ Ⓓ   49 Ⓐ Ⓑ Ⓒ Ⓓ   69 Ⓐ Ⓑ Ⓒ Ⓓ
10 Ⓐ Ⓑ Ⓒ Ⓓ   30 Ⓐ Ⓑ Ⓒ Ⓓ   50 Ⓐ Ⓑ Ⓒ Ⓓ   70 Ⓐ Ⓑ Ⓒ Ⓓ

11 Ⓐ Ⓑ Ⓒ Ⓓ   31 Ⓐ Ⓑ Ⓒ Ⓓ   51 Ⓐ Ⓑ Ⓒ Ⓓ   71 Ⓐ Ⓑ Ⓒ Ⓓ
12 Ⓐ Ⓑ Ⓒ Ⓓ   32 Ⓐ Ⓑ Ⓒ Ⓓ   52 Ⓐ Ⓑ Ⓒ Ⓓ   72 Ⓐ Ⓑ Ⓒ Ⓓ
13 Ⓐ Ⓑ Ⓒ Ⓓ   33 Ⓐ Ⓑ Ⓒ Ⓓ   53 Ⓐ Ⓑ Ⓒ Ⓓ   73 Ⓐ Ⓑ Ⓒ Ⓓ
14 Ⓐ Ⓑ Ⓒ Ⓓ   34 Ⓐ Ⓑ Ⓒ Ⓓ   54 Ⓐ Ⓑ Ⓒ Ⓓ   74 Ⓐ Ⓑ Ⓒ Ⓓ
15 Ⓐ Ⓑ Ⓒ Ⓓ   35 Ⓐ Ⓑ Ⓒ Ⓓ   55 Ⓐ Ⓑ Ⓒ Ⓓ   75 Ⓐ Ⓑ Ⓒ Ⓓ

16 Ⓐ Ⓑ Ⓒ Ⓓ   36 Ⓐ Ⓑ Ⓒ Ⓓ   56 Ⓐ Ⓑ Ⓒ Ⓓ   76 Ⓐ Ⓑ Ⓒ Ⓓ
17 Ⓐ Ⓑ Ⓒ Ⓓ   37 Ⓐ Ⓑ Ⓒ Ⓓ   57 Ⓐ Ⓑ Ⓒ Ⓓ   77 Ⓐ Ⓑ Ⓒ Ⓓ
18 Ⓐ Ⓑ Ⓒ Ⓓ   38 Ⓐ Ⓑ Ⓒ Ⓓ   58 Ⓐ Ⓑ Ⓒ Ⓓ   78 Ⓐ Ⓑ Ⓒ Ⓓ
19 Ⓐ Ⓑ Ⓒ Ⓓ   39 Ⓐ Ⓑ Ⓒ Ⓓ   59 Ⓐ Ⓑ Ⓒ Ⓓ   79 Ⓐ Ⓑ Ⓒ Ⓓ
20 Ⓐ Ⓑ Ⓒ Ⓓ   40 Ⓐ Ⓑ Ⓒ Ⓓ   60 Ⓐ Ⓑ Ⓒ Ⓓ   80 Ⓐ Ⓑ Ⓒ Ⓓ

Each item on this test includes four answer choices. Select the best choice for each item and mark that letter on the answer sheet.

Use this information for questions 1–5.

You are meeting with parents of a fifth grade student to interpret their child's test scores. These scores include the results of a standardized achievement test that shows the student at the 34th percentile in mathematics. The reading test shows a grade equivalent of 6.3. The average reading score reported for the school district is 6.8. The English test shows a grade equivalent of 6.6. A criterion-referenced test shows that a student has mastered 75 percent of the science objectives for that grade level. You also have a folder with representative samples of the student's writing. In your opinion, these writing samples are well above average for the school.

1. How would you explain the mathematics test score?
    (A) "This means that your child did better than all but 34 students on this test."
    (B) "This means that your child did better than all but about 34 percent of the students who took this test."
    (C) "This means that your child did better than about 34 percent of the students who took this test."
    (D) "This means that you child has better mathematics ability than about 34 percent of the students who took this test."

2. One of the parents notices the criterion referenced score information. They inquire whether or not 75 percent means that their child will get a C in science. Which of the following is an appropriate response?
    (A) "Yes—75 percent is in the C range."
    (B) "Yes—this percentage goes along with the percentile on the mathematics test."
    (C) "Yes—in fact a criterion referenced test gives better percentiles than the standardized achievement test."
    (D) "Can't tell—the percent for the criterion referenced test is not a percentile."

3. Which of the following is the most reasonable explanation of why the child's reading score is above grade level but below average for that class.

    (A) "The test company has obviously made an error in reporting the average score for the class."
    (B) "The class did better on average than the entire group of students who took the test."
    (C) "Many people don't realize that half of those who take the test are below average."
    (D) "The averages are different because the number of students in each group is different."

4. The parents ask about the meaning of the 6.6 grade equivalent English score. Which of the following is the most correct response?
   (A) "Your child is above average in English."
   (B) "Your child is below average in English."
   (C) "Your child's English achievement is about average."
   (D) "Your child's English achievement is right at the seventh month of sixth grade."

5. The parents ask for your overall assessment of their child based on these results. Which of the following is the most appropriate response?
   (A) "We can't really draw any meaningful conclusions from these results."
   (B) "The results indicate that your child may do better when evaluated in real world settings."
   (C) "The results indicate that your child does markedly better in English than in mathematics."
   (D) "The results indicate that your child performs better in science than in reading."

6. Which of the following does NOT describe the American family?
   (A) A majority of families have mothers who work.
   (B) An increasing number of children are "latchkey" children.
   (C) Less than 10 percent of American families have a mother (as a home-maker), a father (as the breadwinner), and children.
   (D) Families are groups of people living together who are related to one another.

Use this information for questions 7–8.

There is a school board meeting tonight. There are several items on the agenda including a budget discussion and a discussion of a tracking system for a fifth grade mathematics program. The meeting is open to the public. A teacher in the audience is supporting pro-school board members who want the school budget passed. Registered voters in the community vote on the budget at the same time that they vote for school board candidates. A large group of parents will be at the meeting.

7. A teacher in the audience favors passage of the school budget. Which of the following describes the teacher's most appropriate action?
   (A) Tell parents that the school needs their support and ask them to get out and vote.
   (B) Tell parents to vote yes on the school budget tonight.
   (C) Tell the parents that the voting records are clear and to vote for the pro-school candidates.
   (D) Tell parents that a vote for anti-budget candidates is a vote against school programs.

8. An opponent of the tracking system could most effectively argue against it before the board by saying:
   (A) "The standardized tests used to place students in the program are deliberately designed to track minority students."
   (B) "Tracking programs have been shown to consistently discriminate against minority students."
   (C) "The best teachers are always assigned to the highest and lowest classes."
   (D) "The school administration cannot be counted on to accurately report test scores."

Use this information for questions 9–11.

A teacher has several students in her class who are achieving below grade level. Quite a few students are below grade level in social studies and most of the students are below grade level in reading. About one quarter of the students in the class were born outside the United States and have not mastered English.

9. All of the following are appropriate ways for the teacher to adapt social studies instruction for students with a below grade reading level EXCEPT
   (A) Use instructional materials with a lower reading level.
   (B) Use instructional materials with less difficult concepts.
   (C) Read information about social studies to the student.
   (D) Use recorded tapes with social studies information.

10. Which of the following is the most appropriate way for the teacher to modify plans to meet the needs of students reading below grade level?
    (A) Modify the plans to account for cultural diversity.
    (B) Modify the plans to account for learning style.
    (C) Modify the plans to account for different achievement levels.
    (D) Modify the plans to incorporate alternate evaluation techniques.

11. Which of the following is NOT an effective approach to teaching the LEP students in the class?
    (A) TESL
    (B) Bilingual education
    (C) TEAL
    (D) TOEFL

Use this information for questions 12–15.

An elementary school teacher has the primary responsibility for the arts and rhythmic activities program in his school. Rhythmic and movement activities are very often a part of the curriculum for today's elementary physical education programs. These activities lay the foundation for folk and creative dance units.

12. Which of the following should be the main focus for an elementary school fine arts program?
    (A) Helping students acquire technical skills in drawing.
    (B) Making sure students at least have experience coloring, painting, and using clay.
    (C) Helping students gain appreciation of aesthetics and human creativity of all kinds.
    (D) Allowing students to illustrate their written work in the way they feel most comfortable.

13. The teacher writes a lesson plan that calls on students to give their emotional response to a work of art. Which taxonomy of educational objectives is this lesson related to?
    (A) Psychomotor
    (B) Psychological
    (C) Cognitive
    (D) Affective

14. The teacher would like to integrate a lesson on Haiku with fine arts. Which of the following would LEAST meet the student's needs?
    (A) Use the computer as an artistic tool to illustrate the Haiku.
    (B) Provide a display of classical Japanese paintings for children to color.
    (C) Provide clay as means to illustrate their Haiku.
    (D) Provide paints and brushes for illustrations to the Haiku.

15. Which of the following is most important when planning for rhythmic and movement activities?
    (A) Make sure the music is a lively and catchy tune.
    (B) Make sure you choose partners wisely.
    (C) Make sure you demonstrate each step so each student can see you.
    (D) Make sure the basic approach is a gradual movement from individual to partner to group activities.

Use this information for questions 16–19.

An upper elementary grade teacher is teaching a unit on writing. The unit includes creative writing, personal journals, writing and following directions, and evaluating compositions.

16. Which of the following would be most appropriate for the teacher to use to evaluate students' writing techniques and plan for further writing experiences?
    (A) Administer a standardized grammar test and use the scores as a planning device.
    (B) Use a writing checklist to assess a variety of creative writing samples that include writing summaries and samples.
    (C) Have the students hand in a composition of their choice.
    (D) Have the students answer a series of short answer questions from a specific reading selection.

17. Erin is a student in this class who writes well, understands verbal directions, but often has trouble understanding written directions. Her difficulty might be related to all of the following EXCEPT:
    (A) auditory discrimination
    (B) visual discrimination
    (C) sight vocabulary
    (D) context clues

18. Personal journals that students in the class are writing should NOT be used
    (A) as a record of feelings
    (B) to share their thoughts with others
    (C) as a means of expressing thought
    (D) as a means for writing ideas

19. When writing, it is most important that students in the class
    (A) decide on the best order for presenting ideas
    (B) have a clear beginning
    (C) keep the audience and purpose in mind.
    (D) support the main idea.

Use this information for questions 20–27.

A third grade teacher knows that testing and assessment are among her most important responsibilities. The teacher is preparing to meet with her grade level supervisor to discuss a number of testing and assessment issues in the class.

The teacher is constructing a test to find out how much students learned from a third grade science unit. She wants the test to be properly written. The teacher also wants to try out portfolio assessment in her classroom.

A third-grade student's standardized test result indicates that he is performing at the 2.8 grade level in reading. The teacher wants to be able to explain the meaning of this score to parents at the next go-to-school night.

Repeated testing of another third-grade student, JoAnn, in her class reveals an IQ in the range of 110–115 and standardized achievement test scores two or more years below grade level. The teacher wants to make the appropriate decision about this student.

20. The teacher should explain to the supervisor that she needs to be aware of all of the following when writing the science test EXCEPT:
(A) Errors of measurement
(B) Reliability
(C) Test length
(D) Criterion validity

21. Which inference below could the teacher reasonably draw from the student's reading score?
(A) The student seems to be reading at about the third or fourth grade level.
(B) The student is reading below grade level.
(C) The test was invalid.
(D) The student seems to be learning disabled.

22. Which of the following is the most appropriate interpretation for the teacher to give of JoAnn's test scores?
(A) The student's achievement and potential match.
(B) The student is mildly retarded.
(C) The student is gifted.
(D) The student has a learning disability.

23. The supervisor asks the teacher about the general characteristics of elementary school students. Which of the following possible responses by the teacher would be most appropriate?
(A) All ethnic groups adapt equally well to school.
(B) Boys have more adjustment problems than girls do.
(C) Girls are more physically active than boys are of the same age.
(D) Primary students rebel against the teacher's authority.

24. The supervisor asks the teacher about the relative achievement of boys and girls. Which of the following responses would most researchers agree with?
(A) Boys and girls achieve at about the same level throughout the grades.
(B) Boys do better in primary grades; girls do better through about eleventh grade; and boys do better thereafter.
(C) Girls achieve at a higher level than boys do in elementary school, but the situation is reversed in secondary school.
(D) Boys achieve at a higher level than girls do in elementary school, but the situation is reversed in secondary school.

25. Which of the following responses is the best description the teacher could give of holistic scoring?
(A) Essays are scored using advanced imaging technology.
(B) Essays are scored independently by several readers.
(C) Readers rank essays relative to the "whole" of essays written for that testing cycle.
(D) Readers rank essays based on the overall impression, not on a detailed analysis.

26. The teacher identifies reliability as one of the significant difficulties of portfolio assessment because:
(A) different students may put samples of widely different work in their portfolios.
(B) the scoring machines don't work reliably with the materials in the portfolio.
(C) different teachers may place different emphasis on the portfolios when giving grades.
(D) different teachers may assign widely different grades to the same portfolio.

27. Which of the following is NOT an effective way for the teacher to respond to a test anxious child?
    (A) Give extra time, when practical, for students to finish the test.
    (B) Don't draw attention to the student by providing emotional support.
    (C) Reduce tension before a test with humor.
    (D) Use alternative assessment.

Use this information for questions 28–34.

A primary teacher teaches reading to her students every school day. Right now, the class is reading a science fiction story. In the story, Nayr the alien tries to trick the astronauts away from their spaceship so the alien can look inside. Of course, the teacher is always considering whether she should use a phonics approach or a whole language approach. There is a basal series along with individual reading books in the classroom, and students often read aloud. The teacher also shows students how to read in subject areas such as mathematics and science.

28. The teacher wants to encourage higher level thinking while the students are reading the science fiction story. Which of the following questions would be most appropriate?
    (A) What are other ways Nayr could have gotten inside the ship?
    (B) How did Nayr trick the astronauts?
    (C) Why did Nayr want to go inside the ship?
    (D) How many times did Nayr succeed in getting the astronauts away from their ship?

29. Which of the following would NOT be supported by a basal reading approach?
    (A) Skills are taught and developed in a systematic sequential manner.
    (B) Meeting individual differences and needs of the child.
    (C) A basic vocabulary is established and reinforced.
    (D) Manuals provide a detailed outline for teaching.

30. One of the students has trouble reading the problems in his mathematics book. This difficulty is likely to be the result of
    (A) faulty word identification and recognition
    (B) inability to locate and retain specific facts
    (C) deficiencies in basic comprehension abilities
    (D) inability to adapt to reading needs in content fields.

31. Which of the following goals would not be met through choral reading?
    (A) To help students to feel part of a group
    (B) To appreciate oral reading
    (C) To develop an interest in creative forms of language
    (D) To help students interpret meaning

32. A child has difficulty pronouncing a printed word. The problem may reflect all of the following EXCEPT
    (A) Phonetic analysis
    (B) Sight vocabulary
    (C) Language comprehension
    (D) Context analysis

33. Which of the following was the best reason for the teacher to institute a whole language program in her classroom?
    (A) Everybody's using it.
    (B) It's less work.
    (C) Children comprehend more.
    (D) Children have a better attitude toward reading.

34. Which of the following is NOT furthered by a phonics approach?
    (A) Associate sounds with printed letters.
    (B) Attack new words independently.
    (C) Develop a sight vocabulary.
    (D) Identify multiple word meanings.

35. The gifted and telented (G&T) teacher had always taught students in her own classroom. Then the school implemented a collaborative teaching program, including the G&T teacher. This means that the G&T teacher will
(A) meet with students' parents to discuss the G&T curriculum.
(B) work on an interdisciplinary team to plan the G&T curriculum.
(C) teach both G&T and special education students.
(D) teach with classroom teachers in their classrooms.

36. Weekly planning differs from individual lesson plans in that
(A) weekly plans for lessons and other activities fit into the time periods available during the week while lesson plans detail the lessons.
(B) weekly plans detail the lessons while lesson plans fit into the time periods available during the week.
(C) weekly plans should be prepared each week while lesson plans should be prepared at the beginning of the year.
(D) weekly plans are usually kept by the teacher while lesson plans are usually submitted written in a plan book.

Use this information for questions 37–38.

An intermediate grade teacher wants to teach a varied and challenging social studies program. The teacher is considering a number of different approaches, including the ones below.

37. If the teacher adopted a multicultural approach to teaching social studies the approach would include
(A) a comparison of how different cultures respond to similar issues
(B) how people from different cultures contribute to world events
(C) how people around the world have common characteristics
(D) how events in one part of the globe influence the rest of the world

38. Which of the following map and globe skills would probably be the most challenging to present to these intermediate grade students?
(A) Locating the state, county, and town of the school location.
(B) Coloring a map so no two adjoining states, counties or countries would have the same color.
(C) Reading and using the key on the map.
(D) Transforming factual information about a country to a specific map.

Use this information for questions 39–40.

A group of advanced fourth graders is studying the relationship between the resistance(R) – fulcrum(F) – effort(E) characteristics of levers. They are having difficulty understanding this concept.

39. Which of the following activities would best help students understand these concepts?
(A) Arrange a variety of levers in RFE, FRE, and FER order so the students can demonstrate where to place a lever on a fulcrum to reduce or increase effort.
(B) Have students classify a group of pictorial representations of levers into RFE, FRE, and FER groups.
(C) Read a textbook description of each type of lever and list examples under each type.
(D) Chart the resistance and effort levels of different types of levers.

40. When responding to children's science questions about this lesson, the teacher should do all the following EXCEPT
(A) Encourage activities and materials that stimulate curiosity.
(B) Model good questioning skills.
(C) Answer all questions as quickly and concisely as possible.
(D) Include children's questions in evaluation techniques.

41. Which of the following summarizes Glasser's Reality Therapy approach to classroom management?
(A) Students are left on their own to discover the harsh reality of their own mistakes.
(B) The teacher establishes clear rules and the rewards or punishment for following or breaking class rules.
(C) The teacher explains all positive and negative outcomes in terms of the real world.
(D) Students help develop rules and then accept the consequences of any rule breaking.

42. When a learning theorist says that children can learn vicariously this means that children
(A) can learn by doing.
(B) can learn through a wide variety of activities.
(C) can learn if there is a clear structure.
(D) can learn from others' experiences.

Use this information for questions 43–47.

A fifth grade student has been classified as a special education student. The child study team has determined that the child is learning disabled. The child study team includes an elementary school teacher who may have the student mainstreamed in his class. The team is deciding the appropriate placement for this student, discussing the basis for the placement, and discussing the different strategies to help this student learn.

43. Which of the following describes an appropriate placement strategy for that student?
(A) Place the student in a self-contained class with other learning disabled students and send the student out for music and art specials.
(B) Place the student in a fifth grade class with support from a special education teacher.
(C) Place the student in a self-contained class with other learning disabled students and send the student to a fifth grade class for some subjects.
(D) Place the student in a fifth grade class and meet with the parents to arrange extra tutoring.

44. The team decided to try a learning contract with this student. Contracts to help students change their classroom behavior have an essential element, which is
(A) a parent's signature
(B) a provision for maintaining a log
(C) a statement of expected test scores
(D) a list of short term goals

45. The team also assigned an aide to be with the student when the student is mainstreamed in the elementary classroom. Which of the following represents the LEAST appropriate way for the elementary school teacher to use the aide in an instructional capacity?
(A) Help preschool children dress themselves
(B) Duplicate instructional worksheets
(C) Read to small groups of students
(D) Help manage difficult children

46. The assignment of the child to an appropriate learning environment is most likely based on which of these education laws?
(A) PL-99-457
(B) PL-98-199
(C) The Emancipation Proclamation
(D) PL-94-142

47. Which of the following best describes an effective approach for the teacher to use with this learning disabled student?
(A) Use large print books.
(B) Apply highly relevant skills with a lot of practice.
(C) Provide brief assignments and auditory learning.
(D) Permit them to test out of requirements.

48. Which of the following does NOT describe the impact of physical and mental health on school learning?
(A) Inadequate nutrition can lead to inattentiveness and other problems that interfere with learning.
(B) Alcohol and drug addiction are causes of abnormal physical and emotional development.
(C) Most adolescents rely heavily on peer group approval and respond to "peer pressure."
(D) Alcohol abuse by expectant mothers does little if any damage to the unborn child.

Use this information for questions 49–58.

It is a new teacher's first month in school. The teacher is concerned about maintaining discipline, keeping the students interested and on task, having an effective management style, and just surviving. The principal comes by to observe the class and notices that the teacher calls on only about 40 percent of the students in the class and that more student centered instruction needs to take place. The principal also notices that classroom management needs to be improved and that students are often confused about transitions during the lesson. The principal has a conference with the teacher following the observation.

49. Which of the following would most educators agree should be the teacher's primary focus for the first week of school?
(A) Testing to determine student's readiness to learn.
(B) Intensive reading review to prepare students to learn during the year.
(C) Ensuring that all students have necessary books, materials, and medical clearances.
(D) Instilling the procedures and processes that will foster learning during the year.

50. The best advice this teacher can follow about maintaining interest is to:
(A) Stand where you can see the entire class.
(B) Limit the number of students involved in question and answer sessions.
(C) Ensure that the material being taught is very difficult.
(D) Do not proceed with the lesson if even a single student is not paying attention.

51. The teacher is arranging desks at the beginning of the school year. Which of the following arrangements is LEAST appropriate?

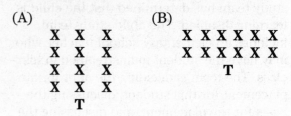

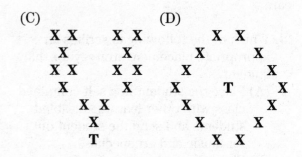

52. Above all, students expect this teacher to be
(A) assertive
(B) understanding
(C) authoritarian
(D) an authority figure

53. According to several researchers, students frequently become discipline problems in order to gain attention. Which of the following is an effective approach for dealing with the attention-seeking student?
(A) Point out misbehavior each time it occurs.
(B) Deliberately ignore appropriate behavior when it occurs.
(C) Send students to the office after several misbehaviors.
(D) Ignore the misbehavior.

54. Which of the following is the most constructive professional advice the teacher could expect the principal to give during the conference?
(A) "Try to call on about 65 percent of the students during any lesson."
(B) "Make a check on a list of names, a seating chart, or something like that, and try to get to everyone."
(C) "Research shows that student participation is important, so try to call on all the students."
(D) "I can see why you don't call on some of these students—they're very difficult—but do your best."

55. During the conference the principal discusses classroom management. The teacher learns that most effective classroom managers first take into account
(A) room size
(B) class size
(C) student characteristics
(D) school curricula

56. The principal also points out that most educators would agree that classroom management is most successful when it:
(A) involves parents
(B) optimizes learning
(C) reduces conflicts
(D) engages students

57. Which of the following is the most appropriate way for a teacher to alert students to a transition from group work to a whole-class activity?
(A) Say, "Times up—put away your work."
(B) Flick the classroom lights.
(C) Stand silently in front of the room and wait for students to realize that you want their attention.
(D) Begin making the presentation and then wait for students' attention.

58. Which of the following would ensure that student-centered instruction is taking place in this classroom?
(A) Student involvement
(B) Students arranged in groups
(C) Cooperative learning
(D) Teacher answering student questions

Use this information for question 59.

59.

SCHOOL GRADING RULES	
A	91–100
B	81–90
C	71–80

A teacher-made, content-valid multiple-choice test is used to assess performance on a social studies unit. One student receives a 92 while another student receives an 88. How confident should the teacher be about assigning grades according to the school rules?
(A) Very confident. The teacher should follow the school grading rules.
(B) Very confident. The difference between the grades is significant.
(C) Somewhat confident. The test is content valid and probably measures important concepts.
(D) Not confident. The errors of measurement in the test probably eliminate the meaning of the difference between the scores.

60. Which is NOT a true statement about the nature vs. nurture controversy?
(A) The nature part refers to heredity.
(B) The nurture part refers to the environment and experience.
(C) Twins split at birth have cleared up this controversy.
(D) The controversy goes on.

Use this information for questions 61–65.

A cluster of primary teachers wants to build its program around the theories of Jean Piaget. Piaget wrote that children learn through a process of equilibration. Piaget used a series of conservation tasks to determine whether or not students fully understood a concept.

61. Which of the following classroom practices are the teachers in this cluster most likely to use?
(A) Teachers teach skills while using manipulative materials.
(B) Students learn a concept through the repeat-practice method.
(C) Students learn concepts vicariously.
(D) Students actively learn concepts through their own experiences.

62. Which of the following is a conservation task that these teachers could use with their children?
(A) The teacher shows the child two groups of attribute blocks. The child can match like shapes.
(B) The teacher gives the child number cubes. The child can place the cubes with the correct number on top when cued by the teacher.
(C) The teacher shows the child a pattern of attribute blocks. The child can successfully duplicate a pattern formed by the teacher.
(D) When one of two matched rows of buttons is spread out, a child knows that the number of buttons has not changed.

63. Teachers in this cluster are likely to involve children in all of the following activities EXCEPT
(A) having students work individually or in small groups.
(B) accelerating students through a series of concepts.
(C) involving students with concrete and pictorial materials.
(D) actively involving students in the learning process.

64. A child is standing outside a room and looks in to see all the students around the teacher's desk. The child looks away for a minute and then looks back to see all the students sitting at their desks. The child knows that no one came in or out of the room, but wonders why there are more children now than there were before. This child is most likely at which of Piaget's developmental stages?
(A) Sensorimotor
(B) Preoperational
(C) Concrete operational
(D) Formal operational

65. All of the following describe how teachers in this cluster would teach science EXCEPT
(A) using cooperative learning to teach science.
(B) having an age appropriate textbook for the class.
(C) using hands-on science experiments.
(D) organizing results through a systematic thinking process.

---

66. Which of the following could be used to screen a child for scoliosis?
(A) a treadmill
(B) a plumb line
(C) a chinning bar
(D) a stethoscope

67. Young children have many experiences with capacity, including sand and water play. Why do so few children carry over these experiences to understanding volume?
    (A) They have not progressed to that stage.
    (B) They usually overfill the containers.
    (C) They usually do not have enough variety of containers.
    (D) No one told them what they were doing.

Use this information for questions 68–72.

An upper elementary grade teacher is conducting an individualized mathematics lesson. Students are working on different skills and concepts. The teacher has these area and perimeter problems on the board for students to solve.

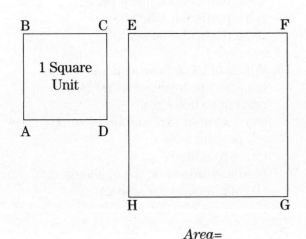

Area=

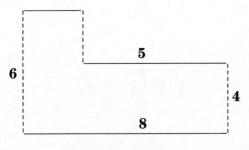

Perimeter =

As the teacher walks around the room, she sees these two examples of student work.

$$\frac{86.4}{6)520} \quad \frac{81.7}{9)736} \quad \frac{18.6}{8)150} \qquad 12 + 9 = 11$$

68. The student who completes the addition problem always gets an answer such as this one. In which area does this student need the most help?
    (A) Lining up decimal points
    (B) Place value
    (C) Addition facts
    (D) Writing number sentences

69. After examining the area problem on the board the student says the area of the larger figure is 2. How could the teacher best help the student see his or her error?
    (A) Suggest the student trace the outside of the small shape and compare that to the tracing of the larger shape.
    (B) Get a ruler and measure both shapes.
    (C) Cut out the small square and see how many fit inside the large square.
    (D) Estimate the increased distance between BC and EF.

70. Which of the following is the least appropriate mathematics objective to teach using manipulative materials?
    (A) Adding single digit numbers
    (B) Solve problems using the strategy "Make an organized list"
    (C) Adding double digit numbers
    (D) Dividing decimals

71. A student continues to make the same type of division error as shown in the accompanying work and gets which of the following answers to 124 divided by 5?
    (A) 2.2
    (B) 20.2
    (C) 24.4
    (D) 22.5

72. After examining the diagram for the perimeter problem, the student says the perimeter is 23 units. Which of the following approaches should the teacher take?
    (A) Say, "Check your addition."
    (B) Trace the shape with her finger, stating the length of each side.
    (C) Count the number of sides of the polygon.
    (D) Get a ruler.

---

73. A teacher wants to teach a middle school mathematics unit. Which of the following approaches would lead to the most successful learning?
    (A) Students are listening to a lesson at their ability level.
    (B) Students are listening to a lesson and challenged above their ability level.
    (C) Students are participating in a lesson at their ability level.
    (D) Students are participating in a lesson and challenged above their ability level.

74. After seeing her class's work, the teacher decides to schedule mathematics first thing in the morning and reading after a recess but before lunch. Which of the following is the correct response to her plan?
    (A) This is poor planning because the students will be late from recess.
    (B) This is good planning, because if her math lesson runs over, she can always cut out recess.
    (C) It doesn't make any difference when she schedules these subjects, as long as she gets them in somewhere.
    (D) This is good planning because the students have a break before the reading.

75. Generally speaking, when this teacher draws up unit plans they are built around
    (A) a particular unit of measure.
    (B) a particular grade level.
    (C) a particular teacher.
    (D) a particular subject.
    (E) a particular subject.

76. Which of the following is the best approach to teaching a first lesson on percent to this class?
    (A) A written explanation of what a percent is
    (B) A 100s chart
    (C) Illustrations on the chalkboard
    (D) Manipulative materials

Use this information for questions 77–78.

A fourth grade teacher is establishing cooperative learning groups in his classroom. At first, the teacher will involve students in cooperative learning activities for 30 minutes each day.

77. All of the following might occur during the cooperative learning activities EXCEPT:
    (A) students getting help from other students.
    (B) students working in groups of two to six.
    (C) group members consulting with the teacher.
    (D) the teacher summarizing students' work.

78. Which of the following activities in the teacher's class is LEAST consistent with cooperative learning groups?
    (A) Group members devise a working plan.
    (B) Group members actively involved in learning.
    (C) Groups of ten to twelve students.
    (D) Teacher presents the project to be worked on.

Use this information for questions 79–80.

A primary grade teacher is planning the next week's lessons. He wants to help students with their coordination and to increase technology based instruction.

79. Which of the following would be the most appropriate activity for the teacher to use to improve the eye-hand coordination?
    (A) Provide numerous highly organized team activities.
    (B) Provide for numerous pyramid-building activities.
    (C) Provide many different sized articles for them to juggle.
    (D) Provide many different sized balls for the student to throw and catch.

80. Which would NOT be an appropriate computer program for this teacher to use with his students?
    (A) Reader Rabbit
    (B) Writer Rabbit
    (C) The Oregon Trail
    (D) Lotus 1-2-3

WRITTEN ASSIGNMENT

Write a lesson plan on the topic below. Use the lined pages that follow. Write your lesson plan on this topic only. A lesson plan on another topic will be rated Unscorable (U).

Assignment

Choose one of these curriculum areas: mathematics, social studies, or science.

Choose either a primary (K–3) or upper elementary (4–6) grade level.

Choose an objective from your curriculum area appropriate to the grade level. Write a lesson plan for teaching that objective.

PRACTICE ATS-W I (ELEMENTARY)

Answer Key

1. C	11. C	21. A	31. D	41. D	51. D	61. D	71. C
2. D	12. C	22. D	32. C	42. D	52. D	62. D	72. B
3. B	13. D	23. B	33. D	43. B	53. D	63. B	73. C
4. C	14. B	24. C	34. D	44. D	54. B	64. B	74. D
5. B	15. D	25. D	35. D	45. B	55. C	65. B	75. D
6. D	16. B	26. D	36. A	46. D	56. B	66. B	76. D
7. A	17. A	27. B	37. A	47. C	57. B	67. A	77. D
8. B	18. B	28. A	38. D	48. D	58. C	68. B	78. C
9. B	19. C	29. B	39. A	49. D	59. D	69. C	79. D
10. D	20. D	30. D	40. C	50. A	60. C	70. D	80. D

PRACTICE ATS-W I (ELEMENTARY)

Explained Answers

1. **C** This choice is the correct interpretation of percentile.

2. **D** It is not possible to predict a grade without more information.

3. **B** This is the correct interpretation of the information.

4. **C** Standardized test scores indicate a range of scores, not one specific score, and 6.6 and 6.8 are in that range. The teacher's correct response is that the child is about average—meaning about average for that school.

5. **B** The only statement supported by the information is that the students may fare better when authentic evaluation is used.

6. **D** Many American families have family members who are not related.

7. **A** This action furthers the teacher's aims and does not run the risk of alienating parents.

8. **B** Because they perform poorer on standardized tests, minority students are disproportionately represented in the lower tracks.

9. **B** Students with a lower reading level can still learn the most difficult concepts.

10. **D** Students often perform better on an alternative evaluation than on a standardized test.

11. **C** TEAL stands for nothing. TESL means teaching English as a second language. Bilingual education means teaching in the second language. TOEFL means teaching of English as a foreign language.

12. **C** The elementary grades are too early in a child's development to have a main focus on artistic proficiency.

13. **D** The affective domain describes this type of objective.

14. **B** All the other choices appropriately involve the students in creative arts activities.

15. **D** Students need to become comfortable, themselves, with these activities before working with others or with groups.

16. **B** Any evaluation of student's writing must be based on actual writing samples. Using a checklist ensures that writing will be consistently evaluated.

17. **A** Difficulty with written directions only is related to some reading or other visual problem. Auditory discrimination refers to hearing.

18. **B** Personal journals are just that—personal—and are not meant to be shared with others. There are other ways to foster written communication among students.

19. **C** Even the most well written piece will not communicate effectively if it is not directed at the intended audience.

20. **D** Criterion validity refers to a test's results to predict how well a person will do something in the future.

21. **A** The errors of measurement in the test lead to a range of scores that spans the third and fourth grade.

22. **D** A student is classified "learning disabled" if he or she performs two or more years below his or her ability.

23. **B** Research shows that about twice as many boys as girls have adjustment problems.

24. **C** Girls generally perform at a higher level in elementary school and gradually lose this ascendancy by high school.

25. **D** Holistic grading is built on the reader's informed impression.

26. **D** Choice D describes the difficulty with the reliability, or grading consistency, of this evaluation approach.

27. **B** Teachers should give test anxious students extra support.

28. **A** This question asks students to devise ways to help Nayr achieve his goal. Question C is a low-level recall question. Questions B and D cannot be answered from the information given.

29. **B** A basal reader contains a single set of stories. Other stories at different reading and interest levels are needed to individualize instruction.

30. **D** Transferring reading skills and reading ability to specific content areas is among the most difficult tasks for students to master.
31. **D** Choral reading is a group phonetic activity and unrelated to meaning.
32. **C** Pronouncing words is a phonetic skill. Reading comprehension has to do with the meaning of the words.
33. **D** Children enjoy reading more when teachers use original books and de-emphasize phonics.
34. **D** Phonics helps students decode words but does not help them identify word meanings.
35. **D** Collaborative teaching generally means that special education teachers work in regular classrooms.
36. **A** A weekly plan allocates available time to lessons.
37. **A** The statement for this choice defines a multicultural approach.
38. **D** This activity, alone, asks students to function at a high cognitive level.
39. **A** Students learn science best through experimentation.
40. **C** The most important part of a response to a question is a complete answer.
41. **D** Glasser's approach features consequences for misbehavior.
42. **D** Vicarious learning means learning from others' experiences.
43. **B** This choice describes the least restrictive environment that meets the student's needs for additional support.
44. **D** Contracts should briefly list short-term goals but none of the other choices listed here.
45. **B** All of the other choices are useful endeavors for aides working in an instructional capacity.
46. **D** This special education act was the first significant federal intervention in public schooling.
47. **C** Learning disabled students benefit most from brief structured assignments and auditory opportunities for learning.
48. **D** Alcohol abuse by expectant mothers can cause enormous damage to the unborn child.
49. **D** While the other choices are important, educators generally agree that this choice is most important.

50. **A** The best advice among the five choices is to stand where you can see the entire class. The other choices represent inappropriate management strategies.
51. **D** In this arrangement it is most difficult for the teacher to see all the students.
52. **D** Students always expect the teacher to be an authority figure.
53. **D** When children are misbehaving to gain attention, reprimanding the student reinforces the behavior.
54. **B** This choice gives a specific suggestion for the teacher to follow.
55. **C** Student characteristics is the most appropriate choice listed.
56. **B** The whole reason for classroom management is to optimize learning.
57. **B** This cueing approach alerts students and gives them time to put away their work.
58. **C** Cooperative learning is truly student centered. All the other activities could take place in a teacher-centered classroom.
59. **D** The teacher should not be confident. Errors of measurement that occur on all teacher made tests eliminate any meaning from the difference in the scores.
60. **C** Research on twins separated at birth and studied later has shed some light on this issue but has not produced definitive findings.
61. **D** Equilibration is supported by the child's own experiences.
62. **D** This choice describes the number conservation task.
63. **B** Piaget indicated that students have to move naturally through series of concepts.
64. **B** Children at Piaget's preoperational stage cannot conserve number.
65. **B** Teachers following a Piagetian model would be much more concerned with developmental level than age level.
66. **B** Scoliosis is a lateral curvature of the spine; a common plumb line can help in an initial screening.
67. **A** The activity with sand and water will not help students learn about volume until they have progressed to the concrete operational stage for volume.
68. **B** The student is having difficulty with place value. The student does not understand that 2 + 9 yields 1 ten and 1 one.

69. **C** This cut and fit activity would clearly show students that the area of the larger square contains about 4 unit squares.

70. **D** Dividing decimals is too symbolically complex to demonstrate with manipulatives.

71. **C** The student gets the whole number portion of the answer correct but then writes the remainder as the decimal.

72. **B** This process will help the student realize that the unlabeled side of the polygon must be included in the perimeter. Subtract 6 – 4 to find that the unlabeled side is 2 units long.

73. **C** Students learn more when a lesson is at their level of ability.

74. **D** It's a good plan because it provides students a break before reading. Reading does not have to be the first subject taught.

75. **D** Unit plans develop a particular subject over time.

76. **D** Manipulatives are invariably the best way to teach a first mathematics lesson to elementary school teachers.

77. **D** Students summarize their own work in the cooperative learning group.

78. **C** Cooperative learning groups are generally no larger than 6.

79. **D** Eye-hand coordination is not fully developed in young children. The activities in choice D will help children develop this skill.

80. **D** Lotus 1-2-3 is an advanced integrated applications package.

WRITTEN ASSIGNMENT

Show your lesson plan to a specialist at the grade level you choose. Ask them to rate your lesson plan 0–3 using this scale.

3 A well developed, complete lesson plan.
Shows a thorough response to all parts of the plan.
Clear objective and lesson plan parts.
A lesson that is free of significant planning errors.

2 A fairly well developed, complete lesson plan.
It may not thoroughly include all parts of an effective plan.
Fairly clear objective and lesson plan parts.
It may contain some significant planning errors.

1 A poorly developed, incomplete lesson plan.
It does not contain most parts of an effective plan.
Contains an unclear objective, poor planning.
It contains some significant planning errors.

0 A very poorly developed, incomplete plan.
It does not contain any elements of an effective plan.
Contains only poor planning.
Contains numerous significant planning errors.

14

PRACTICE ATS-W II (SECONDARY)

This practice test contains the types of items you will encounter on the real test. The distribution of items varies from one test administration to another.

Take this test in a realistic timed setting. You should not take this practice test until you have completed your subject matter review.

The setting will be most realistic if another person times the test and ensures that the test rules are followed. But remember that many people do better on a practice test than on the real test.

You have four hours to complete the multiple-choice items and the written assignment. Keep this time limit in mind as you work. Answer the easier questions first. Be sure you answer all the questions. There is no penalty for guessing. You may write in the test booklet and mark up the questions.

Each multiple-choice item has four answer choices. Exactly one of these choices is correct. Use a pencil to mark your choice on the answer sheet provided for this test.

The written assignment immediately follows the multiple-choice items. Once the test is complete, review the answers and explanations as you correct the answer sheet.

When instructed, turn the page and begin.

ANSWER SHEET PRACTICE ATS-W II (SECONDARY)

1	Ⓐ Ⓑ Ⓒ Ⓓ	21	Ⓐ Ⓑ Ⓒ Ⓓ	41	Ⓐ Ⓑ Ⓒ Ⓓ	61	Ⓐ Ⓑ Ⓒ Ⓓ
2	Ⓐ Ⓑ Ⓒ Ⓓ	22	Ⓐ Ⓑ Ⓒ Ⓓ	42	Ⓐ Ⓑ Ⓒ Ⓓ	62	Ⓐ Ⓑ Ⓒ Ⓓ
3	Ⓐ Ⓑ Ⓒ Ⓓ	23	Ⓐ Ⓑ Ⓒ Ⓓ	43	Ⓐ Ⓑ Ⓒ Ⓓ	63	Ⓐ Ⓑ Ⓒ Ⓓ
4	Ⓐ Ⓑ Ⓒ Ⓓ	24	Ⓐ Ⓑ Ⓒ Ⓓ	44	Ⓐ Ⓑ Ⓒ Ⓓ	64	Ⓐ Ⓑ Ⓒ Ⓓ
5	Ⓐ Ⓑ Ⓒ Ⓓ	25	Ⓐ Ⓑ Ⓒ Ⓓ	45	Ⓐ Ⓑ Ⓒ Ⓓ	65	Ⓐ Ⓑ Ⓒ Ⓓ
6	Ⓐ Ⓑ Ⓒ Ⓓ	26	Ⓐ Ⓑ Ⓒ Ⓓ	46	Ⓐ Ⓑ Ⓒ Ⓓ	66	Ⓐ Ⓑ Ⓒ Ⓓ
7	Ⓐ Ⓑ Ⓒ Ⓓ	27	Ⓐ Ⓑ Ⓒ Ⓓ	47	Ⓐ Ⓑ Ⓒ Ⓓ	67	Ⓐ Ⓑ Ⓒ Ⓓ
8	Ⓐ Ⓑ Ⓒ Ⓓ	28	Ⓐ Ⓑ Ⓒ Ⓓ	48	Ⓐ Ⓑ Ⓒ Ⓓ	68	Ⓐ Ⓑ Ⓒ Ⓓ
9	Ⓐ Ⓑ Ⓒ Ⓓ	29	Ⓐ Ⓑ Ⓒ Ⓓ	49	Ⓐ Ⓑ Ⓒ Ⓓ	69	Ⓐ Ⓑ Ⓒ Ⓓ
10	Ⓐ Ⓑ Ⓒ Ⓓ	30	Ⓐ Ⓑ Ⓒ Ⓓ	50	Ⓐ Ⓑ Ⓒ Ⓓ	70	Ⓐ Ⓑ Ⓒ Ⓓ
11	Ⓐ Ⓑ Ⓒ Ⓓ	31	Ⓐ Ⓑ Ⓒ Ⓓ	51	Ⓐ Ⓑ Ⓒ Ⓓ	71	Ⓐ Ⓑ Ⓒ Ⓓ
12	Ⓐ Ⓑ Ⓒ Ⓓ	32	Ⓐ Ⓑ Ⓒ Ⓓ	52	Ⓐ Ⓑ Ⓒ Ⓓ	72	Ⓐ Ⓑ Ⓒ Ⓓ
13	Ⓐ Ⓑ Ⓒ Ⓓ	33	Ⓐ Ⓑ Ⓒ Ⓓ	53	Ⓐ Ⓑ Ⓒ Ⓓ	73	Ⓐ Ⓑ Ⓒ Ⓓ
14	Ⓐ Ⓑ Ⓒ Ⓓ	34	Ⓐ Ⓑ Ⓒ Ⓓ	54	Ⓐ Ⓑ Ⓒ Ⓓ	74	Ⓐ Ⓑ Ⓒ Ⓓ
15	Ⓐ Ⓑ Ⓒ Ⓓ	35	Ⓐ Ⓑ Ⓒ Ⓓ	55	Ⓐ Ⓑ Ⓒ Ⓓ	75	Ⓐ Ⓑ Ⓒ Ⓓ
16	Ⓐ Ⓑ Ⓒ Ⓓ	36	Ⓐ Ⓑ Ⓒ Ⓓ	56	Ⓐ Ⓑ Ⓒ Ⓓ	76	Ⓐ Ⓑ Ⓒ Ⓓ
17	Ⓐ Ⓑ Ⓒ Ⓓ	37	Ⓐ Ⓑ Ⓒ Ⓓ	57	Ⓐ Ⓑ Ⓒ Ⓓ	77	Ⓐ Ⓑ Ⓒ Ⓓ
18	Ⓐ Ⓑ Ⓒ Ⓓ	38	Ⓐ Ⓑ Ⓒ Ⓓ	58	Ⓐ Ⓑ Ⓒ Ⓓ	78	Ⓐ Ⓑ Ⓒ Ⓓ
19	Ⓐ Ⓑ Ⓒ Ⓓ	39	Ⓐ Ⓑ Ⓒ Ⓓ	59	Ⓐ Ⓑ Ⓒ Ⓓ	79	Ⓐ Ⓑ Ⓒ Ⓓ
20	Ⓐ Ⓑ Ⓒ Ⓓ	40	Ⓐ Ⓑ Ⓒ Ⓓ	60	Ⓐ Ⓑ Ⓒ Ⓓ	80	Ⓐ Ⓑ Ⓒ Ⓓ

Each item on this test includes four answer choices. Select the best choice for each item and mark that letter on the answer sheet.

Use this information for questions 1–4.

While teaching a social studies lesson, a teacher has the students' interest and now wants to maintain their interest. The teacher uses a variety of questions as she teaches and is very interested in changing and reinforcing appropriate student behavior.

1. The teacher has the best chance of maintaining student interest if:
   (A) The teacher is animated.
   (B) The objectives are clear and unambiguous.
   (C) The students understand that what they are learning will help them learn other material later.
   (D) There are no choices available to students.

2. When questioning students, which of the following techniques should the teacher generally follow?
   (A) Make sure students know who will answer a question before it is asked.
   (B) Ask questions of the whole class.
   (C) Ask questions of students who are not paying attention.
   (D) Ask questions of students who usually have the correct answers.

3. Research shows that modeling is one appropriate way of modifying behavior. Which of the following is an example of a good modeling technique?
   (A) Show students how to construct replicas of historic buildings.
   (B) Respond courteously to students' questions.
   (C) Demonstrate students' inappropriate behavior.
   (D) Stress the importance of appearance and show students how to dress.

4. Which of the following would NOT be an appropriate reinforcement of student behavior?
   (A) Grading on the basis of performance
   (B) Praising appropriate behavior
   (C) Explaining that students will lose privileges for poor behavior
   (D) Ignoring inappropriate behavior

Use this information for questions 5–16.

The new eighth grade teacher is in her first month of school. She is having difficulty with discipline and with classroom management. Particular problems seem to arise when she is distributing books and other materials. She does not use a with-it approach to discipline.

While usually quite effective, this teacher can teach in a negative and critical fashion. The teacher does not deal well with parents has had run-ins with them.

At the beginning of the school year the teacher found that a problem student is in her class. Many teachers complain about this student. The teacher leaves school saying, "I better rest up so I'm ready for my problem child." Another teacher in the same situation calls the child's parents to open a line of communication.

5. Her colleague tells the teacher, "Don't take it personally," about the misbehavior of students in her class. Why is this good advice?
   (A) Because the teacher doesn't need to change.
   (B) Because most eighth graders are unmanageable.
   (C) Because students' misbehavior results from students' needs.
   (D) Because the teacher must be more authoritative and not so concerned about students.

6. Which of the following would educators generally agree is the best strategy for this teacher to follow when placing or distributing books and supplies in a classroom?
   (A) Use group monitors to pass them out.
   (B) Have students line up alphabetically at the teacher's desk.
   (C) Place books and supplies available at several locations around the room.
   (D) Place needed books and materials in each student's desk before school.

7. In order to be an effective classroom leader, this teacher should:
   (A) Set up a series of firm, precise rules that students should memorize.
   (B) Make sure peer leaders know the teacher is in charge, not them.
   (C) Discourage cooperative learning experiences.
   (D) Promote competition among class members.

8. It would NOT be appropriate for this teacher to respond to which of the following questions asked by a parent?
   (A) Please show me a folder of my child's work and point out areas of needed remediation.
   (B) Please show me a folder of my child's work and point out areas of possible acceleration.
   (C) Please show me a report of individual student's test scores so that I can tell how my child is doing.
   (D) Please show me how my child is doing compared to the average class performance.

9. Which of the following is LEAST likely to promote good communication with parents?
   (A) Make phone calls to parents.
   (B) Write personal notes on report cards.
   (C) Initiate a series of home/school letters.
   (D) Meet with groups of parents to discuss individual student achievement.

10. As an effective classroom manager, this teacher should take steps to ensure that the majority of class time is devoted to:
    (A) individual work
    (B) on-task activities
    (C) lecturing
    (D) group work

11. Which of the following best describes the discipline approach of "with-it-ness" described on page 429?
    (A) A teacher is always aware of new disciplinary techniques.
    (B) A teacher is always aware of current popular trends among students
    (C) A teacher is always aware of what is happening in the classroom
    (D) A teacher is well respected by other teachers.

12. The critical approach mentioned on page 429 compared to a more positive uncritical approach, will generally result in the following:
    (A) More learning will take place.
    (B) Less learning will take place.
    (C) More homework assignments will be given.
    (D) More parental involvement will take place.

13. The teacher plans to present a lesson using the lecture approach. Which of the following is most likely to enhance instruction?
    (A) The lesson begins with a motivation.
    (B) The teacher focuses on the whole class and avoids making eye contact with individual students.
    (C) The teacher walks around the room while delivering the lecture.
    (D) The teacher chooses a topic above the student's ability level.

14. Which of the following best summarizes the description about two different teacher reactions upon learning that a problem child is in the class?
(A) This is an example of proactive vs. reactive teachers. The teacher is proactive; the other teacher is reactive.
(B) This is an example of proactive vs. reactive teachers. The teacher is reactive, the other teacher is proactive.
(C) This is an example of one teacher knowing the parents and the other teacher not knowing the parents.
(D) This is an example of two proactive teachers with different styles.

15. This teacher will find that discipline in eighth grade is particularly difficult because
(A) students are reaching puberty.
(B) students are peer oriented.
(C) teachers are subject oriented.
(D) teachers are authority figures.

16. If the teacher were teaching high school seniors, she would find that discipline is less difficult than in eighth grade because
(A) it is left to the administration.
(B) it is the parent's concern.
(C) students are less resistant.
(D) teachers are less authoritative.

17. When it comes to getting along in the school, the teacher's colleagues say that a school is a society in itself. This means that:
(A) all races, creeds, and ethnic backgrounds will be represented in a school.
(B) the school reflects the larger community.
(C) students in the school reflect the society in particular and the country as a whole.
(D) it has its own structure of formal and informal relationships, character, and practices.

18. A child is developing within normal parameters in eighth grade. According to Erikson's theory of psychosocial development, what primary emotional crisis is the child experiencing?
(A) Intimacy vs. isolation
(B) Initiative vs. guilt
(C) Industry vs. inferiority
(D) Identity vs. Identity confusion

19. Students are upset about a school board decision to cancel the senior prom. Students can show their displeasure with this decision without the possibility of legal interference from school officials by
(A) Publishing editorials in the school newspaper.
(B) Wearing large buttons that say "PROM POWER" while in school.
(C) Refusing to attend classes.
(D) Placing advertisements in the school newspaper.

20. Which of the following educational practices best reflects B. F. Skinner's model of learning?
(A) Active involvement of students in learning.
(B) Token reinforcement of student's success.
(C) Problem solving as the central focus of instruction.
(D) Manipulative materials to help students learn.

21. A teacher and student are discussing the student's most recent report card. The teacher explains that the student's grades would have been better if all homework assignments were handed in. This teacher is using
(A) threats
(B) positive reinforcement
(C) reverse psychology
(D) negative reinforcement

Use this information for questions 22–26.

A group of high school teachers are meeting with a school psychologist and a social worker to discuss some of their students' problems. One common problem is drug and alcohol abuse, and the teachers report that a number of their students also discuss this problem. One teacher reports that a senior honestly discussed her sexual abuse as a child. The student did not identify who the abuser was.

Other teachers reported that a large number of their students have dropped out of school or are thinking about dropping out of school. During the meeting the group also discussed students with problems and whether or not these students would benefit from an alternative learning environment.

22. Health professionals know that the abuser discussed by the student is most likely
   (A) a teacher or coach
   (B) a relative or family member
   (C) a convicted sexual abuser
   (D) a stranger

23. Which of the following would not be an appropriate intervention for a teacher to use when alcohol abuse, drug use, or child abuse is suspected?
   (A) Go through a student's locker because the student smelled of alcohol.
   (B) Pay particular attention to principles of classroom management.
   (C) Provide awareness programs that focus on drug and alcohol use.
   (D) Report suspected child abuse to proper authorities.

24. Which of the following would most researchers agree represents the percent of students who have used illegal drugs, other than alcohol, before they graduate from this high school?
   (A) 85%
   (B) 70%
   (C) 55%
   (D) 40%

25. Which of the following problems of an adolescent student would probably not be helped by an alternative learning environment?
   (A) Drug abuse
   (B) Alcohol abuse
   (C) Child abuse
   (D) High drop out rates

26. Professional research shows that the most effective way to prevent students from dropping out of school is to
   (A) show a movie describing what happens when a student drops out of school.
   (B) provide students with a list of national statistics on dropouts.
   (C) provide positive support and alternative learning environments.
   (D) provide for parent conferences to discuss keeping students in school.

27. Punishment can be an effective way to change students' behavior when:
   (A) The whole class is involved.
   (B) It involves pertinent extra work.
   (C) It is used for limited and specific reasons.
   (D) It makes the teacher feel better.

28. The school technology committee is listing, in order, the following technological resources according to their importance for school interaction. Which of the resources is at the bottom of their list?
   (A) a CD-ROM player
   (B) a microcomputer
   (C) a graphing calculator
   (D) a minicomputer

29. All the following teacher actions are appropriate examples of cueing EXCEPT
    (A) flickering the lights quickly.
    (B) glancing directly at a student.
    (C) holding up your arm.
    (D) snapping your fingers before asking a question.

Use this information for questions 30–37.

The high school principal called a faculty meeting at the beginning of the school year. The meeting agenda is shown below.

AGENDA
1. *Teacher rights and responsibilities*
2. *Quality schools*
3. *Families in transition*
4. *Board of Education role and responsibility*

During the meeting, the principal asks questions and poses situations about these agenda items.

30. Which of the following describes free speech that a teacher is entitled to exercise?
    (A) Criticizing the decisions of the school board and superintendent in a letter published by a local newspaper
    (B) Disclosing a student's confidential school records to help the student get educational services
    (C) Organizing rallies during school hours that disrupt the school
    (D) Making statements away from school that interfere with teaching performance

31. Teachers enjoy a number of employment related rights including
    (A) immunity from civil suits for job related activities.
    (B) academic freedom to teach what they wish.
    (C) the freedom to associate out of school with any group.
    (D) immunity from dismissal once tenured.

32. Court cases concerning books in school libraries have generally shown that
    (A) schools may not remove books from school libraries.
    (B) parents can prevent school boards from removing books from school libraries.
    (C) individual teachers may prevent their students from reading books in school libraries.
    (D) books may not be removed from school libraries solely because a school official disagrees with its content.

33. Research states characteristics of effective schools include all the following EXCEPT
    (A) a climate of high expectations.
    (B) a high proportion of instructional time spent on task.
    (C) strong and effective leadership.
    (D) eliminating standardized tests.

34. Responsibilities usually attributed to local school boards do NOT include
    (A) employing necessary faculty and staff and designate their responsibilities.
    (B) maintaining school buildings and grounds.
    (C) assigning pupils to schools and control their conduct.
    (D) arranging tuition reimbursement for students who attend nonpublic schools.

35. Which of the groups listed below has overall legal responsibility for education?
    (A) the federal government
    (B) the state government
    (C) local town government
    (D) local school administration

36. Generally speaking, the factor that creates the largest difference in the quality of individual schools is
    (A) teachers' knowledge.
    (B) class size.
    (C) parent/teacher communication.
    (D) the students' SES status.

37. Which of the following statements about the American family is most accurate?
    (A) Less than 30 percent of mothers with children go to work.
    (B) Over 60 percent of married couples have no children.
    (C) Less than 10 percent of American families have children, a mother at home, and a father who goes to work.
    (D) About 30 percent of American families live below the poverty level.

---

38. Which of the following would be the best choice for a formative evaluation of students' writing?
    (A) The Test of Standard Written English
    (B) A portfolio of each student's writing samples
    (C) Iowa Test of Basic Skills
    (D) End of Unit test

39. Which of the following is the LEAST appropriate source of instructional goals and objectives?
    (A) National professional organizations
    (B) Commercial textbooks
    (C) Parents
    (D) School district objectives

Use this information for questions 40–49.

The science teacher is planning a lesson. The teacher plans to begin the lesson by saying, "OK class, today we're going to learn about photosynthesis." The teacher wants to model photosynthesis for the students. She plans to write prerequisite competencies for the lesson on the board. The teacher plans to use an inquiry approach and wants to motivate the students as much as possible.

The teacher plans to give the students activities that will lead them to discover a concept and will ask a number of questions during the lesson. The teacher will end the lesson with an end of chapter test from the teacher's edition of the science text.

40. Which of the following is most consistent with the inquiry approach?
    (A) The teacher deliberately does not try out the experiment in advance.
    (B) The teacher tells the students to avoid analyzing their thought processes.
    (C) The teacher presents a problem to be solved or a situation to explore.
    (D) The students present a problem to be solved or a situation to explore.

41. In all likelihood, the test the teacher will give is a
    (A) formative evaluation.
    (B) standardized test.
    (C) norm referenced test.
    (D) summative evaluation.

42. Which of the following best describes a prerequisite competency?
    (A) The knowledge and skills a teacher must possess to teach an objective
    (B) A subobjective to the main objective of the lesson
    (C) The basis for admitting students when they transfer from another school district
    (D) The knowledge and skills students must possess to learn an objective

43. The type of statement the teacher plans to make at the beginning of the lesson is referred to as
    (A) an anticipatory set.
    (B) an advanced organizer.
    (C) a motivation.
    (D) a objective.

44. Which of the following describes a teacher modeling a skill for students?
    (A) The teacher demonstrates phases of photosynthesis on a drawing of a plant.
    (B) The teacher acts out a phase of photosynthesis.
    (C) The teacher points out phases of photosynthesis on a model of a plant.
    (D) The teacher asks students to draw a diagram of photosynthesis.

45. Which is the best strategy for the teacher to follow once she has asked a question?
    (A) Call on a student immediately and expect a quick answer.
    (B) Call on a student before the question and expect a quick answer.
    (C) Pause before calling on a student and expect a quick answer.
    (D) Pause before calling on a student and give 4 or 5 seconds to answer.

46. Using Bloom's Taxonomy of Educational Objectives as a guide, which of the following descriptions of question types is generally appropriate for classroom instruction?
    (A) Ask questions calling for analysis and synthesis.
    (B) Ask questions calling for knowledge and comprehension.
    (C) Questions should be asked at all levels.
    (D) Ask rhetorical questions.

47. Approximately what percent of questions should a teacher intend to be answered correctly?
    (A) 100%
    (B) 85%
    (C) 70%
    (D) 55%

48. Which of the following best describes the discovery approach to teaching?
    (A) deductive
    (B) skill
    (C) concrete
    (D) inductive

49. According to researchers, which of the following is the most powerful overall motivation this teacher could use?
    (A) praise
    (B) grades
    (C) privileges
    (D) learning

Use this information for questions 50–55.

A department supervisor is reviewing the testing and assessment results for classes in his department. The supervisor uses a standardized test with high reliability to measure achievement in department classes. Students' average normed scores are significantly lower in his department than the average normed scores from comparable departments in districts with the same socioeconomic status.

The supervisor knows that scores on the PSAT (Preliminary Scholastic Achievement Test) are used to determine which high school students receive Merit Scholarships. He is concerned about the impact of these test scores on students in the school.

The supervisor also wants teachers in his department to use authentic assessment, and wonders what changes in assessment approaches he can recommend.

50. What do we know about the standardized test from the description given above?
    (A) The test is shipped on time.
    (B) The test is consistent.
    (C) The test predicts success in college.
    (D) The test can be used repeatedly without fear of cheating.

51. What action, if any, is indicated by the average normed scores reported above?
    (A) No action. The average normed scores are about where they should be.
    (B) The mathematics curriculum and teaching methods should be evaluated.
    (C) The NCTM standards should be reviewed.
    (D) The test company should be contacted and told not to use average scores.

52. Overall, the supervisor knows that
    (A) college success correlates more significantly with PSAT scores than with high school grades.
    (B) the PSAT score is just like an IQ score.
    (C) the PSAT is a projective test.
    (D) girls score lower on the PSAT and boys get more Merit Scholarships.

53. Which factor below will correlate most significantly with overall student achievement in this supervisor's department?
    (A) Socioeconomic status
    (B) Intelligence
    (C) Cooperativeness
    (D) Motivation

54. Which of the following could the supervisor recommend to teachers as a way to implement authentic assessment?
    (A) Collect and evaluate student work.
    (B) Use a standardized test.
    (C) Use only tests that have been authenticated.
    (D) Collect evaluative information from other teachers.

55. The supervisor receives results of a norm-referenced test that indicate that a student has an IQ of 97, leading the teacher to the conclusion that:
    (A) The student has below average intelligence.
    (B) The student's intelligence is in the normal range.
    (C) The student is mildly retarded.
    (D) The standard deviation of the test is 3.

56. Which of the following best characterizes an instructional objective?
    (A) It describes how the teacher will teach the class.
    (B) It describes the average achievement for all students at a grade level.
    (C) It describes the books and materials to be used to teach a lesson.
    (D) It describes what a student should know or be able to do.

57. Class management is most difficult during:
    (A) grades 1–3
    (B) grades 4–6
    (C) grades 7–10
    (D) grades 11–12

Use this information for questions 58–64.

You are teaching a class that is culturally and linguistically diverse. Many of the students in your class have a first language other than English, and many come from homes where English is not spoken. You know that the minority students in your class, as a whole, tend to have lower achievement scores than other students.

You want to familiarize yourself with the difficulties these children have and with the teaching approaches that will be effective in this classroom.

58. The data about the achievement of minority students leads you to the valid conclusion that:
(A) Minority students are less capable learners than other students are.
(B) The parents of minority students care less about their children's education.
(C) Learning expectations should be lowered for minority students.
(D) Minority students have fewer opportunities for enriched learning experiences at home.

59. Which of the following describes an acceptable approach to modifying the objectives or plans for this class?
(A) Modify the plans to teach the class in the foreign language.
(B) Modify the objective to reduce its difficulty level.
(C) Modify the plans to include instruction in English.
(D) Modify the plans to focus on the cultural heritage of those in the class.

60. Which of the following is consistent with you using an ESL approach with a group of LEP students from the class?
(A) Use context clues to help students identify English words.
(B) Teach mathematics in the student's first language.
(C) Help students learn their native language.
(D) Encourage regional and local dialects.

61. Which of the following best depicts the way in which schools have reacted to America's multiethnic and multicultural society?
(A) The academic atmosphere of our schools is not affected by the ethnic and cultural backgrounds of the students.
(B) Recent immigrant groups are accustomed to the academic atmosphere of American schools.
(C) There is no longer a need for schools to deal with the cultural differences of students.
(D) The schools have noted a shift toward cultural pluralism.

62. If you were preparing to conduct a workshop on the changing American family which of the following would be helpful for the workshop organizer to keep in mind?
(A) Families are no longer the predominant influence in the early lives of children.
(B) The nature of the American family has changed for the better.
(C) Schools have no influence on children's values.
(D) School programs developed for these students cannot replace effective parenting.

63. You could help the students in your class who are having difficulty in school by all of the following EXCEPT:
(A) Providing a quiet place to work
(B) Providing exceptions to classroom rules
(C) Providing a flexible schedule
(D) Providing a warm, supportive atmosphere

64. Which of the following is an appropriate alteration to make in your curriculum to accommodate the needs of the recent immigrants in your class?
    (A) Lower the expectations for the group.
    (B) Limit the amount of homework given.
    (C) Teach in the native language.
    (D) Require proficiency in English before students can enter school.

65. Which of the following would generally be the most valid grounds for a teacher's suit against a school district?
    (A) Not granting tenure to a teacher who is pregnant
    (B) Firing a nontenured black female without providing a specific reason
    (C) Firing a tenured white male with more experience than a black male teacher who was not fired
    (D) Actively recruiting black and Hispanic faculty to the exclusion of white faculty members

Use this information for questions 66–74.

A secondary English teacher is planning a class and wants to assess the students' understanding of a lesson while the lesson is underway. The teacher is trying to decide whether to teach a moderate amount or a lot of information and whether to teach below, at, or above the grade level.

The students in the English classes are able students from a lower socioeconomic status. These students are poor children, largely from single-parent families where no one in the family has graduated from high school.

66. Which of the following is an effective instructional strategy for this class?
    (A) Do not be too encouraging.
    (B) Lower learning expectations.
    (C) Deemphasize mastery of the material.
    (D) Provide a structured learning environment.

67. Which of the following most accurately characterizes how the teacher could conduct the desired assessment?
    (A) The teacher should use a standardized test.
    (B) The teacher should observe students during the lesson.
    (C) The teacher should devise and write a quiz for students to complete.
    (D) The teacher should use a test from a textbook publisher.

68. Which of the following activities by a teacher best describes extrinsic motivation?
    (A) Discuss the book *20,000 Leagues Under the Sea*.
    (B) Identify similarities in young children's shoes.
    (C) Discuss the Federal Reserve Bank.
    (D) Identify the points students can earn for participation.

69. When completing an assignment, most successful learning takes place when
    (A) students work independently in school.
    (B) students work independently at home.
    (C) students work in school, supervised by the teacher.
    (D) students do their work on a computer.

70. In response to the teacher's concern about the amount and type of material to teach, which of the following is most likely to result in the most learning?
    (A) Teach moderately above students' grade level.
    (B) Teach moderately below students' grade level.
    (C) Teach moderately at students' grade level.
    (D) Teach a lot of the material at students' grade level.

71. Which of the following activities would engage the student at the highest level of the Taxonomy of Educational Objectives: Cognitive Domain?
(A) Evaluate a book.
(B) Understand a reading passage.
(C) Analyze a written paragraph.
(D) Apply a mathematics formula to a real situation.

72. The teacher is considering four different approaches to mastery and instructional time. Which approach is most likely to result in successful learning?
(A) Expect mastery—use all available time to learn activities.
(B) Expect mastery—use much of the time to discuss feelings.
(C) Don't expect mastery—use all available time to learn activities.
(D) Don't expect masters—use much time for learning activities.

73. Which of the several guidelines below should teachers usually follow when asking questions?
(A) Ask complete questions.
(B) Address questions to individual students.
(C) Ask difficult questions to challenge students.
(D) Address questions to the entire class.

74. A teacher presents an abstract overview of an English topic before teaching the topic to the class. This teacher is using an approach called
(A) anticipatory set
(B) metacognition
(C) inquiry learning
(D) cognitive dissonance

Use this information for questions 75–77.

Many high school teachers in the district find that they have special education students in their classes. These teachers must be aware of the privacy requirements. These teachers must plan lessons based on the student's IEP and must often work with a special education teacher in their classroom.

75. Which of the following is in compliance with federal privacy requirements for confidential records of minor children?
(A) Allow a father who does not have child custody to see his child's confidential school records.
(B) Refuse to let an unrelated legal guardian see the child's confidential records.
(C) Refuse a parent's request to show the child his or her own confidential records.
(D) Inform parents they have no right to see their child's records without the child's permission.

76. Which of the following is the most appropriate action for a special education teacher to take when planning a lesson for students "mainstreamed" under PL 94-142?
(A) Prepare alternative plans for the entire class.
(B) Modify the objective for the special education student.
(C) Prepare alternative plans for the special education student.
(D) Modify plans so that the classroom teacher does not have to work with the special education student.

77. A special education teacher is working with a classroom teacher in a class that includes mainstreamed students. Which of the following best describes the special education teacher's role in the classroom?
(A) Observe the mainstreamed students to identify the out of class support they need.
(B) Teach the entire class cooperatively with the teacher.
(C) Help the mainstreamed students during the teacher's lesson.
(D) Observe the nonmainstreamed students to get tips on their successful learning styles to pass on to the special education students.

---

78. At a "Back-to-School Night" the teacher displays student work and tells parents that it is not a conference time. One parent corners the teacher and asks about her child's progress. Which of the following is the most professional response the teacher could make?
(A) Say, "I'm sorry I am not prepared to discuss your child's progress with others here."
(B) Say, "When would you like to meet to discuss your concerns?"
(C) Say, "Would you please call the office to arrange a conference time?"
(D) Answer the parent's questions as quickly and quietly as possible.

79. Behaviorism was the first significant theory of learning. Which of the following methods would be supported most strongly by behaviorists?
(A) cooperative learning
(B) inductive teaching
(C) practice
(D) inquiry learning

80. Eriksen's stages of psychosocial development describe
(A) the emotional crisis that, when resolved, leads to further development.
(B) Freud's stages of development in more detail.
(C) stages of cognitive development for males and for females.
(D) the social skills needed to be successful at each level of schooling.

WRITTEN ASSIGNMENT

Write an essay on the topic below. Use the lined pages that follow. Write your essay on this topic only. An essay on another topic will be rated Unscorable (U).

Assignment

It used to be that technology was limited to computer classes and business classes. Today, technology is used throughout the curriculum. Choose a secondary subject matter area such as mathematics, history, or English. Write an essay that describes how you would use technology to teach the secondary subject area you have chosen.

PRACTICE ATS-W II (SECONDARY)

Answer Key

1. B	11. C	21. D	31. C	41. D	51. B	61. D	71. A
2. B	12. B	22. B	32. D	42. D	52. D	62. D	72. A
3. B	13. A	23. A	33. D	43. A	53. A	63. B	73. D
4. D	14. B	24. B	34. D	44. B	54. A	64. B	74. D
5. C	15. B	25. C	35. B	45. D	55. B	65. C	75. A
6. C	16. C	26. C	36. D	46. C	56. D	66. D	76. C
7. B	17. D	27. C	37. C	47. C	57. C	67. B	77. C
8. C	18. D	28. D	38. B	48. D	58. D	68. D	78. B
9. D	19. B	29. D	39. C	49. B	59. D	69. C	79. C
10. B	20. B	30. A	40. C	50. B	60. A	70. D	80. A

PRACTICE ATS-W II (SECONDARY)

Explained Answers

1. **B** Research shows that clear and unambiguous objectives is crucial to maintaining students' interest. All of the other choices are either ineffective or not as effective as choice (B).

2. **B** Generally speaking, questions should be addressed to the entire class. The other choices represent inappropriate questioning techniques.

3. **B** Students often emulate behavior they observe in the teacher. A teacher should try to act in a way that he or she wants students to act.

4. **D** All of the other choices describe appropriate reinforcement techniques. Choice C describes negative reinforcement.

5. **C** Students usually misbehave because of who they are.

6. **C** This technique reduces administrative and behavior problems.

7. **B** Peer leaders can interfere with a teacher's effectiveness.

8. **C** A parent has no right to see other students' test scores.

9. **D** There is no reason to discuss individual test scores with groups of parents.

10. **B** Research shows that students learn more when they spend more time on task.

11. **C** This choice is Kounin's definition of "with-it-ness."

12. **B** Research shows that students learn less when teachers are negative and critical.

13. **A** Research shows that this factor, when compared to the other listed factors, is most likely to enhance instruction.

14. **B** The teacher is proactive. Generally speaking, proactive teachers are the best classroom managers.

15. **B** During junior high school and the first years of high school students follow peer leaders.

16. **C** By the last two years of high school, students are less resistant to adult authority.

17. **D** The school has its own society that must be appreciated and "mastered" by beginning teachers.

18. **D** Eriksen describes stages as emotional crises that can have a positive or a negative result. Identity vs. isolation is the crisis most commonly encountered in eighth grade.

19. **B** School officials cannot interfere when students use inoffensive speech, which includes spoken words and symbols or words displayed on their person. School officials can "censor" school papers.

20. **B** Skinner's model of operant conditioning features reinforcement.

21. **D** Negative reinforcement means explaining how to avoid negative consequences.

22. **B** Most abused children are abused by a relative or family member.

23. **A** A teacher should never search students' lockers.

24. **B** Research indicates that about 70 percent of high school students use illegal drugs other than alcohol. This percentage soars when alcohol, an illegal drug for most high school students, is included.

25. **C** The emotional problems caused by child abuse do not respond to an alternative learning environment.

26. **C** Students don't drop out when the schools find some way to keep them interested in school.

27. **C** Punishment is an ineffective way to change students' behavior unless used for very limited and specific reasons.

28. **D** A minicomputer is an extremely powerful computer used primarily by those in the scientific and financial community.

29. **D** Cueing is a device to alert students that something will happen in the next five or ten minutes.

30. **A** Teachers are permitted to criticize school board members and school officials. However, teachers are not permitted to disrupt the school or to engage in the activities described in the other choices.

31. **C** Teachers have freedom of association but the other choices are not teachers' rights.

32. **D** School boards have the right to remove books from school libraries, but the decision cannot be based on a school official or board member disagreeing with the book's content.

33. **D** Standardized tests are used in effective schools.

34. **D** This is not usually a responsibility of local school boards.

35. **B** This responsibility belongs to the states under the Constitution of the United States because the Constitution does not assign this responsibility to the federal government.

36. **D** Research consistently shows that SES correlates most significantly with the quality of an individual school.

37. **C** What used to be the traditional American family now represents less than 10 percent of all families.

38. **B** A sample of the students' writing best enables the teacher to plan future lessons for that student.

39. **C** While parents should participate in schools, they are the least appropriate source of instructional goals from among the choices given.

40. **C** This choice describes the essence of the inquiry approach while the other choices would be inappropriate when using this approach.

41. **D** The test is most likely designed to indicate what students learned about the chapter.

42. **D** A prerequisite competency refers to some skill or ability students must possess to learn an objective.

43. **A** An anticipatory set makes the student aware of the lesson's content. An advanced organizer is an initial abstract discussion of the lesson's content.

44. **B** A teacher models something when he or she actually does it.

45. **D** A teacher should pause before calling on a student and then give a student 4 or 5 seconds to respond.

46. **C** The teacher should ask questions at all levels of the taxonomy.

47. **C** A teacher should ask questions that will be answered correctly about 70 percent of the time.

48. **D** Inductive teaching leads students to discover concepts by leading them from examples to a generalization.

49. **B** Grades remain the main motivation for students to work in school.

50. **B** Reliability means that a test is consistent. It will yield about the same results when given to the same person at different times.

51. **B** Scores significantly lower than those from comparable schools require an evaluation of the curriculum and methods.

52. **D** The PSAT discriminates against women and, as a result, more scholarships go to men.

53. **A** This one factor consistently correlates highest with achievement.

54. **A** Authentic assessment means that teachers observe students or review examples of students' work.

55. **B** IQ scores have a standard deviation of 10 and scores from 90 to 110 are considered in the normal range.

56. **D** Objectives should describe learning outcomes.

57. **C** Class management is most difficult during these years because students reject adult authority.

58. **D** Minority students as a whole are not less capable, but as a group they do have fewer home learning opportunities, which leads to lower achievement scores. All the other choices are false.

59. **D** It is appropriate to alter the objectives or plans to focus on the cultural heritage of those in the class.

60. **A** ESL means English as a second language. This approach encourages the use of English.

61. **D** The cultural identities of students have become more pronounced.

62. **D** The family continues to be the most important influence in the lives of children.

63. **B** A student will not be helped by being allowed to ignore classroom rules.

64. **B** Children from immigrant families will often not benefit from extensive homework because help is usually not available from parents.

65. **C** "Reverse discrimination" is allowable when hiring teachers but not when firing teachers.

66. **D** All other choices are ineffective instructional strategies for these students.

67. **B** Observation of students as they work is the best way to tell how they are doing.

68. **D** Extrinsic motivation is a reward. Choices A, B, and perhaps C could be intrinsic motivations.

69. **C** Students learn more when a teacher supervises work on assignments.

70. **D** Students learn more when they are taught more and when taught at their level.

71. **A** Evaluation is the highest level in this taxonomy.

72. **A** Research shows that students learn most when mastery is expected and all available time is devoted to learning activities.

73. **D** Questions should almost always be directed to the entire class.

74. **D** The approach describes an advanced organizer. An anticipatory set alerts students to a lesson's content.

75. **A** Natural parents have the right to see a child's records.

76. **C** The special education teacher's responsibility is to prepare alternative plans to help the student learn the stated objective.

77. **C** This choice accurately describes why the special education teacher is in the classroom.

78. **B** This nonconfrontational response furthers the teacher's goals.

79. **C** Behaviorists believe that humans learn through practice.

80. **A** This choice accurately summarizes Eriksen's stages.

WRITTEN ASSIGNMENT

Show your essay to an English professor or a high school English teacher. Ask them to rate your essay 0–3 using this scale.

3   A well developed, complete written assignment.
Shows a thorough response to all parts of the topic.
Clear explanations that are well supported.
An assignment that is free of significant grammatical, punctuation, or spelling errors.

2   A fairly well developed, complete written assignment.
It may not thoroughly respond to all parts of the topic.
Fairly clear explanations that may not be well supported.
It may contain some significant grammatical, punctuation, or spelling errors.

1   A poorly developed, incomplete written assignment.
It does not thoroughly respond to most parts of the topic.
Contains many poor explanations that are not well supported.
It may contain some significant grammatical, punctuation, or spelling errors.

0   A very poorly developed, incomplete written assignment.
It does not thoroughly respond to the topic.
Contains only poor, unsupported explanations.
Contains numerous significant grammatical, punctuation, or spelling errors.

PART V

Beginning a Career in Teaching

15 GETTING CERTIFIED IN NEW YORK

New York State Office of Teaching
Cultural Education Center
Albany, New York 12230
(518) 474-3901
(TTY for the deaf: In New York 1-800-622-1220 - Out of New York 1-800-855-2880)

Web address: www.nysed.gov/tcert/homepage.htm
E-mail address: tcert@mail.nysed.gov

This chapter explains how to get certified in New York. The Teacher Certification web page contains complete information about New York State teacher certification. Check the web page frequently for changes in certification regulations.

To obtain a teacher certification application or to get more information about teacher certification you may call the Office of Teaching at the automated information number given above. Access to Office of Teaching representatives is limited. You may also write to the Office of Teaching at the mail or e-mail address given above.

This chapter lists colleges in New York State with approved teacher certification programs.

CERTIFICATION SUMMARY

New York State offers teacher certificates in many different areas. This summary describes the most common certification requirements. More detailed certification requirements are given in the chapter.

New York offers two primary certificate types—provisional and permanent.

Provisional certificates generally require an undergraduate degree, required education courses, student teaching, and passing scores on the LAST and the ATS-W.

Provisional certificates may be obtained by completing an approved teacher certification program at a New York college, by applying directly to the New York State Education Department, through the Interstate Certification Compact or the Northeast Regional Credential. The easiest method is to complete an approved teacher certification program.

Permanent certificates generally require a provisional certificate, a related graduate degree, two years of teaching experience, a passing score on the related CST and passing the video evaluation for the ATS-P.

REQUIREMENTS AND PROCEDURES

FORMS OF CERTIFICATION

There are three forms of certification:

Certificate of Qualification (CQ): The New York Department of Education no longer issues a Certificate of Qualification. This means that you may have less time than in the past to get a permanent certificate. Check with your education advisor to discuss the implication of this action.

Provisional Certificate: This credential enables the holder to provide professional service in keeping with the certificate's title. It is valid for five years and is renewable once for a five year period in accordance with criteria specified in Commissioner's Regulations. The certificate notes that the holder is responsible for knowing the conditions necessary to make the certificate permanent.

Permanent Certificate: This credential is valid for the life of the holder unless annulled for cause. It is issued upon completion, typically, of a master's degree in a field of study functionally related to the subject of the provisional certificate, two years of teaching experience or an academic year supervised internship, and the achievement of qualifying scores on the required assessments.

WAYS TO OBTAIN CERTIFICATION

There are four ways to obtain teacher certification.

We strongly recommend that you try to obtain your teaching certificate through an approved program at a college or university. The approved program route is the most direct and the most trouble free certification route.

Approved Program

A person may complete a teacher education program in a New York college or university and be recommended for a certificate provided that program has been registered by the State Department of Education as leading to the designated certificate. There are more than 2,000 individual programs of preparation in New York. Programs in colleges and universities must give consideration to the certification requirements.

Direct Application

An individual may submit an application, official transcripts of all collegiate study and test scores to the Department. These materials are evaluated in accordance with the pertinent Regulations. If the applicant's preparation, test scores, and moral character satisfy the requirements, the appropriate certificate is issued. If there are deficiencies, the applicant is so informed. This evaluation process for most certification areas is also available through the regional certification offices maintained in the majority of Boards of Cooperative Educational Services; but certificates are issued only by the State Education Department.

Interstate Certification

New York has interstate contracts with 34 other states and jurisdictions. A person prepared in one of the contract states who meets the conditions of the contract is eligible for provisional certification in New York. The conditions are either (1) completion of an approved program of teacher preparation or (2) possession of a valid certificate in the contract state and service under that certificate in three of the most recent seven years.

Northeast Regional Credential

New York is a member of the Northeast Common Market. A person holding a valid certificate in any member jurisdiction may be issued a Northeast Regional Credential, which will authorize that individual's employment in the "receiving" state for a period of two years at the end of which the individual must qualify for a regular state certificate. All applicants for their first New York certificate must obtain a qualifying score(s) on either the NTE Core Battery tests, published and administered by Educational Testing Service, or the New York State Teacher Certification Examinations, developed and administered by National Evaluation Systems.

HOW TO APPLY FOR CERTIFICATION

If you are completing an approved program, your college or university will help you apply for certification. If you are not completing an approved program you need an individual evaluation. Submit the materials described below.

You must submit these documents to begin the certification process.

- a completed certification application with the current application fee
- official transcripts from all your colleges

You must submit these documents before you can obtain teacher certification.

- verification that you completed approved training for identifying and reporting child abuse
- verification of completed testing requirements
- copies of any valid teaching certificates
- affidavit of good moral character

CERTIFICATION TITLES

The titles of the teaching certificates issued by New York are given below.

Certificates for Teaching Common Branch Subjects in the Lower and Upper Elementary Grades:

- PreK–6

- Early childhood annotation

Instruction in Academic Subjects in early secondary grades extension

- English 7–9

- Mathematics 7–9

- General Science 7–9

- Social Studies 7–9

- Language Other Than English 7–9
  (various titles)

Certificates for Teaching Academic Subjects in Grades 7–12

- English 7–12

- Mathematics 7–12

- Social Studies 7–12

- Language Other Than English 7–12
  (various titles)

- Biology 7–12

- Chemistry 7–12

- Physics 7–12

- Earth Science 7–12

Extension Certificates to basic academic subjects certificates

- General Science 7–9 Extension

- Extension to Teach a Language Other Than English in the Elementary Grades (K–6)

- Extension for Instruction in an Academic Subject in the upper elementary grades (5–6)

Certificates for Teaching Special Subjects (PreK–12)

- Art

- Business and Distributive Education

- Dance

- Home Economics

- Health

- Music

- Physical Education

- Recreation

- Speech

- Technology Education

Certificate for Teaching Reading

Certificates for Teaching in Special Education Programs (PreK–12)

- Special Education

- Deaf and Hearing Impaired

- Blind and Partially Sighted

- Speech and Hearing Handicapped

Certificates for School Media Programs (PreK–12)

- School Media Specialist (Library)

- School Media Specialist (Educational Communications)

- School Media Specialist

Certificates for Pupil Personnel Services (PreK–12)

- School Attendance Teacher

- School Dental Hygiene Teacher

- School Nurse-Teacher

- School Counselor

- School Psychologist

- School Social Worker

Certificates for Administrative and Supervisory Service (PreK–12)

- School District Administrative

- School Administrator and Supervisor

- School Business Administrator

Certificate for Teaching English to Speakers of Other Languages (PreK–12)

Extension Certificates for Teaching Bilingual Education

- Bilingual (elementary)

- Bilingual (not elementary)

- Bilingual (PPS/Administrative)

Certificates for Teaching Occupational Subjects

- Agriculture

- Business and Distributive Education

- Home Economics

- Health Occupations

- Technical Subjects (See addendum for specific titles)

- Trade Subjects (See addendum for specific titles)

COLLEGES AND UNIVERSITIES WITH APPROVED TEACHER CERTIFICATION PROGRAMS

The following is a partial list of New York colleges offering state approved teacher certification programs. Read the college catalog and check with the college's education department to be sure that a program is state approved before you begin.

COLLEGE	ADDRESS	PHONE
Adelphi University	Box 701 Garden City, NY 11530	516-877-3462
Alfred University	P.O. Box 786 Alfred, NY 14820	607-871-2214
Bank Street College of Ed.	610 W. 112th St. New York, NY 10025	212-875-4469
Canisius College	2001 Main St. Buffalo, NY 14208	716-888-2397
CUNY - Bernard M. Baruch	17 Lexington Ave. New York, NY 10010	212-387-1731
CUNY - Brooklyn College	School of Education Avenue H & Bedford Ave. Brooklyn, NY 11210	718-951-5214
CUNY - Herbert H. Lehman	250 Bedford Park Blvd. West Bronx, NY 10468-1589	718-960-4993
CUNY - Hunter College	695 Park Ave., Box 393 New York, NY 10021	212-650-3959
CUNY - Medgar Evers	1150 Carroll St. Brooklyn, NY 11225	718-270-6406
CUNY - Queens College	65-30 Kissena Blvd. Flushing, NY 11367	718-997-5220
CUNY - College of Staten Island	2800 Victory Blvd. Staten Island, NY 10314	718-982-3723
CUNY - York College	150-14 Jamaica Avenue Jamaica, NY 11451	718-262-2450
Colgate University	Hamilton, NY 13346	315-824-7253
College of Mount St. Vincent	Riverdale, NY 10471	718-405-3285
College of New Rochelle	Castle Place New Rochelle, NY 10801	914-654-5578
College of St. Rose	432 Western Avenue Albany, NY 12203	518-454-5257

COLLEGE	ADDRESS	PHONE
Columbia - Barnard College	606 West 120th Street New York, NY 10027	212-854-2117
Columbia - Teachers College	525 West 120th Street New York, NY 10027	212-678-4050
Concordia College	171 White Plains Road Bronxville, NY 10708	914-337-9300
Cornell University	Dept. of Ed., Stone Hall Ithaca, NY 14853	607-255-2207
Daemen College	4380 Main Street Amherst, NY 14226	716-839-3600
Dominican College	10 Western Highway Orangeburg, NY 10962	914-359-3577
Dowling College	Idle Hour Boulevard Oakdale, NY 11769	516-244-3171
D'Youville College	Division of Ed., 320 Porter Ave., Buffalo, NY 14201	716-881-7629 716-274-1540
Elmira College	Elmira, NY 14901	607-735-1922
Five Towns College	305 North Service Road Dix Hills, NY 11746-6055	516-424-7000
Fordham University	East Fordham Road Bronx, NY 10458	212-636-6400
Hartwick College	Oneonta, NY 13820	607-431-4841
Hobart and William Smith Colleges	Geneva, NY 14456	315-781-3640
Hofstra University	126 Hofstra University Hempstead, NY 11550	516-463-5745
Houghton College	Houghton, NY 14744	716-567-9672
Iona College	715 North Avenue New Rochelle, NY 10801	914-633-2210
Ithaca College	Muller Faculty Ithaca, NY 14850	607-274-1488
Keuka College	Keuka Park, NY 14478	315-536-5277
LeMoyne College	Syracuse, NY 13214	315-445-4658 718-488-1055
LIU - C.W. Post Center	C.W. Post Campus of LIU, N. Blvd. Greenvale, NY 11548	516-299-3006
LIU - Southampton Center	Southampton Center of LIU, Southampton, NY 11968	516-283-8211

COLLEGE	ADDRESS	PHONE
Manhattan College	4513 Manhattan College Parkway Bronx, NY 10471	212-749-2802
Manhattanville College	Purchase, NY 10577	914-694-2200
Marist College	Poughkeepsie, NY 12601	914-575-3000
Marymount College	Tarrytown, NY 10591	914-631-8586
Marymount Manhattan College	221 East 71st Street New York, NY 10021	212-517-0501
Medaille College	18 Agassiz Circle Buffalo, NY 14214	716-884-3281
Mercy College	555 Broadway Dobbs Ferry, NY 10522	914-674-7350
Molloy College	1000 Hempstead Avenue Rockville Centre, NY 11570	516-678-5000
Mount St. Mary's College	330 Powell Avenue Newburgh, NY 12550	914-569-3268
Nazareth College	Smyth Hall, Rm. 335, 4245 East Ave. Rochester, NY 14610	716-586-2525
New School for Social Research	66 West 12th Street New York, NY 10011	212-229-5600
New York Institute of Technology	268 Wheatley Rd., P.O. Box 170 Old Westbury, NY 11568	516-686-7516
New York University	NYU/SEHNAP, 70 Washington Sq. So., New York, NY 10012	212-998-5033
Niagara University	Niagara University, NY 14109	716-286-8557
Nyack College	Nyack, NY 10960	914-358-1710
Pace University - New York City	1 Pace Plaza New York, NY 10038	212-346-1603
Pace University - Pleasantville	861 Bedford Road Pleasantville, NY 10570	914-773-3833
Pace University - White Plains	78 North Broadway White Plains, NY 10603	914-422-4136
Pratt Institute	200 Willoughby Avenue Brooklyn, NY 11205	718-636-3637
Rensselaer Polytechnic Institute	Troy, NY 12180	518-276-6906
Roberts Wesleyan College	2301 Westside Drive Rochester, NY 14624	716-594-6610
Rochester Institute of Technology	1 Lomb Memorial Drive, Bldg. #1, Rochester, NY 14623	716-475-2666

COLLEGE	ADDRESS	PHONE
Russell Sage College	45 Ferry Street Troy, NY 12180	518-270-2403
St. Bonaventure University	St. Bonaventure, NY 14778	716-375-2201
St. Francis College	180 Remsen Street Brooklyn, NY 11201	718-522-2300
St. John Fisher College	3690 East Avenue Rochester, NY 14618	716-385-8366
St. John's University - Jamaica	Grand Center & Utopia Parkways, Jamaica, NY 11439	718-990-1308
St. John's University - Staten Island	300 Howard Avenue Staten Island, NY 10301	718-390-4545
St. Joseph's College	245 Clinton Avenue, Brooklyn, NY 11205	718-636-6800
St. Lawrence University	Canton, NY 13617	315-379-5861
St. Thomas Aquinas College	Rte. 340, Sparkill, NY 10976	914-398-4154
Sarah Lawrence College	Bronxville, NY 10708	914-395-2374
School of Visual Arts	209 East 23rd Street New York, NY 10010	212-592-2600
Siena College	Loudonville, NY 12211	518-783-2968
Skidmore College	Saratoga Springs, NY 12866	518-584-5000
SUC - Brockport	Room 207, F.O.B. Brockport, NY 14420	716-395-2510
SUC - Buffalo	GC 510, 1300 Elmwood Avenue Buffalo, NY 14222	716-878-4214
SUC - Cortland	P.O. Box 2000, D-206, Cornish Hall Cortland, NY 13045	607-753-2701
SUC - Fredonia	Fredonia, NY 14063	716-673-3449
SUC - Geneseo	Erwin 107 Geneseo, NY 14454	716-245-5560
SUC - New Paltz	OMB 102 New Paltz, NY 12561	914-257-2800
SUC - Old Westbury	P.O. Box 210, Old Westbury, NY 11568	516-876-3099
SUC - Oneonta	Administration Bldg., 337 Oneonta, NY 13820	607-436-3456
SUC - Oswego	611 Culkin Hall Oswego, NY 13126	315-341-2102
SUC - Plattsburgh	Hawkins Hall 107 Plattsburgh, NY 12901	518-564-3066

COLLEGE	ADDRESS	PHONE
SUC - Potsdam	Potsdam, NY 13617	315-267-2535
SUNY - Albany	Education 113 1400 Washington Avenue Albany, NY 12222	518-442-5001
SUNY - Binghamton	Vestal Parkway East Binghamton, NY 13901	607-777-2833
SUNY - Buffalo	553 Baldy Hall, 3435 Main Street Buffalo, NY 14206	716-645-2461
SUNY - Col. of Environmental Science	Syracuse, NY 13210	315-470-6366
SUNY - Stony Brook	Soc. & Behavioral Sci. Bldg. 109 Steele Hall Stony Brook, NY 11794	516-632-7055
Syracuse University	School of Education Syracuse, NY 13244-1120	315-443-4751
Union College	Union Avenue Schenectady, NY 12308	518-388-6361
University of Rochester	421 Lattimore Rochester, NY 14627	716-275-1009
Utica College of Syracuse University	Burrstone Road Utica, NY 13502	315-792-3090
Vassar College	Box 31 Poughkeepsie, NY 12601	914-437-7361
Wagner College	Staten Island, NY 10301	718-390-3464
Wells College	Aurora, NY 13026	315-364-3252
Yeshiva University	245 Lexington Avenue New York, NY 10016	212-340-7788

16 GETTING A TEACHING JOB

There are specific steps you can follow to increase your chances of getting the teaching job you want. There are no guarantees, but you can definitely improve the odds. Let's begin with a discussion of job opportunities.

WHERE ARE THE TEACHING JOBS?

There are teaching jobs everywhere! This writer served on the board of education in a small suburban town with about 80 teachers in a K-8 school district. It was the kind of place most people would like to teach. There were between two and five teaching openings each year, for six years. But you could hardly find an advertisement or announcement anywhere.

About the only people who knew about the jobs were administrators and teachers in the district and surrounding districts, the few people who read a three-line ad that ran once in a weekly paper, and those who called to inquire about teaching jobs. Keep this information in mind. It is your first clue about how to find a teaching job.

The *Occupational Outlook Handbook*, released by the federal government, predicts that teaching opportunities for elementary and secondary school teachers will increase faster than all occupations as a whole during the next 10 years. The book predicts a much faster increase in jobs for special education teachers.

Other sources predict an increased need for mathematics, science, and bilingual teachers during this same period. Experience indicates that the opportunities for teachers certified in more than one area will grow much faster than average as well.

Some publications predict that the population of elementary age school children will increase about 10 percent by 2005. If the number of teachers were to increase at this rate over all, the number of teachers in the United States will grow from about 3,250,000 to about 3,560,000. In the 1990s, the teachers are apportioned approximately as follows: elementary school, 1,600,000; secondary school 1,300,000; and special education, 360,000. New York State mirrors this apportionment.

More than half of New York teachers are over 40. While predictions vary, the number of retirements during the next decade will probably be larger than we have seen in the last 20 years. I have spoken with principals who predicted that all the teachers in their school would retire by the year 2002.

The growth in the school age population and the increased retirement rate will probably produce a large numer of teaching jobs during the next decade. You need only one.

HOW CAN I FIND A JOB?

Before discussing this question, let's talk about rejection. Remember, you need only one teaching job. If you are interested in 100 jobs, you should be extremely happy with a success rate of 1 percent. A success rate of 2 percent is more than you need, and a very high success rate of 5 percent will just make it too hard to decide which job to take.

Rejection and failure are part of the job search process. Be ready; everyone goes through it.

OKAY, I'M READY TO BEGIN. HOW DO I FIND A JOB?

Begin by deciding on the kind of teaching jobs you want and the geographic areas you are willing to teach in. There is no sense pursuing jobs you don't want in places you don't want to go.

Write your choices here.

These are the kind of teaching positions I'm interested in.

_____   _____

These are the countries, places, areas, or locales I'm willing to teach in.

_____   _____

You can change your mind as often as you like. But limit your job search to these choices.

Follow the guidelines presented below. You must actually do the things outlined here. Reading, talking, and thinking about them will not help.

Make and use personal contacts (network)

Find out about every appropriate teaching position

Apply for every appropriate teaching position—go to every interview

Develop a good resume

Develop a portfolio

Use the placement office

MAKE AND USE PERSONAL CONTACTS (NETWORK)

You will not be surprised to learn that many, if not most, jobs are found through personal contacts. You must make personal contacts to maximize your chances of finding the job you want. Take things easy, one step at a time, and try to meet at least one new person each week.

Find a way to get introduced to teachers, school administrators, board of education members, and others who will know about teaching jobs and may influence hiring decisions. The more people you meet and talk to, the better chance you will have of getting the job you want.

Get a mentor. Get to know a superintendent or principal near where you want to teach, and ask that person to be your mentor. Tell them immediately that you are not asking for a job in their district. (That will not stop them from offering you one if they want to.) Explain that you are just beginning your teaching career and that you need help learning about teaching jobs in surrounding communities and about teaching in general. Ask your mentors to keep their eyes and ears open for any openings for which you are qualified. You can have several mentors if you want to. Listen to their advice.

You already have a lot of contacts through your friends and relatives. Talk to them all. Tell them you are looking for a teaching job and ask them to be alert for any possibilities. Ask them to mention your name and your interest in a teaching position to everyone they know.

FIND OUT ABOUT EVERY APPROPRIATE TEACHING POSITION

The contacts you have and are making each week will help you keep abreast of some teaching opportunities. Follow these additional steps. Look in every paper every day distributed in the places you want to teach. Don't forget about weekly papers.

Call all the school districts where you want to teach. Ask the administrative assistant or secretary in the superintendent's or principal's office if there are current or anticipated job openings in the district. If you are in college or a recent graduate, visit or contact the placement office every week and ask your professors if they know about any teaching opportunities. Contact the regional BOCES and the school districts (pages 471–493) for information about jobs and recruitment fairs.

APPLY FOR EVERY APPROPRIATE TEACHING POSITION— GO TO EVERY INTERVIEW

Apply for every teaching position that is of the type and in the location you listed. No exceptions! Direct application for a listed position is probably the second most effective way to get a job. The more appropriate jobs you apply for, the more likely you are to get one. It is not unusual for someone to apply for more than 100 teaching positions.

Go to every interview you are invited to. Going to interviews increases your chances of getting a job. If you don't get the job, it was worth going just for the practice.

Your application should include a brief cover letter and a one-page resume. The cover letter should follow this format: The first brief paragraph should identify the job you are applying for. The second brief paragraph should be used to mention a skill or ability you have that matches a district need. The third brief paragraph should indicate an interest in a personal interview. Every cover letter should be addressed to the person responsible for hiring in the school district.

DEVELOP A GOOD RESUME

A good resume is a one-page advertisement. A good resume highlights the things you have done that prospective employers will be interested in. A good resume is not an exhaustive listing of everything you have done. A good resume is not cluttered.

For example, say you worked as a teacher assistant and spent most of your time on lunch duty and about 10 percent of your time conducting whole language lessons. What goes on the resume? The whole language experience.

Your resume should include significant school-related experience. It should also include other employment that lasted longer than a year. Omit noneducation-related short-term employment. Your resume should list special skills, abilities, and interests that make you unique.

An example of a resume using a format that has proven successful appears in this chapter. This resume combines the experience of more than one person and is for demonstration purposes only.

An outline of a resume you can copy, to begin to develop your own resume, is also included in this chapter. If you are interested in two different types of teaching positions, you may have two resumes. Go over your final resume and cover letters with a placement officer or advisor.

Derek Namost
33 Ann Street
Kearning, NY 12345
(555) 555-5555

Objective: Elementary School Teacher
               Special Education Teacher
               Secondary History Teacher

Education: BS History—Collegiate College (minor in education)   1994
               MS in Education at Long Key College in progress

Certification: Teacher of Special Education
               Teacher of Elementary Education

Experience: **Lincoln School District,**   1998–present
               Elementary School Teacher Fifth Grade

               • Teach in a student-centered elementary school
               • Prepare and teach individualized lessons geared to student needs
               • Use computer software and CD-ROM's to teach mathematics
                 and motivate students
               • Design and implement whole language instruction
               • Integrate instruction in science, language arts, and social studies

               Southern Pines School District,   1994–1998
               Secondary School Special Education Teacher

               • Planned and taught modified classes for classified students
               • Modified the curriculum to meet the individual needs of students
               • Taught modified science and social studies courses to classified students
               • Assisted students with class assignments, self-management, and
                 study skills
               • Collaborated with class and subject matter teachers

               Watson School,   Spring 1994
               Student Teacher, Preschool Class

               • Collaborated in teaching a class of preschool students

Honors: Kappa Delta Pi, Phi Delta Kappa

Coaching/   Coach, varsity soccer team   1995–98
Advising: Advisor, mathematics team   1995–98
               Interested in coaching and advising after-school activities

Special   Extensive experience using computers, including
Skills: Macintosh and IBM computers, multimedia, and CD-ROM's

References: References are available on request

RESUME WORKSHEET

_____

_____

_____

(_____) _____ - _____

Objective:

Education:

Certification:

Experience:

Honors:

**Coaching/
Advising:**

**Special
Skills:**

References:

DEVELOP A PORTFOLIO

Develop a portfolio to show to potential employers. Choose four or five lesson plans you like. Rewrite them extensively to incorporate all the elements of a good lesson plan. Carefully type them in final form and include them in your portfolio. Include examples of your student's work that you believe will be well received by a principal or superintendent. You may want to take pictures of a classroom you've worked in showing class arrangement and bulletin boards. Include other materials to show your familiarity with current teaching methods. Be sure to show your portfolio to your education advisor and a principal before you show it to prospective employers. Make changes in the portfolio as they recommend.

USE THE PLACEMENT OFFICE

If you are a college student or graduate, use the school's placement office. Set up a placement file that includes recommendation letters from professors, teachers, and supervisors. It's handy to have these references on file. If a potential employer wants this information, you can have it sent out from the placement office instead of running around.

College placement offices often give seminars on job hunting and interviews. Take advantage of these.

WHAT TIME LINE SHOULD I FOLLOW?

Let's say you are looking for a job in September and you will be certified three months earlier in June. You should begin working on your personal contacts by September of the previous year. You should start looking for advertisements and tracking down job possibilities during January. Have your placement file set up and a preliminary resume done by February. You can amend them later if you need to. Start applying for jobs in February.

ANY LAST ADVICE?

Stick with it. Follow the steps outlined here. Start early and take things one step at a time. Remember the importance of personal contacts. Remember that you need only one teaching

NEW YORK CITY

The New York City schools enroll about 1,000,000 students and employ about 70,000 teachers. "The City" will always be the largest single source of teaching jobs in New York State. Experts knowledgeable about the New York City schools estimate there may be as many as 5,000 openings for certified teachers every year for the next five years.

The New York City schools offer special tuition support for bilingual teachers in all areas, and for mathematics and science teachers. To find out about these and other incentive programs and to find out about teaching jobs in New York City, call the Office of Recruitment, Personnel Assessment and Licensing at (718) 935-2670.

During my career as a college department chair and dean I helped establish many programs, including a program that helps certify teachers and places these teachers in New York City schools. That program is the Urban Teaching Academy.

THE URBAN TEACHING ACADEMY

The Urban Teaching Academy (UTA) is a college program that offers a wide variety of state approved teacher certification programs. Most UTA students are placed in paid teaching positions in the New York City schools while taking teacher certification courses. The UTA has had an over 90 percent success rate placing its students in paid teaching positions upon graduation.

If you want to teach in New York City call the UTA at one of the numbers below.

Urban Teaching Academy

1-877-UTA-8074
1-877-882-8074

BOCES AND SCHOOL DISTRICTS IN NEW YORK STATE LISTED BY REGION AND COUNTY

BOCES and school districts are listed on the following pages by county in one of the seven regions shown on the map below. The Board of Cooperative Educational Services offices (BOCES) and other region-wide offices in a region are listed first. The school district listings show the number of schools and approximate number of students in each district.

NOTE: Some of the 315 area codes in the listings have been changed to 931.

Another source of information about school districts is the Internet. Refer to the "clickable" map at **www.nysed.gov/emsc/info/cntypick.html.** A click on one of the counties reveals all the school districts in that county. Click on a school district name for extensive information about that district and the schools in that district.

NEW YORK COUNTY MAP

REGION 1: Counties—Allegany, Cattaragus, Chautauqua, Chemung, Erie, Genesee, Livingston, Monroe, Niagara, Ontario, Orleans, Schuyler, Seneca, Steuben, Wayne, Wyoming, Yates

BOCES	Town	Phone
Cattaraugus - All-Erie - Wy BOCES	Olean	716-372-8293
Chautauqua - Erie 2 BOCES	Fredonia	716-672-4371
Erie 1 BOCES	West Seneca	716-821-7000
Genessee Valley BOCES	Batavia	716-344-7515
Monroe 1 BOCES	Fairport	716-377-4660
Monroe 2 - Orleans BOCES	Spencerport	716-352-2410
Orleans - Niagara BOCES	Medina	716-731-4176
Schuyler - Chemung - Tioga BOCES	Elmira Heights	607-739-3581
Steuben - Allegany BOCES	Steuben	607-776-7631
Wayne - Finger Lakes BOCES	Newark	315-332-7400

Region-Wide

	Town	Phone
Diocese of Buffalo School District	Buffalo	716-847-5501
Diocese of Rochester School District	Rochester	716-328-3210

School Districts	Town	Number of Schools	Number of Students	Phone
ALLEGANY				
Alfred Almond Ctl Sch Dist/*Almond*		1	850	607-276-2981
Andover Central Sch Dist/*Andover*		1	475	607-478-8491
Belfast Central Sch Dist/*Belfast*		1	505	716-365-2646
Bolivar-Richburg Sch Dist/*Bolivar*		2	1,100	716-928-2561
Canaseraga Central Sch Dist/*Canaseraga*		1	377	607-545-6421
Cuba-Rushford Central Sch Dist/*Cuba*		3	1,315	716-968-2650
Filmore Central Sch Dist/*Filmore*		1	840	716-567-2251
Friendship Central Sch Dist/*Friendship*		1	465	716-973-3321
Genesee Valley Ctr Sch Dist/*Belmont*		2	836	716-268-7627
Scio Central Sch Dist/*Scio*		1	544	716-593-5510
Wellsville Ctl Sch Dist/*Wellsville*		3	1,735	716-593-5761
Whitesville Central Sch Dist/*Whitesville*		1	305	607-356-3301
CATTARAUGUS				
Allegany-Limestone Ctrl Sch Dist/*Allegany*		3	1,640	716-373-0060
Cattaraugus Central Sch Dist/*Cattaraugus*		2	862	716-257-3483
Ellicottville Ctl Sch Dist/*Ellicottville*		1	756	716-699-2368
Franklinville Ctl Sch Dist/*Franklinville*		2	1,018	716-676-3723
Gowanda Central Sch Dist/*Gowanda*		3	1,495	716-532-3325
Hinsdale Central Sch Dist/*Hinsdale*		1	635	716-557-2227
Little Valley Central Sch Dist/*Little Valley*		1	450	716-938-9155
Olean City Public Sch Dist/*Olean*		7	2,734	716-375-4417
Portville Central Sch Dist/*Portville*		1	1,380	716-933-8701
Randolph Acad Union Free Sch Dist/*Randolph*		1	148	716-358-6866

School Districts	Town	Number of Schools	Number of Students	Phone
Randolph Central Sch Dist/*Randolph*		2	1,082	716-358-6161
Salamanca City Sch Dist/*Salamanca*		4	1,722	716-945-2403
West Valley Ctl Sch Dist/*West Valley*		1	466	716-942-3293
Yorkshire-Pioneer Ctl Sch Dist/*Yorkshire*		4	3,500	716-492-4066

CHAUTAUQUA

School Districts	Town	Number of Schools	Number of Students	Phone
Bemus Point Ctl Sch Dist/*Bemus Point*		2	850	716-386-2375
Brocton Central Sch Dist/*Brocton*		1	881	716-792-9121
Cassadaga Valley Ctl Sch Dist/*Sinclairville*		3	1,525	716-962-5155
Chautauqua Lake Central Sch Dist/*Mayville*		4	1,100	716-753-7138
Clymer Central Sch Dist/*Clymer*		2	600	716-355-4444
Dunkirk City Sch Dist/*Dunkirk*		8	2,298	716-366-9300
Falconer Central Sch Dist/*Falconer*		3	1,550	716-665-6624
Forestville Central Sch Dist/*Forestville*		2	700	716-965-2742
Fredonia Central Sch Dist/*Fredonia*		4	2,057	716-679-1581
Frewsburg Central Sch Dist/*Frewsburg*		2	1,112	716-569-9241
Jamestown City Sch Dist/*Jamestown*		10	6,200	716-483-4350
Panama Central Sch Dist/*Panama*		2	930	716-782-3245
Pine Valley Central Sch Dist/*South Dayton*		2	911	716-988-3293
Ripley Central Sch Dist/*Ripley*		1	500	716-736-2631
Sherman Central Sch Dist/*Sherman*		1	560	716-761-6121
Silver Creek Ctl Sch Dist/*Silver Creek*		2	1,466	716-934-2603
Southwestern Ctl Sch Dist/*Jamestown*		4	1,737	716-484-1136
Westfield Central Sch Dist/*Westfield*		1	1,300	716-326-2151

CHEMUNG

School Districts	Town	Number of Schools	Number of Students	Phone
Elmira City Sch Dist/*Elmira*		13	8,530	607-735-3000
Elmira Hts Ctl Sch Dist/*Elmira Hts*		2	1,226	607-734-7114
Horseheads Ctl Sch Dist/*Horseheads*		7	4,563	607-739-5601

ERIE

School Districts	Town	Number of Schools	Number of Students	Phone
Akron Central Sch Dist/*Akron*		2	1,642	716-542-5532
Alden Central Sch Dist/*Alden*		4	1,995	716-937-9116
Amherst Central Sch Dist/*Amherst*		4	3,200	716-836-3000
Cheektowaga Central Sch Dist/*Cheektowaga*		3	2,281	716-686-3606
Cheektowaga-Maryvale UF Sch Dist/*Cheektowaga*		4	2,500	716-631-7407
Cheektowaga-Sloan UF Sch Dist/*Buffalo*		3	1,400	716-891-6402
Clarence Central Sch Dist/*Clarence*		6	4,000	716-759-0100
Cleveland Hill UFSD/*Cheektowaga*		3	1,509	716-836-7200
Depew Union Free Sch Dist/*Depew*		3	2,710	716-686-2251
East Aurora UFSD/*East Aurora*		4	1,942	716-652-1000
Eden Central Sch Dist/*Eden*		3	1,804	716-992-3629
Evans-Brant Central Sch Dist/*Angola*		7	3,700	716-549-2300
Frontier Ctl Sch Dist/*Hamburg*		6	5,341	716-627-1053
Grand Island Central Sch Dist/*Grand Island*		5	3,194	716-773-8800
Hamburg Ctl Sch Dist/*Hamburg*		6	4,112	716-646-3220
Holland Central Sch Dist/*Holland*		3	1,443	716-537-2231

School Districts	Town	Number of Schools	Number of Students	Phone
Hopevale Union Free Sch Dist/*Hamburg*		1	117	716-648-1949
Iroquois Central Sch Dist/*Elma*		6	2,773	716-652-9300
Kenmore-Tonawanda UFSD/*Buffalo*		13	9,178	716-874-8400
Lackawanna City Sch Dist/*Lackawanna*		4	2,415	716-817-6767
Lancaster Central Sch Dist/*Lancaster*		7	5,099	716-686-3200
North Collins Ctl Sch Dist/*North Collins*		2	780	716-337-0101
Orchard Park Central Sch Dist/*Orchard Park*		6	4,966	716-662-6280
Springville Griffith Inst Sch Dist/*Springville*		4	2,491	716-592-3236
Sweet Home Central Sch Dist/*Amherst*		6	4,029	716-689-5201
Tonawanda City Sch Dist/*Tonawanda*		6	2,718	716-694-7784
West Seneca Central Sch Dist/*West Seneca*		11	7,625	716-674-5300
Williamsville Ctl Sch Dist/*Buffalo*		14	10,570	716-626-7220

GENESEE

School Districts	Town	Number of Schools	Number of Students	Phone
Alexander Ctl Sch Dist/*Alexander*		2	1,200	716-591-1551
Batavia City Sch Dist/*Batavia*		5	2,869	716-344-8217
Byron Bergen Ctl Sch Dist/*Bergen*		3	1,385	716-494-1220
Elba Central Sch Dist/*Elba*		1	625	716-757-9967
Le Roy Central Sch Dist/*Le Roy*		2	1,484	716-768-8133
Oakfield Alabama Ctl Sch Dist/*Oakfield*		2	1,200	716-948-5211
Pavilion Ctl Sch Dist/*Pavilion*		2	1,075	716-584-3115
Pemboke Ctl Sch Dist/*Corfu*		3	1,466	716-599-4525

LIVINGSTON

School Districts	Town	Number of Schools	Number of Students	Phone
Avon Central Sch Dist/*Avon*		3	1,220	716-226-2455
Caledonia Mumford Sch Dist/*Caledonia*		2	1,350	716-538-6811
Dalton Nunda Central Sch Dist/*Nunda*		2	1,100	716-468-2541
Dansville Ctl Sch Dist/*Dansville*		4	2,012	716-335-4000
Geneseo Ctl Sch Dist/*Geneseo*		1	1,200	716-243-3450
Livonia Ctl Sch Dist/*Livonia*		3	2,275	716-346-4000
Mt. Morris Central Sch Dist/*Mount Morris*		1	690	716-658-2568
York Central Sch Dist/*Retsof*		2	1,100	716-243-1730

MONROE

School Districts	Town	Number of Schools	Number of Students	Phone
Brighton Central Sch Dist/*Rochester*		4	3,200	716-242-5080
Brockport Ctl Sch Dist/*Brockport*		5	4,747	716-637-5303
Churchville Ctl Sch Dist/*Churchville*		6	4,505	716-293-1800
East Irondequit Ctl Sch Dist/*Rochester*		6	3,280	716-336-7010
East Rochester UFSD/*E. Rochester*		3	1,401	716-248-6302
Fairport Ctl Sch Dist/*Fairport*		8	7,123	716-421-2000
Gates Chili Central Sch Dist/*Rochester*		7	5,600	716-247-5050
Greece Central Sch Dist/*Rochester*		21	14,200	716-621-1000
Hilton Central Sch Dist/*Hilton*		5	4,464	716-392-3450
Honeoye Falls Lima Sch Dist/*Honeoye Falls*		4	2,461	716-624-7000
Penfield Central Sch Dist/*Rochester*		6	4,809	716-248-3220
Pittsford Central Sch Dist/*Pittsford*		8	5,432	716-381-9940
Rochester City Sch Dist/*Rochester*		48	35,889	716-262-8378

School Districts	Town	Number of Schools	Number of Students	Phone
Rush Henrietta Central Sch Dist/*Henrietta*		9	5,817	716-359-5000
Spencerport Ctl Sch Dist/*Spencerport*		5	4,411	716-352-3421
W. Irondequoit Ctl Sch Dist/*Rochester*		10	3,944	716-342-5500
Webster Central Sch Dist/*Webster*		10	7,470	716-265-3600
Wheatland Chili Ctl Sch Dist/*Scottsville*		2	1,090	716-889-6246

NIAGARA

School Districts	Town	Number of Schools	Number of Students	Phone
Barker Central Sch Dist/*Barker*		3	1,210	716-795-3832
Lewiston Porter Ctl Sch Dist/*Youngstown*		3	2,632	716-754-8281
Lockport City Sch Dist/*Lockport*		11	6,325	716-439-6411
Newfane Central Sch Dist/*Newfane*		5	1,975	716-778-0110
Niagara Falls Sch Dist/*Niagara Falls*		14	8,900	716-286-4205
Niagara-Wheatfield Ctl Sch Dist/*Sanborn*		5	3,893	716-731-7341
North Tonawanda Sch Dist/*N. Tonawanda*		9	5,800	716-694-3200
Royalton Hartland Central Sch Dist/*Middleport*		3	1,850	716-735-3654
Star Point Central Sch Dist/*Lockport*		3	2,550	716-625-7272
Wilson Central Sch Dist/*Wilson*		4	1,597	716-751-9341

ONTARIO

School Districts	Town	Number of Schools	Number of Students	Phone
Canandaigua City Sch Dist/*Canandaigua*		4	4,268	716-396-3700
East Bloomfield CSD/*E Bloomfield*		2	1,191	716-657-6121
Geneva City Sch Dist/*Geneva*		4	2,467	315-781-0276
Gorham Middlesex CSD/*Bushville*		4	1,800	716-554-4848
Honeoye Central Sch Dist/*Honeoye*		1	1,150	716-229-5171
Manchester Shortville CSD/*Shortsville*		2	1,087	716-289-3927
Naples Central Sch Dist/*Naples*		2	1,005	716-374-6381
Phelps-Clifton Springs Ctl Sch Dist/*Phelps*		5	2,159	315-548-5225
Victor Central Sch Dist/*Victor*		4	3,144	716-924-3252

ORLEANS

School Districts	Town	Number of Schools	Number of Students	Phone
Albion Ctl Union Free Sch Dist/*Albion*		3	2,820	716-589-6656
Holley Central Sch Dist/*Holley*		4	1,474	716-638-6316
Kendall Central Sch Dist/*Kendall*		2	1,168	716-659-2741
Lyndonville Central Sch Dist/*Lyndonville*		2	900	716-765-2251
Medina Central Sch Dist/*Medina*		4	2,534	716-798-2700

SCHUYLER

School Districts	Town	Number of Schools	Number of Students	Phone
Odessa Montour Ctl Sch Dist/*Odessa*		3	967	607-594-3341
Watkins Glen Central Sch Dist/*Watkins Glen*		3	1,450	607-535-9718

SENECA

School Districts	Town	Number of Schools	Number of Students	Phone
Romulus Ctl Sch Dist/*Romulus*		1	690	607-869-5391
Seneca Falls Central Sch Dist/*Seneca Falls*		4	1,569	315-568-5818
South Seneca Central Sch Dist/*Interlaken*		2	1,183	607-532-8395
Waterloo Central Sch Dist/*Waterloo*		5	2,010	315-539-1500

School Districts	Town	Number of Schools	Number of Students	Phone
STEUBEN				
Addison Central Sch Dist/*Addison*		3	1,375	607-359-2243
Arkport Central Sch Dist/*Arkport*		1	550	607-295-7471
Avoca Central Sch Dist/*Avoca*		1	725	607-556-2221
Bath Central Sch Dist/*Bath*		3	2,226	607-776-3301
Bradford Central Sch Dist/*Bradford*		1	280	607-583-4616
Campbell-Savona Ctl Sch Dist/*Campbell*		2	1,231	607-527-4548
Canisteo Central Sch Dist/*Canisteo*		2	990	607-698-4225
Corning Painted Post Area SD/*Painted Post*		13	5,534	607-936-3704
Greenwood Central Sch Dist/*Greenwood*		1	265	607-225-4292
Hammondsport Ctl Sch Dist/*Hammondsport*		2	830	607-569-5200
Homell City Sch Dist/*Homell*		5	2,305	607-324-1301
Jasper Troupsburg Central Sch Dist/*Jasper*		2	648	607-792-3675
Prattsburgh Central Sch Dist/*Prattsburgh*		1	610	607-522-3795
Wayland-Cohocton Central Sch Dist/*Wayland*		2	1,950	716-728-2211
WAYNE				
Clyde Savannah Central Sch Dist/*Clyde*		3	1,250	315-923-7747
Gananda Ctl Sch Dist/*Walworth*		2	1,005	325-986-3506
Lyons Central Sch Dist/*Lyons*		2	1,260	315-946-2207
Marion Central Sch Dist/*Marion*		2	1,329	315-926-2300
Newark Central Sch Dist/*Newark*		5	2,810	315-332-3500
North Rose Wolcott Central Sch Dist/*Wolcott*		4	1,920	315-594-3144
Palmyra Macedon Ctl Sch Dist/*Palmyra*		4	2,328	315-597-3401
Red Creek Central Sch Dist/Red *Creek*		2	1,220	315-754-6304
Sodus Central Sch Dist/*Sodus*		3	1,628	315-483-2331
Wayne Central Sch Dist/*Ontario*		5	2,836	315-524-2811
Williamson Central Sch Dist/*Williamson*		3	1,394	315-589-9661
WYOMING				
Attica Central Sch Dist/*Attica*		4	2,001	716-591-0400
Letchworth Central Sch Dist/*Gainesville*		2	1,400	716-493-2571
Perry Central Sch Dist/*Perry*		2	1,300	716-237-6156
Warsaw Central Sch Dist/*Warsaw*		2	1,200	716-786-8000
Wyoming Central Sch Dist/*Wyoming*		1	268	726-495-6222
YATES				
Dundee Ctl Sch Dist/*Dundee*		1	1,001	607-243-5533
Penn Yan Ctl Sch Dist/*Penn Yan*		4	2,230	315-536-3371

REGION 2: Counties—Broome, Cayuga, Chenango, Cortland, Jefferson, Lewis, Madison, Oneida, Onondaga, Oswego, Tioga, Tompkins

BOCES	Town	Phone
Broome - Delaware - Tioga BOCES	Binghamton	607-763-3300
Cayuga - Onondoga BOCES	Auburn	315-253-0361
Delaware - Chenango - Madison BOCES	Norwich	607-335-1200
Jefferson - Lewis - Hamilton BOCES	Watertown	315-788-0400
Oneida BOCES	New Hartford	315-793-8555
Onondaga - Cortland - Madison BOCES	Syracuse	315-433-2602
Oswego BOCES	Mexico	315-963-4251
Tompkins - Seneca - Tioga BOCES	Ithaca	607-257-1551

Region-Wide

	Town	Phone
Diocese of Syracuse School District	Syracuse	315-470-1450

School Districts	Town	Number of Schools	Number of Students	Phone
BROOME				
Binghamton City Sch Dist/*Binghamton*		10	6,086	607-762-8100
Chenango Forks CSD/*Binghamton*		4	2,299	607-648-7543
Chenango Valley CSD/*Binghamton*		3	2,071	607-779-4700
Deposit Central Sch Dist/*Deposit*		2	855	607-467-2198
Harpursville CSD/*Harpursville*		2	1,297	607-693-2503
Johnson City CSD/*Johnson City*		6	2,808	607-763-1234
Maine Endwell Ctl Sch Dist/*Endicott*		4	2,584	607-754-1400
Susquehanna Valley CSD/*Conklin*		5	2,264	607-775-0170
Union Endicott Sch Dist/*Endicott*		8	4,724	607-757-2112
Vestal Ctl Sch Dist/*Vestal*		7	4,265	607-757-2241
Whitney Point Ctl Sch Dist/*Whitney Point*		4	2,200	607-692-8202
Windsor Central Sch Dist/*Windsor*		5	2,106	607-655-8216
CAYUGA				
Auburn Enlarged City Sch Dist/*Auburn*		8	5,500	315-255-5835
Cato Meridian Ctl Sch Dist/*Cato*		3	1,370	315-626-2121
Moravia Central Sch Dist/*Moravia*		2	1,375	315-497-2670
Port Byron Ctl. Sch Dist/*Port Byron*		3	1,390	315-776-5728
Southern Cayuga Ctl Sch Dist/*Poplar Ridge*		2	1,328	315-364-7111
Union Springs Ctl Sch Dist/*Union Springs*		4	1,250	315-889-4101
Weedsport Ctl Sch Dist/*Weedsport*		2	1,100	315-834-6637
CHENANGO				
Afton Central Sch Dist/*Afton*		1	800	607-639-8229
Bainbridge Guilford Ctl Sch Dist/*Bainbridge*		3	1,200	607-967-6321
Georgetown-S Otselic CSD/*South Otselic*		2	525	315-653-7591
Greene Ctl Sch Dist/*Greene*		3	1,479	607-656-4161

School Districts	Town	Number of Schools	Number of Students	Phone
Norwich City Sch Dist/*Norwich*		4	2,500	607-334-3211
Oxford Academy Central Sch Dist/*Oxford*		3	1,060	607-843-2025
Sherburne Earlville CSD/*Sherburne*		3	1,761	607-674-7300
Unadilla Valley Ctl Sch Dist/*New Berlin*		3	891	607-847-6551

CORTLAND

School Districts	Town	Number of Schools	Number of Students	Phone
Cincinnatus Ctl Sch Dist/*Cincinnatus*		2	786	607-863-3335
Cortland City Sch Dist/*Cortland*		6	3,023	607-753-6061
Homer Central Sch Dist/*Homer*		4	2,631	607-749-7241
Marathon Ctl Sch Dist/*Marathon*		2	1,011	607-849-3251
McGraw Central Sch Dist/*McGraw*		2	701	607-836-3636

JEFFERSON

School Districts	Town	Number of Schools	Number of Students	Phone
Alexandria Central Sch Dist/*Alexandria Bay*		1	730	315-482-9971
Belleville Henderson Sch Dist/*Belleville*		1	601	315-846-5411
Carthage Central Sch Dist/*Carthage*		5	3,158	315-493-0510
General Brown Ctl Sch Dist/*Dexter*		3	1,700	315-639-4711
Indian River Ctl Sch Dist/*Philadelphia*		7	3,771	315-642-3441
Lafargeville Ctl Sch Dist/*La Fargeville*		1	525	315-658-2241
Lyme Central Sch Dist/*Chaumont*		1	412	315-649-2417
Sackets Harbor Ctl Sch Dist/*Sackets Harbor*		1	535	315-646-3575
South Jefferson Ctl Sch Dist/*Adams Center*		4	2,200	315-583-6104
Thousand Islands Ctl Sch Dist/*Clayton*		4	1,344	315-686-5521
Watertown City Sch Dist/*Watertown*		8	4,784	315-785-3700

LEWIS

School Districts	Town	Number of Schools	Number of Students	Phone
Beaver River Central Sch Dist/*Beaver Falls*		1	1,201	315-346-1211
Copenhagen Central Sch Dist/*Copenhagen*		1	655	315-688-4411
Harrisville Central Sch Dist/*Harrisville*		1	507	315-543-2707
Lowville Central Sch Dist/*Lowville*		1	1,581	315-376-3544
South Lewis Central Sch Dist/*Turin*		5	1,465	315-348-2500

MADISON

School Districts	Town	Number of Schools	Number of Students	Phone
Brookfield Central Sch Dist/*Brookfield*		1	270	315-899-3324
Canastota Central Sch Dist/*Canastota*		4	1,680	315-697-2025
Cazenovia Ctl Sch Dist/*Cazenovia*		3	1,890	315-655-1317
Chittenango Central Sch Dist/*Chittenango*		5	2,765	315-687-2669
Deruyter Central Sch Dist/*De Ruyter*		1	601	315-852-3400
Hamilton Central Sch Dist/*Hamilton*		2	820	315-824-3300
Madison Central Sch Dist/*Madison*		1	612	315-893-1878
Morrisville Eaton Central Sch Dist/*Morrisville*		2	1,200	315-684-9300
Oneida City Sch Dist/*Oneida*		8	2,500	315-363-2550
Stockbridge Valley Sch Dist/*Munnsville*		1	613	315-495-6512

ONEIDA

School Districts	Town	Number of Schools	Number of Students	Phone
Adirondack Central Sch Dist/*Boonville*		4	1,850	315-942-9200
Camden Central Sch Dist/*Camden*		6	2,887	315-245-2500

School Districts	Town	Number of Schools	Number of Students	Phone
Clinton Central Sch Dist/*Clinton*		3	1,835	315-853-5574
Holland Patent Ctl Sch Dist/*Holland Patent*		4	2,000	315-865-7221
New Hartford Central Sch Dist/*New Hartford*		5	2,967	315-738-9218
New York Mills UFSD/*New York Mills*		1	662	315-768-8127
Oriskany Ctl Sch Dist/*Oriskany*		2	811	315-768-7824
Remsen Central Sch Dist/*Remsen*		2	650	315-831-3797
Rome City Sch Dist/*Rome*		13	6,364	315-338-9100
Sauquoit Valley Ctl Sch Dist/*Sauquoit*		3	1,500	315-839-6311
Sherrill City Sch Dist/*Verona*		5	2,504	315-829-2520
Utica City Sch Dist/*Utica*		12	8,315	315-792-2222
Waterville Ctl Sch Dist/*Waterville*		2	1,300	315-841-3900
Westmoreland Central Sch Dist/*Westmoreland*		2	1,200	315-853-6199
Whitesboro Ctl Sch Dist/*Yorkville*		7	3,948	315-768-9700

ONONDAGA

School Districts	Town	Number of Schools	Number of Students	Phone
Baldwinsville CSD/*Baldwinsville*		8	5,692	315-638-6043
East Syracuse Minoa CSD/*East Syracuse*		8	3,860	315-656-7201
Fabius Pompey Ctl Sch Dist/*Fabius*		3	970	315-683-5301
Fayetteville-Manlius Ctl Sch Dist/*Manlius*		6	4,108	315-682-1200
Jamesville-Dewitt Central Sch Dist/*Syracuse*		5	2,560	315-445-8304
Jordan Elbridge Ctl Sch Dist/*Jordan*		4	1,900	315-689-3978
La Fayette Central Sch Dist/*La Fayette*		3	1,162	315-677-9728
Liverpool Ctl Sch Dist/*Liverpool*		16	9,122	315-453-0225
Lyncourt Union Free Sch Dist/*Syracuse*		1	315	315-455-7571
Marcellus Central Sch Dist/*Marcellus*		3	2,047	315-673-0201
North Syracuse Ctl Sch Dist/*Syracuse*		11	10,200	315-452-3103
Onondaga Central Sch Dist/*Nedrow*		3	1,060	315-492-1701
Skaneateles Central Sch Dist/*Skaneateles*		4	1,803	315-685-8361
Solvay Union Free Sch Dist/*Syracuse*		4	1,748	315-468-1111
Syracuse City Sch Dist/*Syracuse*		37	23,000	315-435-4161
Tully Central Sch Dist/*Tully*		2	1,317	315-696-6200
West Genesee Ctl Sch Dist/*Camillus*		7	5,032	931-487-4562
Westhill Ctl Sch Dist/*Syracuse*		4	2,014	315-476-5329

OSWEGO

School Districts	Town	Number of Schools	Number of Students	Phone
Altmar Parish Williamstown Sch Dist/*Parish*		5	1,850	315-625-7298
Central Square Sch Dist/*Central Square*		8	4,756	315-668-2611
Fulton Sch Dist/*Fulton*		6	4,388	315-593-5510
Hannibal Central Sch Dist/*Hannibal*		3	1,738	315-564-7900
Mexico Central Sch Dist/*Mexico*		5	2,744	315-963-7831
Oswego City Sch Dist/*Oswego*		8	5,208	315-341-5885
Phoenix Central Sch Dist/*Phoenix*		5	2,825	315-695-1511
Pulaski Central Sch Dist/*Pulaski*		2	1,375	315-298-5188
Sandy Creek Central Sch Dist/*Sandy Creek*		2	1,250	315-387-3445

School Districts	Town	Number of Schools	Number of Students	Phone
TIOGA				
Candor Central Sch Dist/*Candor*		2	1,086	607-659-5010
Newark Valley CSD/*Newark Valley*		3	1,682	607-642-3221
Owego Apalachin Ctl Sch Dist/*Owego*		4	2,670	607-687-6227
Spencer Van Etten Ctl Sch Dist/*Van Etten*		3	1,200	607-589-4458
Tioga Central Sch Dist/*Tioga Center*		4	1,321	607-687-8000
Waverly Ctl Sch Dist/*Waverly*		4	1,915	607-565-2841
TOMPKINS				
Dryden Central Sch Dist/*Dryden*		4	2,200	607-844-8694
George Jr Republic Unified Sch Dist/*Freeville*		1	110	607-844-3549
Groton Central Sch Dist/*Groton*		2	1,210	607-898-5801
Ithaca City Sch Dist/*Ithaca*		12	5,858	607-274-2101
Lansing Central Sch Dist/*Lansing*		3	1,196	607-533-4294
Newfield Central Sch Dist/*Newfield*		3	1,128	607-564-9955
Trumansburg Ctl Sch Dist/*Trumansburg*		3	1,509	607-387-7551

REGION 3: Counties—Clinton, Essex, Franklin, Fulton, Hamilton, Montgomery, Saint Lawrence, Saratoga, Schenectady, Warren, Washington

BOCES	Town	Phone
Clinton - Essex - Warren - Washington BOCES	Plattsburgh	518-561-0100
Franklin - Essex - Hamilton BOCES	Malone	518-483-6420
Hamilton - Fulton - Montgomery BOCES	Johnstown	518-762-4633
Herkimer - Fulton - Hamilton - Otsego BOCES	Herkimer	315-867-2023
St. Lawrence - Lewis BOCES	Canton	315-386-4504
WSWHE BOCES	Hudson Falls	518-581-3325

School Districts	Town	Number of Schools	Number of Students	Phone
CLINTON				
Ausable Vly Central Sch Dist/*Clintonville*		3	1,550	518-834-2845
Beekmantown Central Sch Dist/*Plattsburgh*		3	2,200	518-563-8250
Chazy Union Free Sch Dist/*Chazy*		1	617	518-846-7135
Northeastern Clinton Sch Dist/*Champlain*		5	1,642	518-298-8242
Northern Adirondack CSD/*Ellenburg Dep*		2	1,244	518-594-3986
Peru Central Sch Dist/*Peru*		4	2,342	518-643-9494
Plattsburgh City Sch Dist/*Plattsburgh*		6	2,149	518-561-6670
Saranac Ctl Sch Dist/*Dannemora*		5	1,863	518-492-7451

School Districts	Town	Number of Schools	Number of Students	Phone
ESSEX				
Crown Point Central Sch Dist/*Crown Point*		1	415	518-597-3285
Elizabethtown Lewis CSD/*Elizabethtown*		1	450	518-873-6371
Keene Central Sch Dist/*Keene Valley*		1	191	518-576-4555
Lake Placid Ctl Sch Dist/*Lake Placid*		2	912	518-523-2474
Minerva Central Sch Dist/*Olmstedville*		1	190	518-251-2000
Moriah Central Sch Dist/*Port Henry*		1	841	518-456-3301
Newcomb Central Sch Dist/*Newcomb*		1	71	518-582-3341
Schroon Lake Ctl Sch Dist/*Schroon Lake*		1	301	518-532-7164
Ticonderoga Ctl Sch Dist/*Ticonderoga*		3	1,097	518-585-6674
Westport Central Sch Dist/*Westport*		1	285	518-962-8244
Willsboro Central Sch Dist/*Willsboro*		1	415	518-963-4456
FRANKLIN				
Brushton Moira Ctl Sch Dist/*Brushton*		2	983	518-529-8948
Chateaugay Central Sch Dist/*Chateaugay*		1	640	518-497-6410
Malone Central Sch Dist/*Malone*		6	2,752	518-483-7800
Salmon River Ctl Sch Dist/*Ft. Covington*		3	1,650	518-358-2215
Saranac Lake Central Sch Dist/*Saranac Lake*		6	1,855	518-891-5460
St. Regis Falls Ctl Sch Dist/*St. Regis Falls*		1	420	518-856-9421
Tupper Lake Ctl Sch Dist/*Tupper Lake*		2	1,160	518-359-3371
FULTON				
Broadalbin-Perth Ctl Sch Dist/*Broadalbin*		4	1,822	518-883-3442
Gloversville Enlarged Sch Dist/*Gloversville*		7	3,555	518-725-2612
Greater Johnstown Sch Dist/*Johnstown*		6	2,270	518-762-4611
Mayfield Ctl Sch Dist/*Mayfield*		2	1,185	518-661-7800
Northville Central Sch Dist/*Northville*		1	610	518-863-7000
Oppenheim Ephratah CSD/*St. Johnsville*		1	551	518-568-2014
Wheelerville Union Free Sch Dist/*Caroga Lake*		1	194	518-835-2171
HAMILTON				
Indian Lake Ctl Sch Dist/*Indian Lake*		1	229	518-648-5024
Inlet Common Sch Dist/*Inlet*		1	22	315-357-3305
Lake Pleasant Central Sch Dist/*Speculator*		1	111	518-548-7571
Long Lake Central Sch Dist/*Long Lake*		1	125	518-624-2221
Piseco Common Sch Dist/*Piseco*		1	42	518-548-7555
Raquette Lake UN Free Sch Dist/*Raquette Lake*		1	12	315-354-4733
Wells Central Sch Dist/*Wells*		1	192	518-924-2272
HERKIMER				
Bridgewater W. Winfield CSD/*West Winfield*		4	1,700	315-822-6161
Dolgeville Central Sch Dist/*Dolgeville*		2	1,180	315-429-3155
Frankfort Schuyler Sch Dist/*Frankfort*		3	1,290	315-894-5083
Herkimer Ctl Sch Dist/*Herkimer*		2	1,390	315-866-2230
Ilion Ctl Sch Dist/*Ilion*		3	2,075	315-894-9934
Little Falls City Sch Dist/*Little Falls*		4	1,400	315-823-1470

School Districts	Town	Number of Schools	Number of Students	Phone
Mohawk Central Sch Dist/*Mohawk*		2	1,011	315-894-7091
Poland Central Sch Dist/*Poland*		1	801	315-826-0203
Town of Webb Union Free Sch Dist/*Old Forge*		1	445	315-369-3222
Van Hornesville Owen Young CSD/*Van Hornesville*		1	294	315-858-0729
West Canada Valley Ctl Sch Dist/*Newport*		1	1,037	315-845-8802

MONTGOMERY

School Districts	Town	Number of Schools	Number of Students	Phone
Canajoharie Ctl Sch Dist/*Canajoharie*		4	1,185	518-673-4500
Fonda Fultonville Central Sch Dist/*Fonda*		1	1,792	518-853-4415
Ft. Plain Central Sch Dist/*Fort Plain*		2	1,003	518-993-2123
Greater Amsterdam Sch Dist/*Amsterdam*		7	3,642	518-843-3180
St. Johnsville Ctrl Sch Dist/*St. Johnsville*		2	590	518-568-2011

ST. LAWRENCE

School Districts	Town	Number of Schools	Number of Students	Phone
Brasher Falls Sch Dist/*Brasher Falls*		2	1,035	315-389-5131
Canton Central Sch Dist/*Canton*		3	1,894	315-386-8561
Clifton Fine Central Sch Dist/*Star Lake*		1	551	315-848-3333
Colton Pierrepont Sch Dist/*Colton*		1	444	315-262-2100
Diocese of Ogdensburg Ed Off/*Ogdensburg*			5,329	315-393-2921
Edwards-Knox Central Sch Dist/*Russell*		1	800	315-562-8326
Gouverneur Ctl Sch Dist/*Gouverneur*		4	2,004	315-287-4870
Hammond Ctl Sch Dist/*Hammond*		1	395	315-324-5931
Hermon Dekalb Central Sch Dist/*De Kalb Jct*		1	561	315-347-3442
Heuvelton Central Sch Dist/*Heuvelton*		1	775	315-344-2414
Lisbon Central Sch Dist/*Lisbon*		1	787	315-393-4951
Madrid Waddington Sch Dist/*Madrid*		1	860	315-322-5746
Massena Central Sch Dist/*Massena*		6	2,991	315-769-3700
Morristown Ctl Sch Dist/*Morristown*		1	402	315-375-8814
Norwood Norfolk Ctl Sch Dist/*Norwood*		2	1,200	315-353-6631
Ogdensburg City Sch Dist/*Ogdensburg*		6	2,606	315-393-0918
Parishville Hopkinton Sch Dist/*Parishville*		1	675	315-265-4642
Potsdam Central Sch Dist/*Potsdam*		3	1,616	315-265-2000

SARATOGA

School Districts	Town	Number of Schools	Number of Students	Phone
Ballston Spa Ctl Sch Dist/*Ballston Spa*		5	3,837	518-884-7110
Burnt Hills Ballston Lake Sch Dist/*Scotia*		5	3,495	518-399-6408
Corinth Central Sch Dist/*Corinth*		2	1,200	518-654-9005
Edinburg Common Sch Dist/*Northville*		1	130	518-863-8412
Galway Central Sch Dist/*Galway*		2	1,258	518-882-1221
Mechanicville Sch Dist/*Mechanicville*		3	1,477	518-664-5727
Saratoga Springs City Sch Dist/*Saratoga Spgs*		9	6,771	518-583-4708
Schuylerville Central Sch Dist/*Schuylerville*		2	1,635	518-695-3255
Shenendehowa Central Sch Dist/*Clifton Park*		11	8,818	518-887-6251
South Glens Falls Ctl Sch Dist/*S. Glens Falls*		6	2,924	518-793-9617
Stillwater Central Sch Dist/*Stillwater*		3	1,325	518-664-8656
Waterford Halfmoon Sch Dist/*Waterford*		2	856	518-237-0800

School Districts	Town	Number of Schools	Number of Students	Phone
SCHENECTADY				
Duanesburg Central Sch Dist/*Delanson*		2	877	518-895-2279
Niskayuna Central Sch Dist/*Schenectady*		8	4,078	518-377-4666
Rotterdam-Mohonasen CSD/*Schenectady*		4	2,993	518-356-5063
Schalmont Central Sch Dist/*Schenectady*		6	2,360	518-355-9200
Schenectady City Sch Dist/*Schenectady*		17	8,450	518-370-8100
Scotia Glenville Ctl Sch Dist/*Scotia*		6	3,110	518-382-1215
WARREN				
Bolton Central Sch Dist/*Bolton Lndg*		1	251	518-644-3531
Glens Falls City Sch Dist/*Glens Falls*		6	2,805	518-792-1212
Glens Falls Common Sch Dist/*Glens Falls*		1	170	518-792-2557
Hadley-Luzerne Ctl Sch Dist/*Lake Luzerne*		3	1,175	518-696-6100
Johnsburg Central Sch Dist/*North Creek*		1	430	518-251-2814
Lake George Central Sch Dist/*Lake George*		2	1,064	518-668-5456
North Warren Central Sch Dist/*Pottersville*		3	686	518-494-3015
Queensbury Union Free Sch Dist/*Queensbury*		3	3,485	518-793-8811
Warrensburg Central Sch Dist/*Warrensburg*		1	1,100	518-623-2861
WASHINGTON				
Argyle Central Sch Dist/*Argyle*		1	750	518-638-8243
Cambridge Central Sch Dist/*Cambridge*		1	1,191	518-677-2653
Ft. Ann Central Sch Dist/*Fort Ann*		1	674	518-639-5594
Ft. Edward Union Free Sch Dist/*Fort Edward*		2	570	518-747-4872
Granville Central Sch Dist/*Granville*		3	1,460	518-642-1051
Greenwich Central Sch Dist/*Greenwich*		1	1,258	518-692-9542
Hartford Central Sch Dist/*Hartford*		1	585	518-632-5222
Hudson Falls Central Sch Dist/*Fort Edward*		5	2,457	518-747-2121
Putnam Central Sch Dist/*Putnam Sta*		1	40	518-547-8266
Salem Central Sch Dist/*Salem*		1	900	518-854-7855
Whitehall Central Sch Dist/*Whitehall*		2	1,000	518-499-1772

REGION 4: Counties—Albany, Columbia, Delaware, Greene, Otsego, Renesselaer, Schoharie

BOCES	Town	Phone
Capital Area BOCES	Albany	518-456-9215
Otsego - Northern Catskill BOCES	Stamford	607-652-7531
Questar III BOCES	Renesselaer	518-477-8771

School Districts	Town	Number of Schools	Number of Students	Phone
ALBANY				
Albany City Sch Dist/*Albany*		20	9,800	518-462-7200
Berne Knox Westerlo CSD/*Berne*		3	1,239	518-872-0909
Bethlehem Central Sch Dist/*Delmar*		7	4,524	518-439-7098
Cohoes City Sch Dist/*Cohoes*		5	2,167	518-237-0100
Diocese of Albany Ed Office/*Albany*			12,706	518-453-6666
Green Island Sch Dist/*Green Island*		1	295	518-273-1422
Guilderland Central Sch Dist/*Guilderland*		7	5,300	518-456-6200
Maplewood Colonie Common SD/*Watervliet*		1	176	518-273-1512
Menands Union Free Sch Dist/*Albany*		1	221	518-465-4561
North Colonie Ctl Sch Dist/*Newtonville*		8	5,085	518-785-8591
Ravena Coeymans Selkirk Ct SD/*Selkirk*		4	2,523	518-767-2513
South Colonie Central Sch Dist/*Albany*		8	5,758	518-869-3576
Voorheesville Ctl Sch Dist/*Voorheesville*		2	1,370	518-765-3313
Watervliet City Sch Dist/*Watervliet*		2	1,509	518-273-4661
COLUMBIA				
Berkshire Union Free Sch Dist/*Canaan*		1	245	518-781-3500
Chatham Central Sch Dist/*Chatham*		3	1,563	518-392-2400
Copake Taconic Hills Sch Dist/*Hillsdale*		4	1,800	518-325-3151
Germantown Central Sch Dist/*Germantown*		1	802	518-537-6281
Hudson City Sch Dist/*Hudson*		5	2,521	518-828-4815
Ichabod Crane Central Sch Dist/*Valatie*		5	2,552	518-758-7575
New Lebanon Ctl Sch Dist/*West Lebanon*		2	700	518-794-9016
DELAWARE				
Andes Central Sch Dist/*Andes*		1	190	914-676-3167
Charlotte Valley Sch Dist/*Davenport*		1	565	607-278-5511
Delhi Central Sch Dist/*Delhi*		3	1,210	607-746-2101
Downsville Central Sch Dist/*Downsville*		1	350	607-363-2100
Franklin Central Sch Dist/*Franklin*		1	400	607-829-3551
Hancock Central Sch Dist/*Hancock*		2	680	607-637-2511
Margaretville Ctl Sch Dist/*Margaretville*		1	540	914-586-2647
Roxbury-Central Sch Dist/*Roxbury*		1	419	607-326-4151
Sidney Central Sch Dist/*Sidney*		5	1,516	607-563-2153
South Kortright Ctl Sch Dist/*S. Kortright*		1	430	607-538-9111
Stamford Central Sch Dist/*Stamford*		1	540	607-652-7301
Walton Central Sch Dist/*Walton*		3	1,385	607-865-4116
GREENE				
Cairo Durham Ctl Sch Dist/*Cairo*		4	1,670	518-622-8534
Catskill Central Sch Dist/*Catskill*		4	1,691	518-943-4696
Coxsackie Athens CSD/*Coxsackie*		4	1,550	518-731-1700
Greenville Central Sch Dist/*Greenville*		2	1,200	518-966-5065
Hunter Tannersville CSD/*Tannersville*		2	587	518-589-5400
Windham Ashland Jewett SD/*Windham*		1	507	518-734-3400

School Districts	Town	Number of Schools	Number of Students	Phone
OTSEGO				
Cherry Valley Springfield SD/*Cherry Valley*		1	892	607-264-3265
Cooperstown Ctl Sch Dist/*Cooperstown*		2	1,345	607-547-5364
Edmeston Ctl Sch Dist/*Edmeston*		1	585	607-965-8931
Gilbertsville-Mt Upton CSD/*Gilbertsville*		1	675	607-783-2207
Laurens Central Sch Dist/*Laurens*		1	520	607-432-2050
Milford Central Sch Dist/*Milford*		1	501	607-286-7721
Morris Central Sch Dist/*Morris*		1	485	607-263-5110
Oneonta City Sch Dist/*Oneonta*		6	2,270	607-433-8200
Otego-Unadilla Ctl Sch Dist/*Otego*		3	1,400	607-988-1020
Richfield Springs CSD/*Richfld Spgs*		1	750	315-858-0610
Schenevus Ctl Sch Dist/*Schenevus*		1	413	607-638-5530
Worcester Ctl Sch Dist/*Worcester*		1	465	607-397-8785
RENSSELAER				
Averill Park Central Sch Dist/*Averill Park*		6	3,321	518-674-3816
Berlin Central Sch Dist/*Berlin*		4	1,115	518-658-2690
Brittonkill CSD/*Troy*		3	1,414	518-279-4600
East Greenbush Ctrl Sch Dist/*E Greenbush*		7	4,560	518-477-2755
Hoosic Valley CSD/*Schaghticoke*		2	1,224	518-753-4450
Hoosick Falls CSD/*Hoosick Falls*		2	1,501	518-686-7321
Lansingburgh Central Sch Dist/*Troy*		4	2,400	518-235-4404
N. Greenbush Common Sch Dist/*Troy*		1	30	518-283-3800
Rensselaer City Sch Dist/*Rensselaer*		2	1,129	518-465-7509
Schodack CSD/*Castleton-on-Hudson*		3	1,210	518-732-2297
Troy City Sch Dist/*Troy*		9	4,947	518-271-5200
Wynantskill Union Free Sch Dist/*Troy*		1	426	518-283-4600
SCHOHARIE				
Cobleskill-Richmond CSD/*Cobleskill*		4	2,300	518-234-4032
Gilboa Conesville Sch Dist/*Gilboa*		1	450	607-588-7358
Jefferson Central Sch Dist/*Jefferson*		1	330	607-652-7821
Middleburgh Ctl Sch Dist/*Middleburgh*		3	1,047	518-827-6633
Schoharie Central Sch Dist/*Schoharie*		2	1,311	518-295-8132
Sharon Springs Ctl Sch Dist/*Sharon Spgs*		1	427	518-284-2266

REGION 5: Counties—Dutchess, Orange, Putnam, Rockland, Sullivan, Ulster, Westchester

BOCES	Town	Phone
Dutchess BOCES	Poughkeepsie	914-486-4800
Orange–Ulster BOCES	Goshen	914-294-5431
Putnam Northern Westchester BOCES	Yorktown Heights	914-245-2700
Rockland BOCES	West Nyack	914-623-3828
Southern Westchester BOCES	Port Chester	914-937-3820
Sullivan BOCES	Liberty	914-292-0082
Ulster BOCES	New Paltz	914-255-1400

Region-Wide

	Town	Phone
Urban Teaching Academy	Westchester	1-877-882-8074

School Districts	Town	Number of Schools	Number of Students	Phone
DUTCHESS				
Arlington CSD/*Poughkeepsie*		11	8,100	914-486-4460
Beacon City Sch Dist/*Beacon*		6	3,050	914-838-6900
Dover Union Free Sch Dist/*Wingdale*		3	1,675	914-832-4510
Hyde Park Central Sch Dist/*Hyde Park*		7	4,485	914-229-4000
Millbrook Ctl Sch Dist/*Millbrook*		3	1,078	914-677-4200
Northeast Central Sch Dist/*Amenia*		4	1,081	914-373-4101
Pawling Ctl Sch Dist/*Pawling*		2	1,250	914-855-4605
Pine Plains Ctl Sch Dist/*Pine Plains*		3	1,500	518-398-7181
Poughkeepsie City SD/*Poughkeepsie*		8	3,893	914-451-4900
Red Hook Central Sch Dist/*Red Hook*		3	2,151	914-758-2241
Rhinebeck Central Sch Dist/*Rhinebeck*		3	1,259	914-871-5522
Rhinecliff Union Free SD/*Rhinecliff*		1	95	914-876-6414
Spackenkill UFSD/*Poughkeepsie*		4	1,594	914-463-7800
Wappingers CSD/*Wappingers Falls*		14	11,310	914-298-5025
ORANGE				
Chester Union Free Sch Dist/*Chester*		2	857	914-469-2231
Cornwall Central Sch Dist/*Cornwall*		4	2,381	914-534-8039
Florida Union Free Sch Dist/*Florida*		2	709	914-651-3095
Goshen Central Sch Dist/*Goshen*		4	2,373	914-294-2410
Greenwood Lake UFSD/*Greenwood Lk*		2	806	914-782-8678
Highland Falls-Ft Montgmry SD/*Highland Falls*		3	1,060	914-446-9575
Kiryas Union Free Dist/*Monroe*		1	204	914-782-2300
Middletown City Sch Dist/*Middletown*		10	5,576	914-341-5690
Minisink Valley CSD/*Slate Hill*		5	3,830	914-355-5100
Monroe Woodbury CSD/*Central Valley*		8	5,694	914-928-2321
Newburgh City Sch Dist/*Newburgh*		15	11,726	914-563-7221
Pine Bush Central Sch Dist/*Pine Bush*		7	5,680	914-744-2031
Port Jervis City Sch Dist/*Port Jervis*		5	3,433	914-858-3175

School Districts	Town	Number of Schools	Number of Students	Phone
Sugar Loaf Union Free Sch Dist/*Chester*		1	118	914-469-2157
Tuxedo UFSD/*Tuxedo Park*		1	470	914-351-4786
Valley Central Sch Dist/*Montgomery*		7	4,746	914-457-3030
Warwick Valley CSD/*Warwick*		5	3,865	914-987-3000
Washingtonville CSD/*Washingtonville*		5	4,903	914-496-2211
West Point Elem Sch Dist/*West Point*		2	735	914-938-3506

PUTNAM

School Districts	Town	Number of Schools	Number of Students	Phone
Brewster Central Sch Dist/*Brewster*		4	3,091	914-279-8001
Carmel Central Sch Dist/*Patterson*		5	4,413	914-878-2094
Garrison Union Free Sch Dist/*Garrison*		1	270	914-424-3689
Haldane Central Sch Dist/*Cold Spring*		1	785	914-265-9254
Mahopac Ctl Sch Dist/*Mahopac*		5	4,441	914-628-3415
Putnam Valley CSD/*Putnam Valley*		2	1,210	914-528-8143

ROCKLAND

School Districts	Town	Number of Schools	Number of Students	Phone
Clarkstown Central Sch Dist/*New City*		14	8,944	914-639-6486
East Ramapo CSD/*Spring Valley*		15	9,128	914-577-6000
Edwin Gould Ramapo UFSD/*Spring Valley*		1	172	914-578-6700
Haverstraw-Stony Pt CSD/*Garnerville*		8	7,275	914-942-3000
Nanuet UFSD/*Nanuet*		3	1,689	914-627-9888
Nyack Union Free Sch Dist/*Nyack*		5	2,916	914-353-7000
Pearl River UFSD/*Pearl River*		5	2,096	914-620-3900
Ramapo Central Sch Dist/*Hillburn*		7	4,076	914-357-7783
South Orangetown CSD/*Blauvelt*		6	2,621	914-365-4200

SULLIVAN

School Districts	Town	Number of Schools	Number of Students	Phone
Delaware Valley Ctl Sch Dist/*Callicoon*		1	620	914-887-5300
Eldred Central Sch Dist/*Eldred*		2	798	914-557-6141
Fallsburg CSD/*Fallsburg*		2	1,401	914-434-5884
Jeffersonville-Youngsville SD/*Jeffersonville*		1	850	914-482-5110
Liberty Central Sch Dist/*Liberty*		4	1,911	914-292-6171
Livingston Manor CSD/*Livingston Mnr*		1	785	914-439-4400
Monticello CSD/*Monticello*		6	3,544	914-794-7700
Narrowsburg CSD/*Narrowsburg*		1	318	914-252-3100
Roscoe Central Sch Dist/*Roscoe*		1	351	607-498-4126
Tri-Valley CSD/*Grahamsville*		2	1,147	914-985-2296

ULSTER

School Districts	Town	Number of Schools	Number of Students	Phone
Ellenville Central Sch Dist/*Ellenville*		1	2,000	914-647-7100
Highland Ctl Sch Dist/*Highland*		3	1,786	914-691-7241
Kingston City Cons SD/*Kingston*		14	7,608	914-339-3000
Marlboro Central Sch Dist/*Marlboro*		5	2,007	914-236-5800
New Paltz Ctl Sch Dist/*New Paltz*		4	2,288	914-255-1300
Onteora Central Sch Dist/*Boiceville*		5	2,216	914-657-6383
Rondout Valley Ctl Sch Dist/*Stone Ridge*		6	2,781	914-334-8680
Saugerties Central Sch Dist/*Saugerties*		5	3,389	914-246-4934

School Districts	Town	Number of Schools	Number of Students	Phone
Wallkill Central Sch Dist/*Wallkill*		5	3,201	914-895-3301
West Park USD/*West Park*		1	82	914-384-6710

WESTCHESTER

School Districts	Town	Number of Schools	Number of Students	Phone
Abbott UFSD/*Irvington*		1	85	914-591-7151
Ardsley UFSD/*Ardsley*		3	1,732	914-693-6300
Bedford Central Sch Dist/*Bedford*		7	3,080	914-241-6000
Blind Brook-Rye UFSD/*Port Chester*		2	1,050	914-937-3600
Briarcliff Manor UFSD/*Briarclf Mnr*		2	1,143	914-941-8880
Bronxville UFSD/*Bronxville*		3	1,323	914-337-5600
Byram Hills CSD/*Armonk*		4	2,008	914-273-4083
Chappaqua CSD/*Chappaqua*		5	3,204	914-238-7200
Croton-Harmon Sch Dist/*Croton-on-Hudson*		3	1,179	914-271-4793
Dobbs Ferry UFSD/*Dobbs Ferry*		3	1,210	914-693-1506
Eastchester UFSD/*Yonkers*		5	2,080	914-793-6130
Elmsford UFSD/*Elmsford*		3	740	914-592-8440
Greenburgh Ctl 7 Sch Dist/*Hartsdale*		6	2,250	914-761-6000
Greenburgh Eleven UFSD/*Dobbs Ferry*		1	358	914-693-8500
Greenburgh-Graham UFSD/*Hastings-Hudson*		2	282	914-478-1106
Greenburgh-Northcastle SD/*Dobbs Ferry*		1	142	914-693-3030
Harrison CSD/*Harrison*		6	2,753	914-835-3300
Hastings On Hudson UFSD/*Hastings-Hudson*		3	1,345	914-478-2900
Hawthorne Cedar Knolls UFSD/*Hawthorne*		2	295	914-773-7300
Hendrick Hudson CSD/*Montrose*		5	2,467	914-737-7500
Irvington Unified Sch Dist/*Irvington*		3	1,328	914-591-8500
Katonah Lewisboro JFSD/*South Salem*		6	3,513	914-763-5000
Lakeland Central Sch Dist/*Shrub Oak*		9	5,800	914-245-1700
Mamaroneck UFSD/*Mamaroneck*		6	4,133	914-698-9000
Mt. Pleasant Cottage UFSD/*Pleasantville*		2	313	914-769-0456
Mt. Pleasant CSD/*Thornwood*		4	1,691	914-769-5500
Mt. Pleasant-Blythdale UFSD/*Valhalla*		1	119	914-592-7138
Mt. Vernon City SD/*Mount Vernon*		15	9,676	914-665-5201
New Rochelle City SD/*New Rochelle*		10	8,624	914-576-4300
North Salem CSD/*North Salem*		2	1,235	914-669-5414
Ossining UFSD/*Ossining*		6	3,553	914-941-7700
Peekskill City SD/*Peekskill*		7	2,972	914-737-3300
Pelham UFSD/*Pelham*		6	1,982	914-738-3434
Pleasantville UFSD/*Pleasantville*		3	1,521	914-741-1400
Pocantico Hills Ctl Sch Dist/*Tarrytown*		1	354	914-631-2440
Port Chester Rye UFSD/*Port Chester*		7	3,166	914-934-7901
Rye City Sch Dist/*Rye*		5	2,121	914-967-6108
Rye Neck UFSD/*Mamaroneck*		4	1,121	914-698-6171
Scarsdale UFSD/*Scarsdale*		7	3,854	914-721-2410
Somers CSD/*Lincolndale*		4	2,287	914-248-7872
Tuckahoe UFSD/*Yonkers*		2	850	914-337-5376
UFD of Tarrytowns/*Tarrytown*		6	1,977	914-631-9404
UFSD Greenburgh/*Scarsdale*		3	1,076	914-472-7768

School Districts	Town	Number of Schools	Number of Students	Phone
Valhalla UFSD/*Valhalla*		3	1,076	914-683-5040
White Plains City SD/*White Plains*		10	5,903	914-422-2019
Yonkers City Sch Dist/*Yonkers*		36	23,200	914-376-8000
Yorktown CSD/*Yorktown Hts*		6	3,658	914-243-8000

REGION 6: Counties—Nassau, Suffolk

BOCES	Town	Phone
Eastern Suffolk BOCES	Patchogue	516-289-2200
Nassau BOCES	Westbury	516-997-8700
Western Suffolk BOCES	Huntington Station	516-549-4900

Region-Wide

	Town	Phone
Diocese of Rockville School District	Rockville Centre	516-678-5800

School Districts	Town	Number of Schools	Number of Students	Phone
NASSAU				
Baldwin UFSD/*Baldwin*		9	4,952	516-377-9200
Bellmore UF Elem SD/*Bellmore*		2	1,050	516-679-2900
Bellmore-Merrick Ctl High SchDist/*Merrick*		5	4,729	516-623-8900
Bethpage Sch Dist/*Bethpage*		5	2,628	516-733-3700
Carle Place UFSD/*Carle Place*		3	1,540	516-334-1900
East Meadow SD/*East Meadow*		9	7,603	516-228-5200
East Rockaway UFSD/*East Rockaway*		3	1,215	516-887-8300
East Williston UFSD/*Old Westbury*		3	1,483	516-876-4740
Elmont UFSD/*Elmont*		7	3,274	516-326-5501
Farmingdale UFSD/*Farmingdale*		6	5,836	516-752-6631
Floral Park Bellrose Elem SD/*Floral Park*		2	1,900	516-327-9300
Franklin Sq UFSD/*Franklin Square*		3	1,699	516-481-4100
Freeport Unified SD/*Freeport*		8	7,000	516-867-5205
Garden City SD/*Garden City*		7	3,309	516-294-3000
Glen Cove SD/*Glen Cove*		6	3,001	516-759-7217
Great Neck UFSD/*Great Neck*		12	5,846	516-773-1404
Hempstead UFSD/*Hempstead*		10	5,977	516-292-7001
Herricks UFSD/*New Hyde Park*		5	3,556	516-248-3100
Hewlett Woodmere UFSD/*Woodmere*		5	3,056	516-374-8000
Hicksville UFSD/*Hicksville*		8	4,300	516-733-6600
Island Park UFSD/*Island Park*		2	897	516-431-8100
Island Trees UFSD/*Levittown*		4	2,350	516-520-2100
Jericho Unified Sch Dist/*Jericho*		5	2,399	516-681-4100
Lawrence UFSD/*Lawrence*		7	3,853	516-295-7030

School Districts	Town	Number of Schools	Number of Students	Phone
Levittown UFSD/*Levittown*		11	6,632	516-520-8300
Locust Valley Ctl SD/*Locust Valley*		5	2,091	516-674-6350
Long Beach City SD/*Long Beach*		7	4,250	516-897-2104
Lynbrook UFSD/*Lynbrook*		7	2,723	516-887-0256
Malverne UFSD/*Malverne*		4	1,801	516-887-6400
Manhasset UFSD/*Manhasset*		4	2,373	516-627-4400
Massapequa UFSD 23/*Massapequa*		8	6,900	516-797-6600
Merrick UFSD/*Merrick*		3	1,824	516-378-3900
Mineola UFSD/*Mineola*		6	2,752	516-741-5036
New Hyde-Garden City Park SD/*New Hyde Park*		4	1,410	516-352-2227
North Bellmore UFSD/*Bellmore*		5	2,148	516-221-2200
North Merrick UFSD/*Merrick*		3	1,276	516-292-3694
North Shore Central Sch Dist/*Sea Cliff*		5	2,247	516-671-5500
Oceanside UFSD/*Oceanside*		9	5,991	516-678-1200
Oyster Bay East Norwich Ctl Sch Dist/*Oyster Bay*		3	1,411	516-624-6500
Plainedge UFSD/*Massapequa*		6	2,899	516-797-4400
Plainview-Old Bethpage Ctl Sch Dist/*Plainview*		7	4,400	516-937-6322
Port Washington UFSD/*Pt Washington*		6	4,000	516-767-4326
Rockville Ctr UFSD/*Rockville Ctr*		7	3,320	516-255-8920
Roosevelt Sch Dist/*Roosevelt*		6	2,857	516-867-8616
Roslyn Sch Dist/*Roslyn*		5	2,693	516-625-6303
Seaford Sch Dist/*Seaford*		4	2,417	516-783-0703
Sewanhaka Ctl High Sch Dist/*Elmont*		5	7,500	516-488-9800
Syosset Central Sch Dist/*Syosset*		10	5,400	516-364-5600
Uniondale UFSD/*Uniondale*		9	4,874	516-560-8824
Valley Stream 24 UFSD/*Valley Stream*		3	1,046	516-256-0150
Valley Stream Ctl High Sch Dist/*Valley Stream*		4	3,578	516-872-5601
Valley Stream Elem Sch Dist 14/*Valley Stream*		4	2,094	516-568-6100
Valley Stream Sch Dist 30/*Valley Stream*		3	1,277	516-285-9881
Wantagh UFSD/*Wantagh*		5	2,868	516-781-8000
West Hempstead Sch Dist/*W. Hempstead*		4	2,150	516-489-8511
Westbury UFSD/*Old Westbury*		5	3,300	516-876-5016

SUFFOLK

School Districts	Town	Number of Schools	Number of Students	Phone
Amagansett UFSD/*Amagansett*		1	176	516-267-3572
Amityville UFSD/*Amityville*		5	2,913	516-598-6500
Babylon UFSD/*Babylon*		3	2,093	516-661-5810
Bay Shore UFSD/*Bay Shore*		7	5,008	516-968-1117
Bayport Blue Point UFSD/*Bayport*		5	2,105	516-472-4040
Brentwood UFSD/*Brentwood*		17	12,900	516-434-2123
Bridgehampton UFSD/*Bridgehampton*		1	165	516-537-0271
Brookhaven Comsewogue Unif SD/*Pt. Jefferson Sta*		5	3,282	516-474-8100
Center Moriches UFSD/*Ctr Moriches*		2	1,140	516-878-0052
Central Islip SD 13/*Central Islip*		7	6,200	516-348-5112
Cold Spring Harbor CSD/*Cold Spring Harbor*		4	1,557	516-692-8036
Commack UFSD/*E. Northport*		8	5,779	516-754-7210
Connetquot CSD/*Bohemia*		10	6,500	516-244-2204

School Districts	Town	Number of Schools	Number of Students	Phone
Copiague UFSD/*Copiague*		5	4,029	516-842-4000
Deer Park UFSD/*Deer Park*		5	3,450	516-242-6513
East Hampton UFSD/*E. Hampton*		3	1,519	516-329-4100
East Islip Sch Dist/*Islip Terrace*		7	4,394	516-581-1600
East Moriches UFSD/*E. Moriches*		1	590	516-878-0162
East Quogue UFSD/*E. Quogue*		1	343	516-653-5210
Eastport UFSD/*Eastport*		1	947	516-325-0800
Elwood UFSD/*Greenlawn*		4	2,004	516-266-5402
Fire Island UFSD/*Ocean Beach*		1	55	516-583-5626
Fishers Island USD/*Fishers Isle*		1	80	516-788-7444
Greenport UFSD/*Greenport*		1	600	516-477-1950
Half Hollow Hills CSD/*Huntington Sta.*		10	7,203	516-421-6408
Hampton Bays UFSD/*Hampton Bays*		2	1,454	516-723-2100
Harborfields Ctl SD/*Greenlawn*		4	2,725	516-754-5327
Hauppauge UFSD/*Hauppauge*		5	3,394	516-265-3630
Huntington UFSD/*Huntington*		8	3,953	516-673-2038
Islip UFSD/*Islip*		5	2,912	516-859-2200
Kings Park Ctl Sch Dist/*Kings Park*		5	3,309	516-269-3210
Laurel Common Sch Dist/*Laurel*		1	125	516-298-4848
Lindenhurst UFSD/*Lindenhurst*		9	6,703	516-226-6511
Little Flower UFSD/*Wading River*		1	101	516-929-4300
Longwood CSD/*Middle Island*		7	9,105	516-345-2171
Mattituck-Cutchogue Unified SD/*Mattituck*		4	1,308	516-298-8460
Middle Country CSD/*Centereach*		13	10,733	516-738-2700
Miller Place UFSD/*Miller Place*		4	2,664	516-474-2700
Montauk UFSD/*Montauk*		1	350	516-668-2474
Mt Sinai UFSD/*Mount Sinai*		3	2,200	516-473-1991
New Suffolk Common SD/*New Suffolk*		1	26	516-734-6940
North Babylon UFSD/*Babylon*		7	4,505	516-321-3209
Northport-E. Northport UFSD/*Northport*		9	5,304	516-262-6600
Oysterponds Unif SD/*Orient*		1	128	516-323-2410
Patchogue-Medford Unified SD/*Patchogue*		11	8,435	516-758-1000
Port Jefferson UFSD 6/*Port Jefferson*		3	1,100	516-928-0365
Quogue UFSD/*Quogue*		1	92	516-653-4285
Remsenburg-Speonk Unified SD/*Remsenburg*		1	169	516-325-0203
Riverhead CSD/*Riverhead*		7	4,182	516-369-6716
Rocky Point UFSD/*Rocky Point*		3	2,890	516-744-1600
Sachem CSD/*Holbrook*		16	14,500	516-467-8202
Sag Harbor UFSD/*Sag Harbor*		2	737	516-725-5300
Sagaponack Common SD/*Sagaponack*		1	10	516-537-0651
Sayville UFSD 4/*Sayville*		5	3,299	516-244-6510
Shelter Island Unified SD/*Shelter Is*		1	245	516-749-0302
Shoreham Wading River Ctl SD/*Shoreham*		5	2,184	516-821-8100
Smithtown Central SD/*Smithtown*		11	7,751	516-361-2206
South Country CSD/*Patchogue*		6	4,307	516-286-4300
South Huntington UFSD/*Huntington Station*		6	5,442	516-673-1610
South Manor UFSD/*Manorville*		2	1,130	516-878-4441

School Districts	Town	Number of Schools	Number of Students	Phone
Southampton UFSD/*Southampton*		4	1,600	516-283-6800
Southold UFSD/*Southold*		2	804	516-765-5400
Springs UFSD/*E. Hampton*		1	570	516-324-0144
Three Village Central SD/*E. Setauket*		8	6,800	516-474-7530
Tuckahoe Common SD/*Southampton*		1	230	516-283-3550
Wainscott Common SD/*Wainscott*		1	24	516-537-1080
West Babylon UFSD/*Babylon*		7	4,403	516-321-3076
West Islip SD/*West Islip*		8	4,984	516-422-1560
Westhampton Beach UFSD/*Westhampton Beach*		3	1,575	516-288-3800
William Floyd SD/*Mastic*		7	9,700	516-281-3020
Wyandanch UFSD/*Wyandanch*		4	2,300	516-491-1013

REGION 7: New York City Boroughs—Bronx, Brooklyn, Manhattan, Queens, Staten Island

CITY-WIDE	Borough	Phone
Urban Teaching Academy	Bronx	1-877-882-8074
New York City Office of Recruitment	Brooklyn	718-935-2670
Archdiocese of New York School	Manhattan	212-371-1000
Diocese of Brooklyn School District	Brooklyn	718-492-1800

School Districts	Town	Number of Schools	Number of Students	Phone
BRONX				
Bronx High Sch Dist/*Bronx*		23	49,725	718-430-6300
Bronx Sch Dist 10/*Bronx*		44	41,404	718-584-7070
Bronx Sch Dist 11/*Bronx*		30	26,847	718-519-2614
Bronx Sch Dist 12/*Bronx*		24	19,100	718-328-2310
Bronx Sch Dist 7/*Bronx*		22	15,438	718-292-0481
Bronx Sch Dist 8/*Bronx*		28	22,226	718-409-8100
Bronx Sch Dist 9/*Bronx*		35	32,000	718-681-6160
BROOKLYN				
Brooklyn Cmty Sch Dist 17/*Brooklyn*		26	28,000	718-604-4225
Brooklyn Cmty Sch Dist 22/*Brooklyn*		28	28,500	718-368-8000
Brooklyn High Sch Dist/*Brooklyn*		27	53,000	718-258-4826
Brooklyn Sch Dist 13/*Brooklyn*		22	16,300	718-636-3204
Brooklyn Sch Dist 14/*Brooklyn*		26	19,200	718-963-4800
Brooklyn Sch Dist 15/*Brooklyn*		29	21,719	718-330-9300
Brooklyn Sch Dist 16/*Brooklyn*		16	10,900	718-919-4112
Brooklyn Sch Dist 18/*Brooklyn*		18	19,500	718-927-5100
Brooklyn Sch Dist 19/*Brooklyn*		28	24,505	718-257-6900
Brooklyn Sch Dist 20/*Brooklyn*		29	26,700	718-692-5200
Brooklyn Sch Dist 21/*Brooklyn*		28	23,500	718-714-2500

School Districts	Town	Number of Schools	Number of Students	Phone
Brooklyn Sch Dist 23/*Brooklyn*		18	13,700	718-270-8600
Brooklyn Sch Dist 32/*Brooklyn*		19	16,000	718-574-1125
MANHATTAN				
Manhattan Dist 1/*New York*		25	10,500	212-602-9700
Manhattan Dist 2/*New York*		40	21,853	212-330-9400
Manhattan Dist 3/*New York*		21	14,800	212-678-2880
Manhattan Dist 4/*New York*		46	19,543	212-860-5858
Manhattan Dist 5/*New York*		19	14,550	212-769-7500
Manhattan Dist 6/*New York*		27	29,000	212-795-4111
Manhattan High Sch Dist/*New York*		35	48,056	212-501-1100
New York Alt High Sch Dist/*New York*		65	34,000	212-206-0570
QUEENS				
Queens Cmty Sch Dist 25/*Flushing*		30	24,000	718-281-7600
Queens High Sch Dist/*Flushing*		33	71,000	718-281-7500
Queens Sch Dist 24/*Flushing*		26	33,500	718-417-2600
Queens Sch Dist 26/*Flushing*		25	15,583	718-631-6900
Queens Sch Dist 27/*Jamaica*		38	35,000	718-642-5700
Queens Sch Dist 28/*Flushing*		30	25,552	718-830-8800
Queens Sch Dist 29/*Jamaica*		28	26,000	718-978-5900
Queens Sch Dist 30/*Flushing*		27	27,400	718-777-4700
Queens Sch Dist 33/*Brooklyn*		3	1,593	718-935-4259
STATEN ISLAND				
Staten Island Sch Dist 31/*Staten Island*		49	37,400	718-390-1600

NOTES

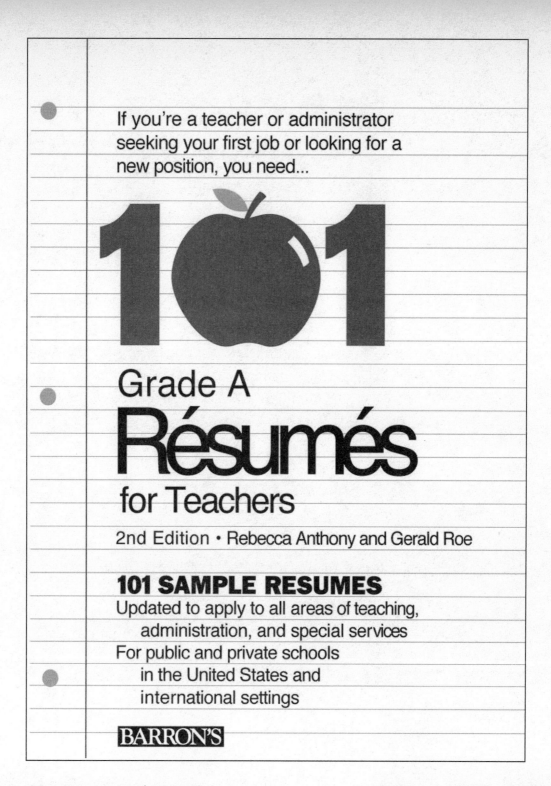

If you're a teacher or administrator seeking your first job or looking for a new position, you need...

101

Grade A
Résumés
for Teachers

2nd Edition • Rebecca Anthony and Gerald Roe

101 SAMPLE RESUMES
Updated to apply to all areas of teaching, administration, and special services
For public and private schools in the United States and international settings

BARRON'S

$12.95 Canada $17.95   ISBN: 0-7641-0129-3

Books may be purchased at your bookstore, or by mail from Barron's. Enclose check or money order for the total amount plus sales tax where applicable and 18% for postage and handling (minimum charge $5.95). Price subject to change without notice.

Barron's Educational Series, Inc.
250 Wireless Boulevard • Hauppauge, New York 11788
In Canada: Georgetown Book Warehouse • 1-800-645-3476
34 Armstrong Avenue • Georgetown, Ontario L7G 4R9
Visit our website at: www.barronseduc.com   (#78) R 11/02

BEGINNING SPANISH FOR TEACHERS OF HISPANIC STUDENTS

Pamela J. Sharpe, Ph.D.

Here at last is a valuable self-instruction program for primary and secondary school teachers who speak English only, but need some practical knowledge of Spanish so that they can work with Hispanic students. The boxed set consists of—

- A 280-page illustrated combination textbook and workbook
- 376 dialogue flashcards bound into a separate book of perforated card stock paper
- Four 90-minute cassettes
- A 92-page audioscript book

The program presents 24 lessons that start with greeting children in Spanish and introducing yourself, giving children basic instructions including taking out and putting away school supplies, participating in learning activities, praising children's good work, correcting their mistakes and behavior, questioning and comforting a child who is injured, participating in holiday celebrations and special events, communicating with Hispanic parents, and much more.

The main book's text and illustration are coordinated to match the dramatized conversations on cassette. It features many quizzes and exercises that will help you learn and retain the Spanish you need to know. The accompanying dialogue cards contain simple line drawings that depict a teacher and students engaged in a variety of classroom activities. Each card coincides with key words and phrases in the lessons and together will help you increase your memory retention.

Pamela J. Sharpe, Ph.D., is Associate Professor of English as a Second Language and Bilingual Education at Northern Arizona University in Yuma.

A quick, practical way to learn Spanish for use in a classroom setting.

ISBN 0-8120-8118-8

$42.95 **Canada $59.95**

Barron's Educational Series, Inc.
250 Wireless Blvd., Hauppauge, NY 11788
Order toll-free: 1-800-645-3476 • Order by fax: 1-631-434-3217
Canadian orders: 1-800-645-3476 • Fax in Canada: 1-800-887-1594

Visit us at www.barronseduc.com

Books and packages may be purchased at your local bookstore or by mail directly from Barron's. Enclose check or money order for total amount, plus sales tax where applicable and 18% for postage and handling (minimum $5.95). Prices subject to change without notice.

#74 8/02